Knotting the Banner

NEW DAOIST STUDIES

DAVID J. MOZINA

Knotting the Banner

Ritual and Relationship in Daoist Practice

道教文化研究中心

Centre for Studies of Daoist Culture
The Chinese University of Hong Kong

The Chinese University of
Hong Kong Press

University of Hawai'i Press
Honolulu

NEW DAOIST STUDIES

Knotting the Banner: Ritual and Relationship in Daoist Practice
    By David J. Mozina

Paperback edition 2024

ISBN: University of Hawai'i Press   978-0-8248-8341-6 (cloth)

                                                      978-0-8248-9867-0 (paperback)

ISBN: The Chinese University of Hong Kong   978-988-237-189-7 (cloth)

Published for North America by:
University of Hawai'i Press
2840 Kolowalu Street
Honolulu, HI 96822 USA
www.uhpress.hawaii.edu

Published for the rest of the world by:
The Chinese University of Hong Kong Press
The Chinese University of Hong Kong
Sha Tin, N.T., Hong Kong
cup.cuhk.edu.hk

Library of Congress Cataloging-in-Publication Data

Names: Mozina, David J., author.
Title: Knotting the banner : ritual and relationship in Daoist practice /
    David J. Mozina.
Other titles: New Daoist studies.
Description: Honolulu : University of Hawai'i Press, 2021. | Series: New
    Daoist studies | Includes bibliographical references and index.
Identifiers: LCCN 2021003492 | ISBN 9780824883416 (cloth) | ISBN
    9780824886707 (pdf) | ISBN 9780824886714 (epub) | ISBN 9780824886721
    (kindle edition)
Subjects: LCSH: Taoism—China—Hunan Sheng—Rituals.
Classification: LCC BL1940.4 .M69 2021 | DDC 299.5/14460951215—dc23
LC record available at https://lccn.loc.gov/2021003492

New Daoist Studies aims to publish exciting new scholarship on the Chinese religion of Daoism. The series was
initiated by Professor Lai Chi Tim, director of the Centre for Studies of Daoist Culture (CSDC), The Chinese
University of Hong Kong (CUHK); and Professor Stephen R. Bokenkamp, Regents' Professor of Chinese, Arizona
State University. It is supported by CSDC, which is itself a joint undertaking of CUHK and the Daoist temple
Fung Ying Seen Koon. Since 2006 CSDC has developed into the world's most dynamic institution for learning
about Daoism and for Daoist studies research and publishing. New Daoist Studies titles share the imprint of two
presses: The Chinese University of Hong Kong Press and University of Hawai'i Press. In the great spirit of Daoism,
the series editors present this cooperative venture as a model for future collaborations.
10 9 8 7 6 5 4 3 2 1

Printed in the United States of America

For my parents Kitty and Chuck, my brother Michael, and Ling

Contents

Series Editors' Preface ix

Acknowledgments xi

How to Use the Companion Website xvii

Prelude 1

Chapter One The Ordinand: Chen Diwen 23

Chapter Two The Deity: Celestial Lord Yin Jiao 75

Interlude 161

Chapter Three The Banner Rite: Recovering the Divine Self 167

Chapter Four The Banner Rite: Inscription of the Talisman 217

Postlude 263

Appendix The Daoist Lineage of the Daxiong Mountain Region 271

Notes 275

Bibliography 315

Index 337

Series Editors' Preface

David Mozina's *Knotting the Banner* is the first book in the New Daoist Studies series to focus on modern Daoist practice. We are extremely excited to introduce it, along with its accompanying website, to the scholarly public.

Knotting the Banner is a tightly focused piece of scholarship. It explores in detail the initial ordination ritual performed by the Hunan Daoist Chen Diwen and the importance of his personal relationship with the primary exorcistic deity of his lineage, Yin Jiao. It carefully traces the roots of Chen Diwen's lineage through several centuries of both Daoist and Buddhist practice in Hunan and clarifies the foundational images of Yin Jiao from Song–Yuan liturgical and hagiographic sources that inform the ordination ritual.

Such a description, however, does not do justice to Mozina's work. Its significance for the field of ritual studies—and religious studies more generally—goes far beyond its undeniable contribution to the study of Chinese religions. Precisely because Mozina's book focuses on one lineage and a single ritual conducted by that lineage, it offers an unprecedented look at the living Daoist tradition, its historical antecedents, and, most importantly, what that tradition might have to teach us about the phenomenology of ritual beyond what we have learned from more fully studied religions.

Mozina was among the group of young scholars interested in Daoist ritual that went to central Hunan in the 2000s in the wake of Patrice Fava's pioneering discoveries there. He was one of the few who stayed on, earning the trust of local priests, painstakingly observing rituals (and making video recordings), gathering documents (including manuscripts that priests show only to trusted outsiders), and amassing oral-historical material of considerable depth and breadth. In the highly charged environment of religion in China, this was in itself a remarkable achievement: Few non-Chinese scholars have the stamina and skill to engage with and persevere in such work. In presenting his findings, Mozina is further attentive to not only the placement of this tradition in Daoist history but also how its ritual practice might add perspectives hitherto unnoticed in the field of ritual studies more generally.

In the words of Vincent Goossaert, research professor of Daoism and Chinese religions at the École Pratique des Hautes Études, whose work will be appearing in our series soon: "Nowhere else I have read an account of a Daoist ritual tradition that balances so convincingly the social and local contexts of the performance, the history and textual basis of the liturgy, and its meaning for participants, notably the priest himself. This allows Mozina to elaborate a 'Daoist theory of ritual' that is not abstract and disembodied but allows us to comprehend clearly the understanding of humanity and divinity that compels Daoists to perform as they do."

This persuasive theoretical construct arises from Mozina's close attention to the writings and words of his Daoist informants. We fully expect *Knotting the Banner* to set a new standard for the collection and presentation of ethnographic material. But it also adds a new dimension—a distinctive understanding of "ritual efficacy"—to theoretical discussions of ritual. We look forward to the discussions it will elicit and the future work, by Mozina and others, that will follow in its wake.

Acknowledgments

This book is about living Chinese religion. It focuses on only one ritual and asks a simple question: how does the ritual work? It finds a not-so-simple answer: human masters and gods talk to each other in a peculiar ritual idiom. The book investigates that idiom and considers the interlocutors, both human and divine, who use the idiom to speak. The ritual is concerned with the relationships that have shaped each interlocutor and the possibility of a new relationship between them. I wanted to write about this dynamic in a way that takes gods as seriously as this ritual designed to interact with them, and honors the faith commitments of many, but not all, of the masters trained in that ritual techné.

The book emerged from extensive fieldwork between 2004 and 2018 in a remote corner of north-central Hunan province. Like the ritual, fieldwork only works if it is predicated on relationships of trust. The trust of the lineage of masters introduced in this book was earned over several years, but it began serendipitously. When I first showed up unexpectedly in December 2003, Jiang Yucheng seemed more fascinated by this strange foreigner than I was by him and his rituals. Slowly at first, he and I formed an enduring friendship I will cherish until the end of my days. He allowed me into his esoteric world filled with exorcisms for the living and funerals for the dead. Jiang Shenzhi granted me full access to the lineage's large cache of manuscripts, many hand-copied by him. I deeply regret that he did not live to see this publication. The next time I bow to his ancestral photograph and tablet,

I will burn a copy of the book to send it to the celestial office in which he is now employed. While I was living among the lineage, sometimes months at a time, Jiang Yeshi, Li Yezhen, Jiang Yeqian, Jiang Yuxian, Li Yuzhang, Cao Yewu, Jiang Yuxiang, and Li Yehe endured hours and hours of silly questions and, sometimes, deep debate spurred by them. The budding master at the center of this book, Chen Diwen, graciously agreed to play a starring role, and put up with incessant inquiries over the years, even on WeChat until the very end of editing.

My hope is that readers will feel something of the living ritual explored in these pages. Like opera, ritual is nearly impossible to write about without crushing its vibrancy. The book weaves into the text still and moving images designed to help the reader experience something of the ritual's sights and sounds, which, hopefully, will help the reader feel something of what is at stake for its participants. This attempt to marry text and image would have been far less feasible without the stellar photography of Doug Kanter. It is testimony to his aesthetic eye that he managed to capture the essence of the ritual in the cover art, and so much of the lived life of these masters in his other images. It will be apparent which photographs are his and which are mine. I also wish to thank photographer Nick Otto for two of his photographs. I look forward to working more with him in the future. The videos were shot by me. All images are presented on a website designed by Michael Burke, whose heroic work on the project continued even after he graduated from Boston College.

Like the protagonists in the ritual, I am enmeshed in several formative relationships that have shaped me and this project. The whole thing began right after passing my comprehensive exams, when I confessed to my graduate mentor at Harvard, Michael Puett, that I had no feel for early Chinese religion. With characteristic enthusiasm, he suggested I try to find a project on living religion. Like a pilgrim, I got on a plane and spent an afternoon with John Lagerwey in his Paris apartment. He promptly put me in contact with Patrice Fava and Alain Arrault, who had just won a Chiang Ching-kuo Foundation grant to study the local religious statuary in Hunan. Patrice had been the first to collect the amazing statuary and go to Hunan to do ethnographic work to contextualize it, and the entire Bureau de Beijing de l'École française d'Extrême-Orient, headed at the time by Alain, was reoriented toward the project. I will forever be thankful that they allowed a green graduate student to tag along on those first research trips to Hunan. The stunning photography featured in Patrice's own book, *Aux portes du ciel*, served as a model for how to introduce local religion to those who have never witnessed it. Alain put me touch with a local scholar he had discovered, Zhang Shihong, who had heard of Jiang Shenzhi and took me to a *jiao* his lineage was performing. One web of relationships led to another.

The problem with studying ritual is figuring out what it means. My general orientation to ritual and religion has been thoroughly shaped by my teachers at Harvard: John B. Carman, Kimberley Patton, and Lawrence Sullivan. Discerning readers will detect Kimberley's imprint on nearly every page of this book. They, and Michael Puett too, made me see that religious traditions have their own theories of ritual no less sophisticated than those from the modern west. With that in mind, I went off to the University of Hawai'i to learn from Poul Andersen about Daoist ritual theory. I tried to emulate his way of reading simultaneously on the sentence level, the social level, and the cosmic level—a skill I believe crucial for reading any ritual.

Another web of intellectual relationships went into writing this book. Conversations over the years with Stephen Bokenkamp, Terry Kleeman, Gil Raz, Josh Capitanio, James Robson, Hsieh Shu-wei, Vincent Goossaert, Ken Dean, Elena Valussi, Lee Fong-mao, Philip Clart, Michael Como, Michael Stanley-Baker, Paul Katz, Hsieh Tsung-hui, Aaron Reich, and Kristofer Schipper have influenced me more than they probably knew at the time. I have been thinking with my dear confidant Mark Meulenbeld, a fellow explorer of local religion in Hunan, since the beginning.

Institutional relationships contributed to this book, too. The Department of Religious Studies of the University of North Carolina at Charlotte provided an uncommonly stimulating environment in which to think about modern western theories of ritual anew. Joseph Winters, Kent Brintnall, and Ann Burlein taught me how to really read western theory, which turns out to be much like reading texts in literary Chinese. During my time in the Theology Department of Boston College, I realized that Chinese ritual masters, both present and past, operate very similarly to theologians in other traditions. I thank my colleagues in the Comparative Theology area and the cohort of innovative doctoral students who provided such fantastic colloquium discussions, as well as a critical mass of bright undergraduates interested in Chinese humanities, several of whom from China, who made my teaching days more edifying for me than for them.

A number of grants made my research possible. Early fieldwork was funded by a Social Science Research Council International Dissertation Research Fellowship, several Foreign Language and Area Studies Academic Year Fellowships, and a Harvard Divinity School Dean's Dissertation Fellowship. Later fieldwork was funded by a Chiang Ching-kuo Foundation Junior Scholar Fellowship, a Faculty Research Grant from the University of North Carolina at Charlotte, and a Junior Faculty Fellowship from Boston College. Several substantive conversations during a National Endowment for the Humanities Summer Seminar titled "An Introduction to Daoist Literature and History," organized by Terry Kleeman and Stephen Bokenkamp at the University of Colorado Boulder, found their way into this book, especially those with Chang Ch'ao-jan, Maruyama Hiroshi, Mark Csikszentmihalyi, and Jason Protass. I am grateful for these opportunities.

It takes yet another set of relationships to bring a book into being. Eleanor Goodman read the entire manuscript with her poet's eyes. I am grateful to the teams at the University of Hawai'i Press and the Chinese University of Hong Kong Press, and especially to editors Stephanie Chun and Grace Wen. Two anonymous reviewers offered encouragement and invaluable feedback on the manuscript, Helen Glenn Court provided meticulous copyediting, and Cynthia Col did the index. I am honored this book appears in the New Daoist Studies Series edited by Lai Chi Tim and Stephen Bokenkamp.

Other kinds of relationships went into producing this book. Joan Wheelis and Dan Brown helped me place an intense project in a larger vision, as did dear conversation partners Rachel Odo, Nathan Rein, Gretchen Skogerson, Qian Ying, Ritika Prasad, Mo Yajun, Aurelia Campbell, Yonder

Gillihan, Zhang Jinfei, Gao Ru, Jocelyn Flint, Matthew Pottinger, Michael Garred, Greg Deegan, Ron Zucca, Jeffrey Franco, Bede Kotlinski, and Mark Francioli. My family in Hangzhou—Zhang Jianxiong, Wang Cuilian, and Zhang Qi—offered great food and cooking tips during visits and WeChat calls. The concern with material culture in the book was inspired by my brother Michael's insightful graduate work on Greek archaeology. My parents, Kitty and Chuck, have given nothing but love and support to a son whose fascination with religion took him away to the far places of the world.

Last to acknowledge is my relationship with Zhang Ling—intellectual partner, soulmate, lover, friend. Every thought, every sentence bears the trace of our incredibly rich life together. Ling provided the book's maps and artwork. More important, she contributed to the book's soul.

How to Use the Companion Website

Access the book's companion website (http://www.davidjmozina.com; username: knottingthebanner; password: yinjiao) to view additional figures and videos (indicated in the book by "web figure" and "web video"). The website also includes color versions of the figures in the book.

Prelude

If one can't perform the Banner Rite, one can't perform any of the rites.

————Master Jiang Yucheng (b. 1973)

Chen Diwen (陳迪文) puffed on cigarettes one after the other as he sat on a stool on the front porch of the modest two-story brick structure in which he lived with his grandparents and wife.[1] The house was perched on the side of a verdant hill above the tiny hamlet of Mount Xiashan (下杉山), one of dozens of poor villages dotting the rugged hills west of Le'an township (樂安鎮) in Anhua county (安化縣) in central Hunan province. He sat under the awning of the house, protected from the steadily pouring rain. From time to time he stepped out onto the dirt path to look further up the hill, peering between the raindrops at a bamboo flagpole that had been erected in a terraced rice paddy, and particularly at the blue cloth banner that billowed from it. It had been some time since he had finished performing the Daoist ritual in which he produced a long talisman written on the three-by-eight-foot banner and then hoisted it onto the pole. He craned to see whether the wind had tangled into knots the five pennant-like streamers cut into the unattached end of the banner (see cover photo). He saw that it had not and that the long, tapered shapes of the streamers continued to flicker almost like flames in the healthy breeze, as they were when he first raised the banner. Chen returned to his stool on the porch and avoided eye contact with the dozens of masters, relatives, and villagers who were attending his ordination into the priesthood that day. Nervously, he continued smoking. The absence of knots in the pennants meant that the deity he had summoned during the ritual had not yet heeded his call.

Chen Diwen felt anxious for good reason. His ordination into the priesthood hinged on the deity's response. For the last four years, Chen had trained with a local master who was a member of the Daoist lineage that dominated the area. As an apprentice, Chen had assisted in the various rites officiated by ordained priests in that lineage. Finally, after his master had agreed he was ready to be ordained, Chen spent forty-nine straight days diligently memorizing and practicing the complicated summoning ritual, making sure he could properly inscribe on the banner the complex talisman the ritual is designed to produce. On that rainy day in February 2004, Chen Diwen performed the Banner Rite (to Summon) Sire Yin (Yingong fanfa 殷公旛法, the Banner Rite) as the first ritual of his own ordination *jiao*.[2] This performance was the first time he had officiated over a ritual in public. If he happened to be unsuccessful and the deity failed to descend from his celestial palace and use the wind to knot the summoning banner, the rest of the three-day ordination *jiao* would likely be aborted and Chen would not be ordained at that time.

The masters in Chen Diwen's lineage recognize a deity called Celestial Lord Yin Jiao (Yin Jiao tianjun 殷郊天君), also known as Thunder General Yin Jiao (Yin Jiao leijiang 殷郊雷將) or Prime Marshal Yin Jiao (Yin Jiao yuanshuai 殷郊元帥), as the agent of their liturgical power. As in much of south China, masters in the region around Le'an township serve their local communities as liturgical specialists. Like many masters in Hunan, they consider themselves members of the broad Zhengyi (正一, Orthodox Unity) tradition. They marry, live in homes rather than in temples, and often hold secular jobs in addition to minding their liturgical responsibilities. They are regularly hired by members of the community to perform an array of ritual services, including rites to thank the high gods for prosperity, funerary rites, and rites to protect bodies and households from demons that cause illness, economic misfortune, and agricultural irregularity. On occasion they are called on to heal bodies and households from demonic infiltration. Technically speaking, it is not the masters who drive demons away; it is Celestial Lord Yin and a host of other heavenly generals and their spirit armies who— under the master's command during ritual—disperse, pacify, or sometimes even destroy disruptive demons and sprites.

The Banner Rite is the ritual way masters in Chen Diwen's lineage attempt to summon the powerful Yin Jiao and submit him to their will. An ordinand cannot be ordained a Daoist priest if he is unable to prove that he can properly perform the Banner Rite. A failed Banner Rite at ordination would signal that the ordinand could not secure General Yin's allegiance and thus could not direct the deity's exorcistic power to fulfill a ritual need. The young master's liturgical performances would lack efficacy, and no one in the community would spend their scant money to hire him. Even if the ordinand practiced the Banner Rite another forty-nine days and tried again, the pressure would be excruciating. A second failed attempt would certainly doom the budding master's reputation before his career even began. All these anxieties swirled in Chen Diwen as he sat chain-smoking and waiting for Marshal Yin to reply.

This book begins with Chen Diwen's palpable anxiety surrounding the Banner Rite. It asks why his performance of the ritual was so intense. It is easy to see that the social condition surrounding the Banner Rite generated much of his concern. The community that would furnish his livelihood was watching, in inescapably empirical terms, whether he could muster enough divine power to merit hiring in the future. His performance of the Banner Rite was a de facto job application, his very aspiration to become a liturgical master was put to a public test.

This book, though, asks why Chen Diwen was so apprehensive from a different point of view. It asks whether anything in the liturgical workings of the Banner Rite itself contributed to his unease. To pose the question this way is really to ask how the Banner Rite works—or fails to work. How might the cosmological, theological, and anthropological assumptions ensconced in Chen Diwen's performance of the liturgy be animated to produce an efficacious or inefficacious result? In other words, what was going on within the world of the Banner Rite such that Chen might compel Yin Jiao to respond favorably—or not? What within the world of the ritual led Chen to agonize? These questions are different ways to frame a classic question in the phenomenology of religion: what is really going on inside a religious moment such that it is experienced in a certain way?

Answering the question posed this way requires a journey deep inside the world of the Banner Rite. Such a journey shows that Chen's apprehension about his performance of the ritual was in large part driven by concern for whether the ritual would accomplish its liturgical goal—successful communication between officiant and deity. Communication here implies a relationship between particular subjects. The Banner Rite is the ritual way that Chen Diwen the ordinand hoped to forge a relationship with his lineage's main martial deity, Yin Jiao, the supplier of his exorcistic power. Using complicated incantations, visualizations, ritual gestures, and inscriptions, Chen strove to convince Yin Jiao that the two should form an intimate bond. If successful, this bond would last for the rest of Chen's liturgical life. Whenever he would need exorcistic power, he would call on Yin Jiao.

But the relationship negotiated in the Banner Rite is far more complicated than one-to-one correspondence. Chen Diwen was not simply a lone ordinand trying to invoke a single deity in straightforward terms. Within the world of the Banner Rite, Chen operated within a web of relationships with divine figures. He was presented as the student of a long, winding lineage of deceased, deified masters who had ritually invoked Yin Jiao for as long as anyone could remember. The lineage has inherited that ritual knowledge from practices dating to at least the late twelfth or early thirteenth century. It is the prestige of the lineage and its maintenance of arcane ritual knowledge that allowed Chen to even dare to approach a deity as fierce as Yin Jiao. For his part, Yin Jiao also exists within a matrix of relationships. He is bound by ties of obligation to his celestial superior, a stellar deity called the Emperor of the North (Beidi 北帝), and to his master, a mysterious figure known as Shen the Realized One (Shen zhenren 申真人), a patriarch of Chen's lineage and the figure to whom Yin Jiao first swore allegiance.[3] Within the world of the Banner Rite, the ordinand Chen Diwen relied on ritual knowledge transmitted through his lineage that taught him how to elicit a response from Yin Jiao by entering into the thick web of divine relationships surrounding the god, and then relying on their authority to communicate his intentions directly to Yin Jiao.

The Banner Rite

Since around 1990, when the local government liberalized official policies on religious expression in Le'an township and its environs, liturgical masters have been reviving ritual traditions suppressed by the Chinese Communist Party for the previous thirty-five years. Locals have slowly raised money to rebuild temples that were desecrated and looted by Red Guards during the Cultural Revolution (1966–1976). Young men like Chen Diwen have once again chosen to be ordained and to make their livings by serving the religious needs of their communities.

While working with Chen's lineage since the mid-2000s, including living with its masters for stints sometimes several months long, I have been struck by how much these masters ground their liturgical identity in their ability to perform the Banner Rite. This single ritual is the touchstone that signals the beginning of every ritual practitioner's transition from an apprentice under tutelage of a master to a full-fledged master capable of officiating over Daoist liturgies, exorcistic rites, and Buddhist funerals.[4] As in Chen Diwen's case, the Banner Rite must successfully be performed by an ordinand on the first day of his ordination *jiao* before the ordination can continue with confidence. An ordinand must publicly show the pantheon of gods and deceased masters of the lineage and his local community that he has mastered the Banner Rite, which is a display of the lineage's most guarded esoteric knowledge. That knowledge has been preserved and passed down the generations in an amalgam of textual and oral forms. The masters of the lineage regard their texts as their most precious heirlooms and make sure to copy them by hand every generation. Their texts are so esteemed that during the Cultural Revolution, when all forms of religious practice were harshly persecuted, the masters surrendered scriptures singing praises of high gods to government officials who searched their residences for religious paraphernalia, but risked arrest and even imprisonment to conceal their ritual texts, chief among them the manual scripting the Banner Rite.

The Banner Rite is a kind of ritual repository for the lineage's most precious secret teachings. It performs the esoteric instructions (*mizhi* 秘旨) for wielding potent exorcistic power for apotropaic or therapeutic ends.[5] The masters of the lineage are very concerned with whether a ritual and a ritual officiant are *ling* 靈 or possess *lingqi* 靈氣—by which they mean ritual efficaciousness driven by "divine power" or "divinely powerful *qi*."[6] In abstract terms, a ritual works if it supplies divine power potent enough to rearrange or change the movements of *qi* comprising the situation addressed by the ritual. A space or body clogged by static or stale *qi* cannot be healthy and prosperous. A ritual such as the Banner Rite is designed to prevent obstructions or unclog a space or body by bringing about an infusion of divine *qi*. These masters imagine both numinous power and unhealthy obstructions of *qi* in terms of subjects. Heavily armed, fierce martial deities literally embody divinely efficacious *qi* by warding off, shooing away, or on rare occasions even destroying demons or sprites that cause disease and misfortune. Chen Diwen and his masters have inherited from their long lineage a special relationship with one of these martial deities—Celestial Lord Yin Jiao. We shall see that Yin Jiao has sworn an oath to serve as martial functionary under the command of the masters of Chen's lineage. Yin Jiao and his spirit army, as well as other celestial generals and their heavenly forces who march under Yin's banner, are responsible for responding to the call of all masters recognized by the lineage.

The Banner Rite performed at an ordination *jiao* 醮 is the most comprehensive version of the ritual, the fullest invocation of the divine, exorcistic power embodied by Yin Jiao and his spirit forces. It requires about an hour and twenty minutes to perform and constitutes a kind of public test of an ordinand after several years of training. Its successful performance is the sine qua non of becoming a full-fledged master. At an ordination such as Chen Diwen's, the Banner Rite is the moment the ordinand forms an intimate relationship with the martial deity, which is what actually allows the master to direct the deity and his exorcistic power. If this initial relationship is not established, any subsequent ritual performance is considered impossible. The banner typically takes anywhere from an hour or so to a few days to knot. A longer wait time or a looser knot signals a less than enthusiastic response from Yin Jiao. Inability to garner a response at all is tantamount to ritual impotency.

The Banner Rite can also be used for many purposes in different liturgical settings. It is performed on the first day of any large *jiao*. Yin Jiao and his minions are summoned to guard the perimeter of any altar space from the disruptive influences of demons and sprites, and to protect the spirit messengers who transmit written memorials and petitions prepared and dispatched by ritual officiants to the various celestial palaces of high gods on behalf of the community or household that sponsors the liturgy. They are also called upon to execute any exorcistic aim of the *jiao,* which might be to defend the community or household from economic strife, interpersonal tension, illness, or consequences of negative karmic action. Shortened versions of the Banner Rite constitute the liturgical heart of any apotropaic or therapeutic "minor rite" (*xiaofa* 小法). Yin Jiao and his forces safeguard individual households from any sort of calamity, often economic, and protect the bodies of its inhabitants—especially women (who are susceptible to complications during pregnancy and childbirth) and children (who are vulnerable to disease)— from what might be demonic meddling. At times, Yin Jiao is charged with healing a household or person who has already been afflicted.

The masters of the lineage dare not breezily presume that their performance of the Banner Rite will in fact summon Yin Jiao and his forces. One need look no further than Chen Diwen's tense smoking to sense how serious this business is. Even seasoned masters are anxious each time they perform the Banner Rite on the first day of a *jiao*. Masters are wary of the possibility that they might mangle parts of the long and complicated ritual. They are also wary that Yin Jiao himself might, for whatever reason, choose not to respond. After all, despite having sworn an oath submitting his services to Chen's lineage centuries ago, Yin Jiao—like all martial deities—can be frighteningly ferocious and obdurate. He is forceful enough to deal with intrusive demons but can also be fickle and capricious. Even a competent performance of the Banner Rite might end in failure. "After all," a master in the lineage notes, "Yin Jiao *is* a god, and he is a little bit unruly [*ye* 野]." This fear is magnified tenfold when the Banner Rite is performed publicly for the first time during an ordination.

The Banner Rite is a decidedly Daoist mode of ritual communication. What enables a mortal such as Chen Diwen to enter a web of divine relationships is successfully establishing a foundation for the communication. That foundation is ontological. By detailed visualizations and complex inner alchemical procedures, an officiant like Chen attempts to recover the divine core of his very self, which shares the same stuff, the same primordial *qi,* as the divine bodies of the Emperor of the North, Shen the Realized One, and Yin Jiao. It is that ontological identity that makes possible communication between a ritual officiant and specific deities.

Once a common ontological ground is established, an officiant like Chen Diwen can converse in the language of the gods. He can literally channel the primordial stuff of his body to express a kind of synesthetic language in a long talisman (*fu* 符) inscribed on the banner. Each utterance of the talisman is an emanation of primordial *qi* from the officiant's body into an amalgam of written graphs, verbal incantations, mental visualizations, and gestures. Such mingling of inscription, voice, mental imagery, and movement communicates with deities because they are infused with the primordial *qi* that ontologically connects the sender with the recipient. If rendered properly, the talismanic language penetrates (*tong* 通) Yin Jiao. He should be moved (*dong* 動) by its message. That message is an entreaty that Yin Jiao be respectful of the web of divine relationships in which he exists. He should abide by the command of his celestial superior the Emperor of the North, he should remember the oath of loyalty he pledged to his master Shen the Realized One, and he should heed his pledge to serve Shen's liturgical progeny—Chen Diwen's lineage of masters. Provided that Chen performs the entire ritual well, Yin Jiao should recognize his duty to his celestial superior, to his master, and to Chen's lineage and agree to serve the ordinand.

The Banner Rite, then, is a sophisticated mode of ritual communication between an officiant such as Chen Diwen and the martial deity Yin Jiao, which mobilizes a web of gods to compel Yin to take up his dutiful position and serve as Chen's exorcistic functionary. This book unpacks this thesis by telling the stories of the two main interlocutors in the ritual—Chen Diwen the ordinand and Yin Jiao the martial deity—and then by drawing out the cosmological, theological, and anthropological concepts animating Chen's inaugural performance of the Banner Rite on that day in 2004. In the spirit of phenomenology of religion, the book articulates what is really going on inside the Banner Rite in Daoist terms. Those are the terms in which Chen Diwen experienced intense anxiety as he sat on his porch after his performance of the Banner Rite.

Ritual, Relationship, and Communication between Subjects

The historian of religion Lawrence Sullivan notes that every ritual is itself a theory of ritual writ large—that is, the symbols of any given ritual, strung together in a particular way in performed action, give a subtle accounting of the nature of ritual.[7] This book demonstrates that the particular theory running through the Banner Rite is that ritual performance itself is first and foremost communication. The interlocutors of that communication are both human and divine subjects thick with their own histories, formative relationships, and ability to participate in the ritual activity in a more or less engaged way—or not to participate at all. The Banner Rite is through and through informed by this notion of ritual, which has in large part come down to it from strands of practice and theory within the great liturgical movements of the Song and Yuan dynasties (960–1368). The masters in Chen Diwen's lineage who perform the Banner Rite today interpret the rite with this notion of ritual in mind.

The idea that ritual is a mode of communication between human and divine subjects has not been at the fore of the classic scholarship on Daoist ritual that informs this book. Kristofer Schipper famously looks at Daoist ritual as a "liturgical structure" or "liturgical framework" that organizes the daily life of local Chinese communities and integrates individuals within them. "The liturgical tradition of Taoism is first of all a great structuring system (*fa* 法) which pursues the autonomy of the social body. The integration of individuals into this body is achieved through ritual (*ke* 科)."[8] Daoist liturgies performed at the major markers of an individual's life— birth, puberty, marriage, death—as well as at public events—new year celebrations, thanksgivings for divine blessings—give shape to the rhythm of local communal life. Partaking in those performances, administered by local "Dignitaries of the Dao" (Daoist priests, *daoshi* 道士), literally incorporates individuals into that "social body," which is itself imagined as a part of the great cosmic body composed of primordial energies from the source of all things, the Dao. The liturgies that have comprised a more or less continuous "practice of the Dao" for two millennia have given shape to the religious and political workings of "non-official China" beyond the control of the state. For Schipper, what is important about ritual is that it provides remarkably durable form or pattern to social life on the ground, and that that local social life stubbornly resists top-down shaping by the state.

Schipper looks so intently at the formal aspects of Daoist ritual that he regards the doing of ritual, not discursive interpretations of that doing, as the very core of ritual:

> When investigating the meaning of Daoist ritual, it soon becomes clear that there is no general value system, but a number of different and overlapping ones. They no doubt reflect different stages and moments in the continuous quest for meaning, and periodically renewed adjustments or additions made to cope with the preoccupations of the times. At the same time, the core of the ritual is preserved. Transformations in meaning do not touch such fundamental ritual actions as singing, the burning of incense and the oblation of sacred, if often unintelligible, writings. It is around these nuclear ritual forms that various interpretational clusters have accumulated.[9]

It is not only the forms, or doing, of ritual action—singing, burning incense, burning liturgical documents like talismans, to name a few—that have endured during the long history of Daoist practice, it is the structure of those forms of doing—the way they are arranged vis-à-vis one another in the sequence of performance—that has persisted. This attention to structure compels Schipper to map out discrete forms of doing into an order or syntax that composes a larger formal set. Discrete "rites" (*fa*) are ordered in a certain way to compose "rituals" (*yi* 儀), and rituals are ordered in a certain way to compose "services" (*hui* 會, *ke*), such as "retreats" (*zhai* 齋) and "sacrifices" (*jiao*). The order of each set is logically similar, which creates a nested symmetry of ritual action that has been remarkably durable. Onto that "formal" structure of ritual syntax practitioners have grafted discursive meanings, which are multiple because they have changed with the vicissitudes of time and place. For Schipper, what Daoist liturgists do and the order in which they do it—rather than what they say about what they do—is the core of Daoist ritual seemingly impervious to major change.[10]

If what is important about ritual is the impact on local society by its performance, and especially the order or syntax of its performance, rather than its interpretation, then the participants in ritual matter for the roles they play in that performance. Noticing that during festivals in Taiwan Daoists often put on plays with string dolls on outdoor stages set up in front of temples, Schipper likens liturgical officiants to puppeteers, and both gods and mediums to puppets.

> The structure that governs the relation between puppet master and puppet—between the one hidden in the shadows who pulls the strings and the other who occupies center stage and, while the show lasts, holds the attention of the audience—is the same structure found in the relation between masters and mediums, men and gods. The gods are puppets. . . . In this game, men play with the gods, and the temple becomes a great dollhouse.[11]

In Taiwan, barefoot ritual masters (*fashi* 法師)—colloquially called "red heads" (*hongtou* 紅頭) for the color of their ritual headgear—perform rites in the vernacular language in which they communicate with various deities or deceased ancestors through mediums. Mediums go into trance, become possessed by specific spirits, and then speak in the spirit's voice or inscribe the spirit's intentions through spirit-writing. The medium is an instrument of the master's power, a tool by which the master communes with otherworldly beings. In addition, just as the barefoot master controls the medium, so does he hold sway over various spirits. Upon ordination, a ritual master makes a covenant with each of the gods, expressed in a sealed ordination document, in which the deity promises protection and aid. The covenant affords the master remarkable power to summon to the vessel of the medium each of the spirits of the pantheon, from lofty deities to lowly demons and orphan souls. The master knows the secret names of those spirits and how to write them in the mysterious language inscribed on talismans. He knows their legends and hails them by reciting vernacular verses alluding to their histories. Spirits are sure to respond. "In spite of respectful words, the summons is real. A law requiring the gods to obey the master is the result of an agreement between the master and the gods [upon the master's ordination]: those who obey will be promoted and honored, the others will be persecuted. They are thus forced to manifest themselves in the medium or the puppet, or to reveal themselves through inspired writing."[12] Higher deities are bound by cosmic law to work for the benefit of mankind, and lower spirits obey masters in their bid to ascend the ladder of merit that leads to a desirable position in the heavens.

Likewise, Schipper argues that Daoist priests (*daoshi*)—those who perform rites in the classical language and, he insists, are direct descendants of the early Celestial Master (Tianshidao 天師道) movement of the second century CE—occupy the role of master over certain deities. During his ordination, a Daoist is conferred a list of functionary deities with whom he has a "personal relationship." They accompany him wherever he goes and protect his body and his ritual performances from demonic attack. Schipper classifies these deities as members of the popular pantheon. Unlike the highest deities, who are hypostases of the Dao and so are regarded as properly "Daoist" gods, popular deities were once lowly, even demonic, spirits who are working their way up the cosmic hierarchy. "These popular gods entered the covenant in order that they might progress in the merit system of the *ke* (liturgy). The *daoshi* is their master and, thanks to his liturgy, the gods may 'pass' (*du* 度). Any of their actions favorable to mankind are duly recorded so that they may gradually transcend their demoniacal identity."[13] For Schipper, the familiar relation between the barefoot ritual master and his medium, between the barefoot ritual master and his spirits, applies here. The Daoist priest is the puppeteer and the deities conferred to him are his puppets. Deities must respond to the summons and directives of the Daoist master.

Schipper's influential ideas about ritual help us get at part of the theory of ritual assumed by the Banner Rite and its liturgists. Ritual is indeed about communication between masters and deities, especially functionary deities such as Yin Jiao with whom the master has a personal relationship struck during ordination. Masters do indeed hail those deities by calling their secret names or writing them out in talismanic language, and by regaling deities by alluding to narratives about their histories. Yet, the Banner Rite insists that the relationship between master and martial deity is more complicated and interesting than that between a puppeteer and his puppet. Although obligated to serve a master, a martial deity is both fearsome and fickle. That he can refuse—and at times does refuse—to obey his obligation is why ordinands such as Chen Diwen are so anxious about whether the ritual succeeds. The master cannot force his functionary deity to respond to his summons, despite divine laws or statutes commanding compliance. For this reason, the master communicates with a host of other deities, who themselves have influence on his functionary, to convince and even coerce the capricious deity to comply. For Schipper, the master and deity are flat characters in a ritual play with an inevitable outcome; they are functions of a virtually unchanging "liturgical structure." But the Banner Rite insists that both master and deity are active participants in an encounter with an uncertain ending, and each uses the symbolic language of the ritual to influence how the ending comes about.

In an incisive critique of Schipper's position that ritual ought to be understood as purely formal syntax vacant of discursive meaning, Poul Andersen argues that ritual has meaning in a relational sense. Ritual means something to someone in a certain context within a larger life world.[14] In other words, ritual involves subjects. By the term "subject," I mean those who have a history, articulable in narrative, in which they are formed by means of relationships with others. Subjects actively participate in endeavors like ritual in such a way that their participation is particular to them in their contexts within a larger life world.[15] Many subjects are involved in a ritual such as the

Banner Rite. Liturgists, lay patrons, artisans, cooks, and even local officials, as well as different classes of deities, deified masters, and demons, all congregate in and around the altar space. But we shall see that the Banner Rite and its liturgists are concerned primarily with two subjects—the ordinand and his martial deity.

These subjects of the Banner Rite are entangled in particular histories. Chen Diwen, who was a sickly child whose grandmother prayed to a deified local master for his health, later found his way into the apprenticeship of another local master. That master introduced Chen to a long lineage of deceased masters who claim to descend from particular Song-era Daoist patriarchs and a quirky Buddhist patriarch. A particular history of Yin Jiao has made its way down to Chen. Narratives and iconography maintained by his lineage recount that Yin Jiao attends to one of the highest of the celestial deities and has passed several lifetimes as a prince of various rulers, most recently of the infamous King Zhou of the ancient Shang dynasty. Yin Jiao began this lifetime as a traumatized boy bent on revenge for his slain mother at the hand of his wicked father, but later gave that up and pledged himself to serve the Dao under the tutelage of a wise master, who happens to be one of the patriarchs of Chen's lineage. The notion of ritual assumed by the Banner Rite and its liturgists, then, is a mode of communication between these two active subjects who are enveloped in histories filled with relationships that have shaped them.

At every turn, Chen Diwen and his masters use the word *goutong* (溝通) —to communicate, to link up—to characterize the Banner Rite. As one master put it, the Banner Rite is performed "to see whether one can communicate with the marshal" (看看自己是否能跟元帥溝通). For Schipper, communication between masters and martial deities is one-way. Ritual language flows from the master who speaks to a deity who receives. The deity, like an actor in a play, has no choice but to obey the speech or written signs. But the Banner Rite and its liturgists recognize that ritual communication is not monologic. It is instead dialogical. It consists of an active call from the officiant and an active response by the deity via the symbolic forms of language supplied by the ritual.

This notion of ritual as communication between subjects resonates strongly with aspects of the linguistic notion of "utterance." Developed by the Russian literary theorist Mikhail Bakhtin (1895–1975), an utterance is any unit of language—from a single word or gesture, to an entire text like a novel or modern dance, to a ritual like the Banner Rite—through which one subject speaks with another. Every utterance is like a little drama in which a speaker conveys some meaning to a listener and a listener responds. An utterance is entirely social. It takes place between speakers in particular situations and saturated by social factors.[16] Chen Diwen is ensconced in his personal history; Yin Jiao is in his. The Banner Rite is not simply a ritual form that Chen enacts in a generic way. Chen in his specific social location addresses Yin Jiao in his, and then Yin addresses Chen in response. Chen Diwen's performance of the Banner Rite—from his initial bowing to the four directions while playing the flute to his raising the inscribed banner to the sky at the end—is how Chen the speaker conveys to Yin Jiao the listener that Chen is a legitimate member of a long lineage with ties to the deity, and that Chen is sincere and competent enough to wield the arcane ritual forms well enough to be taken seriously. Yin Jiao's social location demands that Chen also address the deity's celestial superiors and his master in a bid to convince the fickle god to obey the summons. Unlike a word or sentence bounded by a particular grammatical form, the beginning and end of an utterance are determined by a change in speaking subjects. We shall see that Chen's utterance via his performance of the Banner Rite ends when Yin Jiao responds with his own utterance—knotting the banner or declining to do so.

Seen as an exchange of utterances, a ritual like the Banner Rite is an intersubjective site, a space in which socially located subjects express themselves to one another in ritual language. Intersubjectivity here is not strictly personal or idiosyncratic. Subjects address with ritual forms and respond with forms that are already given. Chen Diwen addresses Yin Jiao with esoteric ritual forms recognizable to the gods, which were learned from his masters, who themselves learned from their masters, and so on. Yin Jiao responds by knotting, or not knotting, the banner—a public form recognized by the gathered human and divine communities. These types of utterances are relatively standardized and repeatable; they are habituated forms constituting the conventional aspect of the ritual language used to communicate messages between members of Chen's lineage and Yin Jiao.

Yet these conventional ritual forms are not neutral; they also reveal something about the individual speakers. The way in which Chen Diwen performs the Banner Rite reveals his sincerity and devotion to his masters and to the lineage's teachings, including their narratives about Yin Jiao. Further, this awareness of how the ritual is performed is expressed in a particularly Daoist way. Chen attempts to recover his true, primordial self, which enables him to imbue the writing of the talisman used to summon Yin Jiao with the power of ancestral *qi*. Chen literally saturates the conventional signs that make up that talisman with rarified *qi* from his true self to create a certain quality of ritual language that empowers it to signify in the celestial realm. In these senses, Chen infuses the more or less standardized, repeatable conventions of the Banner Rite with life and meaning, which are bound up with who he is and with his awareness of who Yin Jiao is. Likewise, Yin Jiao does not simply respond to Chen's performance by knotting or not knotting the banner. The manner in which Yin might knot the banner reveals his enthusiasm for Chen's summons. In this ritual convention, Yin Jiao expresses something of himself to Chen and the gathered community. In these ways, both Chen Diwen and Yin Jiao become authors of ritual utterances the forms of which were not devised by them. They each make the Banner Rite their own.

The theory of ritual running through the Banner Rite and its liturgists insists that ritual utterances are active in the world. They do not simply reflect some situation, like a social or cosmic hierarchy, although they do indeed do that. More important, ritual also allows space for interactions within those hierarchies which can bring about something new. The purpose of the Banner Rite is to provide a mode of communication between two subjects—the officiant and the martial deity—by which they might form an intimate bond. That bond is a promise that the martial deity will respond to the master's ritual summons, and that the master will venerate the martial deity. If struck, the bond will constitute the efficacy of the master's ritual performances, especially in apotropaic and therapeutic rites, for the rest of his days. In its dialogical communication, the Banner Rite transforms an ordinand like Chen Diwen into a master, and Yin Jiao into his personal martial functionary.

Looking at ritual as utterance, as the Banner Rite and its liturgists do, makes us see aspects of Daoist ritual different from those highlighted by Schipper and those he has inspired, especially those who have worked on rituals dealing with martial deities. For example, Mark Meulenbeld gives an account of how Song and later vernacular rituals worked to "domesticate" unruly martial deities like Yin Jiao. Martial gods were the remnants of lowly, "orphan" spirits who possessed mediums, and/or were venerated as local saints. Deemed autonomous and so dangerous, these local spirits were pacified by means of ritual methods that captured and then incorporated them into pantheons of martial deities controlled by ritual masters.[17] Thinking along with Meulenbeld, the Banner Rite can be seen to transform an unruly, undomesticated Yin Jiao into an obedient, domesticated martial deity, who could then be employed by Chen Diwen to subjugate other unaffiliated spirits. This is a perfectly valid reading if one assumes that Yin Jiao has historical roots as a lowly spirit who possessed local mediums, which he certainly might have. But the Banner Rite does not see him that way. We shall see that within the world of the Banner Rite Yin Jiao is imagined as a lofty attendant of a celestial emperor and a virtuous paragon of filial piety. He is fickle and fierce, not at all lowly and demonic. Within the world of the Banner Rite, Yin Jiao is not a passive figure who is important because his status is moved from unaffiliated to affiliated, from wild to controlled. Instead, he is a celestial god with terrestrial jurisdiction and a thick personal history who receives Chen's ritual utterances and actively responds.

Recognition of the particular theory of ritual assumed by the Banner Rite and its liturgists becomes apparent to us scholars when we try to get inside the world of the Banner Rite. Instead of asking how ritual works in the larger society, we might simply ask how it works from its own point of view. This question is the hallmark of the phenomenology of religion. Rather than an agreed upon body of theory, phenomenology of religion is more an orientation, what historian of religion Kimerer LaMothe calls a "practice of understanding."[18] As taught to me, a phenomenological approach is the conscious cultivation of a kind of sensitivity in which we allow a religious phenomenon, such as the Banner Rite, to impress itself upon us. Then we strive to articulate what that phenomenon means within its religious world. This demands that we employ what phenomenologists of religion call *epoché*. This practice has two aspects. First, we try to refrain from overt judgments as to the truth or value of a phenomenon. Second, we try to empathize as much as possible with the phenomenon. We try to relive in our own imaginations what it would be like to experience the phenomenon in all its complexity in order to understand something of the phenomenon from the inside.[19] Of course, *epoché* is at best an ideal. One's ability to refrain from all judgments and fully empathize is limited. Any understanding can only be an approximation. And if not vigilant, well-intentioned empathy can easily become facile, often imperialistic, impressions of what is going on. I found these pitfalls painfully obvious while working on this book. But with frequent reminders of humility, I think we scholars can still cautiously adopt the spirit of the phenomenology of religion. We can glean something valuable about the religious world in which a religious phenomenon occurs. This book shows you the reader what I gleaned from my limited location within the world of the Banner Rite.

Structure of the Book

The structure of the book helps perform the argument that the Banner Rite is a kind of communication between two subjects—Chen Diwen and Yin Jiao—designed to put them in relationship. Subjects have histories during which they themselves have been shaped by meaningful relationships. And subjects play active roles in things like ritual. The first half of the book examines at length the two main subjects participating in the Banner Rite. Chapter 1 peers into Chen Diwen's life before he attempted to summon Yin Jiao. Who were his formative influences and what compelled him to study liturgy from a local master in the first place? How did he learn his craft? How did he discover who Yin Jiao is and how to communicate with him?

We shall be afforded a rare glimpse into one young man's experiences as a liturgical apprentice amid the pressures of life in rural south China at the turn of the twenty-first century. We shall also see that Chen's bona fides as a member of an orthodox lineage with an existing relationship with Yin Jiao is crucial for the Banner Rite's success. Chen comes to the ritual as a sincere ordinand having been trained within a long lineage that recognizes Yin Jiao's own master as one of the patriarchs of its liturgical tradition. By piecing together scraps of evidence from local manuscript culture, we shall learn something of the complicated history of Chen's lineage. We shall see that the lineage actually practices two liturgical traditions—one Daoist with roots in fourteenth-century Hunan, and one Buddhist with roots in twelfth-century Jiangxi province. We shall learn how those strands of practice wound their way to north-central Hunan and then combined into a dual Daoist-Buddhist liturgical tradition. We shall see how that tradition arrived in Chen Diwen's region two hundred years ago, and how it has persisted through the heart-wrenching social and political turmoil of the twentieth century.

Chapter 2 explores who Yin Jiao is and who he has been. Drawing on visual representations and hagiographical literature preserved by the lineage, we shall learn how Chen Diwen and his liturgical brethren believe Yin Jiao became a powerful martial deity, how he came to be defined by his relationship with his celestial superior—the Emperor of the North—and how he concluded an oath of loyal service to his master in the exorcistic arts of the Dao—Shen the Realized One. We shall see that the lineage's images of Yin Jiao and their awareness of his defining relationships have roots in liturgical traditions flourishing during the thirteenth through early fifteenth centuries. Strikingly similar depictions of the god show up in visualization instructions and incantations practiced in certain strands of the Correct Method of the Heart of Heaven (Tianxin zhengfa 天心正法), Divine Empyrean (Shenxiao 神霄), and Pure Tenuity (Qingwei 清微) traditions, as well as in a narrative expressed in a particular Song or Yuan period hagiography. Because these traditions of practice are still relatively understudied, I provide some intellectual and social background for each. Finally, many other depictions of Yin Jiao appear in late imperial sources, especially in vernacular literature, but Chen Diwen's lineage seems to have eschewed them in favor of those from earlier liturgical and hagiographical sources. Although we do not have the sources to understand exactly how the earlier depictions made their way down the centuries to Chen's lineage, we get a strong sense of which strands of Song and Yuan liturgical practice and thought have somehow combined to make up his lineage's Daoist liturgies.

The second half of the book examines how these two subjects encounter each other for the first time during the Banner Rite. These chapters offer a close reading of Chen Diwen's particular performance of the ritual to show the complicated liturgical ways he attempts to communicate with the god and summon him to service. Running through these chapters is a deep engagement with precedents of the Banner Rite's cosmological, theological, and anthropological assumptions in thirteenth- and fourteenth-century practice. By putting Chen's twenty-first-century performance of the Banner Rite—informed by the lineage's liturgical manuals and oral teachings—in conversation with particular ritual commentaries and theoretical treatises by Daoist theologians from the Song and Yuan periods, we see more clearly how the Banner Rite works in Daoist terms. Although this conversation gives a good sense of the intellectual roots of the Banner Rite, these chapters do not offer an intellectual history. Instead they mine surprisingly consonant texts from Heart of Heaven, Divine Empyrean, and Pure Tenuity traditions to lend sophistication and nuance to our accounting of Chen Diwen's performance of the Banner Rite.

Chapter 3 examines the ontological foundation of the ritual communication. In it, we see how Chen employs visualization, incantation, and gesture to burn away his mundane self, take on the divine bodies of several gods, and then recover his divine self, the primordial part of himself that shares in the same ontological reality as denizens of the celestial realm. That common reality allows Chen's divine self to ascend to the heavens and communicate with the divine beings who hold sway over Yin Jiao, chief among them Yin's celestial superior, the Emperor of the North.

Chapter 4 explores the mode of communication from Chen Diwen to Yin Jiao himself. Chen channels ancestral *qi* cultivated in the process of recovering his primordial self to produce a lengthy talisman made up of amalgams of written graphs, verbal incantations, mental visualizations, and gestures. By closely reading the strange writing, speech, imagery, and movement within the fabric of the entire Banner Rite, including the lineage's hagiography and iconography of Yin Jiao, we can make sense of the language the talisman uses to convey messages to the deity about who Chen Diwen is and why Yin Jiao should heed his summons. The language of the talisman does not confidently assume that Yin Jiao will respond, as much influential scholarship on talismans implies. Instead, it shames, cajoles, and even threatens Yin Jiao in hopes that the martial deity might be moved to respond. The talisman itself subtly reveals a fascinating theology that recognizes Yin Jiao as a subject who must be convinced to obey by reminding him of his obligations to his celestial lord the Emperor of the North and to his master Shen the Realized One.

Taken as a whole, this study offers an intriguing Daoist theory of ritual efficacy that accounts for ritual work in terms of the relationship between practitioner and deity, who are both recognized as subjects thick with history and active as participants in ritual.

Chapter One

The Ordinand

Chen Diwen

Communication between us and deities must go through our masters and patriarchs.

——Master Jiang Yucheng (b. 1973)

Only from a source does a stream flow, so when practicing a ritual one must clarify its lineage. If the lineage is not authentic then the general summoned is unorthodox.

——Master Liu Yu (fl. 1258)

Chen Diwen's performance of the Banner Rite to Summon Sire Yin constituted a mode of communication between him and Celestial Lord Yin Jiao in which a relationship between budding master and martial deity might be forged. The Banner Rite itself recognized that the possibility of that communication and relationship begins with acknowledgment that both Chen Diwen and Yin Jiao were subjects. Both were rooted in particular histories that can be expressed as narratives, and those narratives tell how each had been ensconced in consequential relationships that shaped them. Chen and Yin would also maintain a certain agency during the Banner Rite. Far from cogs in some ritual machine or thespians in a play with a foregone conclusion, both subjects would be active participants in the ritual. What they would do—or fail to do—and how they would do it would directly affect the outcome, which Chen's anxiety indicated was anything but certain.

In this and the next chapter, we see something of Chen Diwen's history and of Yin Jiao's. First is Chen's story and the lived experiences that led a young man growing up in rural Hunan at the end of the twentieth century to seek admittance into a local lineage of masters, culminating in his attempt to summon Yin Jiao that day in 2004. What compelled him to study with the local lineage of masters in the first place? How did he learn his liturgical craft? How did he come to know who Yin Jiao is and the proper way to deal with him? We peek into one young man's experiences as an apprentice amid the pressures of life in rural south China at the turn of this century.

Along the way, we see that Chen Diwen's particular story is just the latest chapter of a much larger narrative, that of the lineage of his masters. In the world of the Banner Rite, Chen would never be defined simply as a singular ordinand trying to invoke a martial deity on his own, but instead as a subject operating within a chain of relationships. He was an aspiring member of a long lineage of living and deceased masters who transmitted liturgical know-how down through the centuries. This long line of masters would lend Chen his bona fides for performing the summoning rite. They would witness his performance and act as intermediaries legitimizing and amplifying his requests of the divine realm, as well as his negotiations with Yin Jiao himself.

To understand Chen Diwen as a subject, then, we need to understand something of the history of the lineage to which he belonged. This chapter works outside the scope of local gazetteers to bring that story to light. It examines scant clues culled from dozens of the lineage's liturgical manuals and reads them against recently published works by local scholars in central Hunan and by a handful of international scholars to gain some purchase on how both Daoist and Buddhist liturgical traditions proliferated in parts of central Hunan. With the help of oral histories provided by the eldest living

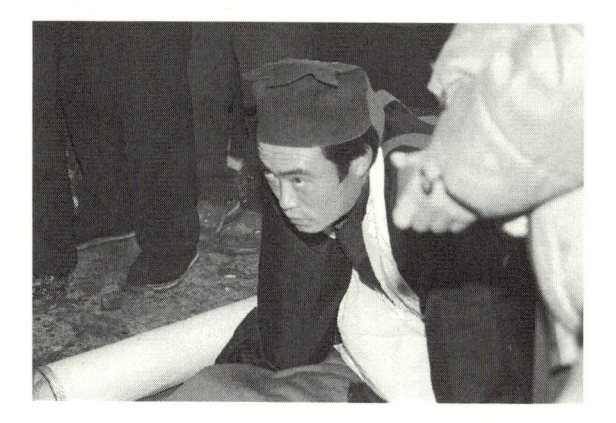

Figure 1.1 Chen Diwen the ordinand. Photograph by the author.

masters in Chen Diwen's lineage, this meticulous detective work shows how these particular traditions eventually came together to form a mode of dual Daoist-Buddhist practice that has characterized the last few hundred years of Chen's lineage, and its cousin lineages in north-central Hunan. It is this story that has defined much of Chen Diwen the ordinand.

Entering the Lineage and Training

Chen Diwen was born on October 4, 1976, nearly a month after Mao Zedong (毛澤東) died, in a tiny hillside hamlet called Mount Xiashan, a few kilometers west of what was then known as Le'an village, a modest market town in southeast Anhua county on the eastern edge of the Daxiong Mountains (大熊山). Chen's maternal grandfather had no sons. Before he gave his daughter away for marriage to a man surnamed Liu, he stipulated that their firstborn son would be a member of his lineage and surnamed Chen. When the child Diwen came along, his parents honored the arrangement and the boy grew up in his grandfather's typical wooden house, perched on the side of one of the steep slopes of Mount Xiashan (web figures 1.1, 1.2).

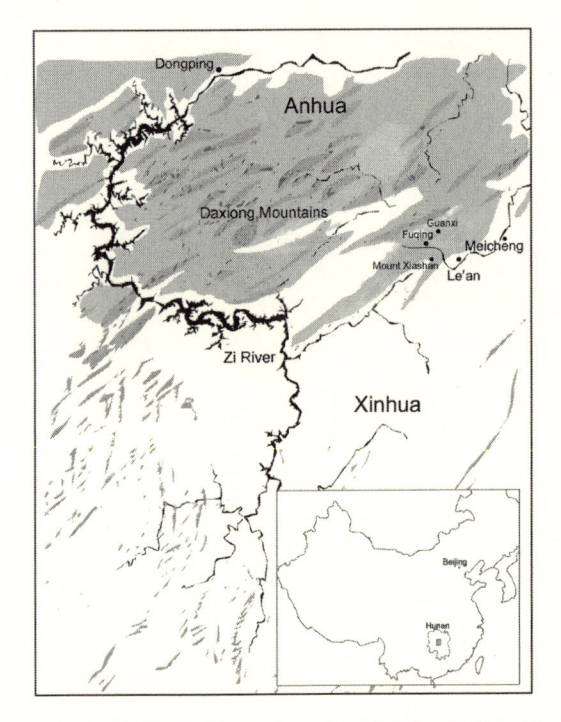

Figure 1.2 The Daxiong Mountain region. Drawing by Ling Zhang.

At the age of six, Chen Diwen began to endure frequent bouts of nausea, difficulty breathing, and chest pain. His grandparents and parents fed him different medicines, but when nothing worked, Chen's maternal grandmother turned to the healing power of a local deity. She was a devout worshiper of a transcendent known as Lord Yang Faqing (楊君法清). According to locals, 250 or so years ago, Yang was a ritual master who gained regional fame for his ability to heal by exorcism and to make rain.

One local master in his eighties recounts that once Yang Faqing hiked to the peak of a mountain to perform a rainmaking ritual with a few apprentices. He told them to ring a gong and beat a drum as he entered a small cave near the top, and that they should not stop playing until he safely returned. Yang then took off his straw sandals and entered the cave. After a while, the sandals he had left outside miraculously turned into two cocks that began to fight. The apprentices were amazed and immediately abandoned their percussion instruments to watch the spectacle. The cave suddenly collapsed, trapping Yang inside. Each day thereafter his wife brought him food and slipped it through a small opening between the fallen rocks. One day she alerted him she would not be able to come feed him for several days. Yang told her not to worry; inside the cave he had plenty of chicken to eat. In disbelief, his wife asked him to prove it. He shoved several insects through the opening in response. At once she understood that he had realized the Dao and become a transcendent. These days Lord Yang Faqing is well known around Le'an as a potent healing deity. It is not uncommon to find wooden images of him on household altars, and local mediums are regularly possessed by him.

During the Cultural Revolution (1966–1976), Chen Diwen's grandmother rescued a carved wooden image of Yang Faqing amid the iconoclastic raids in which government authorities confiscated or destroyed religious imagery in households and temples. Her devotion paid off during one of Chen Diwen's illnesses. She prayed to Yang Faqing over a cup of tea and gave it to her grandson to drink. The charged tea helped significantly and Chen Diwen began a devotion to Lord Yang Faqing that continues today (web figure 1.3).[1]

At age eight, Chen began attending the local primary school, which was located a few hundred meters down the steep hill from his grandfather's house. At age fourteen, he walked four and a half kilometers each way to secondary school in Fuqing village (浮青鄉), the closest market village to Mount Xiashan. When he was seventeen, Chen managed to test into the Anhua No. 13 High School (Anhuaxian di-shisan gaoji zhongxue 安化縣第十三高級中學), located fifty kilometers northwest in Dongping township (東坪鎮), which had become the Anhua county seat in 1951. Chen struggled during the year he boarded there. "The school didn't have a very good reputation for preparing kids for the national college entrance examination," he says with a faint sense of shame, "so I came home."

Chen returned home to an economy that in the early 1990s was finally feeling the positive effects of Deng Xiaoping's (鄧小平) "reform and opening up" (*gaige kaifang* 改革開放) policies instituted in late 1978. An aspect of those reforms, the Rural Household Contract Responsibility System (*Nongcun jiating lianchan chengbao zeren zhi* 農村家庭聯產承包責任制), had reconnected peasants to the land by privatizing agricultural communes in the early 1980s. Peasant households could choose to work parcels of land for their own profit. This opened an avenue for the production of commercial crops. Tangerines and oranges grown on the steep hills of Le'an, already well known in the region, began demanding a modest market outside Hunan and even abroad in Korea and Canada. The Le'an region developed into Anhua county's third largest grower of tobacco. The flue-cured tobacco grown around Siyou village (思游鄉), several kilometers southeast of Mount Xiashan, became recognized for producing excellent tobacco for cigarettes.[2]

Although only a few households were self-sufficient, almost every household grew a substantial percentage of the rice it consumed in paddies alongside mountain streams and on hillside terraces. Sweet potatoes, corn, carrots, beets, beans, lotus root, and red and green chili peppers—ubiquitous in local cuisine—were planted on every square meter of available dry land. Many households raised chickens and hogs. Agricultural life was significantly better than it had been before the reforms, yet Chen Diwen did not wish to become a full-time farmer.

During the mid-1990s, many residents in and around Le'an worked in small factories collecting and exporting all those local tangerines and oranges, and processing all that tobacco. They also worked in modest factories packaging local black tea, fermented foodstuffs, lumber, fireworks, and cement.[3] Others worked in factories producing decorative crafts made of local wood and paper. Their manufactured goods, as well as foodstuffs raised by local farmers, were hawked at the wet market in Le'an on the second, twelfth, and twenty-second days of each lunar month. In 2002, Le'an village became a township (*zhen* 鎮) with jurisdiction over the more than forty-five thousand people living in Le'an village and surrounding villages and hamlets, including Mount Xiashan. That same year, the government implemented a policy mandating that each rural township concentrate its light manufacturing power on a few industries associated with that region. The cadres running

Le'an township decided to focus on its ceramics industry, and small factories producing ceramic goods for commercial businesses, households, and artisans popped up throughout the countryside.[4] In fact, even today several of the wives of masters in Chen Diwen's lineage work in local ceramic factories, where they ornament ceramic and porcelain pieces by hand (web figure 1.4). Making a living in a local factory, however, did not much interest Chen.

During the 1990s, Le'an's greatest commodity was its people. They numbered among the 130 million migrant workers who left their homes in the interior of China to fuel factories making labor-intensive products in coastal cities.[5] During the 1990s and 2000s, one would be hard pressed to find a male or female between twenty and forty years old in Le'an who had not worked at least one several-month stint in a factory on the coast. Daoist masters were among the migrant laborers who followed family members and friends to relatively lucrative employment (web figures 1.5, 1.6).

One of the masters in the lineage that Chen Diwen would enter tells a story typical of an itinerant, unskilled laborer from Le'an in the 1990s and 2000s. He worked odd jobs in Sanzao township (三灶鎮) outside the vibrant city of Zhuhai in Guangdong province near Macao. He next worked a stint for a private security firm in the Haidian district (海淀區) of Beijing as a security guard for hire. After that, he worked two years as a security guard for a gold mining company closer to home in the Anhua county seat in Hunan. He then used his savings to start a small plastics factory at home in Le'an, but that failed miserably, whereupon he headed to Shanghai and worked odd jobs trying to make back his losses. Leaving Shanghai, he spent two years washing airplanes and service vehicles at Baiyun International Airport in Guangzhou, after which he wrangled yet another job as a security guard for a real estate firm in the Bao'an district (寶安區) of Shenzhen, and then worked a stint as a security guard for a real estate firm in the Futian district (福田區). Almost all these employment opportunities were at least partly made possible by Le'an natives who had already established footholds in those companies.

Chen Diwen was one of the few who resisted the lure of higher wages on the coast. Instead, he stayed home during the 1990s and apprenticed as a concrete mixer and bricklayer (*nishuigong* 泥水工) along with the youngest of his two brothers. The local building trades were booming as returning migrant laborers competed to display their newfound wealth by installing shiny white or pink tile facades on their country homes, or even by building new structures from the ground up (web figure 1.7). But Chen's health remained an issue. The constant dust from working with concrete gave him chest pains, so he left the trade.

Chen Diwen worked odd jobs around home, struggling to make a living and contribute income to his grandfather's household. Chronic health issues continued to torment him. At one point, he even felt a little psychologically unstable (*jingshen cuoluan* 精神錯亂) and sought relief from prolonged migraine headaches and nightmares from a local *danqing* (丹青). *Danqing*, which translates to "cinnabar and cyan," describes professional artisans who produce paraphernalia used in local religious rituals. They may paint the scrolls of deities hung around altar spaces, fashion ritual accoutrements made of paper and wood for *jiao* ceremonies and funerals, or carve wooden statuettes of deceased ancestors and masters like Yang Faqing. More than simple artisans, *danqing* are considered religious professionals and perform minor exorcisms. They are often asked to make lustral water and draw talismans designed to dispel mischievous demons that cause headaches, nightmares, and even rat infestations. The *danqing* Chen visited made lustral water for him to drink and it relieved him of his headaches and nightmares. Chen was so grateful that the *danqing* wished to train him in his craft, but Chen did not pursue that path either.

Increasingly desperate and depressed, Chen found himself most interested in the Daoist masters who performed funerals and *jiao* ceremonies for patrons in his local community. "By 1998 I had not done well in high school, my health was not good, and I didn't want to learn a strenuous trade," he remembers. "I was living a relatively difficult life with a body that just couldn't take it, but I liked the [ritual] music, so I began to study Daoism." Like the vast majority of men who would become his liturgical brethren, Chen was initially drawn to the courtly bamboo flute music local masters played as they performed their rituals. He wished to develop this nascent interest and thought working as a Daoist might also benefit his shaky health (web figure 1.8).

On January 9, 1999, Chen Diwen approached a well-known local master named Li Yezhen (李謁真).[6] Born in 1933 in Guanxi (官溪), a hamlet near the market village Fuqing, Li had entered the dominant Daoist lineage in his locale as an apprentice in 1948 at the age of fifteen, but his training was cut short by crackdowns on religious activity by the newly empowered Chinese Communist Party in the early 1950s. During much of the rest of that decade, he served as an administrative director of his village (*cunzhuren* 村主任).

Li Yezhen had a reputation for courage. "During Mao Zedong's time," one of the masters trained by Li recounts, "there were only a few Daoists with enough guts to continue performing rituals. Master Li was one of them." During the early 1960s, when government constraints on religious activities loosened for a few years, Li Yezhen cautiously continued his studies with a local master while serving as a production team leader (*shengchandui duizhang* 生產隊隊長). During the Cultural Revolution, Li is said to have saved many liturgical texts by hiding the most essential manuals scripting the lineage's esoteric rituals and offering only more widely available scriptures to government inspectors. Typical of practitioners of his generation, Li was not officially ordained until 1990.

Li Yezhen's home was not far down the hill from Chen Diwen's, which made for convenient training. Chen also liked it that Li was known for being a good and fair teacher. A master from the lineage notes that "many Daoist masters are eager to teach only because they can make a little money off of their apprentices." During the first year of training, an apprentice does not typically receive compensation for his efforts. Even though he learns on the job by working actual rituals, an apprentice is obliged to hand over to his master any remuneration given by a patron for ritual services. The master may or may not allow the apprentice to keep a portion for his labor. "If you wish to study Daoism, a master will certainly teach you," the master continues, "but he often doesn't care whether he actually knows how to teach. So, there are quite a few apprentices without great ability."

For his part, Li Yezhen saw that Chen Diwen was genuinely interested in becoming a professional priest. Another master in the lineage complains that "the vast majority of new apprentices only want to study well enough to get by; they don't study hard and only want to be able to make some money, and that's it." Li recognized Chen's sincerity, as well as his propensity for music, which is regarded as a prerequisite for entering the lineage.

Chen Diwen bristles when asked what his parents thought about his decision.[7] "They wanted me to continue my schooling," he explains, "so of course they weren't happy." As in most families, Chen's parents believed that success in school offers the surest way out of rural poverty for the entire family. They dreamed that their children would test into college and enter a lucrative profession, and were prepared to take out loans far greater than their economic capacity to pay college tuition. But Chen felt becoming a master would offer another sort of education and a kind of local prestige other than that gained from success in the national educational system. "Being a Daoist in this place," another in the lineage explains, "means that one will receive some respect from people. One won't just be an unknown." Liturgical training affords men high social standing in the local community, even if their incomes remain low relative to what they could earn as secularly educated professionals.

Another master argues that the instruction in literary Chinese and musical arts provided by the lineage is a better education than high school or even college. "After all, one's masters are far more invested than any schoolteacher." Yet another in the lineage adds that the moral aptitude of masters is probably higher than laypeople. "Of course, that's not the case for all Daoists, but our Daoist and Buddhist texts do have a lot of moral theory and we are inculcated by that, so perhaps we approach [moral] problems a little differently from other people."

Li Yezhen assumed primary responsibility for Chen Diwen's training and became known as his transmission master (*chuandushi* 傳度師 or simply *dushi* 度師). As all masters in Le'an do with their apprentices, Li began teaching Chen not by imparting theoretical concepts or ritual techniques but instead by schooling him in music. "First we teach apprentices how to play the bamboo flute (*dizi* 笛子)," Li says. "I record our flute music on a tape recorder, and also record some of the things we sing. Then I make them go home and listen to the recordings on their own. After that they are better able to mimic the music during rituals."

Like all apprentices, Chen Diwen absorbed the rhythms of the rites performed during *jiao* ceremonies for the living and funerals for the dead by learning on the job. "During rituals I would play a little flute, read a few texts, and then listen to my masters sing. I slowly studied and imitated them." Chen regularly served as one of four acolytes (*bangfa* 幫法) who accompany the head officiant (*zhufa* 主法) by supplying flute music along with various cymbal and drum percussion.[8] The lineage is very proud of its flute music, and Chen worked hard to master it (web video 1.1).

Between ritual performances, Chen learned to read and recite the ritual manuals and scriptures. After one of the older masters recited or chanted a line of text, Chen mimicked him, careful to strike the proper pronunciation in the local dialect and the appropriate tone of voice. Chen studied how to use the templates preserved in the lineage's manuals to write the various documents that would be incinerated and so transmitted to divine bureaus during liturgies. "At first I could only understand a little. There were a lot of places in the texts I had to ask a master to explain. If you live to be an old man, you'd study until you're an old man. There's no way you could understand all of it; you could only get better a little at a time. It was definitely hard, but we study slowly. And we could take many years to study, so I didn't feel it was really a slog" (web figure 1.9).

With recommendations from his transmission master Li Yezhen, Chen Diwen asked two older men in the lineage to serve as witnessing masters (*zhengmingshi* 證明師). He approached an established forty-nine-year-old master who went by the Daoist name Jiang Yeqian (蔣謁謙) to serve as his guarantor master (*baojushi* 保舉師), and a precocious twenty-seven-year-old with the Daoist name Jiang Yucheng (蔣玉誠) to act as presenting master (*yinjinshi* 引進師). "These two masters have a witnessing function," Chen explains. "They supervise the transmission master to see whether he is transmitting [the tradition] to his disciple well, whether he has made errors in the transmission or has held anything back." The witnessing masters provide a kind of quality control for the transmission process, a means by which the lineage maintains some sense of pedagogical standards through the generations (web figure 1.10).

The first year of Chen Diwen's apprenticeship was lean. He duly gave his share of earnings from ritual services to Li Yezhen, who allowed him to keep a modest percentage. After that first year, Chen began to make the same money as the ordained masters. He explains that "whether you're an old Daoist or you've just recently entered the lineage, the pay is the same." The exact amount varied depending on the patrons. Families who had done well sending younger members off to labor on the coast might patronize a three-to-five-day funeral. Poorer families living only off the land might scrape together enough for a one-day affair. Every year or so, prominent members of a local ward might organize a three- or four-day *jiao* in gratitude for agricultural and economic blessings bestowed by one of the most recognized gods in the pantheon—the Sagely Emperor of the Southern Marchmount (Nanyue shengdi 南嶽聖帝) or Guanyin Bodhisattva (Guanyin pusa 觀音菩薩).

When Chen Diwen apprenticed during the early 2000s, each of five masters working a funeral or *jiao* ceremony earned on average ¥40 per day ($4.90), which the patrons presented either to the head officiant or to each attending master in red envelopes (*hongbao* 紅包). The head officiant made a little more because he performed several minor rites for patrons during the ritual proceedings. Although wages were not high, they were somewhat reliable. There were usually several funerals to perform every month, even if *jiao* ceremonies were few and far between. Masters in the lineage often continued to practice other trades like carpentry and cement mixing to supplement their incomes.

In 2002, Chen married a young woman surnamed Li from a neighboring hamlet. She supported his budding career, but he knew he had to make a little more money. He finally succumbed to the economic trend and left to work as a migrant laborer. He got a job in a factory making cue sticks for pool and snooker tables in the city of Chenzhou (郴州) in southeast Hunan, and then did the same thing in Liupanshui (六盤水) in neighboring

Guizhou province. In the late 1980s, an enterprising man originally from Le'an founded a modest company manufacturing pool tables, which had grown to include several factories across south China. Chen followed the well-worn tracks of many Le'an natives who had relied on local connections to secure jobs in those factories. After making as much money as he could for more than half a year, Chen returned to his new bride, who had chosen not to work as a migrant laborer, and picked up his training where he left off.

Chen was working toward ordination into a lineage that identifies as both Daoist and Buddhist, as will be described in detail. Although locals commonly address members of the lineage as "officials of the Dao" (*daoguan* 道官), "dignitaries of the Dao" (*daoshi* 道士), or more generically as "masters" (*shifu* 師傅) or "ritual masters" (*fashi* 法師), the masters themselves insist they are "half Buddhist, half Daoist" (*banfo bandao* 半佛半道).[9] On ordination, they receive a Daoist name (also called a presentation name [*zouming* 奏名]), which, we shall see, follows a Daoist lineage poem, as well as a Buddhist name (*foming* 佛名, *shiming* 釋名) following a Buddhist lineage poem.

Outside Chen Diwen's lineage branch, some masters in the region practice a third liturgical tradition generically referred to as the "tradition of masters" or "*shi* tradition" (*shijiao* 師教), a broad label used across south China. In Anhua and Xinhua, the most prevalent *shi* tradition is called the Tradition of the Primordial Emperor (Yuanhuangjiao 元皇教, the Yuanhuang tradition). This local, exorcistic tradition is practiced by ritual masters, such as the renowned Yang Faqing, to whom Chen Diwen's grandmother prayed to heal him as a boy. On ordination, these masters receive a ritual name (*faming* 法名), which typically does not follow a lineage poem but always includes the character *fa*.[10] In the Le'an region, a master might practice either Daoist, Buddhist, or Yuanhuang rites, or a single master might be initiated into all three traditions. One older master in Chen Diwen's lineage claims that generations ago their ancestral masters practiced Yuanhuang as well as Daoist and Buddhist rites, but for some reason the lineage stopped performing and teaching Yuanhuang ritual long before Chen began his study.[11]

Chen Diwen's Daoist Lineage

Chen Diwen was training to be ordained into a lineage that had a long history in the Meishan (梅山) region of central Hunan.[12] Since at least the Northern Song dynasty (960–1127), the term Meishan denoted the northern reaches of the Xuefeng Mountain (雪峰山) range, especially the part of the range known as the Daxiong Mountains, which lie to the east of the Zi River (資水) (see figure 1.2). This region had nominally been incorporated into the Han empire in the third century BCE, but remained a rather autonomous frontier area mostly populated by Yao (瑤 / 猺 / 徭 / 傜) and Miao (苗) native peoples. During subsequent centuries, a few intrepid Han settlers attempted from time to time to put down roots in the rugged mountains, but those efforts were sporadic and unsuccessful. Throughout the medieval period, native chieftains' grip over the territory remained strong. After the fall of the Tang dynasty, a wave of Han migrants fleeing the wars that ravaged Jizhou (吉州) in Jiangxi arrived in the 920s and even pledged themselves as "guest households" (*kehu* 客戶) of the Meishan Yao, a practice that seems to have died out by the founding of the Song dynasty in the mid-tenth century. The Song empire claimed sovereignty over the Meishan region, but it continued to be de facto ruled by native chieftains. Indeed, Meishan natives boldly plundered Han commerce between the Xiang River (湘江) valley to the east and the towns and villages of Shaozhou (邵州) on the upper reaches of the Zi River. In 977, the Song court disallowed all relations with the Meishan natives and prohibited Han settlement of their territories.

A violent uprising of Meishan natives in the early 1060s prompted county magistrates to advocate policies to subjugate them and open the Meishan territory to Han settlers. After some debate at the court of Emperor Song Shenzong (宋神宗) (r. 1067–1085), Zhang Dun (章惇) (1035–1106), a favorite of the eminent statesman Wang Anshi (王安石) (1021–1086), announced in January of 1073 an accord by which the Meishan natives agreed to consign their territory and submit as subjects of the Song empire. Shortly after, the territory of Meishan was divided into two counties—Anhua in the north and Xinhua (新化) in the south—that endure with slightly different borders today. After this "opening of Meishan" (*kai Meishan* 開梅山), a second wave of Han migration from Jizhou, especially Taihe (泰和) county, in Jiangxi promptly poured into Xinhua. In the early Ming dynasty, another flood of Jiangxi merchants, many of whom also from Ji'an (formerly Jizhou), migrated to Xinhua.

The ritual tradition Chen Diwen was studying seems to have been bound up with these massive waves of Han migrants from Jiangxi. Members of the liturgical lineage are identifiable to one another by a twenty-character lineage poem (*paixushi* 派序詩) included in one of their manuscripts:

道德流來遠	*Dao de liu lai yuan*	The Way and its Power flows from afar,
通真玄妙深	*Tong zhen xuan miao shen*	Its penetrating truth mysterious, marvelous, fathomless.
三千功行滿	*San qian gong xing man*	Accomplish three thousand merits and achievements,
飛身謁玉京	*Fei shen ye yu jing*	Your flying body will pay respects at the Jade Capital.[13]

The Daoist name bequeathed to a new master on his ordination includes one character from this poem, which denotes the generation of the lineage to which he belongs. For example, Chen Diwen's transmission master was given the Daoist name Li Yezhen. The middle character *ye* 謁 corresponds to the eighteenth character of the poem, or the eighteenth generation of the lineage. Should Chen Diwen be ordained, he would be given a Daoist name with the *yu* 玉 character, which corresponds to the nineteenth character of the poem, or the nineteenth generation, marking him as belonging to the generation after his master.

Unfortunately, sources I have so far uncovered do not reveal who might have composed the poem, or whether he did so in Hunan or elsewhere. Because I have not happened upon any Daoist master who identifies with this poem outside the Daxiong Mountains of Anhua and northern Xinhua, it is entirely possible the broad lineage identifying with it was initiated in this region, but we cannot be sure.[14] If we estimate that every twenty-five years constitutes a generation, then the first generations of the lineage defined by the poem would have been active sometime in the sixteenth century, the middle of the Ming dynasty (1368–1644). We do have a record of Daoist names from the sixth *tong* 通 and seventh *zhen* 真 generations—the mid- to late seventeenth century, the early Qing dynasty (1644–1911)—in ritual manuscripts from the Zhenshang (圳上) region in northern Xinhua.[15] Thus the lineage has been flourishing over a fairly wide area in the mountains of northern Xinhua and Anhua since at least that time. Different clans living in different places within this wide swath of rugged geography have over the centuries formed dozens of local sublineages, often without knowing one another (see appendix).

Something of the history of Chen Diwen's Daoist lineage can be gleaned from an 1888 colophon in a ritual manual preserved by his masters. The colophon records information about the Daoist office (*zhi* 職) of the user of the manual, a certain Xiao Xingxiang (蕭行祥), a member of the fourteenth *xing* 行 generation:

> [My] office is associated with the disciples of the Orthodox Unity Celestial Masters of the Transcendent Mount Longhu in the blessed land of Jiangxi. They transmitted liturgies and established teachings which spread to the Jade Void Palace in scenic Xinhua on the Zi River, in one of the locales under the jurisdiction of the Provincial Administration Commission of the Changbao Circuit based in Changsha in Hunan.[16] [The liturgies and teachings of the Jade Void Palace] branched out to the disciples of our venerable patriarch, the Realized One Fang Shenzhi, of Chuliang within the third sector of Shima village. The tradition spread continuously. In the east our grand patriarch Master Gong Sanjiao and patriarch Master Gong Qianhui transmitted the tradition to Shanxi channel. [My] transmission master Fu Gongyu branched out to Liujia dike in Fuqing, Anhua county.[17]

> 職系江西福地龍虎仙山正一天師門下。傳科設教，流遺上湖南星沙長寶道承仙〔宣〕布政司所隸等處濱水勝地新化縣玉盧宮，分派石馬鄉第三都上楚良老祖深智方真人門下。教流有餘。東師太祖三教冀先生、師祖千輝冀先生，教傳山溪沖。度師功玉扶先生，枝分安邑浮青劉家壩。

The colophon states that the Zhengyi (Orthodox Unity) tradition of the Celestial Masters on Mount Longhu was transmitted to the Jade Void Palace (Yuxugong 玉虛宮) on the Zi River in Xinhua county. Something of the story of the Jade Void Palace and its reputed founder, Zeng Rushou (曾如壽), has been pieced together from scant clues in local gazetteers, genealogies, ritual manuscripts, stelae, and oral histories by several scholars working in central Hunan.[18] Some sources date Zeng Rushou to the tenth and eleventh centuries, others to the fourteenth century. Whichever the case, the general contours of his story are fairly consistent across sources.

Zeng Rushou was a disciple in the lineage of Zhang Jinghua (張景華), who according to some sources was a descendant of the famous thirtieth-generation Celestial Master, Zhang Jixian (張繼先) (fl. 1092–1126).[19] Perhaps to escape political turmoil, Zhang Jinghua left Mount Longhu and went to Mount Wenxian (文仙山) (also known as Mount Wenjin 文斤山) in southern Xinhua, where he studied with a certain Tan Guanmiao (譚觀妙). The two of them established the Abbey of Cultured Transcendents (Wenxianguan 文仙觀), which seems to have maintained a rule of celibacy. They trained many disciples, including a certain Wang Guilin (王桂林), who in turn trained three prominent students.[20]

The third of those students, Zeng Rushou, eventually left—or was forced out of—the Abbey of Cultured Transcendents, perhaps because of its apparent insistence on celibacy. He traveled to Mount Longhu in Jiangxi and studied the rites directly from the Celestial Masters for close to eight years. After returning to Xinhua, he founded the Jade Void Palace near the Xinhua county seat (present-day Shangmei township 上梅鎮) sometime during the Zhizheng (至正) reign period (1341–1368) at the end of the Yuan dynasty. Shortly after the Ming conquest, the Office of the Daoist Association (Daohuisi 道會司) was established in the temple.[21] Six notable disciples were trained at the Jade Void Palace and took the tradition to different locales and established six "houses" (*fang* 房)—families of hereditary Daoists each associated with a branch temple.[22] From each of these six houses and their temples, sublineages and subtemples branched out to more and more locales in central

Hunan from the early Ming through the next centuries.[23] To this day, Daoist lineages in central Hunan trace their roots to Zeng Rushou's Jade Void Palace, and many can do so through lineage branches that extend back to one of these six patriarchs or the temples with which they were associated.[24]

It is very likely that Chen Diwen's lineage descends from one of these six patriarchs and his temple, though this is not specified in his lineage's cache of manuals. The 1888 colophon quoted states simply that one of the lineages originating in the Jade Void Palace stretched north to the village of Chuliang within the third sector of Shima village in Xinhua county (present-day Hailong village [海龍鄉], several kilometers north of Zhenshang township deep in the Daxiong Mountains). Given that Chen's lineage shares the same generational poem as lineages throughout northern Xinhua and southeastern Anhua, and that they all trace their lineages back to the Jade Void Palace, it stands to reason they also share connections to one or more of the six houses of the Jade Void Palace. The He (賀) clan of Songshan village (松山村), not far from Hailong, preserves two ritual manuals that mention that their lineage originally comes down from the Jade Void Palace of Zeng Rushou through the branch temple Daotang Abbey, associated with the first of the six houses.[25] It seems very likely that Chen Diwen's lineage, liturgical cousins of the He clan, does so as well.

The colophon mentions that a venerable patriarch named Fang Shenzhi (方深智) taught many disciples in the village of Chuliang (Hailong). According to the lineage poem, Fang Shenzhi was of the tenth *shen* 深 generation of the lineage, which dates him to the mid-eighteenth century. From Chuliang, the tradition was passed to a patriarch named Gong Sanjiao (龔 三教) of the eleventh *san* 三 generation—the late eighteenth century—and then to Gong Qianhui (龔千輝) of the twelfth *qian* 千 generation—the turn of the nineteenth century—who transmitted the tradition south to Shanxi channel, which seems likely to be today's Shanxi village (山溪村). The colophon author's transmission master, Fu Gongyu (扶功玉) of the thirteenth *gong* 功 generation—the early nineteenth century—then brought the tradition east to Fuqing village in Anhua county, where Chen Diwen's masters serve today.

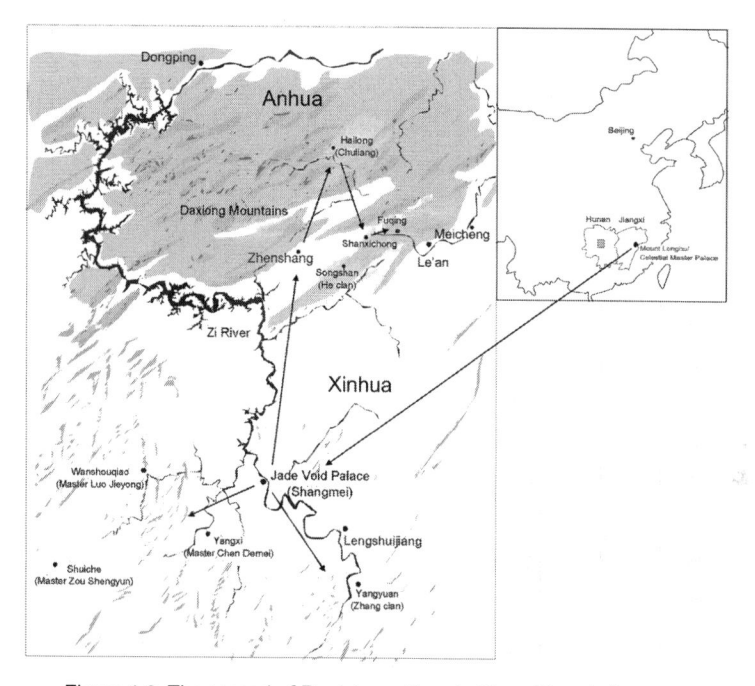

Figure 1.3 The spread of Daoist practices to Chen Diwen's lineage.
Drawing by Ling Zhang.

Other ritual manuals preserved by Chen Diwen's lineage show that the Fang, Gong, and Fu clans were not the only ones who extended this Daoist lineage to Fuqing. In the same village of Chuliang where Fang Shenzhi lived, a prominent Luo (羅) clan produced several members of the tenth *shen* generation. Together with Fang, the Luos are revered as patriarchs by Chen Diwen's lineage. In the late eighteenth century, the patriarch Luo Shenhui (羅深惠) trained a native of Fuqing, Jiang Sanlu (蔣三祿) of the eleventh *san* generation. As we shall see, Jiang's clan later taught the teachings to a Li clan member. Since at least the early nineteenth century until today, the two clans have collaborated in ritual performances, together trained disciples, and sometimes intermarried. It is this Jiang-Li lineage that Chen Diwen entered in 1999 (see appendix).

From cobbling together these scant sources, three general stages in the transmission of the Zhengyi Daoist liturgical tradition to Fuqing are apparent: first, from the Celestial Master headquarters on Mount Longhu in eastern Jiangxi province to the Jade Void Temple in Xinhua; second, from the Jade Void Temple to the region around Chuliang (Hailong) in the mountains of northern Xinhua; and, third, from Chuliang southeastward to Fuqing just over the Anhua county border (see figure 1.3).

This story of the lineage history is complicated by the influence of the Quanzhen 全真 Daoist tradition on rural enclaves in central Hunan during the mid- to late Ming through the Qing dynasties. Founded in the twelfth century by disciples of Wang Zhe (王喆) (1113–1170), the Quanzhen order established a presence in many major Daoist institutions during the following centuries. During the Ming dynasty, many Daoists from the Quanzhen center on Mount Wudang (武當山) in Hubei moved south into Hunan to staff Quanzhen institutions in Changsha, Nanyue (南嶽), Liuyang (瀏陽), Taoyuan (桃源), Taojiang (桃江), and Liling (醴陵).[26] The Quanzhen order had experienced something of a renewal when it was reevaluated by the Ming court, which had previously lavished favor on the Zhengyi tradition as represented by the Celestial Masters on Mount Longhu in Jiangxi. During the waning years of the Ming, Confucian literati joined forces with Quanzhen monastics in solidarity with the Ming during the Manchu conquest. Later, Qing emperors admired the strong discipline and moral precepts of the Quanzhen order and privileged it. Meanwhile, key Quanzhen masters anachronistically fashioned a stable Longmen (龍門, Dragon Gate) lineage designed to situate Wang Changyue (王常月) (?–1680), the influential abbot of the White Cloud Abbey (Baiyunguan 白雲觀) in Beijing, as the national teacher of the orthodox Daoist teachings of Qiu Chuji (丘處機) (1148–1227), the well-known first-generation patriarch of the Quanzhen order. This effectively created a national Daoist lineage that enjoyed the prestige of the court.[27]

In their study of the Zhang clan altar in Yangyuan village in Xinhua, Lui Wing Sing and Li Xinwu found that more than three hundred masters in Xinhua, both living and recorded in liturgical manuals, have taken the Quanzhen Longmen lineage poem as their generational poem while continuing to practice Zhengyi ritual. By way of example, Lui and Li show that a Daoist lineage in Shuiche township (水車鎮) in Xinhua, which traces itself back to Zhang Jinghua of Mount Wenxian through the third of the six branch houses of the Jade Void Palace, switched from a lineage poem associated with Zhang Jinghua of the Zhengyi Celestial Master tradition to the Quanzhen Longmen poem sometime during the end of the Ming or early Qing.[28] Similarly, the Zhang clan of Yangyuan village, which practices both Daoist and local *shi* rites and recognizes a patriarch rumored to have been associated with the patriarch of the fourth house of the Jade Void Palace, integrated the generational characters of the Quanzhen Longmen lineage poem into their Yuanhuang liturgical names (*fahao* 法號).[29] Master Luo Jieyong of Luguan township in Xinhua explains that his lineage—liturgical descendants of the sixth house of the Jade Void Palace—also adopted the Quanzhen Longmen lineage poem.[30] And Patrice Fava's work on the lineage of Masters Chen Demei (陳德美) and Wan Yilin (萬益林) in Yangxi township (洋溪鎮) in Xinhua reveals that that lineage also uses the Quanzhen Longmen poem.[31]

These reports confirm Lui and Li's assertion that, from at least the late Ming, the influence of the monastic Quanzhen order had penetrated central Hunan enough that local lineages whose masters married and lived at home—so-called hearth-dwelling Daoists (*huoju daoshi* 火居道士)—and practiced rituals associated with the Zhengyi tradition began identifying with the Quanzhen Longmen monastic lineage, even though they did not recognize Quanzhen patriarchs such as Wang Zhe and Qiu Chuji and continued to worship a recognizably Zhengyi pantheon. This seems to exemplify what Monica Esposito calls the "Longmen fashion"—a trend in which non-Quanzhen Daoists claimed affiliation with the Longmen lineage, especially during the "Longmen renaissance" of the late Ming and early Qing.[32] Perhaps attracted to the growing prestige being accumulated by the Quanzhen order, local Zhengyi masters in Hunan began to identify themselves as Longmen by using the Longmen lineage poem for their liturgical names.

Lui and Li suggest that this adoption of Longmen identity by local Zhengyi masters was a near universal phenomenon in central Hunan. It seems the poems that lineages had been using neared exhaustion by the late Ming, and they found in the Longmen poem a suitable way to organize their liturgical progeny. But here we must be cautious. Chen Diwen's lineage poem, which also seems to have been fashioned during the mid- to late Ming, is not the Longmen poem. Living masters of Chen's lineage are aware that Quanzhen Daoism has a presence in Hunan, but they insist they have no connection to it. Their poem is shared by the several lineages I have personally encountered around Le'an and Meicheng townships in southeastern Anhua, as well as by lineages around Zhenshang township in the mountains of northern Xinhua.[33] It seems adoption of the Longmen poem by local Zhengyi Daoists in central Hunan was not as ubiquitous as Lui and Li propose.

At this point, we can only speculate as to why certain lineages chose not to adopt the Longmen generational poem in the late Ming. As we have seen, it is extremely common that lineages in Xinhua and Anhua can trace their provenances to the Zhengyi tradition of Zhang Jinghua of the Abbey of Cultured Transcendents through his liturgical descendant Zeng Rushou, founder of the Jade Void Palace, and often to Zeng Rushou through one of the Jade Void Palace's six houses. Perhaps certain of the six houses refused the allure of the Longmen fashion raging during the late Ming and early Qing. Based on my fieldwork and the field reports by other scholars working in Hunan, I notice that the lineages that adopted the Longmen poem are clustered in the central and southern parts of Xinhua county and trace themselves back to patriarchs or temples associated with the third, fourth, and sixth of the six houses of the Jade Void Palace. Lineages around Zhenshang township in the mountains of northern Xinhua, which share the generational poem used by Chen Diwen's lineage and other lineages in southeastern Anhua, trace themselves back to the first of the six houses (see figure 1.3). Perhaps lineages associated with certain houses were especially influenced by the Quanzhen monks that came down to central Hunan from Mount Wudang during the Ming and early Qing. Perhaps lineages in the southern part of central Hunan were more exposed to the Quanzhen influence because of their nearness to the Quanzhen center of Nanyue to the east. Or perhaps Daoist lineages that adopted a strong Buddhist identity, as was the case for

Chen Diwen's lineage and others in northern Xinhua, felt no need for Quanzhen prestige. All these historical questions await future research.

Chen Diwen's Buddhist Tradition

As mentioned, Chen Diwen was training to enter a lineage that identifies as half Buddhist, half Daoist. In practice, masters of the lineage make most of their living performing funerary rites they classify as Buddhist. Demand for them is more regular than for Daoist rituals, which occur only when members in the local community organize a *jiao* or when a particular household requires minor rites for apotropaic protection or exorcistic healing, which typically require only a few hours to perform.

Documents used during ordinations are peppered with language identifying masters with both traditions. The memorials written out during ordination *jiao,* which are then burned to send up to the high gods to notify them of the event, routinely describe the lineage as that which "studies the arts of Buddhism and the mysteries of Daoism, the mysteries of which vow to traverse death by means of rebirth and aspire to aid people and benefit their affairs" (習佛教之藝，道教之玄，玄願度死以超生，欲濟人而利物). Buddhist ritual "arts" deal with death by working toward a favorable rebirth for the deceased, while Daoist ritual "mysteries" are designed to benefit the health and welfare of the living. The ordination certificate, which identifies an ordinand to the celestial bureaucracy and is delivered to the heavenly registry by burning, includes a poem with lines extolling both traditions:

For the Buddha, the Dharma, and the sangha, all phenomena are empty,	佛法僧伽萬相空
For the treasures of the Dao, the scriptures, and the masters, there is the writ of five thousand words [the *Daode jing*].	道經師寶五千文
The profound meanings of these two lineages are to be understood with care,	兩門奧義精心悟
The mysterious profundities of their teachings and texts are to be sought attentively.[34]	教典玄微仔細尋

The ordinand is to take refuge in the three treasures (*sanbao* 三寶) of Buddhism—the Buddha, the Dharma, and the sangha—as well as in the three treasures of Daoism—the Dao, the scriptures, and the masters. Again, these two sets of treasures are not imagined as Buddhist meditation practice on the one hand and Daoist ritual practice on the other. Instead they mark off two kinds of ritual labor, the boundaries of which are clearly expressed in the format of a manual called the *Esoteric Transmissions for Daoist and Buddhist [Rites] and Their Templates* (*Fo Dao michuan ji kuanshi* 佛道秘傳及款式). The first half of the manual consists of secret instructions necessary for Daoist rites on behalf of the living; the second half is composed of various esoteric instructions for Buddhist funerary ritual.[35]

Chen Diwen's lineage recognizes the monk Pu'an (普庵) as its Buddhist patriarch, and their ritual manuals routinely refer to him as "ancestral master" (*zushi* 祖師). Recent fieldwork by a handful of scholars has discovered that Buddhist practice stemming from Pu'an has thoroughly penetrated the liturgical practice of Zhengyi Daoists and practitioners of local *shi* rites all over south China.[36] Pu'an (1115–1169), given name Yu Yinsu (余印肅), was a native of Yichun (宜春) in Yuanzhou (袁州) in northwestern Jiangxi province. He was a thirteenth-generation Chan master in the Linji (臨濟) tradition who left his family to enter nearby Longevous Prosperity Monastery (Shoulongsi 壽隆寺) at age twenty and received full precepts at age twenty-seven. The following year, he traveled to Mount Wei (潙山) in Hunan and studied with the Chan master Huanglong mu'anzhong (黃龍牧庵忠) (1084–1149). There he had an awakening experience, after which he returned to the Longevous Prosperity Monastery in Jiangxi. In 1153, he was appointed abbot of the Chan Monastery of Compassionate Transformation (Cihua chansi 慈化禪寺) on Mount Nanquan (南泉山) in northwestern Jiangxi. One day, while reading a commentary on the *Flower Garland Sutra,* he had a powerful awakening experience. As his fame spread, many pilgrims sought him out. In 1166, he oversaw a massive renovation and expansion of the Monastery of Compassionate Transformation, which was completed shortly before his death in 1169. He was subsequently honored with seven posthumous titles by emperors throughout the Ming dynasty.

Several canonical and noncanonical sources vividly record that Pu'an was known not only for the building of an influential Buddhist monastery but also for his exorcistic skills. He is said to have routinely cured the sick with herbal medicines and healed those suffering from contagious diseases by intoning incantations and inscribing talismans. He successfully brought about rain and sunshine, cut down trees afflicted by demons, and destroyed licentious cults.[37] An anonymous, noncanonical text, the *Record of Numinous Effects by Ancestral Master Pu'an* (*Pu'an zushi lingyan ji* 普庵祖師靈驗記), is filled with tales of Pu'an's mastery of exorcistic ritual techniques, even those usually associated with Daoism rather than Buddhism. In one legend, the governor of Yuanzhou in Jiangxi, cocky about his knowledge of thunder rites (*leifa* 雷法), suspected that Pu'an was a demon and intended to subdue him. When asked by the governor whether he could summon thunder, Pu'an was reticent, replying only that he was willing to learn. The governor borrowed Pu'an's altar and attempted to summon thunder for three days without success. As he left humiliated, Pu'an teased him, "Let me send you off with heavenly drums" (將天鼓相送). He pointed to the sky with his cane and immediately loud claps of thunder rolled down and lightning lit up the sky as rain and hail fell.[38] Stories of Pu'an's exorcistic prowess persist. Ye Mingsheng and John Lagerwey have collected numerous oral stories about Pu'an and his formidable powers in northwestern Fujian.[39]

Chen Diwen's lineage sees itself as an heir to Pu'an's exorcistic tradition. Like their ancestral master said to have learned many exorcistic techniques, even thunder rites associated with Daoism, members of Chen's lineage practice what scholar Tam Wai Lun calls "the ritual tradition of popular exorcistic Buddhism" (*minjian de quxie fojiao yishi chuantong* 民間的驅邪佛教儀式傳統) or "liturgical Buddhism" (*yishi zhong de fojiao* 儀式中的佛教).[40] These forms of Buddhism, which have permeated large swaths of south China, are usually practiced by lineages of masters living at home rather than by monks living in a monastery. These masters employ esoteric techniques to ensure favorable rebirth and to exorcize malevolent forces by intoning the powerful Pu'an Incantation (*Pu'an zhou* 普庵咒) and wielding an array of ritual implements. About the "Pu'an water" (*Pu'an shui* 普庵水) liberally used to purify spaces, bodies, and implements during funeral rites, an ordination manual preserved by Chen Diwen's lineage claims that "the *samadhi* water of Pu'an is cool and refreshing; it can command earth and heaven to make snow and frost. Wicked killer *qi* and evil spirits all withdraw, and heterodox demons and those outside the teaching all wither away" (普庵三昧水清涼，能令地天作雪霜，惡煞凶神皆退避，邪魔外道悉消亡). Wielders of talismans associated with Pu'an are said to "be able to fly up to the Nine Heavens to pursue and capture *po* and *hun* souls; they are especially able to report along the ten stages [of the bodhisattva path]; and they are able to guard a body and protect a household, heal illness and shoo away nefarious demons, pray for rain and good weather, and exorcize evil and remove killer *qi*" (可以飛達九天，攝魄追魂，猶能通傳十地，可以護身鎮宅，可以治病除邪，能禱雨祈晴，可驅凶退煞).[41]

Popular exorcistic Buddhist traditions can seem like a chaotic bricolage of Buddhist, Daoist, and local *shi* traditions like the Yuanhuang tradition. Yet, like all the lineages I have come across in southeastern Anhua, Chen Diwen's lineage is quite clear about the boundaries between liturgical traditions.[42] Liturgical texts are marked as either Daoist or Buddhist, like the *Esoteric Transmissions for Daoist and Buddhist [Rites] and Their Templates* mentioned above. What members of Chen's lineage mean by calling themselves half Buddhist, half Daoist is that they have been inducted into a lineage that has preserved esoteric knowledge about how to officiate over two ritual traditions used for two different purposes. When hired to protect or heal the living, the lead officiant dons Daoist vestments and uses Daoist texts to perform Daoist rituals. When called upon to ferry the deceased through the trials of purgatory and safely on to the next rebirth, the lead officiant usually wears different vestments to officiate over Pu'an-related rituals scripted in Buddhist texts (web figures 1.11, 1.12).[43]

Snippets from a Buddhist text preserved by Chen Diwen's lineage give clues as to how Pu'an's exorcistic Buddhism made its way to Chen's liturgical ancestors. A ritual manual copied in the late 1980s from some older manual by the most senior member of the lineage records information about the provenance of his Buddhist office (*zhi* 職):

[My] office is associated with the Prefectural Buddhist Registry on Mount Nanquan in Yichun district, Xuandou [Yuanzhou] prefecture,[44] [under the jurisdiction] of the Provincial Administration Commission of Jiangxi founded during the Qing dynasty. Based on precedents from the Han, [Northern] Zhou, Tang, Song, and Yuan periods, the Hongwu emperor of the great Ming dynasty took charge of setting up [this ministry]. He often visited the Court of Burning Incense. By his royal benevolence, he granted the temple the name Great Chan Monastery of Compassionate Transformation, Protector of the State out of Vast Compassion. A building in the eastern [compound] of the monastery branched out. One branch took up residence in Goose Brook in the third sector of Shima south of Chu [Hunan].[45]

職係前清定鼎江西道承宣布正使司玄都〔袁州〕府宜春縣南泉山僧綱司。歷自漢周唐宋元基，大明洪武主開設。屢朝香火院。皇恩敕賜廣慈護國大慈法〔化〕禪寺。東一樓遺發，派寓於楚南石馬三都上鵝溪。

Just as an officiant assumes a Daoist office upon ordination, he also assumes a Buddhist office, which the text asserts is affiliated with Pu'an's Monastery of Compassionate Transformation on Mount Nanquan. In the Qing administrative system, this monastery fell under the jurisdiction of the Provincial Administration Commission governing Yichun district within Yuanzhou prefecture in northwestern Jiangxi. The text claims that the Hongwu (洪武) emperor (Zhu Yuanzhang 朱元璋, r. 1368–1398) of the Ming dynasty had earlier decreed the Prefectural Buddhist Registry be instituted at the monastery. During the Ming and Qing dynasties, the government administration of each prefecture included a Buddhist registry, which monitored the number, qualifications, and conduct of all Buddhist monks in its jurisdiction.[46] Reflecting renewed imperial support for Buddhism during the Ming dynasty, the text mentions further favor by the Hongwu emperor, capped by his bestowing on the temple the name Great Chan Monastery of Compassionate Transformation, Protector of the State out of Vast Compassion. According to a genealogy compiled in 1806 and preserved in the monastery, Zhu Yuanzhang actually ordered the building of a Dragon Pavilion (Longting 龍亭) within the monastery, and then graced the pavilion with a stele on which his handwritten inscription read "The first Chan grove under Heaven" (天下第一禪林). According to the genealogy, it was in fact the Chenghua (成化) emperor (r. 1465–1487) who granted the monastery the title mentioned in the ritual manual preserved by Chen Diwen's lineage.[47] Despite the historical infelicities that came down through Chen's lineage, its manual traces the Buddhist liturgical practice of Chen's lineage back to Pu'an's monastery, which had garnered some importance during the early Ming dynasty and remained a regionally important temple through the Qing.

The manual goes on to state that the Monastery of Compassionate Transformation branched out to establish subsidiary temples. One of them, the Western Spring Monastery (Xiquansi 西泉寺), was built in the Daxiong Mountains of northern Xinhua near Goose Brook (E'xi 鵝溪), several kilometers northwest of today's Zhenshang township. A colophon to the manual explains that the

> Western Spring Monastery on Daxiong Peak was founded during the Chenghua reign period by a monk named Hongqing of the Southern Spring Mountain Monastery [Monastery of Compassionate Transformation] in Yichun county in Jiangxi. The monastery is located west of the Southern Spring Mountains [in Jiangxi] so it was called the Western Spring Monastery.[48]
>
> 大熊峯之西泉寺，係江西宜春縣南泉山寺之僧名弘清者于成化年間所建，寺居南泉山之西，故名曰西泉寺。

A recent ethnographic investigation of old temples in the Daxiong Mountains by local scholar Li Wuhan attests that the Western Spring Monastery was founded in 1465 by a monk named Hongqing (written 宏清 instead of 弘清 as in our manual). Only the front gate and a few stone pillars survive, along with tombs around the grounds. A 2003 promulgation from the Loudi (婁底) municipal government states that tombs were dug on the grounds of the monastery from 1465 until 1917, interring twenty-six generations of monks (*heshang* 和尚) and nonmonastic ritual masters.[49]

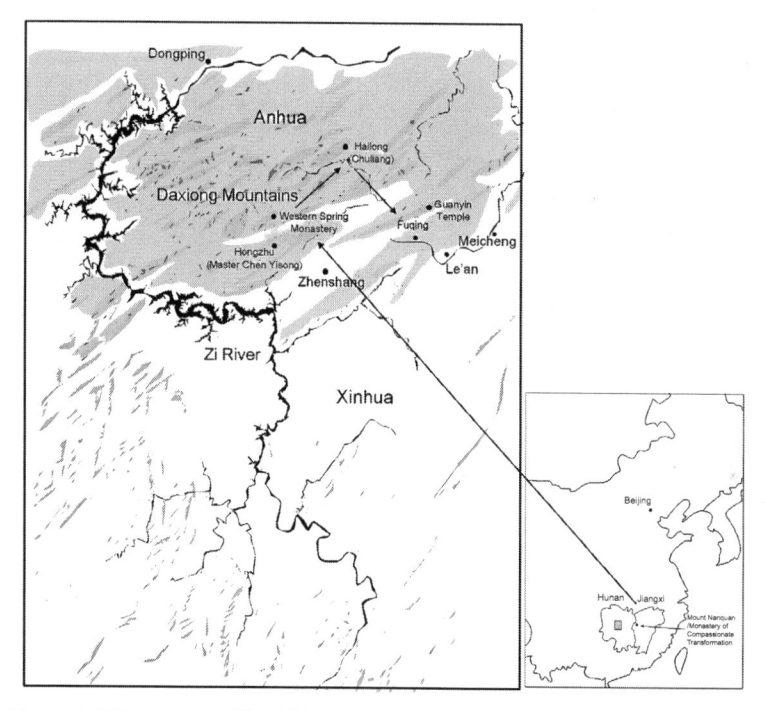

Figure 1.4 The spread of Buddhist practices to Chen Diwen's lineage. Drawing by Ling Zhang.

The manual preserved by Chen Diwen's lineage states that the Western Spring Monastery in Xinhua county in Hunan was a temple that branched out specifically from "a building in the eastern [compound]" (*dong yilou* 東一樓) of the Monastery of Compassionate Transformation on Mount Nanquan. This little phrase might be a subtle clue indicating that part of the tradition of dual Buddhist and Daoist exorcistic ritual practiced by Chen's lineage originates in Pu'an's Chan monastery itself. Tam Wai Lun argues that the kind of dual exorcistic ritual currently practiced in northwestern Jiangxi by "incense and flower monks" (*xianghua heshang* 香花和尚)—nonmonastic ritualists who, much like the masters of Chen Diwen's lineage, consider themselves half Buddhist, half Daoist—is likely not a bastardization of traditional Chan practice by local nonmonastic ritualists. Instead, Buddhist and Daoist exorcistic practices might very well have been taught by Chan monks based in Pu'an's Monastery of Compassionate Transformation and its branch temples such as the Western Spring Monastery. Construction of the Monastery of Compassionate Transformation was completed in 1169; it was then destroyed by fire in 1292 but grandly reconstructed in 1295 with the support of the Yuan court. In the reconstruction, the compound was expanded and organized into an eastern and a western section, each composed of twelve administrative (or perhaps living) quarters (*dongxi ershisi liao* 東西二十四寮).[50] The Western Spring Monastery was built on an east-west plan seemingly similar to its parent temple, and the eastern and western buildings accommodated different ritual practices. Li Wuhan reports that during the Ming dynasty the compound of the Western Spring Monastery covered more than two thousand square meters, and that the western buildings were of the Buddhist tradition and the eastern of both Buddhist and Daoist traditions.[51] Chen Yisong (陳益松)—a practitioner of Daoist, Pu'an Buddhist, and local *shi* rites in Hongzhu village (洪竹村) deep in the Daxiong Mountains—corroborates Li Wuhan's account. Relying on manuals preserved by his lineage, Chen says that "the eastern buildings taught both popular Buddhist and Daoist traditions, while the western buildings taught the Buddhist tradition."[52] Given that eastern buildings in the Western Spring Monastery were associated with both Buddhist and Daoist ritual, we might surmise that the modest line in our manual mentioning that the Western Spring Monastery branched out specifically from a building in the eastern section of Pu'an's Monastery of Compassionate Transformation is a subtle clue that the exorcistic practice associated with Pu'an in Xinhua and Anhua has combined Buddhist and Daoist elements since the flourishing of Pu'an's monastery in Jiangxi during the late thirteenth and fourteenth centuries.

A colophon to our manual provides a genealogy from the founder of the Western Spring Monastery, the monk Hongqing, through the next several generations of leading monks at the monastery:

> Hongqing passed [the practices] to Dening, who then passed them to Wenhai, who in turn passed them to Chengyu, who passed them to Chuanyi in the fourth generation, who passed them to Faxian in the fifth generation, who passed them to the monk Yangde in the sixth generation. Yangde also studied at the Red Furnace Monastery in Suzhou prefecture

within the metropolitan area of the Southern Capital. He passed on [the practices] to the Universal Transformation Monastery on Mount Longzhu, from which [the practices] were transmitted to the Shrine of the Patriarchs' Prosperity.[53]

弘清傳與德寧，續傳文海，再傳成余，四傳傳遺，五傳法現，六傳養德和尚。養又參學於南京蘇州府紅爐寺，續傳龍珠山普化寺，再傳祖興庵。

The text claims that Pu'an's exorcistic tradition passed from Hongqing down several generations to monks I have not been able to corroborate, and finally to a monk named Yangde (養德). The colophon includes a note that Yangde, originally surnamed Chen (陳), was a native of Mount Sijia near Xi Brook (錫溪四甲山) in Xinhua and that he lived from 1585 to 1663. He is buried behind the Western Spring Monastery.[54] Yangde seems to have been a rather influential figure. The text makes a point of noting that he studied in a monastery in faraway Suzhou, which seems to attribute some worldliness to him, but I have been unable to find any corroboration of this or explanation of its possible significance. Several lineages across northern Xinhua and southeastern Anhua trace their exorcistic Buddhist practices back to Yangde, and sometimes back to Hongqing through the same lineage of monks listed in Chen Diwen's manual.[55] We can imagine that Yangde was instrumental in radiating the tradition of Pu'an exorcistic Buddhist practices out from the Western Spring Monastery. At least one vector went northeast to the Universal Transformation Monastery (Puhuasi 普化寺, also written 普華寺) on Mount Longzhu near present-day Hailong,[56] and then to the Shrine of the Patriarchs' Prosperity (Zuxing'an 祖興庵), which I have not been able to locate (see figure 1.4).

A passage from the body of the manual picks up the story:

One branch of the tradition [from the Western Spring Monastery] spread to the Universal Transformation Monastery in Chuliang, whence it was transmitted to the Shrine of the Patriarchs' Prosperity, from which a branch split off to the lineage of our revered patriarch, Luo Shenhui the Realized One, of Hainan Creek. Luo Shenhui personally transmitted [the tradition] to the lineage of our great patriarch Master Jiang Sanlu of Wangjia Lane in

Fuqing, Anhua county. From there [the tradition] was handed down from master to master, transmitted from generation to generation. One branch of the tradition spread to Guanyin Monastery channel near Guanxi, and was then transmitted to Ningdian Bridge in Fuqing, where three generations of my lineage have resided and tended our altar.[57]

一支教寓於楚良普化寺，傳至祖興庵，支分海南溪老祖深惠羅真人門下。親傳安邑浮青王家坊師太祖蔣三祿先生幕下。由是師師相授，代代續傳。一支教演於官溪觀音寺冲，轉傳於浮青盋滇橋，三代建壇居住。

A branch of Pu'an's tradition spread from the Western Spring Monastery to other Buddhist temples to the east, and was eventually assumed by a patriarch of Chen Diwen's lineage, Luo Shenhui, who lived in the village of Chuliang (Hailong) (see figure 1.4). Luo is marked by his Daoist name, which according to the lineage's Daoist generational poem puts him in the tenth *shen* generation of the Daoist lineage, roughly the mid- to late eighteenth century. Here we see that as Pu'an's brand of exorcistic Buddhist practice—which we have gleaned was very likely a blend of Buddhist and Daoist practices—was transmitted among local Buddhist temples, it was also taught to nonmonastic, "hearth-dwelling" masters like Luo Shenhui, who, recall, identified with Daoist traditions that had emanated from the Jade Void Palace in Xinhua. It is therefore not surprising that a large number of nonmonastic masters were buried along with monks on the grounds of the Western Spring Monastery. The exchange of ritual techniques between monks and different stripes of local masters must have been vigorous. The text then states that Luo Shenhui personally transmitted these Buddhist practices to his disciple Jiang Sanlu, a resident of Fuqing and member of the eleventh *san* generation, which dates him to around the turn of the nineteenth century. Here we have indication that the Buddhist tradition practiced by Chen Diwen's lineage made its way to Fuqing by at least the beginning of the nineteenth century.

Finally, the text states that from Jiang Sanlu the practices spread throughout the Fuqing area. One strand made its way to the locale around Guanyin Temple (Guanyinsi 觀音寺), a sizable temple near the tiny hamlet of

Guanxi where Chen Diwen's master Li Yezhen lived.[58] From there, the tradition came down to the generations of masters above the copyist of the text, Jiang Shenzhi (蔣身志) (1928–2018), a direct descendant of Jiang Sanlu. The text locates those masters in a hamlet associated with Ningdian Bridge, just north of Fuqing village, where Jiang Shenzhi lived until his death. These short passages buried within a Buddhist liturgical manual suggest that, by at least the late eighteenth century, Buddhist exorcistic ritual had migrated out of regional temples connected with Pu'an's legacy to Chen Diwen's liturgical ancestors who identified as Daoist masters.

Just as Chen Diwen's lineage has used a Daoist generational poem to create Daoist liturgical names marking its members' place in the lineage, it has also used a Buddhist generational poem to fashion Buddhist liturgical names down the generations. That poem reads:

道正印國	*Dao zheng yin guo*	The correctness of the Dharma is impressed upon the empire,
師紹慈嗣	*Shi shao ci si*	Its masters carry on compassion through the generations.
妙智宗祖	*Miao zhi zong zu*	The Patriarchs in their sublime wisdom
玄悟真如	*Xuan wu zhen ru*	Mysteriously awakened to Suchness.
守戒持行	*Shou jie chi xing*	They held fast to the precepts and practiced them,
益鎮宏規	*Yi zhen hong gui*	Bringing benefit and calm as did the Great Paragon [the Buddha].
茂衍慶源	*Mao yan qing yuan*	Flourishing, continuing is the celebrated source,
克彰法本	*Ke zhang fa ben*	Ably manifesting the root of the Dharma.
從聞思修	*Cong wen si xiu*	Obey what you have heard and mindfully practice.
續佛慧命	*Xu fo hui ming*	The wise commands of successive Buddhas,
常住法位	*Chang zhu fa wei*	The changeless status of the Dharma,
廣揚教化	*Guang yang jiao hua*	Spread enlightenment far and wide,
福潤群生	*Fu run qun sheng*	Blessings saturate all sentient beings.
通編維方	*Tong bian wei fang*	Penetrating texts sustain the region,

無藏盡義	*Wu zang jin yi*	But no canon exhausts their meaning.
萬海同春	*Wan hai tong chun*	The myriad seas together celebrate springtime,
祥雲畢集	*Xiang yun bi ji*	Auspicious clouds gather.
桂乳流傳	*Gui ru liu chuan*	The nectar of the sweet osmanthus flower is passed down
馨香戀世	*Xin xiang lian shi*	Amid the sweet incense in the world of attachment.
竺泉華原	*Zhu yuan hua yuan*	Wellspring of India, fount of China,
光明耀輝	*Guang ming yao hui*	Brilliant and dazzling.[59]

Just as in the Daoist lineage poem, each generation of Chen Diwen's lineage takes one character of this poem for the Buddhist name bequeathed at ordination. For example, Chen's master, who was assigned the Daoist name Li Yezhen, was also given the Buddhist name Li Mingzhen (李命真). The middle character *ming* 命 corresponds to the fortieth character of the Buddhist poem, or the fortieth generation of the Buddhist lineage. Should Chen Diwen be ordained, he would be given a Buddhist name with the *chang* 常 character, which corresponds to the forty-first generation and would mark him as belonging to the generation after his master.

Although the Buddhist lineage poem generates liturgical names the same way as the Daoist poem, the Daoist poem is primarily used to mark the generations of the lineage. Daoist names are used to invoke the entire lineage of ancestral masters, even for a Buddhist liturgy. Typically, Buddhist names are only used by officiants to sign petitions recited and burned during funerary rites, or by copyists to sign Buddhist manuscripts. In fact, in the cache of texts preserved by Chen Diwen's lineage, I can find no mention of a Buddhist name prior to the last five generations. Even the copyist of the Buddhist lineage poem, Jiang Shenzhi, who made the copy in the late 1980s, notes that stanzas are likely missing and that the text should be checked against other texts, to which it seems he did not have access.[60] Clearly, the Buddhist poem is not maintained nearly as fastidiously as the Daoist one (web figure 1.13).

The copyist's trepidation was well founded. The Buddhist poem used by Chen Diwen's lineage is actually two poems that have been combined. The first thirty-six characters—from *dao* 道 to *xiu* 修—are originally one poem; the second forty-eight—from *xu* 續 to *hui* 輝—are another. Both poems are recorded in the 1806 genealogy we encountered, which was, recall, preserved in Pu'an's Compassionate Transformation Monastery in Jiangxi. This text indicates that the thirty-six-character poem was associated with a certain Chan Master Guoming (國明禪師), about whom we know nothing more than what the text states—that he was a Song dynasty monk of renowned Shaolin Monastery (少林寺) in Henan. The forty-eight-character poem is a supplement to the first. It is attributed to Chan Master Jin Bifeng (金碧峰禪師), who, the genealogy states, was a disciple of a certain Chan Master Jieyuan (界源禪師), a fourteenth-generation Linji monk.[61]

According to canonical sources, Jin Bifeng was a well-known monk who lived during the late Yuan and early Ming dynasties. Originally from the town of Yongshou (永壽) in Qianzhou (乾州) in Jiangxi, he traveled widely from Sichuan to Shanxi and founded a temple—the Numinous Vulture Shrine (Lingjiu an 靈鷲菴)—on famed Mount Wutai (五臺山) in northern Shanxi. Emperor Yuan Shundi (元順帝) (r. 1333–1370) honored him in Beijing and, intriguingly, asked him to pray for rain. After the Ming conquest a few years later, Zhu Yuanzhang summoned the monk to Nanjing and inquired about his knowledge of the nature of demons. The emperor decreed that a temple just outside a southern gate of the capital be renamed Bifeng Monastery (碧峰寺) and serve as the monk's residence. Jin Bifeng died shortly after at the age of sixty-five.[62]

Gleaning the 1806 genealogy from the Compassionate Transformation Monastery, it seems the first poem was exhausted by the monks of the monastery by the late Yuan or early Ming. They acquired the second poem as a supplement from the renowned Jin Bifeng. The original poem and its supplement then made their way from the Monastery of Compassionate Transformation to the Western Spring Monastery in Hunan. Eventually, those poems were used by lineages of nonmonastic masters in northern Xinhua who seem to have learned Pu'an's ritual tradition from monks of the Western Spring Monastery and its branch temples. In addition to Chen Diwen's lineage, we have evidence that at least one other lineage branch in northern Xinhua still uses the poem, that of Master Chen Yisong, which practices Pu'an Buddhist, Daoist, and local *shi* rites. That lineage also shares the same Daoist generational poem with Chen Diwen's lineage.[63]

Much more evidence is needed to determine how widespread, dominant, or varied Pu'an-related Buddhist practice has been in northern Xinhua and Anhua, and why lineages in southern Xinhua seem not to have picked it up. For now, our scant sources suggest three general stages in the transmission of Pu'an's exorcistic Buddhist practice to Chen Diwen's liturgical ancestors in Fuqing: first, from Pu'an's Monastery of Compassionate Transformation in Jiangxi to the Western Spring Monastery in the Daxiong Mountains of northern Xinhua; second, from the Western Spring Monastery northeastward to temples near Hailong in Xinhua; and, third, from those temples to nonmonastic masters around Hailong, whose lineage then transmitted the practices eastward to the Fuqing area in Anhua (see figure 1.4).

The Jiang and Li Clans of Fuqing

Our genealogical investigations of Chen Diwen's lineage show something of its dual pedigree. Its Daoist ritual tradition is rooted in the Jade Void Palace in southern Xinhua, which seems to have claimed some sort of relationship with the Celestial Masters on Mount Longhu in eastern Jiangxi. Its Buddhist ritual tradition originated in Pu'an's complicated exorcistic Buddhist tradition—which might have included Daoist elements—from the Western Spring Monastery in northern Xinhua, which was a subsidiary of Pu'an's Monastery of Compassionate Transformation on Mount Nanquan in western Jiangxi. These two streams of practice seem to have converged in the Daxiong Mountains of northern Xinhua.

From the Daoist manuals preserved by Chen's lineage, we know that the Zhengyi Daoist tradition practiced in the Jade Void Palace made its way north to the town of Chuliang, where it was practiced by masters of the tenth *shen* generation of the lineage, including Fang Shenzhi and Luo Shenhui, during the mid- to late eighteenth century. Passages from the lineage's Buddhist manuals state that Pu'an Buddhism spread from the Western

Spring Monastery to smaller temples in the Chuliang area and then to Luo Shenhui. That Luo Shenhui is prominently mentioned as a patriarch who received and transmitted both Daoist and Buddhist rites suggests that Chen Diwen's lineage has been simultaneously practicing Zhengyi Daoist and Pu'an Buddhist ritual since at least the latter half of the eighteenth century.

Indications are that the intermingling of these ritual traditions among Chen's liturgical ancestors in the Daxiong Mountains had begun even earlier. During their fieldwork, Lui Wing Sing and Li Xinwu acquired the text of a public notice hung on the occasion of the funeral of a certain Daoist Li Xuanming (道士李玄明), which took place in 1731 in a hamlet near Dongping (today the Anhua county seat) on the Zi River about thirty-five kilometers northwest of the Western Spring Monastery. The composer of the notice, a certain Xie Xuanying (謝玄應), is introduced in the document as affiliated with a branch lineage of Pu'an's Monastery of Compassionate Transformation.[64] The names of the composer of the notice and the deceased suggest they both were masters of the eighth *xuan* 玄 generation of Chen Diwen's Daoist lineage. Given that the composer Xie Xuanying is also identified as an officiant of a branch of Pu'an's Monastery of Compassionate Transformation, the evidence is subtle but compelling that Chen Diwen's lineage has been practicing both Zhengyi Daoist and Pu'an Buddhist ritual since at least the early eighteenth century.

Branches of the lineage spread over the Daxiong Mountains and eventually eastward to Fuqing. Chen's masters take the ancestral masters mentioned in the Buddhist ritual manual as patriarchs of their branch of the Daoist-Buddhist lineage in Fuqing (see appendix). Their manuals show that Luo Shenhui of the tenth *shen* generation, who lived in Chuliang (Hailong), passed the tradition down to Jiang Sanlu of the eleventh *san* generation, who was a native of Fuqing. One of Chen Diwen's masters tells a story about these two patriarchs:

When Master Jiang Sanlu was young, he and his mother worked many years as servants in the household of the Realized One Luo Shenhui [in Chuliang]. Sanlu was very bright and Luo Shenhui took a liking to him, and so took him as a disciple. He mastered the rites quickly. The Realized

One Luo Shenhui had two sons who also studied with him, but they weren't as bright as Master Jiang Sanlu and learned the rites more slowly. The Realized One Shenhui was so fond of Master Jiang Sanlu that he adopted him as his own son. That is how Master Jiang Sanlu came to know so splendidly this Daoist-Buddhist dual tradition [*Fo Dao liangjiao* 佛道兩教] of ours. Later he returned to Fuqing and taught the tradition.[65]

The ritual tradition from Chuliang (Hailong) seems to have made its way to Fuqing through other avenues as well. Recall that the 1888 colophon to the Daoist liturgical manual indicates another line of transmission from Chuliang to Fuqing. Master Fang Shenzhi of the tenth *shen* generation in Chuliang passed the tradition down two generations to members of the Gong clan in Xinhua, who then transmitted it to Fu Gongyu in Fuqing, a master of the thirteenth *gong* generation, which dates him to the early to mid-nineteenth century. This text indicates that at least one other branch of the tradition from Chuliang was transmitted to Fuqing in addition to that descending from Jiang Sanlu (see appendix).

During the nineteenth century, multiple clans in the Fuqing area had received the dual Daoist-Buddhist ritual tradition from Chuliang through at least two lines of transmission. Those clans came to define different branches of the tradition in and around Fuqing. Consecration documents hidden within wooden statues of familial and liturgical ancestors from the Fuqing area indicate that several of these local clans practiced together and often intermarried. For instance, at the turn of the nineteenth century, two members of the twelfth *qian* generation—a certain Fang Qianming (方千明), a descendant of Fang Shenzhi of Chuliang, and a certain Gong Qianshen (龔千神) of the Gong clan—were liturgical brothers as well as in-laws. Furthermore, Gong Qianshen served as the transmission master of a certain Jiang Gongchan (蔣功禪) of the thirteenth *gong* generation, who was a descendant of Jiang Sanlu. Liturgical training and marriage bound these clans into a network of masters that came to dominate the hills and hamlets in and around Fuqing village (see appendix).

Among these clans, the Jiang clan seems to have enjoyed relatively high status, which it maintains today. It has been keen to collect, preserve, recopy, and redact an impressive trove of more than two hundred ritual texts, including those from other clans, such as the Fu, which produced the Daoist manual containing the 1888 colophon. The cache of the Jiang clan includes dozens of nineteenth-century texts, the oldest of which dates to the Daoguang (道光) period (1821–1850). Certain masters of the Jiang clan have been especially respected in the Fuqing area and even beyond.

Discussions with living members of Chen Diwen's lineage about the last several generations of deceased masters listed in a liturgical manual invoking them to oversee rituals reveal the ways in which the Jiang clan of Fuqing became closely associated with the Li clan of Guanxi, of which Chen's master, Li Yezhen, was a member.[66] Chen's masters explain that Jiang Sanlu passed down the tradition to several masters of the twelfth *qian* 千 generation of the lineage, among whom were Jiang Qianling (蔣千靈), Jiang Qianzhen (蔣千珍), Jiang Qianhe (蔣千和), who were likely his sons or nephews (see appendix). Jiang Qianzhen transmitted the tradition to Jiang Gongchuan (蔣功傳) (b. 1804) and Jiang Gongqing (蔣功清) of the thirteenth *gong* generation. Jiang Gongqing taught the rites to Jiang Xingshi (蔣行時) (b. 1832) of the fourteenth *xing* 行 generation, as well as to a certain Li Xingchun (李行春) of the Li clan in Guanxi. The Li clan had been practicing the Daoist-Buddhist tradition from Chuliang since at least the previous *gong* generation in the early nineteenth century, but by the *xing* generation in the mid-nineteenth century it was sharing masters with the Jiang clan. Jiang Xingshi taught the rites to his son Jiang Manzeng (蔣滿鋥), one of several Jiang brothers and cousins to be ordained into the fifteenth *man* 滿 generation of the lineage, as well as to Li Manjuan (李滿鋗) (b. 1860) of Guanxi. Jiang Manzeng and Li Manjuan were close friends and together trained many masters of the sixteenth *fei* 飛 generation, including Li Feimao (李飛茂), Chen Diwen's third-generation master. Li Manjuan even married off his daughter to Jiang Manzeng's son, Jiang Feiqing (蔣飛清) (1888–1971). An exceptionally ambitious young man, Jiang Feiqing studied with both his father Jiang Manzeng and his father-in-law Li Manjuan but took Li Manjuan as his transmission master.

By all accounts, Jiang Feiqing, courtesy name (*zi* 字) Jiang Bayong (蔣 拔庸), was a powerful master and effective politician (web figure 1.14). Chen Diwen's masters explain that he organized a group of masters from across Anhua to petition the county government to form the Anhua Daoist Association (Anhua daojiao xiehui 安化道教協會) in July 1941. A government report found in the Anhua County Archives states that Jiang and his fellow masters sought an officially recognized Daoist association in order "to unite the disciples of Daoism across the county, to promote the benefits of Daoist study, to organize and strengthen its regulations, to propagate its doctrines, and to advance the true spirit of the Three Principles of the People" (團結全縣教徒,增進學益,整飭教規,宣揚教義,發揚三民主義真精神). Couching the petition in the political vision of Republic of China founder Sun Yat-sen (孫逸仙) must have made much sense during the summer of 1941, just a few months before the horrific second Battle of Changsha against the Japanese army. Jiang Feiqing had experience as a supervisor of military services (*bingyi dudaoyuan* 兵役督導員), helping organize local conscription into the Nationalist army during the Anti-Japanese War, and as a security group head (*baozhang* 保長) who had responsibility for one hundred households in Fuqing. He was well poised to lead a preparation committee, which seems to have functioned as a liaison between the would-be members of the Anhua Daoist Association and a county government eager to ensure that the new organization would join forces in resisting the Japanese while "studying doctrines and ameliorating superstition" (研討教義,改善迷信). After a series of negotiations, the petition was approved on April 24, 1942. From the 102 masters or their representatives in attendance that day outside the county office of the Nationalist Party in Meicheng, Jiang Feiqing was elected as the association's first executive director (*changwu lishi* 常務理事) (web figures 1.15, 1.16).[67]

Masters of the Jiang and Li clans continued to work together to train the seventeenth *shen* 身 generation. Jiang Feiqing served as transmission master for several masters, including his son Jiang Shenzhi (1928–2018). Jiang Feiqing's liturgical brother, Li Feimao, transmitted the rites to Li Shenming (李身銘), the master of Chen Diwen's master, Li Yezhen (1933–2007). The *shen* generation was the last generation of the lineage to have received training relatively unencumbered by government restrictions. Practicing in the sleepy hills of the Daxiong Mountains, the masters of Fuqing escaped the anti-superstition movements of the Republican period. Until his death in January 2018 at age eighty-nine, Jiang Shenzhi was the last surviving member of the *shen* generation. His generation's most prolific copyist, codifier, and redactor of the lineage's ritual manuals, Jiang occupied an elevated place in the lineage as the last living link to the past before Liberation (web figure 1.17).

When Chen Diwen's future master Li Yezhen began training in 1948 as a would-be-member of the eighteenth *ye* 謁 generation, religious practice was flourishing in the Fuqing area. He initially took Jiang Shenzhi as his transmission master. Jiang had already gained a reputation as a precocious and powerful master even though he had just been ordained in 1946. But Li's training soon became difficult. From the early 1950s, cadres of the Chinese Communist Party branded local religious practice "feudal superstition" (*fengjian mixin* 封建迷信) and tried to restrict it. Jiang recalled, "From 1951 through the 1980s our practices were not permitted. There were households that requested we offer rites for them and so we would perform one-day rituals under the cover of darkness, but we had to conceal them from the government, and not let the government know." Uneven waves of repression ensued as the 1950s unfolded. At times, masters were able to perform rites for villagers; at other times they were fined, occasionally interrogated, and even detained in custody. "The fine was ninety yuan," Jiang remembered, "but at the time that was a lot; everyone was so poor then."

Li Yezhen became an administrative director in his home village of Guanxi while surreptitiously trying to continue his training as best he could. Eventually, though, he had to stop. His master Jiang Shenzhi was under close scrutiny by the government. After all, Jiang's father, Jiang Feiqing, had been the leader of the Nationalist-sanctioned Anhua Daoist Association, a local administrator, and a local security group head who occupied a higher class than most in Fuqing. He was just the kind of rural "capitalist" and Nationalist sympathizer the Communists targeted. After the land reforms were completed in 1953, Jiang Feiqing was branded a local despot (*eba* 惡霸) and his son was suddenly tainted. For several years, Jiang Shenzhi could not find meaningful work. When government-propagated class struggle subsided a bit in the last years of the 1950s during the Great Leap Forward, Jiang was finally able to find employment as an accountant (*kuaiji* 會計) for the local advanced agricultural producer's cooperative (*gaojishe* 高級社), and then for the local people's commune (*renmin gongshe* 人民公社). He was later, ironically, posted to a low-level job in the local government offices, but his livelihood was always precarious due to association with his father.

During the early 1960s, government repression of religious activities lessened for a while. While working as a production team leader in Guanxi, Li Yezhen furtively took advantage of the space to resume studies with another master in the lineage, Li Shenming, given that Jiang Shenzhi was still under scrutiny and dared not practice. The Cultural Revolution, however, got under way in 1966 and the lineage faced the greatest crisis in its collective memory. Jiang Feiqing was criticized and humiliated in a public ceremony to shame and punish counterrevolutionaries. After several years of polite requests to talk about that time, Jiang Shenzhi finally opened up to me during the summer of 2010:[68]

> In 1967 they were going after counterrevolutionaries. They falsely accused my father of being a counterrevolutionary and beat him up pretty badly. They put on him some groundless charges saying he was the "head of the third middle brigade" [*sanzhongdui zhongduizhang* 三中隊中隊長]. The government hired a few thugs to come over and beat him up. Only in the 1980s was the injustice redressed when the government paid a little in damages.

Jiang Feiqing's ties to the Nationalist government made him vulnerable to accusations of being the leader of a counterrevolutionary organization. He never recovered from the humiliation and died soon after, in 1971. When telling the story, Jiang Shenzhi sighed heavily, mournful that he could not even give his father a proper funeral according to the rites of his lineage.

Government authorities were set on rooting out all religion, which was branded a feudal vestige and so an impediment to the economic and social progress envisioned by the Communist Party. Jiang Shenzhi recalled,

> During the Cultural Revolution, all the temples and shrines as well as anything related to religion [*zongjiao* 宗教] were destroyed. All the households of Daoists were searched. During that time, it was "establish the four new things and do away with the four old things" [*li sixin po sijiu* 立四新破四舊].[69] They incessantly tried to confiscate any of our texts having to do with religion, but since the texts were easily hidden, not that many were actually confiscated. But nearly all our ritual accessories—Buddhist and Daoist painted scrolls and statues; our cymbals, flutes, gongs, wooden fish, conch, and drums—were confiscated. My father stashed our old manuals in the homes of good friends who were not Daoists. Since they weren't Daoists no one went to search their houses, so the texts were safe. But still some texts were confiscated, destroyed, lost, or misplaced.

Li Yezhen and other members of the lineage who lived through the Cultural Revolution recalled that they would surrender to the authorities only woodblock-printed scriptures such as the *True Scripture of the Three Officers* (*Sanguan zhenjing* 三官真經) and the *Diamond Sutra* (*Jin'gang jing* 金剛經), which were public texts. But they were sure to hide away the hand-copied ritual texts containing the esoteric instructions (*mizhi*) for performing rituals, including the Banner Rite.

Yet some masters resisted. Jiang Shenzhi remembered:

> At the time no one at all came out to oppose the government. No one dared. But still there were a few gutsy Daoists who would secretly perform minor rites for people. After someone died, they would perform a simple one-day ritual and burn a numinous mansion [*lingfang* 靈房], but no one dared to perform many funerals.

Some patrons and masters, as well as a few apprentices, such as Li Yezhen, risked heavy penalty to ferry the soul of a deceased through the courts of judgment in the underworld, and to burn a bamboo and paper model of a house—the ritual way to provide the soul a temporary home in the underworld before rebirth. Without texts, they performed from memory.

Without musical instruments, they lightly struck ceramic teacup covers with chopsticks to simulate percussion while whispering invocations and chants.

Through the 1970s, the masters of Fuqing scrambled to make ends meet. Some worked as painters of household items and modest decorations (*youqigong* 油漆工). Because they were literate, some were able to work as accountants for production teams (*shengchandui kuaiji* 生產隊會計), as irrigation works technicians (*shuili jishuyuan* 水利技術員), and as "barefoot doctors" (*chijiao yisheng* 赤腳醫生)—villagers who were trained by urban doctors sent down to the countryside. Barefoot doctors labored to prevent epidemics by administering immunizations and improving sanitation. They could diagnose simple ailments and attempt to cure them with both Western and Chinese medicines and techniques. The end of the Cultural Revolution upon Mao Zedong's death in 1976 and the institution of Deng Xiaoping's policies of "reform and opening up" in 1978 were not immediately felt in Fuqing. Government repression of religious activity remained strong and the masters of Fuqing continued to live secular lives.

Only in the late 1980s and early 1990s did the freeze on religious expression begin to thaw, but unevenly. One master recalls, "Here in Fuqing things began to loosen up about 1990, but in other places it was in the late 80s, and still others as late as 1996. Actually, the cadres of each locale were all different. They could fine you at any time because the government still had not actually permitted you to practice. So, you had to look at the situation of each cadre." Although wary of their precarious situation, masters and villagers cautiously began to practice more openly. Local scholar Zhang Shihong reported that in 1992 the Anhua County Bureau of Culture (Anhuaxian wenhuaju 安化縣文化局) published a pamphlet titled "Materials for Singing at Funerals and Burials" (*Binzang yanchang ziliao* 殯葬演唱資料), which dictated the kinds of hymns the government deemed appropriate for funerals. Local cadres summoned all the masters in the area and distributed the pamphlet, charging an administrative fee for a permit allowing them to perform funerary rites. Although the pamphlet proclaimed more intense governmental scrutiny of funerary ritual, the document de facto signaled the government no longer considered traditional funerary rites counterrevolutionary superstition. With certain oversight and a taxation mechanism, the government in effect sanctioned traditional funerary activity. In 1993, the county government again cracked down on masters who performed funerals and families who hired them, fining them ¥100 to ¥300 (roughly $17 to $51). But the measure only succeeded in bolstering funerary activity. Families of the deceased simply added the fine to the cost of the funeral—already a large expense—and went on practicing.[70]

Masters in Chen Diwen's lineage recovered their hidden ritual manuals and piece by piece bought or made new musical instruments. Jiang Shenzhi in particular took it upon himself to codify, recopy, and redact their entire repertoire of Daoist and Buddhist ritual manuals. He included dozens of secret instructions that had previously been taught only as oral transmissions. Jiang feared poor mastery of this ritual knowledge by disciples who were spending extended periods working outside the locale as migrant laborers and so had less exposure to the oral tradition.

Having taught himself how to paint ritual scrolls as a young master before Liberation, Jiang Shenzhi also fashioned new paintings of deities, which were once again hung on the walls of altar spaces constructed for Daoist rites and Buddhist funerals. He based the paintings on ink-drawn templates that were squirreled away with the ritual manuals (web figure 1.18). Lay patrons and local craftspeople rebuilt small temples dedicated to local tutelary gods—temple kings (*miaowang* 廟王) and gods of the soil (*tudigong* 土地公, *tudipo* 土地婆), who respectively protect the people and land of each hamlet (web figure 1.19). Locals began rebuilding large temples like the Guanyin Temple near Guanxi (web figures 1.20, 1.21).

Most important, the lineage began training Daoists again. Li Yezhen finally completed his training under the guidance of his transmission master, Li Shenming. Forty-two years after he had originally entered the lineage as an apprentice in 1948, Li was ordained in 1990 and took his Daoist name, Yezhen, the first member of the eighteenth *ye* generation. Jiang Shenzhi, who had been his original transmission master, served as one of his two witnessing masters. Several others who had begun training during the Mao era were also ordained into the *ye* generation during the 1990s. The next generation after that was instituted when Jiang Shenzhi began training his teenage grandson. A precocious apprentice with a fierce sense of responsibility to the lineage branch his family had led for more than two centuries, Jiang Yucheng was ordained in 1991 at age eighteen, the inaugural member of the nineteenth *yu* 玉 generation, the first generation to be completely trained and ordained after the Mao era (web figure 1.22). But scars from the past remained. Jiang Shenzhi's son never entered the lineage due to the toll brought by the political pressure on his father and grandfather, Jiang Feiqing.

Members of the lineage adjusted to the shifting political reality in Fuqing. In 1990, one of Jiang Shenzhi's apprentices was, remarkably, elected village head (*cunzhang* 村長). Two years before, the Communist Party had across the nation instituted grassroots elections of village-level leaders by the villagers themselves. The villagers' committee (*cunmin weiyuanhui* 村民委員會), composed of several elected officials led by the village head, was nominally a self-governing entity outside the Party. The Fuqing village head elected in 1990 had entered the lineage as an apprentice in 1963 but would not be ordained as Li Yeshi 李謁詩 until 1997. He explains that as village head he took responsibility for maintaining levels of economic production, handling disputes among locals, relaying party propaganda, collecting the agricultural tax, and directing local family planning and afforestation policies (web figure 1.23).

When asked how he managed to serve as village head while training to be a master, Li Yeshi recounts,

> When I was village head I didn't publicly perform rites in the Fuqing area, but I would go to [northern] Xinhua and other places outside Fuqing to perform. And I never became a Party member. In 1991, the government wanted me to join the Party, but I had selfish motives. At the time I was studying how to perform funerals. Had I joined the Party, it would not have been very easy to be a Daoist. At that time, those sorts of activities were still rather impermissible, and I really liked being a Daoist so I refused to join the Party. Furthermore, joining the Party wouldn't have increased my wages. At most I might have been selected branch secretary [*cunzhishu* 村支書],[71] but the status was in reality about the same as village head, as were the wages. Had I become a Party member, a lot of things would

have been controlled by the Communist Party. Of course, the [elected] village head was still controlled, but you could choose what to listen to, and if worse came to worst you could just quit being village head. Also, the government had no right to prohibit you from being village head because it was the people who elected you. But were I to become branch secretary of the Party, the government could prohibit me from serving because the branch secretary is appointed by the government. Therefore, I didn't join the Party so I could be village head and be a Daoist.[72]

These striking remarks illustrate one way in which masters of Chen Diwen's lineage refashioned their relationships with a government that had oppressed them for decades. Like water, they sought out cracks in the system in which to practice their liturgical tradition within the new political reality.

They also looked for ways to rehabilitate the political status of that liturgical tradition, to redefine it once again as acceptable religion (*zongjiao* 宗教) rather than reviled superstition (*mixin* 迷信). Li Yeshi explains that the masters of Fuqing have been well aware that the distinction between religion and superstition is largely political:

Performing a funeral won't affect the government's political power, and it won't affect public order. It is a kind of freedom of belief [*xinyang ziyou* 信仰自由]. Now of course during the Mao era, the constitution also included freedom of belief, but Mao Zedong, in order to eradicate superstition, did not permit anything "superstitious," including anything "religious." The government said all of it was "superstition" and not "religion." Later, society developed and the government came to realize that our liturgical tradition is not superstition but instead a kind of religion. They also realized it wouldn't affect the government. These days we perform funerals next to the government offices and they pay no attention. The government does not advocate religion and it does not curb it. But if you organize, if you influence the government, then it will definitely control you. Take Falun gong (法輪功), for example. It is, in fact, also a kind of belief, a kind of religion. Had they not gone to Tiananmen (天安門) to sit in meditation, not gone to Zhongnanhai (中南海) to plead, not gone to disturb the government, then the government definitely would not have sought to control them.

Li Yeshi's voice carries a hint of both trepidation and disgust as he refers to the sit-in by a thousand Falun gong practitioners outside the headquarters of the central government and the Chinese Communist Party, just off Tiananmen Square in Beijing, on April 25, 1999.[73] The protest immediately brought the ire of the Party's top leaders, and the government soon flooded the national media with a coordinated propaganda campaign. The leaders of Falun gong, especially its founder Li Hongzhi (李洪志), were charged with harming their followers and even causing some deaths by encouraging them to ignore medical prescriptions in favor of Falun gong practices. Falun gong cultivation was said to cause serious mental illness. Falun gong was labeled a "heterodox teaching" (*xiejiao* 邪教) indulging in excessive worship of its leader Li Hongzhi, mind control, false doctrines, and corrupt money making, all of which were intended to damage society and even overthrow the government (web figure 1.24).[74]

Not certain how much truth the media stories actually contained, Li Yeshi feels that Falun gong was, in any event, foolish to challenge the government so baldly. Mindful of the lessons to be drawn, he argues that the kind of Daoism and Buddhism his lineage practices actually aids the social agenda of the party-state, especially in its battle against graft.

> Daoist and Buddhist books exhort people to do good, and so if Daoism and Buddhism continue to develop, they should be a help to the government. If everyone believed in religion [*xinjiao* 信教], they would definitely do more good deeds and would not have a lot of selfish interests, so there is absolutely no subversive effect on the government.

Not unlike his liturgical forebear Jiang Feiqing during the Republican period, Li Yeshi defines the lineage's Daoist-Buddhist practice in politically correct terms—morally upright, staunchly patriotic, and politically benign religion over and against immoral, treacherous, and corrupt superstition.[75]

Conclusion

Chen Diwen had little idea of the long and rich history of the lineage he had entered. From the older masters he heard a few stories about the great Jiang

Feiqing, and only bits and pieces about the trauma his transmission master's generation suffered during the Cultural Revolution. Like all the masters in the lineage, young and old, Chen knew next to nothing about the twists and turns by which the lineage made its way to Fuqing. He had little idea that the Daoist strand of the tradition had descended from the Jade Void Palace in Xinhua through one of six subsidiary temples sometime during the fifteenth century. He did not know how Pu'an's Buddhist rites had come down to him, although he often sang incantations, read ritual manuals, and transcribed liturgical petitions mentioning the Western Spring Monastery and his ancestral master Pu'an. He did not know Jiang Sanlu had likely brought the dual Daoist-Buddhist tradition to Fuqing from his master Luo Shenhui in northern Xinhua during the late eighteenth century. They were simply names among dozens of other ancestral masters invoked from the lineage's ritual manuals during liturgies.

Although Chen Diwen did not know much of his lineage's history, he did understand that he had walked through a gateway into a grand liturgical tradition that had a special relationship with Celestial Lord Yin Jiao. He knew that all his hours mastering the flute and percussion instruments, all his efforts learning to sing incantations and write out liturgical documents, were designed to culminate in an ordination. And he knew at that ordination he would have to conjure the formidable martial deity by performing the Banner Rite to Summon Sire Yin.

As we shall see, Chen Diwen's performance of the Banner Rite is a mode of communication between him and Yin Jiao in which a relationship between budding master and martial deity might be forged. The possibility of that communication and relationship begins with recognition that both Chen Diwen and Yin Jiao are subjects rooted in particular histories, that each are already ensconced in their own experiences and relationships. For his part, Chen would bring his entire personal history to the Banner Rite. From his healing by a local transcendent during his youth, to his disenchantment with the quest to make money away from home, to his interest in the music of the local liturgies, and finally to his years training with his masters, Chen worked hard to become a member of the lineage. Each of those experiences would contribute to the sincerity and earnestness with which he would test his knowledge and skill by attempting the Banner Rite.

But Chen Diwen's history was not limited to his personal story. The lineage he sought to enter was full of historical vicissitudes, in which certain Daoist and exorcistic Buddhist practices came together in a coherent liturgical repertoire. In terms of the Banner Rite, Chen's identity was largely defined by the lineage, and his status as an aspiring member would be of crucial importance in determining the success or failure of the rite. Chen would not undertake the ritual on his own, but instead with assistance from the long line of deceased masters who had transmitted the rites down to his age. "Our masters support [*zhichi* 支持] us in our ritual affairs," he and his masters frequently say. They mean that officiants, and especially rookies like Chen, never perform the rites alone. "Because our rites have come down to us from our masters," Jiang Yucheng explains, "communication between us and deities must go through our masters and patriarchs, it must be relayed by our masters. Every time we perform a ritual event, we must invite the masters of the lineage to witness it." Chen Diwen would meticulously invite the entire pantheon of deceased masters to witness his performance of the Banner Rite. He would request they endorse his attempt to communicate with and summon Yin Jiao, relying on their experience as proven interlocutors with the celestial realm to help broadcast his message to the appropriate heavenly bureaus. He would especially rely on the lineage's direct connection with one of its patriarchs, Shen the Realized One, who, as Yin Jiao's master, wields considerable influence over the mercurial god.

Young Chen Diwen would attempt to officiate over the Banner Rite as a subject formed by his experiences in this life and by his place within a long lineage of powerful ancestral masters. The Banner Rite could not succeed without his sincere intention born from his personal experience. Nor could it work without the stated support of the deceased masters of the lineage, whose teachings gradually formed him over his years of training. Who Chen Diwen came to be, then, would be crucial for the success of his performance of the Banner Rite.

But what about the other subject participating in the Banner Rite, Celestial Lord Yin Jiao? Just as Chen's personal history and liturgical relationships bear on the Banner Rite, so do Yin Jiao's history and his particular, divine relationships. Who is this fearsome martial deity with whom Chen would try to communicate, over whom Chen would dare assert control? With what relationships is he bound up? And what would compel him to entertain Chen's ritual call and perhaps agree to submit to his command? To Yin Jiao and his story we now turn.

Chapter Two

The Deity

Celestial Lord Yin Jiao

I bow to the Realized One as my master and till the end of my days I shall not forget.

——Marshal Yin Jiao

When summoning and employing thunder gods, how could one not know whence they came?

——Master Bai Yuchan (fl. 1194–1229)

Chen Diwen would attempt to communicate with Celestial Lord Yin Jiao using the Banner Rite to establish a relationship with his lineage's main martial deity, the supplier of its exorcistic power. The potential relationship here is one between subjects. Chen has a personal story and was defined by a long lineage of masters in central Hunan who have maintained a relationship with Yin Jiao for as long as any living master can remember. Chen plays an active role in the Banner Rite. Yin Jiao also has a story, also has been defined by certain consequential relationships, and also plays an active role in the Banner Rite. This chapter asks who Yin Jiao is. What is his story? What are the relationships that have shaped him? More precisely, who is he according to the written and visual representations of the god preserved by Chen Diwen's lineage? This portrayal of Yin Jiao was not invented by the lineage.

In fact, it resonates strongly with depictions of the god in certain ritual texts and hagiographic literature from the Southern Song and Yuan periods.

The chapter does not attempt to give an exhaustive history of the figure Yin Jiao. Indeed, an adequate account of the origin and development of the god and his cult would require its own lengthy monograph. The chapter also does not show why certain depictions of Yin Jiao rather than others were picked up by Chen Diwen's liturgical ancestors, or why Yin Jiao, as opposed to any of the other martial deities, became their main exorcist. We simply do not have the sources to tell those stories. Unlike book-length works that have included the examination of ritual to shed light on the development of representations of individual gods and on the social contexts of their cults, the chapter contextualizes the lineage's depiction of Yin Jiao in its liturgical history to reveal the god's active role in a ritual.[1] In this study, history is the handmaiden of liturgy. Delving into past representations of Yin Jiao in their liturgical contexts helps us understand how Chen understands and interacts with the god in the Banner Rite.

However, the lineage's representations of Yin Jiao are rooted in the incredible religious vibrancy of the Song and Yuan dynasties, a time when new liturgical traditions were both enthusiastically borrowing from and anxiously competing with one another. Out of that vibrancy, certain images of Yin Jiao appearing in ritual and hagiography came together to form the particular visual depiction and literary story of the god that has come down to Chen Diwen. Through textual and iconographical analysis, this chapter locates some of those literary and visual representations in several of the liturgical movements of the Song and Yuan—the Correct Method of the Heart of Heaven, cults to the Emperor of the North (Beidi *pai* 北帝派), rites having to do with the Fengdu (酆都) underworld, Divine Empyrean thunder rites, and Pure Tenuity ritual. Because these traditions are still relatively understudied and so might be new to many readers, the chapter provides brief backgrounds of each. From this, it is clear that the lineage's particular portrayal of Yin Jiao that emerged from this complicated liturgical context was decidedly not influenced by depictions of the deity put forth in Yuan and Ming vernacular literature.

Putting the lineage's particular image of Yin Jiao in historical context highlights his role as an active participant in the Banner Rite. It also clarifies why Chen Diwen exerts so much energy entering into relationships with the deities who have shaped Yin Jiao as a subject—his celestial superior the Emperor of the North and his master Shen the Realized One. Further, it illustrates how certain cosmological and theological ideas from the Song–Yuan period are alive and working in the Banner Rite.

According to Chen Diwen's Lineage

Chen Diwen first learned something about Yin Jiao from visual images of the god while training as an apprentice at *jiao* and funerals. He noticed that a conspicuous painted scroll depicting Yin Jiao was always hung in the southeast corner of the altar space (*tan* 壇) for both Daoist *jiao* and Buddhist funerals. As

Figure 2.1 Marshals Yin Jiao (top) and Wang Lingguan (bottom), painted by Jiang Shenzhi in 1994. Photograph by the author.

all masters do when preparing for a liturgy, masters in Chen's lineage construct a dedicated space within which the ritual action will take place. Altar spaces are usually set up in the foyer of a patron's home or in the main room in the Guanyin Temple in Guanxi when a *jiao* is occasionally held there for the entire community. The walls of the altar space are adorned with scrolls of deities arranged as in a throne room. High gods sit along the northern wall facing south. On the eastern and western walls, scrolls depicting groups of deities are arranged as courtiers saluting the divine rulers. Behind these courtiers, a quartet of martial deities—Yin Jiao and Wang Lingguan (王靈官) on the eastern wall, Ma Sheng (馬勝) and Zhao Gongming (趙公明) on the western wall—protect the boundary between altar space and the profane world.

The scrolls of Yin Jiao used by Chen Diwen's lineage always depict him with a boyish face and two tufts of knotted hair called "forked buns" (*yaji* 丫髻) because the clumps of hair form the Y shape of two tree twigs. This hairstyle is associated with young children—the character *ya* 丫 is a metaphor for a young child, especially a girl—and lends an innocent quality to Yin Jiao. That innocence is juxtaposed with a ferocity evinced in his donning a necklace of twelve skulls and a headband fastening a skull across his forehead, as well as in his wielding two weapons—a great halberd and a golden bell.

Chen Diwen also learned something of Yin Jiao from other kinds of images. Paper representations of major deities of the pantheon, called "image robes" (*xiangyi* 像衣／相衣), hang from the rafters as if floating above the altar space. Image robes are fabricated by "paper horses" (*zhima* 紙馬), local artisans who supply props made of paper and bamboo used by masters in liturgies. Rows of hanging image robes make the altar space feel crowded with invited deities who have descended to witness the liturgy. The masters of the lineage explain that these images are gifts of garments to their divine guests. They are burned in offering at the end of the ritual program. The image robe of Yin Jiao depicts him much like the painted scroll bounding the altar space. He has a boyish face and forked buns of hair and brandishes a halberd and golden bell. The image robe of Yin Jiao always portrays him with bare feet, which also suggests his youthfulness.

Figure 2.2 Image robes for Yin Jiao (center with bell) and other deities.
Photograph by author.

These visual images of Yin Jiao were the first way Chen Diwen became acquainted with the deity, but Chen also repeatedly read a hagiography about him. "When I was preparing to perform the Banner Rite [for my ordination], I borrowed the text from Master Jiang Shenzhi. First, I went through it with an older Daoist who gave his explanations, then I read it myself." Chen paid close attention to the details of Yin Jiao's life recounted in the *Genealogical Investigation of the Practice over Ten Lifetimes of the Celestial Lord Yin Jiao, Great Year the Controller of Killer Spirits of the Earth Ministry* (*Disi tongsha taisui Yin Jiao tianjun shishi xiuxing maikao* 地司統煞太歲殷郊天君十世修行脈考), or *Genealogical Investigation*.[2] The text was redacted (*zhengli* 整理) by Jiang Shenzhi in the early 1990s when he was working hard to recopy and edit key texts as the lineage again began to train and ordain masters. He based his redaction on an older hagiography of Yin Jiao preserved by the lineage and on hagiographical elements within ritual manuals for summoning him, including the *Banner Rite [to Summon] Sire Yin,* the text scripting the Banner Rite.[3] Jiang Shenzhi labored to make sense of the older hagiography in light of the ritual manuals and vice versa. He left several minor discrepancies, like seams in the fabric of the text, apparently in respect for disparate details about Yin Jiao that had come down through the lineage.

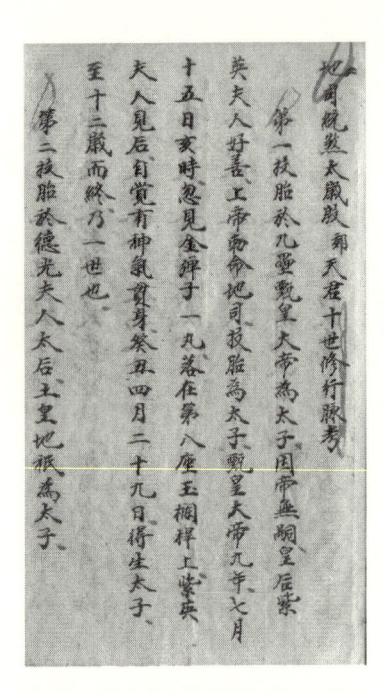

Figure 2.3 First page of the *Genealogical Investigation*, redacted by Jiang Shenzhi in the early 1990s. Scan by the author.

The Lifetimes

According to the *Genealogical Investigation,* Yin Jiao has had ten lifetimes and into each he was born a crown prince. He was first born to the Great Emperor August Zhen of the Nine Realms (Jiulei Zhenhuang dadi 九壘甄皇大帝), whose title suggests he was an ancient ruler of the nine regions of the earth corresponding to the nine celestial spheres.

> Because the Emperor had no heirs and the Empress Lady Ziying dedicated herself to goodness, the Emperor on High decreed that the Earth Minister be born as their crown prince. During the *hai* hours [between 9 and 11 p.m.] on the fifteenth day of the seventh month of the ninth year of the Great Emperor August Zhen's reign, [Lady Ziying] suddenly saw a golden pellet descend onto the eighth section of a jade balustrade [in the palace]. After Lady Ziying saw it she felt divine *qi* penetrate her body. She gave birth to the crown prince on the twenty-ninth day of the fourth month of a *guichou* year. He died at age twelve. This was his first lifetime.[4]

因帝無嗣，皇后紫英夫人好善，上帝敕命地司投胎為太子。甄皇大帝九年七月十五日亥時，忽見金彈子一丸，落在第八座玉欄杆上。紫英夫人見後，自覺有神氣貫身。癸丑四月二十九日得生太子，至十二歲而終，乃一世也。

In his later lifetimes, the deity called the Earth Minister (*Disi* 地司) manifested as crown princes to subsequent rulers in antiquity. His second life was spent as the son of the Earth Emperor of Earth Spirits (Tuhuang diqi 土皇地祇), another ruler of the earthly bureaus, and the Empress Lady Deguang (Deguang furen taihou 德光夫人太后). In lifetimes three through nine, he was born to several obscure rulers.[5]

In his tenth lifetime, the Earth Minister was born as Yin Jiao, the crown prince of the infamous King Zhou (Zhouwang 紂王), the last ruler of the ancient Shang 商 dynasty, and his wife Jiang Luzhen (姜鹿貞), also called Jiang Ren (姜衽). The text carefully delineates Yin Jiao's various names. His other given name was Shu (樞) and his childhood name was Jin Dingnao (金叮哤), the little Golden Chatterer. His courtesy name was Zhongfang (忠芳), Loyal Youthfulness, and his ritual name was Jin Nezha (金哪吒). His alternative name was Juye (巨野), Great Wild, an allusion to the mountain forest to which he was abandoned as an infant.[6]

The hagiography tells how King Zhou, wicked and corrupt, banished the queen Jiang Luzhen from the main palace for questioning his habit of making disastrous political decisions on the counsel of his favorite concubine, Su Daji (蘇妲己). Queen Jiang was exiled to the "chilly palace" (*lenggong* 冷宮) on the edge of the grounds where disfavored queens and concubines were relegated.

In the back of the grounds, [Queen] Jiang offered incense and told Heaven of the matter to help bring good fortune to the realm. One day she saw bootprints on a muddy path within the grounds. She followed the prints, which wound around to the very back of the grounds where she offered incense and prayed. Suddenly she felt clear and bright as if divine *qi* penetrated her body, and she became pregnant. It is said this was the result of the decent into the world by [the god of] the star Purple Tenuity. This is the meaning of the saying "The [god of the] star Purple Tenuity mounts his horse and descends into Fengdu in order to warn of the King's [breaking] the prohibitions against lasciviousness."[7]

姜於後園，焚香告天，以助國祚。一日姜見園內泥道上，有靴走腳腳印。姜隨其腳印，套走至後園，焚香禱告。忽覺神清氣爽，似有神氣貫體，由此懷孕。此謂紫微星臨凡所致也。言紫微星跨馬下酆都，為警其色戒之說也。

Maintaining the pattern of divine conception in Yin Jiao's prior lifetimes, the text identifies his paternity as the god of Purple Tenuity (Ziwei 紫微), who resides in the celestial palace within the stellar Walls of Purple Tenuity (Ziweiyuan 紫微垣), the constellation surrounding the Northern Extremity (Beiji 北極), the constant point in the northern sky around which all heavenly bodies revolve. Yin Jiao's mother was penetrated—literally "pierced" (*guan* 貫)—by divine *qi*, defined as the awesome force of Purple Tenuity's descending by horseback to the depths of Fengdu, the realm of the dead, in order to alert of King Zhou's perilous behavior. The text designates Yin Jiao's birth as the divine response to the most calamitous political moment in ancient history.

King Zhou, infuriated that Yin Jiao was not his child, leaves the boy to perish in the narrow alleys of the capital city, but horses and cattle avoid trampling him. The king then abandons him in the mountain forests outside the city in hopes that tigers and wolves will devour him, but even they dare not harm the divinely conceived child. Instead, a white deer suckles him and white birds swaddle him with their wings. Eventually, a general named Marquis Yin (Yinhou jiangjun 殷侯將軍) rescues him, and a wet nurse from his household, He Tugu (賀徒姑), raises him as her own.

At age twelve, Yin Jiao finally learns that King Zhou had killed his mother and abandoned him to die in the great wild (*juye* 巨野). In hopes of allaying his fury, Yin Jiao plans to avenge his mother by destroying the cruel king and his regime. He searches for skilled military men and finds a likeminded man-at-arms named Jiang Rui (蔣銳), with whom he roams about the realm seeking support. They travel to Mount Qingcheng (青城山) in Sichuan where they come across a man named Peng Chengrun (彭澄潤) living in a cave.[8] A native of Chengdu prefecture, Peng Chengrun goes by the alternative name Yixuan (一玄), One Mystery, and by the courtesy name

Shouzhen (守真), Holding Fast to Truth. He also bears the taboo name Xia (霞), Rosy Cloud. At age nine, Peng Chengrun went to Mount Qingcheng and cultivated the great elixir (*xiulian dadan* 修煉大丹) in Shuilian Cave (水濂洞).[9] He eventually realized true reality and took an alternative name thick with alchemical overtones—Sire Shen the Realized One Who Wondrously Transformed by the Golden Tripod (Jinding miaohua Shengong zhenren 金鼎妙化申公真人).

Shen the Realized One burns incense and prays to Heaven day and night for a "worthy general" (*liangjiang* 良將) to whom he can transmit his techniques of self-realization. One moonlit night, Shen tosses and turns in his cave until finally he falls asleep. He dreams that outside his cave the local god of the soil and his attendant declare that the following day a worthy general with a boyish appearance named Yin Jiao will come through a mountain pass about twenty-four miles away. Shen wakens overjoyed and grateful to the gods. At dawn, he commands his attendant boy to disguise himself as a gatherer of medicinal herbs and wait for the young general at the pass. Sure enough, at about noon the attendant spots travel-worn Yin Jiao and Jiang Rui resting under an ancient pine tree. He inquires about their journey and Yin Jiao tells them of their mission. The attendant boy promptly invites the weary travelers to Shen's thatched hut outside Shuilian Cave to rest and rejuvenate.

While hosted by Shen the Realized One, Yin Jiao explains he is looking for military men to help him take revenge on his father King Zhou and rectify the country. Shen suggests that there is no need to travel afar to acquire an army. At that moment, encamped on nearby Mount Zao (燥山), is a certain Wang Huaiyu (王槐慾), who goes by the moniker General Magpie (Yaque jiangjun 鴉鵲將軍) and commands twelve thousand men. Overjoyed, Yin Jiao sets out for Mount Zao. While reconnoitering the encampment, however, Yin Jiao is stunned by the might of the force. "Daggers and swords glinted and flashed, an air of murder wafted about. Arrows were like locusts, shears were like rain" (刀光劍影，殺氣騰騰，箭矢如蝗，剪石如雨).[10] Deeply humbled, Yin Jiao returns to Shen the Realized One and tells him that all the prince's might cannot possibly rival what he has seen. Yet if he could somehow acquire the fierce General Magpie, then revenge would certainly be assured. Yin Jiao realizes he did not know how to do so.

As Yin Jiao sighs with worry, Shen cautiously tells him that although he is admirably loyal for wishing to rectify the county, Heaven will not allow patricide:

> You must know that just as Heaven covers all and Earth carries all, a father raises a child and a mother gives it birth. Parental favor is as boundless as the vast sky. Even if you smash your own body and pulverize your bones, it would still be insufficient to repay one ten-thousandth of your parents' toil. Even though you said you wish to avenge your mother, that is also not permitted by Heaven.[11]

> 當知天覆地載，父鞠母生，父母之恩，昊天罔極。縱然粉骨碎身，究難報劬勞於萬一耳。雖曰為母報仇，亦天之不許耳。

Shen the Realized One then makes his offer to Yin Jiao:

> I hope only that the Prince might reconsider and turn toward goodness, that you might forget enmity toward your father and genuinely put the country first. If you can take refuge in the rectifying Dao, assist my lineage, and offer incense, then bow to Heaven as witness and vow an oath. If you follow my counsel then how difficult could it be to subdue the insignificant General Magpie? My Daoist methods can raise thunderbolts, hold up the sun and moon, overturn rivers and seas, and summon rain and wind. With these powers why would I worry Wang Huaiyu [General Magpie] would not bend the knee under me?[12]

> 但願太子能回心向善，不記父怨，純以社稷為重。能皈依正道，佐助本宗，玄化香火，叩天作證，立出誓言。能從吾勸告，區區鴉鵲將軍，有何難降者乎？以吾之道法，雷霆可舉，日月可攜，翻江倒海，喚雨呼風，何愁王槐慾不屈膝於吾之足下乎？

As soon as Yin Jiao hears these words, he awakens and takes Shen as his master. He diligently studies the profound Dao and follows all his master's directives.

For some time, Shen gleefully observes how sincerely Yin Jiao is submitting to his regimen. Then Shen requests the high gods and his deceased masters witness an oath between him and Yin Jiao. Shen kneels, takes incense in his hands, and declares to the gods and masters,

> Your disciple Shen Yixuan practiced on Mount Heming and retained true reality in Shuilian Cave.[13] Now the crown prince of King Zhou of the present dynasty has come to my cave seeking a master to study the Dao to help hand down the mysterious winds [of the Dao] through the ages. Although it is said that the rites are permitted to be passed down, how dare I, your humble minister, act on my own authority so presumptuously? For this reason, I first make a petition to inform [the high gods and deceased masters] and then make this oath: Today I pass on [the methods] according to the great law. I dare not issue falsity nor hide the truth lest I fall into Fengdu for eternity and suffer karmic retribution. Should the General [Yin] turn his back on me may heavenly thunder destroy him.[14]

> 弟子申一玄，鶴鳴山修煉，水濂洞存真。今有當朝紂王太子，來吾洞中，求師學道，佐助玄風，永垂千古。雖曰法許流傳，臣何敢擅專妄舉？為此先申啟告，再立誓言：今依大法傳授，不敢出偽隱真，否則永墮酆都，輪迴報應。倘將若負吾，天雷誅滅。

Yin Jiao then takes incense in his hands, looks up, and declares to the gods and deceased masters:

> Your disciple Yin Jiao is the crown prince of King Zhou and the Queen. I was born their son on behalf of Heaven, and zealously intended to keep peace in the country. But it happened that my father the King was without morals. He abandoned me to the great wild and relegated my mother to the chilly palace. Fortunately, I encountered the general Marquis Yin, who rescued me and nurtured me in my hapless life. When I was eighteen years old, my heart harbored hatred for my father and I wished to find strong military men to take revenge. When I met my master, he exhorted me to realize this action would be a great crime against Heaven. I have already turned my heart toward goodness. I have vowed to obey my master's instructions and to the end will not be of two minds. Should I violate this oath, I will be willing to suffer Heaven's punishment.[15]

弟子殷郊系紂王正宮太子，代天作子，意欲助安社稷。原為父王無
道，棄郊於巨野，貶母於冷宮。幸遇殷候將軍，收歸撫養殘生。今
叨一十八歲，心懷恨父，欲求強兵報怨。蒙師勸告，知此舉為吾之
逆天大罪。現已回心向善，誓願恪遵師訓，終始不二。如違盟言，
自甘天罰。

Then Yin Jiao unties his silk waistband and knots it as a sign of their shared
intention. He prostrates himself, bows to his master, and receives the transmission.

But Shen is not yet completely certain that Yin Jiao will uphold his
promise. He exhorts his disciple,

> You are of the golden branches and jade leaves of royalty and of utmost
> honor. After completing [your training, I worry that] you might not pay
> attention to my words, that you might [instead] command fierce soldiers,
> establish yourself as king, and arrogate power to disorder governance. If
> so, my plans would then have been wasted and, contrary to my efforts, I
> would have done harm. If you wish to study the Dao from me, you must
> crawl between my knees and again swear the oath, and then I shall pass [my
> teachings] to you. My disciple, should your heart thereafter come to regret
> [this], you will surely be struck dead by thunder.[16]

汝系金枝玉葉，極貴極尊。成就之後，不顧貧道之言，汝統狂兵，
自立國王，專權亂政。吾乃枉費心機，反成無益。既然從吾學道，
但從吾膝下一過，再立誓言，吾乃付度。弟子他時心若退悔，定有
雷誅。

Yin Jiao bows his head and kowtows. Then Shen "opens a golden well"
(*dakai jinjing* 大開金井)—that is, he draws the graph for "well" (*jing* 井) on
the ground and straddles it—as Yin Jiao, in a gesture of utter submission,
crouches down onto the graph between Shen's legs. There Yin Jiao swears
another oath:

> I bow to the Realized One as my master and till the end of my days I shall
> not forget. I untie my silk waistband and divide it between us. I hold the
> silk and swear to Heaven: should I break the covenant and back out of my
> oath then I shall certainly spend my next lifetime as a dog.[17]

自拜真人為師，歿世不忘。解下絲縧，各分一半。郊以絲縧向天立
誓，如有背盟悔誓，吾來世永為犬也。

The Emperor on High hears Yin Jiao's devotion and bestows upon him a halberd, a golden bell, and a secret incantation. Shen the Realized One then sends Yin Jiao off to Mount Zao along with his attendant boy and another numinous boy (*lingtong* 靈童). They find General Magpie's army as fearsome as before, but this time Yin Jiao violently rings his golden bell, brandishes his halberd, and declaims his incantation. The army of twelve thousand immediately surrenders. General Magpie himself admits defeat and pledges his axe to Yin Jiao. In audience before Shen, Yin Jiao and General Magpie swear an oath to each other on a golden tablet.

Later, Shen gives Yin Jiao a pellet of golden elixir (*yili jindan* 一粒金丹), which he promptly consumes. After practicing in a cave for three years, Yin Jiao attains the Dao and realizes true reality on the ninth day of the third month in a *wuchen* year. Later that year, an imperial edict arrives, written in celestial script from the Great Emperor of Purple Tenuity of the Northern Extremity (Beiji Ziwei dadi 北極紫微大帝)—Yin Jiao's divine father. A short time later, a great whirlwind carriage pulled by a crane and a *luan*-bird descends to the earth and the Emperor of Purple Tenuity confers titles on the protagonists in the story. Yin Jiao is given the title Celestial Lord Yin Jiao, Ferocious Worthy of the Earth Ministry, Great Year of Utmost Virtue, Top Marshal Who Assists in the Rite by Cutting Off Ears of Demons as Trophies, Top General Who Manifests Penetrating Power by Embodying the Dao and Protects the Country before the Emperor of the Northern Extremity (北極御前顯應通靈體道護國上將、助法戲魔上帥、地司至德太歲猛烈尊神、殷郊天君). Yin Jiao's trusty companion Jiang Rui is given the title Deputy General, the Emissary Who Manifests Penetrating Power to Quickly Capture [Demons] (亞將軍顯應通靈急捉使者). Shen the Realized One and General Magpie are also given titles, and Magpie's twelve thousand soldiers receive official posts.[18]

Hagiographic Insights

This remarkably detailed hagiography, along with the visual images of Yin Jiao maintained by the lineage, conveyed crucial bits of information about the deity who would play a central role in Chen Diwen's performance of the

Banner Rite. First, the visual images portray Yin Jiao as a youthful, almost cute deity veiling a terrible ferocity. His boyish face, girlish hairdo, and bare feet belie the ruthlessness with which he terrorizes demons with his halberd and golden bell, as evidenced by the string of skulls around his neck and forehead. Second, the narrative about Yin Jiao's prior births places the god in cosmological context. Before his first, twelve-year lifetime as a crown prince, he existed as a deity governing the Earth Ministry. The hagiography picks up this association at the end the narrative. Part of the title granted Yin Jiao by the Emperor of Purple Tenuity names the prince the Ferocious Worthy of the Earth Ministry, Great Year of Utmost Virtue. Since at least the Southern Song dynasty Yin Jiao has been associated with the Earth Ministry, a cosmological bureau charged with administering the earthly realm.

Third, the narrative repeatedly ties Yin Jiao to the stellar deity Great Emperor of Purple Tenuity of the Northern Extremity, whose name is often abbreviated as the Emperor of the North. Yin Jiao's mother was miraculously impregnated by the god of the star of Purple Tenuity, which the text describes as due to the god's mounting his horse and descending to the world. An alternative name of the Banner Rite is the Banner Rite of Celestial Lord Yin Jiao in which Purple Tenuity Mounts His Horse (*Yin Jiao tianjun Ziwei kuama fanfa* 殷郊天君紫微跨馬潘法).[19] At the end of the narrative, the Emperor of the North confers Yin Jiao's title, designating the martial god as serving the throne of the Northern Extremity. Yin Jiao is a close subordinate of the Emperor of the North. Yin Jiao's very presence in the world is an expression of the power of that lofty stellar god in the world.

Fourth, the heart of the hagiography tells how Yin Jiao and his master Shen the Realized One form a symbiotic relationship. Shen prays for a capable disciple and Yin Jiao, turning his lust for patricidal revenge into devotion for the Dao, becomes the dutiful apprentice who eventually receives his master's alchemical teachings, realizes the Dao, and attains great exorcistic might. Their relationship is cemented in their great oath. Shen pledges to the gods and previous masters that he will withhold nothing of the teachings and practices from Yin Jiao. In turn, Yin Jiao vows to serve the Dao by becoming a member of Shen's lineage, even humiliating himself in deference to his master. Both swear to uphold the oath under threat of divine punishment.

None of this key information about Yin Jiao was invented by the Jiang-Li lineage over the past two hundred or so years, or even in the Ming–Qing period by Daoists in central Hunan descending from the Jade Void Palace or by Buddhist practitioners originating from the Western Spring Monastery. Instead, it derived from the Song–Yuan period, a time when exorcistic rituals employing martial deities flourished.

The Revelation and Its World

The earliest datable glimpse we have of Yin Jiao is in the story of his revelation to a master during the Southern Song dynasty (1127–1279). The tale is narrated in a preface to a ritual text for employing Yin Jiao—the *Great Rite [for Summoning] the Earth Minister of the Heart of Heaven* (*Tianxin disi dafa* 天心地司大法, or the *Great Rite*)—included in the huge compendium of late Tang through early Ming ritual texts, the *Collected Fundamentals of the Dao and Ritual* (DZ 1220 *Daofa huiyuan* 道法會元). The preface of the *Great Rite* was signed in the autumn of 1274 in Changsha by a master named Peng Yuantai (彭元泰). In December of 1290, Peng, bearing the title Sincere and Orthodox Realized One of Universal Beneficence from Surging *Yang* (Chongyang puhui chengzheng zhenren 沖陽普惠誠正真人), added a colophon from the Academy of Scholarly Worthies (Jixianyuan 集賢院), the imperial organ in the Yuan capital, which was staffed with academicians who oversaw the Daoist clergy and tried to entice reclusive scholars into state service.[20] That the 1290 colophon includes a title for Peng Yuantai, and that he composed the piece in the imperial Academy, suggests that he had gained such stature that the Yuan government recognized him and perhaps even summoned him to the capital to contribute his ritual text to the imperial collection.

Peng Yuantai's preface recounts a revelation of Yin Jiao to a deceased patriarch of Peng's lineage, a certain master in Sichuan called Liao Shouzhen the Realized One, the Transcendent Elder of Southern Flourishing (Nanchang xianbo Liao zhenren Shouzhen 南昌仙伯廖真人守真), which is the same title Chen Diwen's lineage uses to invoke him as one of its ancestral masters.[21] Liao Shouzhen received the ritual instructions for employing Yin Jiao from the god himself three generations before Peng Yuantai, which would date the revelation to sometime during the late twelfth or early thirteenth century.[22] The *Great Rite* mentions one patriarch in the lineage prior to Liao Shouzhen: Shen Xia the Realized One, Executor of the Rite amid the Wondrous Transformations of the Golden Tripod (Jinding miaohua zhifa Shen zhenren Xia 金鼎妙化執法申真人霞), almost the exact title for Shen that appears in Chen Diwen's hagiography and ritual manuals.[23] Unfortunately, we know next to nothing about Shen the Realized One and can only guess who he might have been or whether he in fact existed.[24]

In Peng Yuantai's narrative, Liao Shouzhen diligently chanted the *Scripture of Salvation* (*Duren jing* 度人經), which had retained its medieval popularity during the Song period, and practiced the Great Cavern Rite (Dadong fa 大洞法), a higher-level practice in the classic Shangqing (上清) tradition.[25] Liao was perplexed as to why heavenly flowers fell about while he was deeply concentrated in seated meditation. The Emperor of the North commanded a host of transcendent ministers to descend to assist Liao in his practice, including the Emperor's attendant (*shiyu* 侍御) Yin Jiao. Yin served as Liao's personal exorcist. "No matter the day or time [Yin Jiao] could be employed as desired, completely obeying the Realized One's wishes" (行無擇日，用不選時，如意指使，悉順真人之意焉), and "wherever he went, disease and pestilence were wiped out and evil spirits went into hiding" (所到則瘟疫消滅，神煞潛藏). To cement the bond, Yin Jiao himself issued Liao Shouzhen a single talisman as the credential (*xin* 信) authorizing his putting Yin Jiao to service.[26]

Peng Yuantai's narrative of the revelation and his descriptions of Yin Jiao throughout his preface and colophon make three important observations about the god. First, Yin Jiao is a celestial deity emanating from the cosmogony and closely associated with the Emperor of the North, who rules the northern sky and the underworld. Second, Yin Jiao is decidedly not a terrestrial deity. He is neither a deceased human spirit or demon from the underworld nor an earth spirit roaming the realm of the living, even though, as we shall see, he has jurisdiction over an earthly bureau. Third, Yin Jiao is called a "thunder god" (*leishen* 雷神), a major category of exorcistic deity that became popular during the late Northern Song and cut across almost all exorcistic traditions during the Southern Song.

Peng Yuantai's observations about the nature of Yin Jiao in his 1274 preface and 1290 colophon meshed nicely with theories of exorcistic deities circulating about the Southern Song during the thirteenth century. Those theories defined exorcistic deities in terms of their cosmic locations—where they emerged in the universe, where they resided, and to which high deities they owed allegiance. For example, the prominent Southern Song master Liu Yu (劉玉) (fl. 1258) of Jiangxi delineated four categories of exorcistic deity: celestial deities (*tianshen* 天神), thunder gods, deities of the underworld Fengdu, and earth spirits (*diqi* 地祇):[27]

> When summoned, celestial [exorcistic] deities invariably descend from the gate of Heaven. When summoned, thunder gods invariably come from the central Heaven and arrive through the *xun* 巽 door. When summoned, [the deities of] Fengdu come out from the Earth door. Only the marshals and generals of the Earth spirits suffuse [the world], and so only they exist right in front [of the master]. When summoned, they are [already] in the realm of the living and so come easily and completely without obstruction.[28]

> 召天神必自天門而降，召雷神必自中天而來巽戶而至，召酆都則自地戶而出。維地祇帥將昐〔胮〕蜜只在眼前，召之則在于陽間，平步而來，略無障礙。

Liu Yu is concerned with where in the cosmos different martial deities with exorcistic functions derive. Some hail from the heavens; some called thunder gods are from the central Heaven, which alludes to their headquarters in Divine Empyrean cosmology; some are from Fengdu, the underworld realm of the dead; and some called earth spirits exist all around us in the realm of the living. Different exorcistic deities reporting to different cosmic bureaus under different divine rulers were summoned by different ritual methods. Masters like Liu Yu could learn many different ritual methods employing various exorcistic deities. Indeed, he seems to have studied Divine Empyrean, Fengdu, and earth spirits methods. We shall see that in the religious vibrancy of the thirteenth century, rituals for employing various stripes of exorcistic deities easily cut across lineages of liturgical practice.

Cosmology

For Peng Yuantai, Yin Jiao is first and foremost a celestial deity who emerged during the cosmogony but has jurisdiction over a terrestrial bureau called the Earth Ministry. Yin Jiao's nature as both of the heavens and concerned with the earth seems paradoxical, and Peng labors to explain it:

> The Earth Ministry is the Earth Ministry of the Heart of Heaven. Above there are the Nine Heavens and below the Nine Earths. When Heaven and Earth were converged [in the primordial chaos], *yin qi* and *yang qi* were intermingled. Then *yang qi* rose and *yin qi* sank. It is said that gods gathered in extreme *yang,* and demons gathered in extreme *yin.* Gods and demons are the numinous powers of these two [modes of] *qi.* The Thunder God of the Nine Heavens [Yin Jiao] is *qi* of extreme *yang* that dwells under the *kun* earth.[29] When *yang* begins its return it does so from the position of *kan* [extreme *yin*]. Therefore, we know that *yang qi* works latently to cause the myriad things to sprout and to bring about the four seasons; it surveils malignant spirits and subdues epidemic forces. The Emperor on High bestowed upon [Yin Jiao] a crown and received him at the Jade Steps [of the celestial court]; he considers Yin Jiao's merits greatest and his position highest of all the gods who attend to him. [Yin Jiao's] divine power is boundless and his numinous might is unfathomable. If we investigate his traces [in the world, we see] he was born in high antiquity. If we discuss his divinity, [we see] he comes from the Anterior Heaven.[30]

> 夫地司者乃天心地司。上曰九天，下曰九地，天地相合，陰陽交感，陽升陰降。所謂神九至陽，鬼九至陰，鬼神二炁之靈者。九天雷神乃至陽之炁，居於坤土之下，一陽來復，自乎坎位。乃知陽炁潛施，發生萬物，以成四時，鈴轄煞神，降伏瘟部。上帝賜冠冕，朝見於玉階，以為侍從之神，其功最大，其位最高，神通無窮，威靈莫測。究其迹，生於上古，議其神，自乎先天。

The text situates Yin Jiao and his power in a kind of cosmological paradox explained by cosmogonic logic. After the primordial One of undifferentiated *qi* split into two—*yang qi* rising to form levels of Heaven and *yin qi* sinking to form levels of Earth—Yin Jiao, like other gods, emerged in the extreme *yang* of the heavens. Yet he dwells under the Earth in the realm of extreme *yin,* where demons emerged opposite gods. Yin Jiao is of "extreme *yang qi*" amid the deepest realm of *yin qi* under the Earth. Just as *yang* begins its inexorable increase at the moment of greatest *yin*—high noon begins its rise in the dead of night, summer begins to emerge at the winter solstice—so does Yin Jiao supply the spark of vivifying *yang qi* in the darkest realm of death and decay where all things return. Among roaming demons that cause illness and death, he reigns germinating the myriad things and keeping at bay the forces of pestilence. The text signals this idea of *yang* within *yin* by referencing the trigram *kan* ☵, a solid *yang* line in the bosom of two broken *yin* lines, which graphically expresses the latent *yang* force within the extreme *yin* of the north, winter, and midnight, supplying propulsion for the cyclical movement of the cosmos.[31]

This idea of *yang* within *yin,* high within low, is also captured by Yin Jiao's title, Earth Minister of the Heart of Heaven (Tianxin disi 天心地司). Yin Jiao tends to the demonic forces of the dark reaches under the earth, yet he himself is of the Heart of Heaven. In Peng Yuantai's preface, the Emperor on High (Shangdi 上帝)—which in this context refers to the Emperor of the North—receives Yin Jiao at court, lauds his awesome power, and considers his "merits greatest and position highest of all the gods who attend to him." The text sketches Yin Jiao as a lofty celestial deity who emerged from the Anterior Heaven (Xiantian 先天) before the differentiation of primordial *qi* and the cyclical movements of the world began. He serves as the personal attendant of the mighty Emperor of the North and manifested in this world as an imperial prince in high antiquity.

In his 1290 colophon to the *Great Rite,* Peng Yuantai expands on Yin Jiao's various forms. "In the ritual, the marshal who takes charge of the rite is Inspector Commissioner of the Three Heavens. He was an imperial prince in high antiquity who realized the Dao and apprehended truth. He is known for his great achievements and his transformations are difficult to measure" (是法者，主法之帥乃三天斜察使，上古帝子，悟道成真，功高所著，變化難量).[32] Peng stresses that Yin Jiao is a lofty celestial god who emanated from the Three Heavens—the first realms generated by the Dao during the cosmogony and within which pure deities arose. Later, he manifested in this world as an imperial prince in high antiquity—the image that later sources, including the hagiography preserved by Chen Diwen's lineage, would interpret as the crown prince of ten kings during ten lifetimes, including the crown prince of King Zhou of the Shang.

The term "Heart of Heaven" in Yin Jiao's title associates him with the Correct Rites of the Heart of Heaven, a major liturgical movement that arose during the Northern Song dynasty (960–1127). Before we examine this aspect of Yin Jiao's nature, it would help to contextualize briefly the Heart of Heaven movement in relation to older traditions dedicated to the Emperor of the North.

Emperor of the North

By the time Peng Yuantai was writing in the late thirteenth century, the Emperor of the North had already been worshipped for quite a long time. Sometime during the Period of Disunion (220–589), a Great Emperor of Purple Tenuity of the Northern Extremity emerged from ancient cults devoted to the stars of the Northern Dipper. He assumed his position as a high stellar god overseeing all other astral deities.[33] In Shangqing texts, the divinity, often simply called the Emperor of the North, took on the role of demon queller. In chapter 10 of his *Declarations of the Perfected* (*Zhen'gao* 真誥), Tao Hongjing (陶弘景) (456–536) introduces various secret rituals for calling upon the Emperor of the North, which he deemed to be among the original Shangqing revelations to Yang Xi (楊羲) in the late fourth century. In one ritual, the practitioner intones an elaborate incantation requesting the Emperor of the North to dispatch his trusty attendant Tianpeng (天蓬). Heavily armed and flaunting a blue tongue, green teeth, four eyes, and a grey beard, Tianpeng rides a carriage drawn by a dragon and a mythical *kui* 夔 beast, a dragon-like monoped. "Should mischievous demons dare to come show themselves, [Tianpeng] will seize his axe as large as the sky and chop off their heads and limbs" (敢有小鬼，欲來見狀，攫天大斧，斬鬼五行).[34] We shall see that versions of this same incantation, which came to be known as the *Tianpeng Incantation* (*Tianpeng zhou* 天蓬咒), have continued to be used by Daoist masters, including those in Chen Diwen's lineage, to the present day. The Emperor of the North's secret rituals were hidden away in the Six Heavens of Fengdu (Fengdu liutian 酆都六天), a celestial realm of demonic forces divided into six sectors, each governed by a heavenly palace. Should the practitioner know the names of the six palaces, he would be able to fend off demonic harassment and live a long life.[35]

Widespread cults to the Emperor of the North flourished during the Tang period. Scholar Li Yuanguo credits a prominent Daoist named Deng Ziyang (鄧紫陽) (d. 739) as the founder of a lineage specifically devoted to the Emperor of the North.[36] Strewn across scant canonical and epigraphic sources are several stories about Deng Ziyang, who seems to have enjoyed the patronage of Emperor Tang Xuanzong (唐玄宗) (r. 712–756), even receiving the title Celestial Master (Tianshi 天師) from him. In one story, Deng Ziyang was chanting the *Tianpeng Incantation* one night on Mount Magu (麻姑山) in southern Jiangxi when the armored god suddenly appeared. Tianpeng announced that the master's devotion had been noticed by the Emperor of the North, who commanded Tianpeng to reveal to Deng a text replete with methods for becoming a transcendent, employing demonic spirits, and curing disease.[37] In another story, Deng Ziyang was traveling from Mount Magu to visit his relatives. While on the road, he had somehow acquired a spirit sword. As he rested on the bank of a creek, he recited the *Tianpeng Incantation* incessantly. Moved by the master's devotion, the Emperor of the North dispatched a spirit to reveal to Deng a sword method (*jianfa* 劍法). Later, Deng Ziyang lived on the Southern Marchmount (Nanyue 南嶽) in Hunan, where he taught all his ritual methods.[38]

During the second half of the Tang, rites devoted to the Emperor of the North were promoted by the government, spread across south China, and penetrated other ritual traditions. A descendant of Deng Ziyang named Deng Qixia (鄧啟霞), who had reputedly received a Shangqing register on Mount Mao (茅山) and a Zhengyi register on Mount Longhu, wove Emperor of the North rites into those two ritual traditions during the late ninth century. By that time, Emperor of the North methods had also become entrenched in Sichuan. The influential Daoist Du Guangting (杜光庭)

(850–933), who lived in Sichuan during his later years, learned Emperor of the North methods and promoted them.

In the Tang–Song period, we get a fleshed-out story of the origins of the Emperor of the North. Chapter 37 of *The Wondrous Scripture of the Upper Chapters on Limitless Salvation of the Lingbao Tradition* (*Lingbao wuliang duren shangpin miaojing* 靈寶無量度人上品妙經) is dedicated to him. The Celestial Worthy of Primordial Commencement (Yuanshi tianzun 元始天尊), the highest deity of the Lingbao tradition, explains:

> This Great Emperor of the Northern Extremity leads the stars, asterisms, demons, and deities of the three realms. None of the many spirits and numinous powers fail to kowtow and request his orders. The spirits of the Five Marchmounts, four rivers, mountains, and streams all bow twice and humbly attend to him, requesting [orders to make] floods, droughts, wind, or rain. The [Emperor of] the Northern Extremity is my fifth manifestation. He is positioned in direct line within the imperial house [in that] the Jade Emperor is his ancestor. [The Emperor of the Northern Extremity] arose during the primordium of the great void.[39]
>
> 此北極大帝，總制三界星宿鬼神。萬神千靈，莫不叩頭請命。五嶽四瀆山川之神，皆再拜伏候，乞請水旱風雨。北極是吾第五化身，位居皇極正統，玉帝為祖，立太空之元。

The text casts the Emperor of the North as an instantiation of the Celestial Worthy of Primordial Commencement himself who, according to Lingbao cosmology, emerged from the primordial One during the cosmogony. The Emperor of the North takes his place among the very highest and oldest of stellar deities. He resides in his stellar palace within the Walls of Purple Tenuity asterism near the fixed center of the northern sky. From there, he commands the seven stars of the Northern Dipper to improve humans' well-being by subduing demons that cause disease.

In another text, we learn how the Emperor of the North came to rule the underworld of Fengdu. In the *Wondrous Scripture of Divine Incantations for Subduing Demons by [the Power of] the Emperor of the North, as Spoken by the Most High Celestial Worthy of Primordial Commencement* (*Taishang Yuanshi tianzun shuo Beidi fumo shenzhou miaojing* 太上元始天尊說北帝伏

魔神咒妙經), the Celestial Worthy of Primordial Commencement found Fengdu in chaos and its demonic denizens wreaking havoc in the realm of the living. He dispatched celestial gods to pacify the underworld realm, but in their purity they were no match for the forces of illness and death. Frustrated, the Celestial Worthy turned to the Emperor of the North, who led a great army of heavenly soldiers headed by Tianpeng and the generals of the seven gods of the Northern Dipper. In a horrific battle, the Emperor of the North trapped demonic soldiers in great nets strewn across the sky and the earth, and unleashed on them "killing *qi* of the great mystery" (*taixuan shaqi* 太玄殺氣). His forces destroyed the underworld army in seven days. Returning to his heavenly throne, the Emperor of the North then established governance over Fengdu. He installed a celestial deity to surveil each of its six caverns and dispatched three hundred thousand heavenly soldiers to patrol the realm of the living.[40] A later chapter in the text tells us the Emperor of the North even offered rewards for unsuccessful or marginalized Daoists to take up positions in his new bureaucracy. "Mortals of the lower realm! If you seek learning without success you should accord with my utmost Way. You should first [use my] talisman and seal to subdue marginal sprites and cure myriad maladies. You will then be recruited as officials of the demon registers of Fengdu. You will be admitted into the transcendent ranks and your names will be recorded on jade slips" (下元生人，求學未能，契吾至道，先須符印，降伏外魔，攝治萬病。召酆都鬼錄之官，進品仙階，名書碧簡).[41] The celestial Emperor of the North thus came to administer Fengdu.

Heart of Heaven Devotion

It is in this context of flourishing cults to the Emperor of the North during the Tang–Song transition that the Correct Rites of the Heart of Heaven movement arose, and it is out of the Heart of Heaven movement that the vision of Yin Jiao in Peng Yuantai's *Great Rite* of 1274 emerged. A coherent origin story of the Heart of Heaven tradition has been reconstructed from interweaving sources by several scholars.[42] One evening in 994, a retired prefectural official named Rao Dongtian (饒洞天) living on Mount Huagai

(華蓋山) in central Jiangxi saw a brilliant, multicolored light emanating from one of the summits toward the sky. The next morning, he hiked to the spot where the light had come forth and found an altar dedicated to the Three Pure Ones (Sanqing 三清), the most primordial of the Daoist divinities. There he dug into the earth and found buried golden plates engraved with the "secret templates of the Heart of Heaven" (*Tianxin bishi* 天心秘式), but he could not make sense of them. Later he met a deity who told him to seek out a master of some renown named Tan Zixiao (譚紫霄). Tan had been a courtier of the fourth ruler of the Min (閩) kingdom, Wang Chang (王昶) (r. 935–939), during which time Tan had been given a set of talismans written on wooden slips found buried in the ground by a medium, Chen Shouyuan (陳守元), who had acquired high standing at court but could not figure out how to activate the talismans. Tan Zixiao mastered them and declared he had obtained the "correct method of the Heart of Heaven of Zhang Daoling." After the fall of the Min kingdom in 945, Tan Zixiao fled to Mount Lu (廬山) in northern Jiangxi, where Rao Dongtian sought him out. Tan helped Rao master the ritual templates engraved on Rao's golden plates and directed him to seek an audience with the god of Mount Tai (泰山), who requested the celestial court bestow on Rao a detail of spirit soldiers. Rao Dongtian came to be recognized as the first patriarch of the Correct Method of the Heart of Heaven liturgical tradition.

The rites supposedly passed from Rao Dongtian through four generations of masters to Deng Yougong (鄧有功), who also lived on Mount Huagai and is responsible for two of the three foundational Heart of Heaven texts. Sometime during the late eleventh or early twelfth century, he composed a compilation of the methods of the Heart of Heaven, *The Correct Rites of the Heart of Heaven of the Shangqing Tradition* (*Shangqing tianxin zhengfa* 上清天心正法). From versions he obtained from various temples in the region, Deng Yougong also edited a text titled the *Demon Code of the Spinal Numinous Writ of the Shangqing Tradition* (*Shangqing gusui lingwen guilü* 上清骨髓靈文鬼律), which contains a "demon code" (*guilü* 鬼律) governing the earthly behavior of demons, spirits, deities, and even masters; "jade protocols" (*yuge* 玉格) regulating the initiation of masters; and "liturgical templates" (*yishi* 儀式) listing priestly titles and templates for ritual documents. Deng Yougong attributed the original demon code on which his edition was based to Rao Dongtian himself.[43] The third foundational Heart of Heaven text was compiled by Yuan Miaozong (元妙宗) and submitted to the throne in 1116. Yuan had been summoned to the capital in 1115 to assist in the collation of a new canon of Daoist texts under Emperor Song Huizong (宋徽宗) (r. 1100–1125). Realizing that the new canon was deficient in methods for healing by exorcism with talismans, Yuan compiled a text of oral instructions for writing efficacious talismans, the *Secret Essentials of the Most High for Assembling the Realized Ones for Assisting the Country and Saving Its People* (*Taishang zhuguo jiumin zongzhen biyao* 太上助國救民總真祕要), which gives a complete and systematic account of the Correct Rites of the Heart of Heaven.

Heart of Heaven Practice

The foundational Heart of Heaven texts make clear that the liturgical movement was firmly rooted in older cults to the Northern Dipper and its lord the Emperor of the North. Yuan Miaozong writes:

> I have heard that the rites of the Heart of Heaven refer to the rites of the Northern Extremity and the Central Dipper. The Northern Extremity is the central point of the heavens where all phenomena in the cosmos gather. And the Northern Dipper is the Central Dipper asterism in the sky where all *qi* is bestowed. For these reasons it is the Heart of Heaven and so these rites originate from there.[44]
>
> 臣聞天心之法，北極中斗之法也。北極者，天之中樞，萬象之所會；北斗者，天之中斗，萬炁之所稟。故為天之心，則其法本之於此也。

The term "Heart of Heaven" denotes both the point of Northern Extremity and the Central Dipper asterism. The Northern Extremity is the pivot in the sky near the seventh star of the Northern Dipper (Polaris, Beichen 北辰) which was believed to remain fixed at the center of the heavens as all other asterisms revolved around it. The Central Dipper asterism is the Northern

Dipper, composed of seven stars ruled by seven ancient lords in charge of individual fate and lifespan.[45] The ruler of the Heart of Heaven is, of course, the Emperor of the Northern Extremity, the lord of the Walls of Purple Tenuity asterism. A master of the Correct Rites of the Heart of Heaven should learn several inner cultivations (*neixiu* 內修) designed to request and tap the awesome power of the Emperor of the North to exorcize demons. The master should daily imbibe *qi* emanating from the Three Radiants (Sanguang 三光)—the sun, the moon, and the stars of the Northern Dipper. He should visualize transforming his body into the body of Zhang Daoling (張道陵). And he should "walk along the guideline" (*bugang* 步罡/綱) by visualizing ascent along the stars of the asterisms of the northern sky, especially the Dipper, on the way to petition the Emperor of the North in his Palace of Purple Tenuity.

If the Emperor of the North assented to a petition, he would express his exorcistic power in the world by dispatching his trusty general Tianpeng—the lord of the hidden ninth star of the Northern Dipper—and his retinue of thirty-six assistant generals. Tianpeng was often accompanied by the great exorcists Heisha (黑煞, the Black Killer) and Xuanwu (玄武, the Dark Warrior). The cult to Xuanwu would be promoted by the Song ruling house and later by the Ming imperial family. When these three were joined by another celestial general, Tianyou (天猷), they formed the so-called Four Saints (Sisheng 四聖).[46] These saintly generals and their spirit soldiers were headquartered in the Department of Exorcism of the Northern Extremity (Beiji quxieyuan 北極驅邪院), the same celestial bureau to which practitioners of the Correct Rites of the Heart of Heaven were assigned. The Emperor of the North presided over the Department of Exorcism, and Zhang Daoling served as its commissioner (Quxie yuanshi 驅邪院使).[47] The Heart of Heaven master could also borrow spirit soldiers from the realm of the dead under Mount Tai. But because these soldiers were in fact deceased souls and not members of the celestial Department of Exorcism of the Northern Extremity, they should be returned to the ruler of their realm, the Great Emperor of the Eastern Marchmount (Dongyue dadi 東嶽大帝), immediately after use.[48] The Heart of Heaven master would petition the Emperor of the North and wield all these fearsome deities with three core talismans—that of the

Three Radiances (Sanguang fu 三光符), Heisha (Heisha fu 黑煞符), and the Heavenly Guideline (Tiangang fu 天罡符)—along with two seals and a set of nine additional talismans called the "spinal numinous writ" (*gusui lingwen* 骨髓靈文).

The Heart of Heaven texts stress that the methods revealed to Rao Dongtian and deciphered by Tan Zixiao were continuous with the earlier Zhengyi and Shangqing traditions.[49] Yuan Miaozong writes,

> [Heart of Heaven rites] have all emerged from the lineage of the Orthodox Unity; [they] function as the central administration for investigating and punishing crimes. Ever since Sire Rao [Dongtian] achieved secret merits of old—the bamboo records [of which] reside in Heaven's memory— and the gods bestowed upon him the true registers and he received secret instructions from [Tan] Zixiao, [Rao's] lineage has transmitted these rites. They have thereby been made known to the world.[50]
>
> 同出乎正一之宗，為劾治之樞轄。自昔饒君凤著陰功，簡在天意， 神付真籙，受訣紫霄，嗣系遞傳其法，遂明之于世。

Another text claims that Deng Yougong maintained that the Heart of Heaven methods were first revealed by the Most High Lord Lao to Zhang Daoling, the first Celestial Master and patriarch of the Zhengyi tradition.[51] When Heart of Heaven masters visualized transforming their bodies into those of deities, they invariably took on the body of Zhang Daoling. By aligning with the Zhengyi tradition, the codifiers of the upstart Heart of Heaven movement positioned it as a later revelation of the most ancient of orthodox Daoist traditions. The strategy seems to have worked both ways. The thirtieth Celestial Master, Zhang Jixian, learned Heart of Heaven methods and was said to have presented them along with various thunder rituals to Emperor Huizong.[52] The *Correct Rites of the Heart of Heaven of the Shangqing Tradition* even includes a talisman claiming to have been transmitted by the thirtieth Celestial Master himself. During the Yuan dynasty, the Zhengyi establishment on Mount Longhu in Jiangxi incorporated the Heart of Heaven jade protocols, which listed registers and regulated the initiation and promotion of its masters, into its own Zhengyi *Jade Protocols of the Celestial Platform* (*Tiantai yuge* 天台玉格).[53]

The Heart of Heaven texts make a similar claim for the Shangqing tradition. Expressions from that tradition color the titles and content of all the core texts, which Poul Andersen attributes to the likelihood that early Heart of Heaven codifiers were avid Shangqing practitioners. Detailed visualizations, some directly quoted from Shangqing texts, pepper Heart of Heaven texts. Deng Yougong claims that Yang Xi, the recipient of the original Shangqing revelations during the late fourth century, transmitted the basic tradition of using talismans, which appeared anew in the world via the Heart of Heaven revelations to Rao Dongtian.[54]

These textual claims positioned the Heart of Heaven's devotion to the Emperor of the North and his attendant generals in the orthodox terms of traditional Zhengyi and Shangqing practice. The gods entreated by Heart of Heaven methods might have been demon quellers, but they were celestial demon quellers, pure gods like the Most High Lord Lao and the True Ones of the Shangqing heavens. This point permeates the Heart of Heaven core corpus and later texts associated with the tradition. For example, Lu Shizhong 路時中 (fl. 1120–1130)—a famous and widely traveled Heart of Heaven master who developed a derivative ritual program he called the Great Rites of the Jade Hall (Yutang dafa 玉堂大法)—makes a clear distinction between celestial martial deities and those of the underworld. "The Master said: Those called 'infantry generals' who mean to kill and subdue [demons], and those called 'officer generals' who are in charge of infantry generals' posts, are together called 'spirits.' These spirits are not the demonic spirits of the dark underworld" (師曰：兵將者所以示殺伐之意，官將者所以主領其職也，總而歸之，則謂之神。神者，非陰幽鬼神也).[55] All celestial spirits associated with the Department of Exorcism of the Northern Extremity—from the Emperor of the North to the Four Saints down to the least exalted of the spirit soldiers—should receive pure, bloodless offerings of incense, flowers, wine, tea, fruit, wheat noodles, lamps, candles, and paper money.[56] It was even the duty of the spirit chef charged with feeding the spirit generals and soldiers of the Department of Exorcism to make sure their food was free of any traces of rats, ants, flies, bugs, cats, dogs, and other pollutants.[57]

When Peng Yuantai produced his *Great Rite* in 1274 in Changsha, he claimed he put to paper ritual instructions that had orally come down to him over four generations from Liao Shouzhen of Sichuan. Peng and his lineage were undoubtedly steeped in Heart of Heaven liturgical traditions which had been flourishing in south China for more than two hundred years, and which were themselves rooted in much older traditions worshipping the Emperor of the North. In Peng's preface, it was the Emperor of the North who responded to Master Liao's difficulties while meditating. But instead of dispatching any of the Four Saints—Tianpeng, Heisha, Xuanwu, or Tianyou—the Emperor of the North sent down Yin Jiao. Just like those celestial generals, Yin was revealed as directly subordinate to the Emperor of the North and as a heavenly martial deity who deals with demons but is resolutely not of the underworld. He serves the Emperor of the North by directing the Earth Ministry with celestial power. In this sense, Yin Jiao is defined by allegiance to his superior, a trope that has persisted as the image of the god made its way down to Chen Diwen's lineage.

Heart of Heaven Orthodoxy

Peng Yuantai insists on Yin Jiao's lofty status throughout his 1274 preface to the *Great Rite*. He belabors the point that Yin Jiao ought not to be confused with terrestrial deities even though he directs the Earth Ministry. One feels through the page Peng's consternation that floating around thirteenth-century south China were homonymous ritual texts for summoning terrestrial entities instead of the celestial Yin Jiao.

> I once saw three books filled with ritual texts also called *Rites of the Earth Ministry*. Within [their pages] were scattered fiendish demons such as the nine-headed horse face and the snake-headed elder of fire, for all of whom there were talismanic graphs. We know neither the origins of the texts nor who revealed and passed them down. Performing such rites to deal with sprites and fiends such as these would be just like using fire to put out a conflagration or using water to divert a flood. There is a common saying

that goes: "One goes a thousand miles to seek refuge with Zhou Jiu only to have one's arms broken by Zhou Jiu." [Using those rites] is only worth a laugh![58]

嘗見有法書三部，亦曰地司法也，其間混雜兇惡之鬼，至於九頭馬面、蛇頭火伯等，悉有符籙，不知其來歷，自誰降傳。若使此法以治若等妖怪，正謂以火救焚，以水退水。俗云：「千里投周九，反被周九打折手。」良發一笑耳。

The rites and talismans recorded in these dubious texts of no reliable provenance can merely summon demons to deal with demons, employ like to remedy like—an absurd logic for Peng Yuantai. Implied here is that only the might of a celestial martial deity like Yin Jiao can possibly neutralize demonic forces. Tragically, gullible practitioners have been duped by charlatan masters lacking a legitimate Heart of Heaven pedigree.

Most likely, younger pupils [are attracted to these inferior rites because they] fancy lengthy texts, but in reality they listen to slanderers and sycophants and distance themselves from accomplished men. Within those rites, masters of mediums gather to insult people; [their rites] very much run counter to the orthodox, grand core of the great Dao. Figures of this kind [the fiendish demons depicted in these inferior ritual texts] are the slain souls of Fengdu. When could they ever leave there [to execute the rites]? Alas! Some claim that when summoning the Marshal [Yin Jiao] from before the Nine Emperors below the Nine Earths [of the underworld], they actually see him coming from there. Others claim that he is summoned from the direction of the Great Year [star] which regulates the year. Both [kinds of claimants] either have not received oral transmissions from masters or have presumptuously interpreted masters' teachings. How could [these claimants] succeed and achieve resonance [with Yin Jiao]?[59]

盖後學愛多文，實聽讒佞，遠至人。巫師於斯法中集合侮人，殊乖大道正大之體。若此之輩，酆都戮魂，何日出耶？嗚呼。又謂召元帥，自九地之下九皇之前，見元帥自此來者，又謂自直年太歲方召者，皆不得師傳，妄釋其說，何可得而至感？

Peng Yuantai suggests that these shady rites are performed not by legitimate Heart of Heaven masters but by "masters of mediums" (*wushi* 巫師),

likely ritual masters who interpreted the speech and behavior of mediums used during rites, whom in another place Peng calls "seeds of Fengdu" (*Fengdu zhongzi* 酆都種子).[60] Peng declares such rites "insulting" to its patrons and hopelessly counter to orthodox Daoist practice, though it is not clear whether it is the use of mediums or something else in the ritual that offends the Dao. Instead, it is the Great Rite [for Summoning] the Earth Minister of the Heart of Heaven received by Peng Yuantai that is in line with the Dao, a claim echoing earlier Heart of Heaven concerns with establishing its own orthodoxy. The Great Rite is efficacious because it employs celestial Yin Jiao who moves freely about the cosmos rather than demons who are by definition slain souls trapped in the Fengdu underworld. How could they possibly escape their chthonic confines to execute the ritual? Peng Yuantai is irked that even some who summon Yin Jiao get it wrong. They erroneously think that he physically emerges from the underworld or from the direction of the star Great Year (Taisui 太歲).[61] For Peng Yuantai, these errors are brazen interpretations by sophomoric practitioners within Heart of Heaven lineages or by those who recklessly practice outside the constraints of an orthodox Heart of Heaven lineage's received wisdom.[62]

Peng Yuantai's sardonic tone implies cults to deities and demons of the Fengdu underworld were rife during the late Southern Song.[63] Although we lack sources that would provide a clear picture, it seems that sometime during the Tang–Song transition recognizable Fengdu ritual methods emerged from older cults to the Emperor of the North in his guise as ruler of the Fengdu underworld. Those methods proliferated throughout south China, and by the Southern Song became rather diverse and complicated. The influential Divine Empyrean master and champion of inner alchemical techniques Bai Yuchan (白玉蟾) (fl. 1194–1229) is said to have commented,

> In antiquity there were no Fengdu rites. During the late Tang there was a certain master Wu Dayuan (吳大圓) who began to transmit these rites to the world and use them to summon and interrogate demonic spirits. Those rites had only eight generals, three talismans, and four incantations, and there was a seal of the Department of the Chief Overseer of Fengdu. Later people added [to these rites] and they became unbearably varied and long

winded. How could there be orthodox rites when people do this sort of thing?[64]

古無酆都法，唐末有大圓吳先生始傳此法於世，以考召鬼神。其法中只有八將三符四呪，及有酆都總錄院印。後人增益，不勝繁絮。似此之類，安有正法？

It seems that Fengdu masters themselves agreed with Bai Yuchan's assessment. During the late twelfth through the mid-thirteenth century, a lineage of masters in Sichuan tried to organize the mass of cluttered Fengdu rites and theorize them. Lu Ye (盧埜), his master Zheng Zhiwei (鄭知微), Zheng's master Zhu Ximing (朱熙明), and Lu Ye's disciple Xu Bida (徐必大) collected and learned as many Fengdu rituals as they could.[65] Xu Bida remarked that Zheng Zhiwei gathered and compared diverse ritual texts from more than fifty Fengdu masters.[66] Lu Ye took the lead compiling, editing, and annotating the manuals they amassed into a handful of texts preserved as chapters 264 through 268 in the *Collected Fundamentals of the Dao and Ritual*.

Rites of Fengdu

Lu Ye and his companions tried to systematize and institutionalize Fengdu rituals by taking notes from the successful Heart of Heaven movement. They produced the *Numinous Text on the Black Code for Restraining Demons from the Great Darkness of Fengdu in the North* (*Beiyin fengdu taixuan zhimo heilü lingshu* 北陰酆都太玄制魔黑律靈書) and the *Liturgical Protocols of the Black Code of the Great Darkness Fengdu* (*Taixuan fengdu heilü yige* 太玄酆都黑律儀格), which were roughly equivalent to one of the Heart of Heaven's core texts, the *Demon Codes of the Spinal Numinous Writ of the Shangqing Tradition*. The Fengdu masters' "black code" (*heilü* 黑律) polices the behavior of demons and masters much like the Heart of Heaven "demon code." The Fengdu "liturgical protocols" intersperse various ritual instructions with initiation grades of Fengdu practitioners and ranks of denizens of the underworld, from generals to wandering souls and demons—a seeming combination of the Heart of Heaven "jade protocols" and "liturgical templates." Around these pieces Lu Ye added ritual texts, perhaps composites of manuals from the large cache of texts he and members of his lineage collected.

Then Lu Ye and his associates gave their black code an origin story. In the preface to the *Numinous Text on the Black Code for Restraining Demons*, Lu Ye's master Zheng Zhiwei recounts a version of the story in which the Emperor of the North conquers Fengdu. The emperor appoints his imperial censor (*yushi* 御史), a deity named Wei Boxian 魏伯賢, to govern the unruly demons with the Talisman for Commanding the Nine Springs (Jiuquan haoling fu 九泉號令符), the Seal for Surveilling Demonic Spirits (Toucha guishen yin 斜察鬼神印), and, most important, the black code. Later, three of the Emperor of the North's divine officials tidied up the black code—here called the Shangqing code—and revealed it first to the original Celestial Master, Zhang Daoling, in the second century and then later to the famous court Daoist Du Guangting, who spent his final years in Sichuan during the early tenth century. This Fengdu black code existed alongside codes of other ritual traditions, but the Fengdu code was not to be trifled with.

> If the Divine Empyrean jade protocols could be called the compassionate, benevolent code, the Fengdu black code could be called the stern, severe code. Nothing of the code may be violated. Those who perform the orthodox rites [implement the black code] must be solemn and respectful in guarding and upholding them. First make oneself correct and only then will one be able to subdue demonic spirits according to the punishments [listed in the black code]. Do not allow them to trouble the nine dark [realms]. In this way one may enter the ranks of the transcendents.[67]

神霄玉格可稱慈仁律，酆都黑律可稱嚴重律。夫律皆不可犯。行正法者，當謹畏守持。先正己而後可以責伏鬼神，勿令累及九玄，斯可進秩仙班。

Again taking a page from the Heart of Heaven playbook, Lu Ye and his redactors identified the Emperor of the North as the ultimate source of the black code while tying it to the prestige of the orthodox Zhengyi tradition and, more subtly, to the Shangqing tradition, and then to their own backyard in Sichuan. Their black code was to be as respected as other codes and ritual programs popular in south China, especially those associated with the Heart of Heaven and the Divine Empyrean traditions. But the black code should also be regarded with utmost seriousness, and even feared, because it was severe enough to discipline the dangerous demons of the underworld.

Fengdu masters wielded frightening power. At the Emperor of the North's court, they occupied the same level as exalted gods like Zhenwu, and the black code gave them control over no fewer than forty-four methods for slaying demons.[68] Fengdu masters must take care not to abuse that power, which was not easy when working with twitchy demonic agents. The spiritual functionaries serving Fengdu masters were keen on acting from their observations of masters' facial expressions or emotional states before any formal commands might actually be issued. A strange look by a master or piece of innocent gossip could easily lead to real harm. Lu Ye tells a cautionary tale about a certain Fengdu master, who seems to have been his own master's master, Zhu Ximing:

> Once Realized Lord Zhu, the founder of the lineage, held a gathering for friends and became upset with someone. He didn't say anything but had the random thought: "People in the world like this one who do not have faith in Daoist ritual methods should be killed." Immediately that person was unable to sit still. By the time he got home he was spitting up blood and then he died. From this we know that those who receive Fengdu ritual methods are guarded by vicious demons. While [the master] is in the midst of a thought, [the demon guards] act without [formal] command.[69]
>
> 昔朱真君教主嘗聚朋友，心怒一人，不發言，但興念云：「世間如此不信道法者，可殺之。」其人竟坐不住，及歸，吐血而死。是知受酆都法者，惡魔護衛，意念之間，不令而行。

This volatile power ultimately came from the Emperor of the North by virtue of his conquest of Fengdu. Like Heart of Heaven masters with whom they shared roots, Fengdu masters visualized the Emperor of the North, summoned Tianpeng by reciting the *Tianpeng Incantation,* and called upon the rest of the Four Saints and thirty-six generals of the Department of Exorcism in the Northern Extremity. Although they took up official posts in Fengdu and might occasionally interrogate or quell demons, the Emperor of the North and his minions were fundamentally celestial deities who permanently resided in the central heavens. "The Great Emperor of the Jade Void of the Northern Extremity of Purple Tenuity—who governs all the stars above, manages the myriad rites in the middle [the realm of the living], and commands Fengdu below—is the lord of all the heavenly asterisms" (紫微北極玉虛大帝，上統諸星，中御萬法，下治酆都，乃諸天星宿之主也).[70] The Emperor of the North governs the civil and martial officials of Fengdu as a manifestation of the lofty Great Emperor of the Purple Tenuity asterism.[71] In the realm of the living, he administers the various ritual methods used by mortals.[72]

Yet Fengdu masters also dealt directly with demonic functionaries in the Fengdu bureaucracy. Lu Ye explains that civil officials are deceased souls of ancient emperors, lords, loyal officials, and righteous men, and that martial posts are filled by terrifying demons. These denizens of the underworld are often "impetuous, ferocious demons" (cao'e xiongkuang zhi gui 操惡兇狂之鬼) who demand bloody sacrifice and are not easily controlled.[73] Further, Fengdu masters might also summon the Demon Kings of the original six Fengdu caverns, who are the most dicey of all. They easily burst from the underworld in a rampage and harm living people, for which the master would be held responsible. "Should the ritual officiant wish to summon the Great Demon Kings who Rule the Palaces of the Six Caverns to personally go on an offensive to fight demons, [the officiant] should request that Great Marshal Tianpeng serve as military supervisor, otherwise the [Demon Kings'] demon soldiers will come up from the nine dark [realms] and invariably harm living beings. [In that case,] the ritual officiant's punishment would be death" (法官欲召六洞主宮大魔王，親征戰鬼，當請天蓬大元帥為監軍，不然鬼兵出九幽，必害生命，法官罪當死).[74]

These sorts of Fengdu traditions were in the water when Peng Yuantai transcribed the Great Rite text in 1274. He chafed when he discovered ritual texts having to do with the Earth Ministry but employing demons instead of Yin Jiao, or when they conflated Yin Jiao with underworld spirits. He sought to clarify that Yin Jiao administers the Earth Ministry from on high, not from below as a deity of Fengdu. Peng Yuantai's efforts seem not to have been terribly effective. In his 1290 colophon to the Great Rite, he comments,

"Three texts were circulating in Hunan, all compiled by the seeds of Fengdu. I have already burned several copies. By no means should those who see them in the future collect them and take an interest in them. You will understand why once you see them" (湖湘有三部文者，皆是酆都種子所撰，區區已焚數本，將來有見者，切勿因而動念，見而可知矣).[75]

Moreover, it seems Fengdu rites had indeed gotten complicated and verbose, just as Bai Yuchan had described several decades earlier. Peng Yuantai asserted that his Great Rite was simple and elegant compared with the three large books filled with shabby texts for employing demons. "With one talisman and with one incantation, as well as with reliance on the heavenly power of our ancestral master Liao the Realized One, one may employ [Yin Jiao]" (一符一咒，中間籍祖師廖真人在天之靈，可以役使).[76]

Peng Yuantai was out to defend the proper, straightforward method to employ celestial Yin Jiao against the muddled methods bandied about by those he took as heterodox charlatans. It was in his zeal to safeguard the orthodoxy of this image of Yin Jiao and the particular ritual method orally passed down to him within his Heart of Heaven lineage that Peng originally took brush to paper, seemingly risking censure.

> I am performing this utmost virtue [of writing out the Great Rite] because I desire to do away with the heterodox and assist the orthodox in order to align with those who understand. If you see texts like the [aforementioned] three, rid them and burn them so as to avoid being bound and condemned for drifting toward an interest in demons. In my brief work [the *Great Rite* text], I humbly comprehend the exceeding virtue of the Most High. Therefore, I must certainly be exempted from the so-called offense of leaking [the contents of the rite].[77]
>
> 愚作至德，蓋欲除邪輔正，以契知音。若有三部文者，見而捨之焚之，免招譴責，流入鬼趣。少副區區體太上好生之德，所謂漏泄之愆，必可逃也。

Perhaps Peng Yuantai's vehement insistence on the orthodoxy of his Great Rite, even to the point of breaking the protocol of secrecy, was driven by the fact that the Fengdu ritual methods and his own Heart of Heaven methods had grown from the same cult to the Emperor of the North, or that the black code was so very similar to the Heart of Heaven demon code. Battles among siblings are often the fiercest.

Thunder Gods

In his 1274 preface to the *Great Rite*, Peng Yuantai depicts Yin Jiao as a celestial attendant of the Emperor of the North, not as a Fengdu deity, despite his post as lord of the Earth Ministry. Peng also cryptically refers to him as Thunder God of the Nine Heavens (Jiutian leishen 九天雷神), but does not elaborate.[78] Peng goes on to tell a story about how his lineage's patriarch, Liao Shouzhen, met Yin Jiao's deputy general Jiang Rui. Both Jiang Rui and Yin Jiao are called thunder gods of the Emperor of the North.

> Later, [Liao] the Realized One achieved the Dao and traveled throughout the realm. One day he commanded the Marshal [Yin] to vanquish a demon. The Marshal had been present [with him] for some time when he said, "The demon has been vanquished!" The Realized One asked, "But you have not left my side. How could it have been done so fast?" The Marshal replied, "My deputy general Jiang Rui responded to your command and already wiped out the demon." The Realized One asked, "May I know about this deputy general?" The Marshal replied, "He is also a thunder god of the Emperor of the North." The Realized One was thereupon delighted and promoted [Jiang Rui] to Emissary who Manifests Penetrating Power to Quickly Capture [Demons]. The Realized One drew a talisman according to [Jiang Rui's] likeness and handed it to him as a credential of his agreement to aid in Marshal [Yin's] rite.[79]

> 後真人得道，徧歷江湖。一日命元帥滅魔，良久，帥現曰：「魔已滅矣！」真人曰：「帥未離左右，何其速耶？」帥曰：「有副將蔣鋭應命，已行戩滅矣。」真人曰：「副帥可得聞乎？」帥曰：「亦北帝雷神也。」於是真人喜而遷秩為顯應通靈急捉使者。真人因形以符，付之為約信，以輔元帥之法。

For Yin Jiao's trusty companion Jiang Rui, we get an alternative story from the one in the hagiography preserved by Chen Diwen's lineage. Jiang Rui receives the same title in both narratives, but Peng Yuantai casually labels him and Yin Jiao thunder gods of the Emperor of the North. Although subtle, this is a comment on the divine nature of Yin Jiao and his entourage.

Recall Liu Yu, master Lu Ye's disciple who studied Divine Empyrean, Fengdu, and earth spirit methods and was active in 1258. If we presuppose that the general categories of exorcistic gods he sketched—celestial deities, thunder gods, Fengdu deities, and earth spirits—were floating around thirteenth-century south China, then it seems Peng Yuantai recognized that Yin Jiao and his retinue function as thunder gods as well as celestial martial deities. Although Peng works hard to distinguish celestial Yin Jiao from deities of Fengdu, he seems to embrace a certain fluidity between celestial deities and thunder gods, perhaps because both were associated with heavenly realms. This fluidity is not surprising in an age when practitioners often mastered several ritual methods. Thunder gods like Yin Jiao and Jiang Rui work their exorcistic power with lightning-quick efficiency, which is due to easy communication with the master based on an intimate relationship cemented by an oath and signified by a credential, such as the talisman Liao the Realized One gave to Jiang Rui. But before we examine the nature of Jiang Rui and Yin Jiao as thunder gods, we would do well to learn something about thunder rites, which had become wildly popular by Peng Yuantai's day.

Divine Empyrean Thunder Rites

The notion of thunder as an ambivalent force in the world had been a deeply rooted idea in the Chinese imagination for at least a millennium before the Southern Song.[80] At times considered an expression of the natural processes of the cosmos, at others a miraculous intervention in the world by celestial deities, thunder and its concomitant lightning could either be welcome signs of rain and relief from drought or harmful and even deadly forces brought down by heavenly displeasure. Morality tales of heaven using thunder and lightning to strike down culprits of hidden crimes or punish unfilial sons are countless. Ritual methods arose to harness thunder's generative power to make rain and its destructive power to vanquish illness-causing demons. By the late Tang dynasty and into the Song, practitioners of "thunder rites" or "rites of the Five Thunders" (*Wulei fa* 五雷法), as the ritual methods came to be generically called, developed techniques by which to summon various deities embodying the power of thunder, such as Sire Thunder (Leigong 雷公) and his four brothers. Thunder rites were developed in myriad ways by each of the new Song exorcistic movements, including the Heart of Heaven tradition, and seem to have become nearly ubiquitous.

Amid the popularity of thunder rites during the Northern Song, the Divine Empyrean movement stands out for its interpretations of thunder ritual, which were amplified by its breathtaking success at the imperial court. In 1116, a remarkable master named Lin Lingsu (溫州) (1076–1120) was presented to Emperor Song Huizong. Lin managed to persuade the emperor that the form of ritual Lin practiced was superior to all older Daoist traditions because it was revealed from the absolute highest Heaven, a theretofore unknown celestial region called the Divine Empyrean. Further, Lin convinced Huizong that the emperor himself was the human manifestation of the divine sovereign of the Divine Empyrean, the Great Emperor of Everlasting Life (Changsheng dadi 長生大帝), who had been born as Huizong to lead the world anew according to the Dao.

Filled with zeal, the emperor promulgated Lin Lingsu's religion throughout the empire. He ordered all prefectures to build Divine Empyrean temples dedicated to himself, the Great Emperor of Everlasting Life; he had new court liturgies fashioned; and for a few years he even abolished Buddhism and ordered monks and nuns be nominally absorbed into the Daoist clerical hierarchy. Divine Empyrean teachings took pride of place in a new compilation of the Daoist canon that had been under way since 1114.[81] Although Lin Lingsu's impact was profound, he left the court under mysterious circumstances in 1119 and died soon afterward.

Lin's associate at court, a young Daoist by the name of Wang Wenqing (王文卿) (1093–1153), carried on. Often identified by the honorific title court attendant (*shichen* 侍宸), granted by Emperor Huizong, Wang penned or was in some way responsible for several texts that would become foundational for the Divine Empyrean tradition. Wang claimed that he received direct transmission from a mysterious figure named Wang Zihua (汪子華), who allegedly practiced on the Southern Marchmount in Hunan during the Tang dynasty. In 762, the Shangqing goddess Wei Huacun (魏華存) revealed the Divine Empyrean teachings to him. In 789, at the age of seventy-seven,

Wang Zihua ascended to Heaven, where the Emperor on High granted him the title Fire Master of the Thunderclap (Leiting huoshi 雷霆火師).[82]

In an exchange with a disciple, Wang Wenqing gave an account of how he received transmission from the Fire Master. While traveling on the Yangzi River, Wang met the Fire Master, who promptly taught him the "way one's spirit flies to pay audience to the [Divine] Emperor" (*feishen yedi zhi dao* 飛神謁帝之道). Later, during his visit to the Cavern of Purity and Truth (清真洞) in Jinling (金陵, present-day Nanjing), where famous master Ye Fashan (葉法善) (616–c.720) of the Tang period practiced Daoist cultivation, Wang Wenqing became lost in the wild and accidentally entered a hut. He realized it was a "residence of thunder" (*leizhai* 雷宅), and inside found a text he called a "thunder book" (*leishu* 雷書). After he finished copying the text on tree leaves, an old woman appeared, telling him, "This is the place where thunder resides. You cannot stay here for long" (此乃雷霆所居之地，不可久留). Three years later, Wang met the Fire Master again. He told the Fire Master about the previous experience and presented him the thunder book. The Fire Master marveled, "You are truly a destined transcendent! The old woman was the Mother of Lightning. Because you have obtained the text, I should speak to you about my teaching" (子真宿仙也，昔老姥乃電母也。子既得其文，予當語汝於此). Thus Wang Wenqing received direct transmission from the Fire Master.[83]

Although other tales about the founding of the Divine Empyrean tradition are in circulation,[84] this story, apparently told by Wang Wenqing himself, seems to have had lasting impact. It firmly established Wang the Fire Master and his disciple Wang Wenqing as progenitors of the tradition, the original transmitters of the teachings from the Divine Empyrean Heaven. Those teachings included a nuanced description of the Divine Empyrean itself, elegantly sketched out by Wang in a preface to a text called the *Numinous Writ of the Jade Pivot on the Great Rite of the Five Thunders from the Jade Ministry of Upper Clarity* (*Shangqing yufu wulei dafa yushu lingwen* 上清玉府五雷大法玉樞靈文). Wang recounts the words of Wang the Fire Master, who explained to him that after the cosmogony the ruler of the Divine Empyrean realm, called the True King Jade Clarity of the Divine Empyrean on High (Gaoshang shenxiao yuqing zhenwang 高上神霄玉清真王)—the same deity who, under the title Great Emperor of Everlasting Life, later manifested as Emperor Huizong—was moved by the desperate suffering of beings in the lower realms and sought to learn how to save them. Thus the True King Jade Clarity's father and the most ancient divinity in the cosmos, the Celestial Worthy of Primordial Commencement (Yuanshi tianzun), "taught him the secret instructions for using the Five Thunders to defend against deviant forces and cut down sprites" (教以五雷禦邪斬妖之訣). The Celestial Worthy of Primordial Commencement retreated into the void and the True King Jade Clarity set out to help those in the realm of the living. He taught his secret methods to "elders on the Five Marchmounts" (*Wuyue zhangren* 五嶽 丈人), including, it is implied, Wang the Fire Master.[85]

The Five Thunders wielded by the True King Jade Clarity are classes of martial deities organized within a vast celestial bureaucracy. Continuing in Wang the Fire Master's voice, the text explains that the True King Jade Clarity rules from his Thunder City (Leicheng 雷城) in the central heavens through a hierarchy of offices. The highest among them, the Headquarters Office of the Five Thunders (Wulei dusi 五雷都司), is the hub of the Divine Empyrean administration. The Commissioner of the Five Thunders (Wuleishi 五雷使) in charge of the Headquarters Office directs the Five Thunders— thousands of civil and martial thunder gods divided into five categories: celestial thunder gods (*tianlei* 天雷), divine thunder gods (*shenlei* 神雷), dragon thunder gods (*longlei* 龍雷), thunder gods of the watery realms (*shuilei* 水雷), and local tutelary thunder gods (*shelinglei* 社令雷).[86] This last category comprises deceased souls of a given locale. After living a loyal, righteous, filial, or brave life, deceased local heroes transform into expressions of thunder in all its wild and ambivalent power. If attentively worshiped with blood sacrifice, these local thunder gods can quell demons and make rain, but if neglected they can also wreak havoc by causing floods and damaging trees. Local thunder gods are so fierce that masters attempting to employ them must petition the god of the local city walls and moats (the city god, *chenghuang* 城隍) to supervise them.[87]

The Headquarters Office of the Five Thunders and its classes of thunder gods maintain jurisdiction over three subordinate offices that receive communications from the realm of the living. The Office of the Jade Pivot (Yushuyuan

玉樞院) is staffed by three hundred of its own officials and thunder gods, and receives petitions to deal with floods, droughts, inundations by pests, warfare, and famine. Under the Office of the Jade Pivot, the Headquarters Office of the Thunderclap (Leiting dusi 雷霆都司), also called the Northern Extremity, is governed by the Emperor of the North and assists with floods and droughts. About this office, Wang the Fire Master mentions that "the Heart of Heaven has thunder gods too, but it does not maintain autonomous control" (天心有雷，但不專耳). The Emperor of the North's office plays a subordinate role to the Office of the Jade Pivot and must wait for orders from it—a subtle Divine Empyrean assertion of its superiority over the Heart of Heaven and other traditions revering the Emperor of the North. Also under the Office of the Jade Pivot, the Office of Penglai (Penglaisi 蓬萊司), headed by the Commissioner of Waterways (Dushui shizhe 都水使者) and staffed by its own thunder gods, specializes in water-related issues, from the proper flow of streams and rivers, to the distribution of clouds and air circulation, to rainmaking in times of drought. This office must also wait for orders from the Office of the Jade Pivot.[88]

In laying out Wang the Fire Master's descriptions of the celestial bureaucracy, Wang Wenqing co-opted liturgical rivals such as the Heart of Heaven tradition by respectfully demoting them within its hierarchy, just as earlier liturgical movements had done. Wang Wenqing's vision placed thunder at the center of the cosmology. The effects of thunder—mainly rain making and exorcism—were the primary ways the rarified, celestial True King Jade Clarity interacted with the world. Thunder gods arrayed in their various ranks reporting to various offices were the embodiments of thunder, the primary agents of divine power in the mundane world.

Nature of Thunder Gods

Wang Wenqing's Divine Empyrean cosmology and vision of thunder gods fanned out rapidly across various lineages of practice, apparently even in his own day. In a sign of their adoption into the Zhengyi liturgical program, the thirtieth Celestial Master, Zhang Jixian, was said to have personally known both Wang Wenqing and Lin Lingsu and studied thunder rites during the twilight of the Northern Song. Famed Divine Empyrean master Sa Shoujian (薩守堅) (fl. 1141–1178?) was reported to have received revelations from those three masters and in turn trained many disciples.[89] Later in the Southern Song, prominent master Chen Nan (陳楠) (d. 1213) and his student Bai Yuchan combined Wang Wenqing's vision of thunder with inner alchemical (*neidan* 內丹) techniques to contribute significantly to a tradition of practice known as the Southern Lineage of the Golden Elixir (Jindan nanpai 金丹南派). Bai Yuchan himself wrote an introduction to the *Preface to the Abstruse Directives of the Thunderclap from Wang the Fire Master* in which, as we saw, Wang Wenqing narrated his version of the Divine Empyrean revelation story.[90] Amid this rapid development of Wang Wenqing's vision across lineages and traditions of practice, a general theology of thunder gods developed in which their natures were fleshed out in hagiographical passages replete with vivid images of their appearances and tendencies.

Thunder gods were first and foremost fierce. The *Numinous Writ of the Jade Pivot on the Great Rite of the Five Thunders from the Jade Ministry of Upper Clarity*—which was, recall, attributed to Wang Wenqing and based on Wang the Fire Master's revelations—provides a graphic description of the figure who would become the most prominent thunder god, Marshal Deng (Deng yuanshuai 鄧元帥). In high antiquity, Deng Bowen (鄧伯溫) was a general who followed the Yellow Emperor (Huangdi 黄帝), the progenitor of Chinese civilization, into victorious battle over his great opponent Chi You (蚩尤). Deng Bowen was enfeoffed for his heroics. After the Yellow Emperor ascended to Heaven, Deng retired to Mount Wudang and studied Daoist cultivation techniques for a hundred years and was eventually able to manipulate his *qi* so well that he could levitate. Seeing that the ministers of the worldly ruler were unable to tame immoral and violent people who bullied the weak, Deng Bowen repeatedly made an oath to become a thunder god to battle evil. The vigor with which he recited his oath moved Heaven.

> One day [Deng Bowen] suddenly transformed into [a figure with] a phoenix's beak, silver teeth, vermillion hair, and a blue body. In his left hand he held a thunder spear, in his right a thunder awl. He was one hundred feet tall. From his two armpits sprung wings that, once unfurled,

cast in shadow everything within several hundred miles. His two eyes emitted two rays of fiery light that shone a hundred miles. His hands and feet were dragon talons. He flew about the great void gulping down devilish fiends and vanquishing spritely dragons.[91]

忽一日變鳳觜、銀牙、朱髮、藍身。左手持雷鑽，右手持雷鎚。身長百丈，兩腋生翅，展開則數百里皆暗，兩目放火光兩道，照耀百里，手足皆龍爪。飛遊太虛，吞唸精怪，斬伐妖龍。

The Emperor on High granted Deng the title Great Deity of the Statutes and Commands (Lüling dashen 律令大神) and designated him a "divine thunder god," one of the five classes of thunder deities. When sacrificing to Marshal Deng, a practitioner should retreat to his meditation room, draw an image of the god, and present five ounces each of sheep, chicken, and goose blood along with five sheep heads, seasonal fruit, and clean wine.[92]

This graphic image of Marshal Deng is typical of thunder gods. Through devoted practice, they often acquired fantastical bodies exuding ferocity that could make rain, stop natural disasters, and destroy illness-inflicting demons. Thunder gods demand bloody sacrifice and are far more fierce than the demons they hunt. Along with Marshal Deng, two other metamorphosed deities—Marshals Xin Zhongyi (辛忠義) and Zhang Jue (張珏)—became the most well known of the thunder gods. The three of them report to the Headquarters Office of the Five Thunders in the highest echelon of the Divine Empyrean bureaucracy.

Thunder gods work with lightning speed. The *Hidden Texts of the Thunder Crystal of the Anterior Heaven* (*Xiantian leijing yinshu* 先天雷晶隱書), likely a Yuan collection of Divine Empyrean rites from the Southern Song, some traceable back to Wang Wenqing himself,[93] instructs practitioners to be mindful of thunder gods' blinding efficiency when summoning them to receive commands for a task:

> Visualize that the marshals stand respectfully with folded hands waiting for [your] command, and then that they take up [your] intention and carry it out. The nature of these thunder gods is most intense. They are not able to stop for long. As soon as they are summoned and arrive, [you should] immediately dispatch them. Do not offer empty formalities. The reason is that thunder gods come and go as suddenly as thunder and lightning.[94]

存帥拱立俟命，任意行持。其雷性最烈，不能停久，召至即遣，毋
致虛文。雷神往來，欻如雷電故也。

Another text prefaced and perhaps written by Wang Wenqing, the
Great Rite of the Five Thunders for Interrogation and Execution in the [*Office
of the*] *Jade Pivot in the Divine Empyrean on High* (*Gaoshang shenxiao yushu
zhankan wulei dafa* 高上神霄玉樞斬勘五雷大法), quotes Wang the Fire
Master: "Whenever one wishes to carry out [a rite], one's heart and mouth
must correspond. The divine nature of thunder generals and marshals is ferocious and fierce; they respond immediately to a single breath" (火師曰：凡
欲行持，須心口相應。雷神將帥神性猛烈，一呼一吸，立便感應).[95] Thunder
gods are so frenetic that a master wishing to employ them must take care that
his words match his intentions, lest the thunder gods manically mistake his
meaning and cause unintended consequences. One title for Marshal Deng—
the Great Deity of Sudden Flames (Huhuo [or Xuhuo] dashen 欻火大神)—
captures the god's speediness in a pun. The character *hu/xu* 欻, meaning
"suddenly," is also pronounced *chua,* onomatopoeia for the crashing sound
of a sudden burst of wind, or the sound made when striking a match. The
wordplay conveys the sense that Marshal Deng moves as suddenly as the
bursting "*chua*" sound of combustion.[96]

Divine Empyrean masters come to manage rowdy thunder gods by
forming intimate relationships with them. Masters should know something
about their backgrounds, as they would of any close acquaintance. In the
Heartfelt Records of the Three Marshals of the Thunderclap (*Leiting sanshuai
xinlu* 雷霆三帥心錄), Bai Yuchan recounts how he formed an intimate bond
with the three major thunder gods—Marshals Deng, Xin, and Zhang.[97] One
night while Bai was reading a now lost text called the *Thunder Annals* (*Leidian*
雷典), a mysterious man came to his room and asked about the origins of the
three marshals. Sensing something unusual about the man, Bai sat him down
and explained that the three marshals originally lived in antiquity during
the reigns of the Three Sovereigns and Five Emperors.[98] Marshal Deng was
in fact the younger of two sons born to the sage king Fuxi (伏羲). Marshals
Xin and Zhang were actually the sons of the great-great-great-grandson of
the Yellow Emperor. Given that the thunder marshals were born during the
time when these sage kings succeeded one another, Bai reckoned that all

three marshals were originally members of the same royal family. Therefore, all three should be called upon by a single inner alchemical practice using a single talisman. Bai bemoaned that many masters in his day fundamentally misunderstood the single origin of the three marshals and so mistakenly tried to summon each using different talismans. "It is not strange," he scoffed, "that their ritual performances are not efficacious!" (行持不靈無怪).[99]

Then Bai Yuchan experienced something remarkable:

When I finished speaking the sun and moon shone, thunder and lightning illumined [the sky], and the wind and rain howled. The Great Deity [of Sudden Flames Marshal Deng] descended, the Supervisor-in-Chief [Marshal Xin] appeared, and the Emissary [Marshal Zhang] came forth. To a person they were deeply convinced [by my explanation] and paraded around my seat three times. Together they struck a solemn oath: "We three gods always support the mysterious transformations [of the Dao]. The hearts of men and the ritual techniques of the Dao are deep and can hardly be illuminated. From time to time there are those with efficacy and [we] are sure to examine their sincerity. Now you, Sire, have in a short time displayed what is arcane and expounded upon what is deep, and have exhaustively gone through all [the knowledge] that can be relied upon. Because [you] use this [knowledge] without doubt, what [we] will confer upon you is indeed not light. [You] may be called the mainstay in the sea of ritual techniques and the crossing bridge for future disciples. When a talisman [you inscribe] arrives [to our attention] and is implemented we shall put all our might toward the task." Suddenly things were still and dead quiet, the sky was no longer clouded over, and the four modes of *qi* were clear and calm. My divine guests had all departed. I realized fully [what had happened] and so wrote [this] down on paper to instruct future disciples.[100]

言既畢,日月明,雷電耀,風雨聲。大神降,都督形,使者出,躬服膺,繞座三匝。共立弘誓曰:「吾等三神,素扶玄化。人心道法,杳杳莫明,間有靈者,格其誠耳。公今一旦顯微闡幽,歷窮所據。用之既勿疑,授之顧不輕。可謂法海之砥柱,後學之津梁。符到奉行,吾當力是。」俄忽之間,寂無遺響,天無浮翳,四炁朗清,神客並失。予亦大悟,因筆于牘,以示後人。

Bai Yuchan implies that the *Thunder Annals* text he was reading that night included the origin stories of Marshals Deng, Xin, and Zhang, and that the mysterious man who showed up to his room was really an emanation of the three marshals who came to test him. For Bai, knowing the origins of the thunder gods with whom one deals is crucial for efficacious practice. Understanding that the marshals were originally "of one house" in antiquity provided license for Bai's single talisman for summoning all three, which was part and parcel of his elegant inner alchemical practices. Because Bai knew the personal histories of Marshals Deng, Xin, and Zhang, the thunder gods allowed him to enter into an intimate relationship with them. They struck an oath with Bai in which they promised to respond to his talismanic summons with all their power. Bai's thunder rites turned on an unmediated relationship between thunder gods and the master, which arose from his familiarity with the gods' pedigrees. "When summoning and employing thunder gods," Bai exclaims, "how could one not know whence they came?" (役召雷神，可不知其所從來乎).[101]

The Pervasiveness of the Divine Empyrean Vision

From the time Liao Shouzhen was said to have received his revelation of Yin Jiao in the late twelfth or early thirteenth century in Sichuan, and to the time Peng Yuantai wrote out his *Great Rite* text in 1274 in Changsha, various traditions of thunder rites inspired by Wang Wenqing's Divine Empyrean cosmology had been proliferating throughout south China. In this context, it is not surprising that Peng referred to Yin Jiao by the title Thunder God of the Nine Heavens, and casually mentioned that both Yin Jiao and his assistant general Jiang Rui were thunder gods of the Emperor of the North. Heart of Heaven practices had appropriated Divine Empyrean–style thunder gods much like Wang Wenqing's Divine Empyrean cosmology had appropriated the Emperor of the North. Scholar Li Zhihong goes so far as to assert that Peng Yuantai's *Great Rite* was a Heart of Heaven–Divine Empyrean hybrid.[102] To my reading, the appropriation of Divine Empyrean notions of thunder gods by Peng's lineage seems either to have been undeveloped or so thorough that his preface exudes no whiff of Divine

Empyrean cosmology. Yin Jiao is presented as the Earth Minister of the Heart of Heaven, a celestial deity who emerged from the primordial Anterior Heaven and serves as the personal attendant of the most high Emperor of the North, like previous celestial attendants Tianpeng and the other of the Four Saints. If Yin Jiao and Jiang Rui are thunder gods, they serve within a decidedly Heart of Heaven cosmology blissfully free of Wang Wenqing's thick Divine Empyrean bureaucracy in which the Emperor of the North and his thunder gods are subordinate to a headquarters office ruling the five categories of thunder gods.

Yet in subtle ways, Peng Yuantai's depiction of Yin Jiao and Jiang Rui does draw on the characteristics of Divine Empyrean thunder gods. First, Yin Jiao is fierce. "Wherever [Yin Jiao] went, disease and pestilence were wiped out and evil spirits went into hiding," wrote Peng in his preface. Although Yin Jiao was indeed ferocious, Song and Yuan sources did not always present him with a fantastical body like those of Marshals Deng, Xin, and Zhang. The youthful body and boyish look that came down to Chen Diwen's lineage seems to symbolize what Peng Yuantai emphasized—Yin Jiao's primordial, divine nobility. And nowhere does Peng hint that the celestial Yin Jiao accepts bloody sacrifice, although he does command thunder gods who do.

In Peng Yuantai's *Great Rite* ritual manual, the officiant is instructed to begin summoning Yin Jiao and his spirit troops by intoning the *Incantation for Communicating with Purple Tenuity* (*Ziwei chongzhou* 紫微衝呪):

Fierce Clerk Lord of Years [Yin Jiao], lead your many deities: Yellow Banner who guides in front and Leopard Tail who follows from behind; [gods of the] seventy-two *hou* and twenty-four *qi;* evil killers in the front ranks and sinister divinities in the reserve guard; [the god of Yin Jiao's] yellow halberd that punishes sprites and [the god of his] golden bell that assaults ghouls; emissaries of the five directions and mighty spirits of pestilence and poison; and [finally] local tutelary deities of the nine realms and blood-consuming soldiers. The Emperor on High [the Emperor of the North] has decreed that you all are immediately to descend to assist me with the great Way to wipe out sprites and fiends. Those who dare disobey will be decapitated and [their heads] will be presented [to me]. [According to] the statutes and commands of the Mysterious Troops, [you, Yin Jiao, will] ceaselessly exorcize pestilence/quickly subdue [demons]/or kill demons [depending on the purpose of the ritual]. Hastily the statutes and commands of the Great Emperor Purple Tenuity of the Northern Extremity order Marshal Yin of Great Might, the [God] Great Year of the Earth Ministry to descend.[103]

歲君猛吏，總領眾神：黃旛前引，豹尾後隨；七十二候，二十四炁；惡煞當先，兇神翊衛；黃鉞誅妖，金鐘擊祟；五方使者，疫毒威靈；九州社令，血食之兵。上帝有命：疾速降臨，助吾大道，掃滅妖精，敢有拒逆，斬首來呈，玄都律令，驅瘟／急降／煞鬼無停。急急北極紫微大帝律令，勑召地司太歲大威力元帥殷某速降。

By the authority of the Emperor of the North, the officiant aims to muster the "fierce clerk" Yin Jiao and his fearsome retinue. Although Yin Jiao does not himself indulge in bloody sacrifice, he commands "local tutelary deities of the nine realms" of the living and "spirit soldiers who consume bloody sacrifice." Here, these local tutelary gods might simply refer to local heroes transformed into territorial protectors after death. Given the pervasiveness of Divine Empyrean cosmology, however, they might also denote a specific category of thunder deities—local tutelary thunder gods. Recall that this fifth category of thunder power comprises deceased heroes of a given locale who lust after bloody sacrifice. They are so unruly that practitioners, and even high thunder gods like Marshals Deng, Xin, and Zhang, must enlist the local city god to supervise them. In Peng Yuantai's *Great Rite,* it is possible that Yin Jiao commands these local, blood-thirsty tutelary thunder gods, essentially mimicking the role of the three high thunder gods of the Divine Empyrean.

Like thunder gods, Yin Jiao and Jiang Rui work fast because they have a close relationship with the master. Yin Jiao remains at Liao Shouzhen's beck and call. "No matter the day or time, Yin Jiao could be employed as intended, completely obeying Liao the Realized One's intentions." Thunder gods and masters communicate easily. A second colophon to Peng Yuantai's *Great Rite,* written by a certain Chen Yizhong (陳一中) in 1316, mentions that "the secret of the rite is that it is only one talisman and one incantation; when I clack [my teeth] they sound like a drum and [Yin Jiao] responds to my heart's desire" (其祕止一符一咒，叩之如鼓應聲，隨心應感).[104] As we saw in Bai

Yuchan's narrative, thunder gods resonate with practitioners' every intention and desire after practitioners have learned something about their identities, histories, or appearances, thereby forging a relationship. When Liao Shouzhen learned that Yin Jiao's deputy general Jiang Rui so quickly smote the demon that Yin was commanded to subdue, Liao immediately asked, "May I know about this deputy general?" Yin Jiao responded by revealing his and Jiang Rui's pedigree—they are thunder gods of the Emperor of the North. Liao Shouzhen reciprocated by promoting Jiang Rui and a lasting relationship was struck, which was symbolized by a talisman. After he promoted Jiang, Liao "drew a talisman according to Jiang Rui's likeness and handed it to him as a credential of his agreement to aid Marshal Yin's rite." Likewise, when Yin Jiao initially appeared to Liao, Yin "issued a single talisman to the Realized One as his credential for putting Yin Jiao to service."

These similarities between Yin Jiao, Jiang Rui, and thunder gods of the Divine Empyrean tradition are subtle. Peng Yuantai was far more concerned with protecting Yin Jiao from being mistaken for a fierce Fengdu deity than fleshing out how Yin was a fierce yet intimate thunder god. It is possible that Peng was simply calling Yin Jiao and Jiang Rui thunder gods in a generic way, that the term *leishen* was so diffuse in the late thirteenth century that it did not necessarily have any resonance with Divine Empyrean visions of thunder gods. But I doubt that was the case. Divine Empyrean practice had indeed been deeply influential since it rocketed to prominence during the first decades of the twelfth century at Emperor Huizong's court. The Divine Empyrean influence on the image of Yin Jiao was more conspicuous in other ritual texts from the Southern Song, Yuan, and Ming dynasties. It seems a safe bet that the seeds for that increasing influence were planted by Peng Yuantai's time.

A Foundational Image

Amid the sea of competing and appropriating liturgical traditions swirling during the late thirteenth century, Peng Yuantai sought to clarify exactly who Yin Jiao is and who he is not. It is tempting to interpret Peng as trying to understand Yin Jiao in terms of Liu Yu's contemporary categories of exorcistic deities. Peng seemingly labored to describe Yin Jiao as belonging somewhere between Liu Yu's celestial deity and thunder deity, as opposed to a deity from Fengdu or an earth spirit. It is equally tempting to surmise that Peng subtly tried to characterize Yin Jiao and his associate Jiang Rui according Wang Wenqing's categories of thunder deities. Perhaps Peng described them as divine thunder gods who move easily between the heavens, the underworld, and the realm of the living, or as thunder gods reporting to the Emperor of the North's Office of the Thunderclap in the Northern Extremity.

In any event, Peng Yuantai argued with verve that Yin Jiao is first and foremost a celestial deity who emerged from the Anterior Heaven during the early stages of the cosmogony. He is exalted as the first among the Emperor of the North's court attendants recognized by Peng's Heart of Heaven lineage, which was rooted in older cults to the Emperor of the North. Despite having been charged with overseeing the terrestrial Earth Ministry, Yin Jiao ought not be confused with exorcistic deities from the Fengdu underworld. Yin Jiao and his associate Jiang Rui are instead lofty thunder gods. Like the thunder deities made famous by Divine Empyrean lineages, Yin Jiao and his retainer are especially fierce. They respond, as fast as lightning, to the will of a worthy practitioner after striking a close relationship with him, denoted by a talismanic credential.

It is remarkable how much of the spirit of this first extant depiction of Yin Jiao has made its way into the hagiography maintained by Chen Diwen's lineage. There Yin Jiao is represented as a personal thunder god closely associated with the Emperor of the North, and not at all associated with Fengdu. With titles almost identical to those in Peng Yuantai's 1274 text, Liao Shouzhen and a master above him, Shen the Realized One, show up in the lineage's ritual manuals listing ancestral masters to be invoked during liturgies. This early depiction of Yin Jiao and his associations seems to be a foundational source for Chen Diwen's lineage.

Visual Depictions

We have seen how derisively Peng Yuantai referred to practitioners outside his Heart of Heaven lineage as deluded "masters of mediums" and "seeds of Fengdu" who blithely confused the celestial Yin Jiao with inferior, blood-thirsty deities of the underworld. Peng's strong language suggests that various ritual methods for calling Yin Jiao were, despite his best efforts to eradicate them, somewhat common among different ritual traditions by the late thirteenth century. Yin Jiao was in fact becoming a more or less popular exorcistic deity across south China. He was summoned in different ritual methods as they prolifereated during the Southern Song and through to the Yuan and early Ming dynasties.

During this time, ritual practitioners freely learned methods associated with different liturgical traditions. A few of the masters we have met are good examples. The thirtieth Celestial Master, Zhang Jixian, is said to have studied Heart of Heaven and Divine Empyrean rites, and to have traveled to Sichuan, where he learned other rites dedicated to the Emperor of the North. Bai Yuchan learned a strain of thunder rites associated with Wang Wenqing and combined them with inner alchemical techniques he learned from Chen Nan. At some point, he declared himself a Divine Empyrean master. During the early to mid-thirteenth century, Lu Ye of Sichuan and his disciples became proficient in Fengdu, Divine Empyrean, and earth spirits rites. Heart of Heaven rites were becoming so diffuse within the religious landscape that they eventually receded as an easily recognizable liturgical tradition, all while contributing much to Zhengyi liturgies newly reworked by the Celestial Masters on Mount Longhu as they steadily gained imperial favor. Amid this jumble of appropriations and reappropriations, Yin Jiao found his way into almost all contemporary ritual schemes.[105]

The ways in which Yin Jiao appears in different canonical texts show this intense intermingling. On one hand, we find manuals for summoning Yin Jiao that resemble Peng Yuantai's Heart of Heaven *Great Rite*. Yet even some of those hang together with other manuals from other liturgical traditions. The *Great Rite for [Summoning] Marshal Yin of the Earth Ministry for*

Judicial Investigations (*Jiucha disi Yin shuai dafa* 糾察地司殷帥大法, or *Judicial Investigations*) contains two manuals for summoning Yin Jiao from two lineages, followed by two manuals obviously influenced by Divine Empyrean–style thunder rites.[106] On the other hand, Yin Jiao was absorbed into the pantheons of various liturgical traditions and became a minor martial deity assisting their rites. In Divine Empyrean texts, Yin Jiao was plucked out of his Heart of Heaven cosmology and inserted into a Divine Empyrean pantheon headed by Celestial Lords Deng, Xin, and Zhang.[107] Yin is similarly included with thunder gods in an immense pantheon listed in a text compiled and partially composed by Jiang Shuyu (蔣叔輿) (1162–1223), who developed the Great Rites of Lingbao (Lingbao dafa 靈寶大法) tradition. Jiang integrated elements of Divine Empyrean, Heart of Heaven, Zhengyi, Great Rites of the Jade Hall, and Loyalty and Filiality (Zhongxiao 忠孝) traditions within a classical Lingbao liturgical frame.[108] In Jiang Shuyu's text, Shen the Realized One is also listed as a master right after Lin Lingsu and Wang Wenqing.[109] In a text associated with the cult of the Emperor of the North and dated to no earlier than 1377, Yin Jiao shows up as one of many martial gods in a pantheon including thunder gods from the Divine Empyrean, gods from Fengdu, and earth spirits.[110]

Yin Jiao was also included in various ways in the most comprehensively syncretistic movement of all—the Pure Tenuity tradition.[111] First codified by Huang Shunshen (黃舜申) (1224–after 1286), the Pure Tenuity movement fashioned a comprehensive ritual system from Divine Empyrean, Great Rites of Lingbao, and esoteric Buddhist practices. A Pure Tenuity manual was dedicated to summoning Yin Jiao and his entourage.[112] Other Pure Tenuity manuals simply absorbed Yin Jiao into their extensive pantheons, as did Divine Empyrean texts.[113]

Iconography

In this context of intense liturgical borrowing and innovation, it is not surprising that Yin Jiao was depicted rather differently in separate ritual manuals dedicated to him. He was seen as a boyish warrior, an adult warrior from the heavens, a fearsome figure with a dynamic body, and a Daoist priest.

Several texts portray him as a boyish figure who nevertheless exudes violence. Peng Yuantai's *Great Rite* text instructs the practitioner to visualize him with "hair in forked buns; an azure face; the appearance of a child; nine skulls hanging around his neck; a single skull fastened to his forehead; a naked body [from the waist up]; a red kilt fastened by a belt; bare feet; a yellow halberd in the right hand and a golden bell grasped with the left" (丫 髮，青面，孩兒相，項帶九骷髏，額帶一骷髏，躶體，風帶紅裙，跣足，右手黃鉞，左手執金鐘).[114] A similar youthful image is found in the *Judicial Investigations* text mentioned. Two undated ritual manuals included within that text seem to hang in the same Heart of Heaven tradition as Peng Yuantai's *Great Rite*, which is perhaps the reason the images of Yin Jiao are so similar. In the first manual, the practitioner is instructed to visualize the god as having

> the appearance of a child; an azure face; red hair with horn-like forked buns bundled up with floss silk ribbons; an azure body; short, bare legs; a black, green, and red robe; a red kilt bound across the waist; twelve skulls hanging around his neck; a golden bell in his left hand; a yellow halberd grasped with his right; and a body short and stout. [He is] standing in a black cloud with [his retainers] Yellow Banner and Leopard Tail in attendance on either side.[115]
>
> 孩兒相，青面，紅髮，丫角，乾結處綿頭帮，青身體，露哨腿，皂 線緋袍，紅裙扎腰，項帶十二骷髏，左手金鐘，右手執黃鉞，身肥 短。立黑雲中，有黃旛、豹尾立侍左右。

The second manual in the *Judicial Investigations* text, labeled only as "from another lineage" (*you yipai* 又一派), instructs the practitioner to visualize Yin Jiao in similar terms, with an "azure face; the appearance of a child; hair in a pair of forked buns; twelve skulls hanging from his neck; a yellow halberd grasped with his right hand; a golden bell grasped with his left; a black, loose robe; and shod in boots" (青面，孩兒相，雙丫髮，項下十二骷髏，右手執黃 鉞，左手執金鐘，皂綽袍，穿靴).[116]

In these sources, Yin Jiao's youthful appearance and childlike hairstyle lend an innocent quality, but his skull accessories, yellow halberd, and golden bell exude the menacing air of a great warrior. This image of Yin as childlike yet mature, innocent yet lethal has proved enduring. We saw that the visual imagery of Yin Jiao adorning the altar spaces constructed by Chen Diwen's lineage looks very similar (see figures 2.1, 2.2).[117] Perhaps not coincidentally, sources depicting Yin Jiao in this way all mention Liao Shouzhen as a patriarch. It is tempting to surmise from these few sources that ritual traditions, past and present, recognizing Liao as an ancestral master might share this imagery.

In other sources, Yin Jiao is similarly depicted as a warrior but with no indication of boyishness. The undated *Esoteric Rite [for Summoning] Great Year* (*Taisui bifa* 太歲祕法) instructs the practitioner to visualize Yin Jiao with "the appearance of a celestial being; a jade-green face; twelve skulls around his neck; a red robe tied around his waist with a black belt; bare feet; a yellow halberd in his left hand and a golden bell in his right" (天人相，碧色面，項帶十二骷髏，緋袍，皂帶纏於腰間，跣足，左手黃鉞，右手金鐘).[118] The *Upper Clarity Great Rite [for Summoning] the Fierce Thunder [God Yin Jiao] of the Martial Spring* (*Shangqing wuchun lielei dafa* 上清武春烈雷大法), a Pure Tenuity text, depicts Yin Jiao with "an azure face; hair tied up into a topknot on the crown of his head; red beard and sideburns; and vermillion dress. The great god has a single skull on his head and nine skulls around his neck; his left hand holds a golden bell and his right a yellow halberd; and he rides a nine-headed, golden ox" (青面，束髮，頂中作髻，紅髭鬢，朱衣。大神項上一髑髏，項下九髑髏，左手持金鐘，右手執黃鉞，乘九頭金牛).[119] In these portrayals, Yin Jiao retains his skull accessories, yellow halberd, and golden bell, but instead of childlike features he takes on a red beard and sideburns, or the vague, but seemingly adult, features of a celestial being.

In yet other ritual texts, Yin Jiao possesses a frightening, fantastical body. The *Esoteric Rite from the Emperor of the North [for Summoning] Marshal Yin of the Earth Ministry* (*Beidi disi Yin yuanshuai bifa* 北帝地司殷元帥祕法) instructs the practitioner to visualize that a four-armed Yin Jiao wreathed in a rainbow-colored cloud enters the altar space from the south. He has "an azure face and body; a golden crown atop vermillion hair; a red robe with a black belt wound around his waist; the sun held in the palm of his upper left hand; the moon held in the palm of his right; a halberd-axe in his lower right hand; a golden bell in his lower left; and twelve skulls hanging from his neck" (青面青身，金冠朱髮，緋袍皁綠，絞紮腰間，上左手托日，右手托月，下右手鉞斧，下左手金鐘，項上懸掛十二骷髏).[120] Interestingly, an almost identical image found its way into an illustrated preface to a sixteenth-century edition of the *Precious Scripture of the Jade Pivot Spoken by the Celestial Worthy of the Nine Heavens who Transforms All with the Sound of Thunder Responding to the Prime* (DZ 16 *Jiutian yingyuan leisheng puhua tianzun shuo yushu baojing* 九天應元雷聲普化天尊說玉樞寶經), preserved in the Tenri University Library in Japan.[121]

An even more frightening depiction is given in the *Thunder Rite for [Summoning] the Martial Spring [Thunder God] Great Year* (*Taisui wuchun leifa* 太歲武春雷法). The practitioner is to visualize Yin Jiao with

> a naked body; azure face; azure body; sallow hair standing on end; one skull on the crown of his head; eight skulls hanging around his neck; leopard leather covering his buttocks; two hands coming out from his two eyes—a golden bell in the right and a seal in the left; two middle hands with Yellow Banner in the left and Leopard Tail in the right; two lower hands with a halberd in the left and a fiery sword in the right; a shooting ray of golden light from his "seal hall" [the third eye between his eyebrows]; bare feet; and lightning fires all about his body and under his feet.[122]

> 赤體，青面，青身，焦黃髮豎起，項上骷髏一箇，項帶骷髏八箇，豹皮護臀，兩眼出兩手，右金鐘，左印，中兩手，左黃旛，右豹尾，下兩手，左戟，右火劍，印堂中金光一條射人，赤腳，足下及徧身俱是飛火。

These descriptions of Yin Jiao are a far cry from the portrayals of him as a boyish warrior. These representations maintain his azure face, skull accessories, halberd, and bell, but portray him as a terrifying figure with wild hair, a third eye shooting rays of light, and many arms—some even protruding from his eyes! Yin Jiao looks far more like the classic Divine Empyrean thunder gods—Marshals Deng, Xin, and Zhang—who came to test Bai Yuchan that cloudy night in the early thirteenth century. The iconographical evidence suggests that Yin Jiao took on some of the features of Divine Empyrean thunder gods as he was appropriated across liturgical traditions during the Southern Song, Yuan, and early Ming.

Finally, Yin Jiao was portrayed as a rather mild-mannered Daoist master in the *Great Rite Decreed by the Emperor for Praying to the Precious Pearls Five Thunders* (*Diling baozhu wulei qidao dafa* 帝令寶珠五雷祈禱大法), which appears to have been written during the Yuan or early Ming but claims to document a rite taught during the Southern Song. The preface states the rite was transmitted by and to practitioners in lofty places. A certain Zhu Meijing (朱梅靖), who served as a ritual master on the domestic staff in the imperial palace and as an academician in the Academy of Scholarly Worthies before retiring to Mount Qingcheng in Sichuan, transmitted the rite to three masters, one of whom was an unranked commissioner in the Bureau of Military Affairs, and another the thirty-sixth Celestial Master, Zhang Zongyan (張宗演) (1244–1291).[123] The text recognizes the famous Shangqing goddess Wei Huacun as the founder or matriarch (*zhufa* 主法) of the rite, but the prevalence of the three main thunder gods of the Divine Empyrean and frequent mentions of Wang the Fire Master suggest the rite itself was likely shaped by Wang Wenqing's vision of the Divine Empyrean. Pithy instructions state that Marshal Yin "has the taboo name Jiao, has the appearance of a Daoist priest, wears a yellow robe, and has a red face" (諱郊，道士相，着黃衣，面赤).[124]

It is curious that this depiction is so different from all other extant portrayals of Yin Jiao, especially because this text is heavy with Divine Empyrean features. It seems as if the masters who practiced the rite during the Southern Song or compiled and edited the text during the Yuan or early Ming somehow sanitized the exotic and fearsome iconography of Yin Jiao that had already been widely associated with him. Indeed, the text does not provide descriptions of any of the thunder gods summoned. Given that the preface mentions the high political positions of the rite's practitioners, it is tempting to surmise that the rite might have been made more genteel for practice in the upper echelons of the imperial bureaucracy. Or perhaps it might have been the Celestial Masters who were responsible for this iconographic transformation of Yin Jiao into a Daoist priest.[125] But these possibilities must remain conjecture.

Scholarly Interpretations

Modern scholarship comments on the diverse visual representations of Yin Jiao in several ways. Nikaidō Yoshihiro suggests that certain elements of Yin Jiao's iconography derive from depictions of the fierce wisdom kings (*vidyārāja*) in esoteric Buddhism. For instance, the skulls come from depictions of Yamāntaka (Daweide mingwang 大威德明王), the child image from Acalanātha (Budong mingwang 不動明王), the golden bell from Ucchuṣma (Jin'gang yecha mingwang 金剛夜叉明王), and so forth.[126] For Nikaidō, Yin Jiao's iconography is an amalgamation of various esoteric Buddhist elements. Ch'en Chun-chih thinks with Lee Fong-mao's distinction between a deity's original form (*benxiang* 本相) and subsequent morphed forms (*bianxiang* 變相). Ch'en suggests that Yin Jiao's childlike, innocent depiction in Peng Yuantai's *Great Rite* and other texts reflects the deity's original form, whereas his more ferocious images depict the deity's various morphed forms from that original.[127] Kao Chen-hung, in his dissertation, uses the same rubric to explain Yin Jiao's diverse iconography.[128]

Without more sources, it is difficult to move beyond resemblances between Yin Jiao's iconography and that of various esoteric deities. It is not easy to know why an original image of Yin Jiao might have morphed into various other images, or which cultural, social, or liturgical circumstances might have invited a particular morphing rather than another. In other words, why might masters of different liturgical traditions have chosen to adopt or fashion a certain image of Yin Jiao over others?

I can only hypothesize that during the Song, Yuan, and early Ming, masters practicing within different ritual traditions in different places subscribed to different theologies and had different liturgical needs that compelled their choices. Perhaps for Peng Yuantai, who vehemently advocated for his Great Rite as orthodox and for its image of Yin Jiao as authentic, the martial god's childlike appearance exudes his high status in the celestial realm as a primordial deity and his noble position in the earthly realm as a youthful crown prince in high antiquity. His young, innocent look stands in sharp contrast to those grotesque deities of Fengdu like the nine-headed horse face and the snake-headed elder of fire, whom Peng loathed as fiendish and whose manuals he branded heterodox and deserving to burn.

Such a young, innocent, childlike look is also the image that the Ming–Qing imperial palace chose to depict when including Yin Jiao in its imperial Daoist shrine, the Hall of Reverent Peace (Qin'an dian 欽安殿). Built as a part of the imperial palace in the early fifteenth century by the Yongle (永樂) emperor (r. 1402–1424), the hall housed the guardian deity of the Ming dynasty, Zhenwu, and throughout the Ming and Qing periods it was the site where many Daoist rituals took place. In two side chambers of the hall, two walls are painted with the images of twelve martial deities, one of whom is Yin Jiao. He is depicted as a child with hair buns, a white face, bare arms, and bare feet; he wears a red kilt fastened by a belt and holds a yellow halberd in his right hand.[129] This image strongly resembles the depiction of the deity in Peng Yuantai's *Great Rite,* even if it depicts Yin Jiao without a golden bell, azure face, or skulls around his neck and forehead—features eliminated perhaps because they were deemed unfit for the imperial shrine.

Just as Peng Yuantai, amid a sea of different portrayals of Yin Jiao, might have stuck to his lineage's image for internal reasons, and just as the Ming–Qing designers and painters for the Hall of Reverent Peace in the imperial palace depicted Yin Jiao according to their preference, so has Chen Diwen's lineage adhered to its preferred representation. It inherited the childlike image of Yin Jiao—almost identical to the depiction in Peng Yuantai's *Great Rite*—and it seems never to have adopted any of the deity's other forms. It is not that the lineage has been unaware of the existence of more ferocious images of the god. At some point, the lineage acquired a text made from woodblocks cut in 1891 and printed by a commercial press called the Hall of Shared Celebration (同慶堂). The text describes Yin Jiao with "a blue face, purple hair, and protruding fangs" (藍面紫髮現獠牙).[130] Although masters have seen depictions of Yin Jiao different from the one they use in their rituals, they have never stopped using the childlike image of the god. I suspect this is because that particular image is rooted in the Banner Rite and in the particular hagiography of Yin Jiao that has come down to them, whereas Yin as a fantastical, fearsome deity in the woodblock text belongs to the world outside their esoteric, liturgical sphere. Just as Peng Yuantai insisted centuries before, the orthodoxy and authenticity of the lineage's internal practice takes priority.

Hagiographical Depictions

During the religious fervor of the Southern Song, Yuan, and early Ming, visual imagery of Yin Jiao was variously depicted in ritual manuals taught and used by practitioners who were creatively accommodating one another's liturgical methods. Various narratives about Yin Jiao were also being knitted into hagiographical tales. Almost certainly, numerous hagiographies about Yin Jiao circulated, but only one has survived. It is found in the *Reprinting of Illustrated Comprehensive Records in Search of the Gods since the Origins of the Three Teachings (Chongkan huitu sanjiao yuanliu soushen daquan* 重刊繪圖三教源流搜神大全), or *In Search of the Gods*. The hagiography in this collection cannot be precisely dated, but it is reasonable to believe it took shape sometime during the Yuan–Ming period.[131]

A hagiography is a complicated genre. In his study of medieval hagiographies about the extraordinary exploits of transcendents in Ge Hong's (葛洪) (283–343) *Traditions of Divine Transcendents (Shenxian zhuan* 神仙傳), Robert Campany resists the modern compulsion to read hagiographies as purely literary creations born of an author's imagination more or less untethered from the lived world, or as relatively clear windows into the practices and social relationships of lived religious life of the time. He argues instead that they are descriptive of assumptions about beliefs and practices in the social world in which they emerged, as well as prescriptive for cultivating a certain religious life within that world. By the very ways in which the story is told, the hagiography both reflects something of its social, intellectual, and spiritual context, and works to bring forth some religious ideal in its readers and their institutions.[132]

The story about Yin Jiao included in *In Search of the Gods* is a hagiography in that it seems designed to inspire emulation within the social and religious assumptions of its day. It is hard not to read the short tale as a kind of moral encouragement to emulate the virtues—filial piety, loyalty, vigor, and righteousness—for which Yin Jiao is an exemplar. But the story also reflects something of its lived religious world. The raison d'être of the story is to describe the origin of the figure who would become a great martial deity and to convey how he achieved this status. In the ritual life of masters of the time, knowing where martial gods came from, their trials and tribulations, and how they acquired their appearances and titles were of utmost importance. Recall the night during the Southern Song when Bai Yuchan was reading a text about the origin stories of Marshals Deng, Xin, and Zhang. Disguised as mysterious visitors, the three gods tested Bai's knowledge about their pedigrees and their deeds, which he believed were recorded as their "heartfelt records" (*xinlu* 心錄) kept in the internal records of the celestial archives.[133] For Bai Yuchan, reading such tales about the origins and exploits of thunder gods was the means by which a master came to know the gods to be summoned. That intimate knowledge allowed the master to strike a relationship with specific thunder gods, often consummated by an oath, which in turn assured that the fierce gods would quickly respond to the master's summons. "When summoning and employing thunder gods, how could one not know whence they came?" Bai exclaims. For him, that knowledge was the foundation of efficacious ritual practice.

In Search of the Gods probably enjoyed a wide audience when it was originally printed during the Yuan–Ming period. It was presumably read by different consumers in different ways. Some lay readers might have read the narratives as fantastic stories with entertainment value. Others might have been inspired to live more virtuously, like the moral paragons in the stories. Many masters might have read the stories as prescriptions for their own ritual lives filled with rites for summoning martial gods like Yin Jiao. Like Bai Yuchan, many would have read the narratives in terms of their liturgical traditions. So it does not seem odd that large swaths of the narrative in *In Search of the Gods* made their way into lineages, which is exactly what happened in Chen Diwen's lineage. Somehow, through what Campany calls "the hagiographic reshaping process," narratives from *In Search of the Gods* were woven into esoteric hagiographical texts and carefully copied by hand down the generations.[134] We do not have the sources to show how and when that occurred in the history of Chen's lineage. We do not know whether a copy of *In Search of the Gods* itself was directly accommodated by Chen's ancestral masters during the late Yuan and early Ming as they fanned out from the Jade Void Palace in central Hunan, or whether later ancestral masters accommodated subsequent versions of the narrative printed during the Ming and Qing. But we can appreciate the obvious similarities between Yin Jiao's narrative in *In Search of the Gods* and in the hagiography preserved by the lineage, and hypothesize that those details about Yin Jiao have endured because they have bolstered a ritual in which masters in the lineage have been invested.

It seems as if the hagiography about Yin Jiao in *In Search of the Gods* might have always resonated with ritual texts. Among its undoubtedly many sources, it seems to draw on a few features of the god that found modest expression in two of the ritual manuals we have examined. Recall that in his 1274 preface to the *Great Rite,* Peng Yuantai portrayed Yin Jiao as an awesomely powerful celestial god emanating from the Anterior Heaven. Even in his post in charge of the Earth Ministry, Yin Jiao serves as a direct attendant to the Emperor of the North and enjoys "the highest rank in the heavenly court," is "Thunder God of the Nine Heavens who is composed of extreme *yang qi,*" and was "born an imperial prince in high antiquity who realized the Dao and apprehended truth."

The *Upper Clarity Great Rite [for Summoning] the Fierce Thunder [God Yin Jiao] of the Martial Spring (Upper Clarity Great Rite),* a Qingwei text, seems to add a little detail to these features in an incantation that would come to be widely known as the *Yin Jiao Incantation (Yin Jiao zhou* 殷郊咒). With slight variations, this passage commonly occurs in Qing and twentieth-century ritual manuals preserved by lineages that invoke Yin Jiao, including the *Banner Rite* used by Chen Diwen's lineage. In the Qingwei *Upper Clarity Great Rite,* the practitioner is instructed to declaim loudly

> [I] respectfully plead to the General [Yin Jiao] who commands fortune and directs the *qi* [of vitality], the great General who pacifies people and kills demons. [You] practiced ten lifetimes as crown prince and apprehended orthodox truth after [consuming] one pellet of golden elixir. [Gods of]

heavenly stars and earthly lights converge under your banner. The Emperor of the Earth and [demons of] pestilence submit under your whip. You do not violate loyalty and filiality, and punish those who rebel. The Emperor [of the North] bestowed upon you a bell and halberd with which to vanquish sprites and fiends. . . . Immediately follow the statutes and command of the Great Emperor of Purple Tenuity of the Northern Extremity.[135]

仰啟統運主炁將，鎮元殺鬼大將軍，十世修行為太子，一粒金丹成正真，天星地曜歸麾下，土皇瘟疫伏驅馳，忠孝不違伐叛逆，帝賜鐘鉞斬妖精……急急如北極紫微大帝律令。

In lauding Yin Jiao, the incantation declares that he was born a crown prince in ten separate lifetimes before he realized ultimate truth by ingesting a golden elixir, which seems to be a fuller articulation of the sentiment Peng Yuantai expressed, that Yin Jiao was born an imperial prince in high antiquity who realized the Dao and apprehended truth. Like Peng's text, the incantation boasts of Yin Jiao's great standing among high gods and of his terrible power over demonic forces. But the incantation includes a few strands not appearing in Peng's text. Yin Jiao is loyal and filial, and mercilessly punishes those who rebel against these virtues. And the Emperor of the North bestows on Yin Jiao his bell and halberd, which are so conspicuously featured in the god's iconography from the Song to today.

Hagiographic Resonances

The *Upper Clarity Great Rite* and Peng Yuantai's *Great Rite* mention only a few threads of Yin Jiao's story. *In Search of the Gods* takes these threads and several others and weaves them into a coherent hagiography. We do not know whether the author was a master and so would have had easy access to ritual manuals summoning Yin Jiao, nor whether stories about the god were in the public water during the Yuan–Ming period. In any case, the author drew on his sources to produce and print a substantial narrative.

In Search of the Gods fleshes out the trope that Yin Jiao was a crown prince by specifying he is actually the son of the last ruler of the ancient Shang dynasty, King Zhou. One day his queen steps on a giant footprint and instantly becomes pregnant. Yin Jiao is born wrapped in a lump of flesh. In his wickedness and corruption, King Zhou abandons the lump of flesh in the wild, but animals avoid harming it, birds shield it from sunshine, and a white deer suckles it. The hagiography goes on to recount how Shen the Realized One, whom Peng Yuantai's *Great Rite* recognizes as ancestral master, happens upon the lump of flesh in the wilderness, recognizes it as a "transcendent embryo" (*xiantai* 仙胎), and cuts it open to reveal the infant. Shen names the boy Jin Nezha (唫哪吒) and also gives him the Daoist name Jin Dingnu (唫叮奴) and the nickname Yin Jiao. Shen entrusts the infant to a certain Transcendent Auntie He (He Xiangu 賀仙姑) who raises him.

The hagiography continues to give the backstory of Yin Jiao's characteristic iconography. When the child is seven, Auntie He informs him that he is the son of corrupt King Zhou and that his father killed his mother, which fills the boy with a lust for revenge. Shen the Realized One is touched by Yin Jiao's filial piety for his mother and so trains the boy in the military arts. Shen allows Yin to choose his weapons and the young warrior promptly selects a golden bell and a yellow halberd. Yin Jiao engages in several battles and gains power and soldiers. In one battle, he rides something resembling a seahorse (*haima* 海馬) and subdues two strongmen who become his assistant generals.[136] In another, he defeats twelve wailing demons with skull heads, which he cuts off and hangs around his neck. Shen informs him that when knocked together the skulls would make demons howl and tremble and cause human foes to suffer headaches and weak hands, thus compelling both to retreat without putting up a fight. Leading his newly acquired army, Yin Jiao supports King Wu of the Zhou against corrupt King Zhou. From a strong sense of loyalty, vigor, filial piety, and righteousness (*zhong fen xiao yi* 忠憤孝義), Yin Jiao slays the female fox spirit Daji, who manifests as King Zhou's bewitching concubine and caused the death of the queen. In recognition of Yin Jiao's filial piety toward his mother and of his great courage, the Jade Emperor grants him the title Marshal Yin of the Earth Ministry who Conquers with Mighty Power, Great Year of Utmost Virtue, Patrolling Emissary of the Nine Heavens (地司九天遊奕使至德太歲殺伐威權殷元帥).[137]

The hagiography locates Yin Jiao as both divine child and royal prince at the heart of one of the empire's foundational political myths. Born to the house of King Zhou yet divinely conceived and miraculously begotten as a "transcendent embryo," Yin Jiao is fated to play a major role in the Zhou's righteous conquest over the Shang. The story emphasizes the youthfulness of Yin Jiao, and the heart of the story sketches his close relationship with his rescuer Shen the Realized One, the wise and upright master who teaches the boy how to fulfill his destiny. Throughout, Yin Jiao is portrayed as a moral paragon. Driven by filial piety for his murdered mother, he places his loyalty first in Shen and then in the Zhou cause, renouncing his own claim to the Shang throne. His uprightness is recognized by Heaven with appropriate title.

The hagiography that came down to Chen Diwen through his lineage is largely based on the narrative articulated in *In Search of the Gods,* which itself seems to have engaged images of Yin Jiao manifested in Peng Yuantai's 1274 *Great Rite* and in the Qingwei *Upper Clarity Great Rite.* Recall the lineage's hand-copied hagiography of Yin Jiao, the *Genealogical Investigation,* which accounts for all ten of Yin Jiao's lifetimes as if fleshing out the line in the *Upper Clarity Great Rite* proclaiming that Yin Jiao "practiced ten lifetimes as crown prince." We learn something of his first lifetime, that Yin Jiao's mother, Lady Ziying, was impregnated by divine *qi* as she saw a golden pellet descend onto a jade balustrade in the palace and then gave birth to the son of an ancient ruler, the Great Emperor August Zhen of the Nine Realms. We get the names of each of Yin Jiao's subsequent fathers, including his second, the Earth Emperor of the Earth Spirits, thus lending further information about Yin Jiao's association with the earthly realm and his future post as director of the Earth Ministry. In the *Genealogical Investigation,* we get a fuller version of Yin Jiao's tenth conception than that depicted in *In Search of the Gods.* After having been rejected by King Zhou, the Queen Jiang Luzhen follows bootprints left by the Emperor of the North to the rear of the palace grounds, where she is impregnated by his divine *qi,* imagined as occurring while the stellar god was descending on horseback to alert the depths of Fengdu of King Zhou's recklessness. This moment conveys that Yin Jiao's authority as director of the Earth Ministry flows from the Emperor of the North, who reigns over the Fengdu underworld. The hagiography uses the footprint trope we saw in *In Search of the Gods* to account for Yin Jiao's intimate association with the Emperor of the North, who does not appear in the

Yuan-Ming hagiography but abounds in Peng Yuantai's ritual text and in the Qingwei manual.

The lineage's *Genealogical Investigation* also fleshes out the narrative that Yin Jiao attained ultimate truth. Peng Yuantai writes only that Yin Jiao "was born an imperial prince in high antiquity who realized the Dao and apprehended truth." The incantation in the Qingwei *Upper Clarity Great Rite* states that Yin Jiao "practiced ten lifetimes as crown prince and apprehended orthodox truth after [consuming] one pellet of golden elixir." The hagiography recounts how after he made his solemn oaths to Shen the Realized One, Yin Jiao attained the Dao and achieved perfection after ingesting a pellet of golden elixir given by his master and then practicing in a cave for three years. The enlightenment story signals the fruition of the intimate relationship between apprentice and master.

Many more details about Yin Jiao in *In Search of the Gods* have, twisting and turning, made their way down the centuries to the lineage's hagiography. In both texts, Yin Jiao brims with youthfulness. Both tell in strikingly similar terms how King Zhou abandoned the infant in the wilderness and how wild animals protected and nurtured him. The Yuan–Ming hagiography describes how Shen the Realized One discovers the "transcendent embryo" and entrusts the infant to the care of Transcendent Auntie He, whereas the lineage's hagiography has Marquis Yin finding the boy and a wet nurse from his household, He Tugu, raising him. In both texts, the boy learns about the fate of his mother and is driven to avenge her. We have seen how this picture of youthfulness is today depicted in the lineage's visual imagery of Yin Jiao used in its altar spaces.[138]

Further, both texts stress Yin Jiao's filiality, loyalty, vigor, and righteousness, but in diverging ways. In *In Search of the Gods,* Yin Jiao vows to avenge his mother, loyally follows Shen the Realized One, and righteously fights for the Zhou cause against his father and inheritance, finally slaying the fox spirit responsible for his mother's demise. In the lineage's *Genealogical Investigation,* Yin Jiao begins down the path of revenge but Shen makes him see that patricide is, even when driven by revenge for one's mother, ultimately unfilial and counter to the way of heaven. Yin Jiao instead becomes Shen's loyal apprentice and learns the rites. The text spares no detail describing the series of oaths by which Yin Jiao pledged his eternal loyalty to Shen, cementing their master-apprentice relationship.

Chen Diwen knew nothing of these remarkable textual resonances as he studied Yin Jiao's story in the *Genealogical Investigation* during his training. But he did know that mastery of Yin Jiao's narrative was crucial for successfully summoning the god during the Banner Rite. Chen paid attention to the narrative details about Yin Jiao's ten lifetimes and especially noted Yin's oaths of perpetual loyalty and service to his master. Like Bai Yuchan almost eight hundred years before, Chen Diwen knew that knowing about Yin Jiao's pedigree and great deeds was constitutive of ritual success.

Campany makes the point that scriptures teach by putting forth cosmological or doctrinal systems, and ritual manuals teach by putting forth systems of procedures, whereas hagiographical narratives teach by yielding stories that ground those cosmologies, doctrines, and procedures in the lives of subjects in particular times and places. "Neither mode of thought is reducible to the other; they are complementary ways of knowing and conveying, each reinforcing and legitimating the other."[139] For Chen Diwen and his lineage, their hagiographical narrative about Yin Jiao—what they call his "genealogical investigation" (*maikao* 脈考) or "genealogy of origin" (*chumai* 出脈)—is the indispensable counterpart to the Banner Rite. Successful performance of the ritual method as notated in the *Banner Rite* manual requires knowledge about Yin Jiao's origins and exploits articulated in the *Genealogical Investigation* hagiography. The hagiography does not simply supply background knowledge to the Banner Rite; it is actively incorporated into the ritual. Lines from the hagiography are intoned in incantations throughout the ritual sequence—at places word for word. Indeed, the success or failure of Chen Diwen's summoning of Yin Jiao during the Banner Rite would turn in no small part on how well Chen knew Yin Jiao's pedigree. Intimate knowledge of Yin would be crucial for forming a relationship with the martial god and compelling him to obey the summons. Without that knowledge, the risk of ritual failure would be much greater.

Depictions in Vernacular Fiction

During the Yuan and Ming dynasties, narratives about Yin Jiao were not confined to short hagiographies. The god also showed up in lengthier works of vernacular fiction, a developing genre that became wildly popular during the Ming. That Yin Jiao should appear in several of these works was not odd. Mark Meulenbeld shows that ritual practices from the Song and Yuan periods informed the episodes narrated in several later vernacular novels. As much as they were creative works of fiction, novels were often also narrative accompaniments to ritual that fleshed out the backstories of gods involved in ritual performances. These "paraliturgies" worked much like the hagiography of Yin Jiao in *In Search of the Gods* worked with Yuan ritual, and like the *Genealogical Investigation* works with the Banner Rite.[140]

Here we examine depictions of Yin Jiao in three works of vernacular fiction. Although images of the god in these works might have drawn on earlier ritual practices, they seem not to have much influenced the hagiography and iconography of Yin Jiao that have made their way into Chen Diwen's liturgical tradition. His liturgical ancestors seem to have preferred an older depiction of Yin Jiao sketched in Peng Yuantai's *Great Rite* of 1274 and in the Qingwei *Upper Clarity Great Rite,* and then elaborated in the Yuan–Ming hagiography of Yin Jiao in *In Search of the Gods.*

The Plain Tale

Yin Jiao makes an appearance as a lead character in a plain tale (*pinghua* 平話) narrative called the *Plain Tale of King Wu's Conquest of King Zhou* (*Wuwang fa Zhou pinghua* 武王伐紂平話), or the *Plain Tale.*[141] Popular during the fourteenth century, the plain tale was a form of vernacular fiction based on versions of major episodes in Chinese history, mostly of famous kings and emperors in antiquity. Plain tales were short, tightly structured texts with an educational and moral bent compiled from a wide variety of sources and meant to be read.[142] The *Plain Tale* was printed, with exquisite illustrations, between 1321 and 1323 by the well-known commercial publisher Yu Zhi'an (余志安) (fl. 1304–1345) in Jian'an (建安, present-day Jianyang 建陽) in northwestern Fujian.[143]

The shape of Yin Jiao's story in the *Plain Tale* resembles the general contours of his hagiography in *In Search of the Gods*. Both texts portray Yin Jiao as King Zhou's crown prince who as a young boy learns of his mother's murder by his father. Morally virtuous and righteously bellicose, Yin Jiao vows to avenge her, builds an army, and joins the forces of King Wu in the Zhou uprising to overthrow King Zhou's corrupt Shang dynasty. Yet the two texts have rather different agendas. The hagiography in *In Search of the Gods* aims to sketch the morally upright, martially powerful nature of Yin Jiao in the context of the story of the Zhou conquest of the Shang. The historical episode is the occasion of Yin Jiao's excellence. The three-chapter *Plain Tale* sketches Yin Jiao as a main character among other main characters in the story of the conquest. Yin Jiao functions as but one of the dramatis personae in a detailed recounting of that ancient event.

The *Plain Tale* presents a more complex view of King Zhou and of his concubine Daji. Here Yin Jiao's father is depicted as an upright, intelligent, eminently capable ruler who has the misfortune of becoming smitten with the stunningly beautiful prefect's daughter. Shortly before her betrothal to the king as a secondary wife, Daji is possessed by a fox spirit with nine tails and golden hair. The bewitched Daji manipulates King Zhou and he becomes the notoriously cruel tyrant known to history. The text describes how he desecrates temples, orders ill-advised building projects, and decapitates ministers for giving advice contrary to Daji's wishes. When the king's primary wife, Queen Jiang, reprimands him for sending her off to seclusion after Daji frames the queen for trying to murder her, the king pushes the queen from a building to her death.

Like the hagiography in *In Search of the Gods*, the *Plain Tale* depicts Yin Jiao as the manifestation of a deity, but with much less nuance. Rather than relating a "transcendent embryo" story, the *Plain Tale* simply asserts that Queen Jiang gave birth to a prince who was actually the stellar god Great Year manifested as a person to respond to King Zhou's transgressions. Yin Jiao's divine origin is bound up with his destiny to destroy the Shang king.[144] The *Plain Tale* goes on to detail the boy's childhood in the palace. After his mother is killed when he is a year old, Yin Jiao is nurtured by a bevy of wet nurses. When the boy grows into a brilliant and ardent ten-year-old,

Daji fears the wet nurses might tell him the truth about the demise of his mother. She persuades the king to destroy them all by pitting them against one another in cruel, gladiator-like games. A nurse surnamed Feng (馮) who avoided the bloody spectacle is able to tell young Yin Jiao the sordid truth before taking her own life in the king's prison. After the spirits of his mother, nurse Feng, and the other victims appear to him begging for vengeance, Yin Jiao confronts his father King Zhou and Daji only to be sentenced to death. Just before the axe falls, a giant of a man whisks the boy away from the public execution square. Yin Jiao vows to raise an army and avenge his mother by destroying King Zhou, Daji, and their henchmen.

The *Plain Tale* does not mention Shen the Realized One or any other mentor figure, nor does it portray Yin Jiao as a warrior with his familiar yellow halberd, golden bell, and skull accessories. Instead, it explains that Yin Jiao becomes powerful during a revelatory dream. One night while sleeping in a temple, Yin Jiao encounters a divine soldier who declares, "In the future you will certainly destroy the immoral lord; I give you a method by which you will definitely prevail" (你後必破無道之君；吾與汝一法，必勝矣).[145] The deity then gives Yin Jiao the Axe for Destroying King Zhou (po Zhou zhi fu 破紂之斧), an awesome weapon weighing a hundred pounds. Yin Jiao awakes with the axe in his hands and the strength to wield it. Divinely enabled, the young warrior joins the forces of King Wu and his marshal Jiang Shang (姜尚), aka Jiang Ziya (姜子牙), in the Zhou rebellion against the throne and is appointed a general. The text spills plenty of ink recounting several of Yin Jiao's deft military exploits as the Zhou forces approach and storm the capital.

In the climactic final scene of the *Plain Tale,* Yin Jiao fulfills his pledge to avenge his mother and wet nurses. Unlike the hagiography in which Yin Jiao kills only Daji, here he vanquishes both her and King Zhou. He uses his mighty axe to decapitate his father as prophesied in his dream in the temple. Reckoning with Daji is filled with much more drama. On the block, the beguiling villain bewitches two executioners with her beauty so they cannot fulfill their duty. Yin Jiao steps in and covers Daji's face with white silk so she cannot charm him. As she receives the death blow she disappears, leaving behind only sparks. Wielding a sprite-subduing seal (*xiangyao zhang* 降妖章) and a sprite-subduing mirror (*xiangyao jing* 降妖鏡), Jiang Ziya is able to detect Daji, who had transformed back into her original form of a nine-tailed fox spirit. Yin Jiao promptly traps it in a silk bag and bludgeons it until it disappears.

Although written during the Yuan dynasty at about the same time Yin Jiao's hagiography in *In Search of the Gods* was taking shape, the *Plain Tale* paints a very different portrait. Yin Jiao is still the youthful prince-cum-warrior who righteously avenges his pitilessly slain mother during the Zhou campaign against the Shang. Yet in the *Plain Tale*, Yin Jiao is notable for great military exploits along his path to a final reckoning with the cruel Daji rather than for any sort of story about how he became a martial deity. The *Plain Tale* mentions, almost in passing, that Yin Jiao was born a manifestation of a stellar god—here the star Great Year instead of the Emperor of the North. But that divine association underscores the boy's destiny to overthrow the Shang dynasty rather than establishing Yin Jiao as a god. The *Plain Tale* mentions neither details about the boy's miraculous birth nor his apprenticeship with any sort of master like Shen the Realized One. Yin Jiao's familiar iconography is markedly different. Instead of a halberd, bell, and skull necklace, Yin Jiao wields the axe to destroy King Zhou. That the axe and the strength to wield it were divinely imparted underscore that Yin Jiao is destined to fulfill his vow of vengeance; they do not symbolize any sort of fate to become a martial god. The *Plain Tale* presents a very different image of Yin Jiao from the one in the Yuan–Ming hagiography and Chen Diwen's liturgical ancestors seem to have preferred the latter.

Journey to the North

When genres like the plain tale gave way to full-fledged vernacular novels during the first half of the sixteenth century, Yin Jiao again found himself playing a role. He made an appearance in *Journey to the North* (*Beiyou ji* 北遊記), a twenty-four-chapter narrative recounting how Zhenwu, the True Warrior, endured a series of contests on his path to realizing the Dao and canonization as the High Emperor of the Dark Heavens (Xuantian shangdi 玄天上帝). The earliest extant edition of the text was printed in 1602 by Yu Xiangdou (余象斗) (fl. late 1500s–1637), a member of the same Yu clan of notable publishers in northwest Fujian who had printed the *Plain Tale* in the early 1300s. Yu Xiangdou likely based the 1602 edition on an even earlier edition.[146]

Journey to the North tells the story not of Yin Jiao's role in the Zhou conquest of the Shang, but of his own meritorious deeds assisting the protagonist Zhenwu. In chapter 21, Zhenwu and his entourage are traveling across a mountain when they encounter thirteen spritely fiends (*yaojing* 妖精) called the Thirteen Great Guardians (Shisan taibao 十三太保).[147] Having always demanded that locals offer them thirteen boys and girls in sacrifice, these blood-thirsty demons easily overpower Zhenwu and his armed entourage. Zhenwu manages to escape the carnage and flees to the temple of the Three Pure Ones for counsel. The Three Pure Ones issue an edict decreeing that the Great Guardians' master, the guardian god of the north-south border, here called Yin Gao (殷高) instead of Yin Jiao, should assist Zhenwu in subduing the demons. Yin Gao obeys the edict and joins forces with Zhenwu.

When they reach the Great Guardians' mountain, they find two minor demons, Yellow Banner (Huangfan 黃嬌 [嬌]) and Leopard Tail (Baowei 豹尾), blocking the road. Yin Gao recognizes that the demons originally belonged to him.

> Yin Gao immediately performed a method by which he spit out deadly *qi* and his body became enveloped by a golden radiance. He revealed his true form as [the god] Great Year with three faces and four arms. The two sprites could not escape and displayed their true forms: two leopard tails attached to his spear.[148]

> 殷高即作法，將殺氣吐出，遍體金光，現出太歲真形，三面四手。那二妖不能走動，露出真形，卻是鎗裡兩把豹尾。

Armed with his spear readorned with its original leopard tails, Yin Gao proceeds to attack the encampment of the Thirteen Great Guardians but is unable to subdue them. Attempting to allay Zhenwu's anxiety, Yin Gao seeks counsel from his master Sa the Realized One (Sa zhenren 撒真人). Recognizing that Zhenwu is a manifestation of the Jade Emperor, Sa volunteers to join them in the fight. The next day they meet the thirteen in battle.

> Just when [the Thirteen Great Guardians] tried to capture Yin Gao by their usual method, Sa the Realized One spurted a mouthful of ritually [transformed] precious water. Then he drew out two cords, red and white, and tossed them in the air. The Thirteen Great Guardians were all skewered together to form a string and displayed their true forms to be thirteen skull bones. Sa the Realized One inserted a pellet of fire elixir into each skull and instructed Yin Gao to wear one skull on his head and hang twelve from his neck.[149]

> 正要行法捉殷高，撒真人將法寶水含口中一噴，取出白紅二索，丟起空中，把那十三太保盡穿作一串，露出真形，卻是十三個骷髏骨。撒真人於骨中每一個入火丹一丸，分付殷高，頭代一個骷髏，頸挂十二個骷髏。

Later, an edict arrives from the Jade Emperor canonizing Yin Gao as Marshal Yin, the Top General of Luminous Militarism, the Worthy of Upmost Virtue, the [God] Great Year of the Earth Ministry Who Takes Charge of Killing (地司統殺太歲至德尊神光武上將殷元帥).

The tale about Yin Jiao in *Journey to the North* is essentially an etiological account of how he gained a familiar title. Along the way, we learn how Yin Jiao recovered two of his attendants—Yellow Banner and Leopard Tail—who are mentioned both in visualization instructions and in incantations in earlier ritual texts in the Daoist canon.[150] We also get an alternate backstory of Yin Jiao's iconic skulls, which dominate his visualized imagery in canonical sources.[151] Yet Yin Jiao's overall story in *Journey to the North* is quite different from the Yuan–Ming hagiography in *In Search of the Gods* and its ritual antecedents.[152] Yin Jiao gains his merit by assisting Zhenwu along his path rather than by fulfilling a vengeful vow during the Zhou conquest. Yin Jiao is presented as a tutelary deity guarding the north-south border and as master of the unruly Thirteen Great Guardians, albeit a rather impotent one. When he shows his true form as the god Great Year, he displays a fantastical body with three faces and four arms, which resembles the terrifying images visualized in a few of the canonical sources.[153] *Journey to the North* connects Yin Jiao to a powerful master, Sa the Realized One, but is concerned with demonstrating the master's great exorcistic power rather than with bearing witness to any kind of intimate relationship or oath between apprentice and master. If the tale in *Journey to the North* is a weaving together of various images of Yin Jiao expressed in earlier ritual texts, it chooses certain images rather than others to narrativize.

Canonization of the Gods

Yin Jiao's most famous appearance in vernacular fiction is in the hundred-chapter novel *Canonization of the Gods* (*Fengshen yanyi* 封神演義). The authorship and date of the work are debated. One argument claims the text was written in the late sixteenth or early seventeenth century by a certain Xu Zhonglin (許仲琳) (fl. 1567–1620). Another contends that it was likely written by a Daoist named Lu Xixing (陸西星) during the Jiajing (嘉靖) reign (1522–1567). Yet another asserts that the earliest known edition must date to 1624 or 1625.[154] The questions of who wrote the text and when are overshadowed by the fact that *Canonization of the Gods* became immensely popular during the late Ming and early Qing dynasties.

Drawing heavily on many sources, including the *Plain Tale, Canonization of the Gods* tells the story of the Zhou conquest of the Shang dynasty within a divine frame. King Zhou insults the goddess Nü Wa (女媧) who in retaliation works to bring down his Shang dynasty by supporting the establishment of the Zhou dynasty by King Wen and his son King Wu. She engineers the issuance of a new heavenly mandate by the high council of Daoist gods and enlists a host of unruly spirits, most notably the fox spirit Su Daji, to corrupt King Zhou and weaken his rule. Terrific battles between forces loyal to the Shang and to the Zhou are fought by bitterly divided divine generals and warriors, Daoist masters, and fantastic creatures, each using martial arts and divine weapons powered by different methods. At the fated conclusion of the bloodshed, the fallen spirits on both sides are registered on a list of canonizations (*fengshen bang* 封神榜), which honorably recognizes them with titles for their various roles in establishing the newly mandated regime.

Yin Jiao plays a role familiar to readers of the *Plain Tale* but with creative embellishment for which *Canonization of the Gods* is known. The teenage crown prince finds his mother, Queen Jiang, gruesomely mutilated and dying on the order of King Zhou, who was manipulated into punishing his wife for treason by his fox-possessed concubine Daji. Enraged, Yin Jiao vows to avenge her and immediately slices in two a general in league with Daji's plotters, planning to then go after Daji. King Zhou orders Yin Jiao and his younger brother, Yin Hong (殷洪), executed on the spot. Aided by a few upright generals, the two boys narrowly escape the capital only to be caught by King Zhou's forces and brought back. The decree comes down from King Zhou to decapitate his sons at the palace gate. As the king's general is about to perform his duty, two transcendents create a dust storm around the captive princes and whisk them away to safety. One of the transcendents, Guangchengzi (廣成子), takes Yin Jiao as his Daoist apprentice and trains him on Mount Jiuxian (九仙山).

After mentoring Yin Jiao for several years, Guangchengzi decides that his apprentice ought to assist the new commander of the Zhou forces, Jiang Ziya, so that Yin Jiao might finally seek his revenge. While Yin Jiao is roaming about the mountain looking for a weapon, he discovers an intriguing cave in which he happens upon seven cooked beans. Upon eating them,

> His Highness [Yin Jiao] became confused. Without knowing why, [he noticed] the bones throughout his body crackling. An arm suddenly came out of his left shoulder. Panicking, His Highness turned pale from fright as he suddenly saw another arm on his right. After a moment three heads and six arms suddenly sprouted. Yin Jiao was gawking and dumbfounded with terror, and for quite a while he stood speechless. Suddenly he saw [Guangchengzi's] lad Baiyun come forth and call to him, "Brother apprentice, the master asks for you." At that moment Yin Jiao perked up somewhat, pondered [what had happened] and became clear and bright. His face was like indigo and his hair like cinnabar. There were fangs

protruding from the top and bottom [of his mouth] and there had grown another eye [in his forehead]. Swaying back and forth, he arrived at [his master's] cave.[155]

殿下心疑，不覺渾身骨頭響，左邊肩頭上忽冒出來一隻手來。殿下著慌，大驚失色，只見右邊又是一隻。一會兒忽長出三頭六臂，把殷郊只諕得目瞪口呆，半晌無語。只見白雲童兒來前叫曰：「師兄，師父有請。」殷郊這一會略覺神思清爽，面如藍靛，髮似硃砂，上下獠牙，多生一目，晃晃蕩蕩，來至洞前。

Guangchengzi is delighted with his apprentice's new form. He bequeaths to Yin Jiao a square-shaped halberd (*fangtian huaji* 方天畫戟), a Heaven-overturning seal (*fantian yin* 番天印), a soul-sinking bell (*luohun zhong* 落魂鐘), and a pair of male and female swords (*cixiong jian* 雌雄劍). As the battle-ready Yin Jiao is about to leave, his wise master says to him, "I have given to you all my treasures. You must follow [the mandate of] Heaven and respond to [the needs of] humanity. You are to advance east through the five passes and assist King Wu of Zhou to raise an army to save people and punish crimes. Do not change your intention and harbor no doubt in your heart. Should you incur the wrath of Heaven, it will be too late to repent!" (吾將此寶盡付與你，須是順天應人，東進五關，輔周武，興弔民伐罪之師。不可改了念頭，心下狐疑，有犯天譴，那時悔之晚矣). Yin Jiao replies sincerely, "The words of my master are misplaced. King Wu of the Zhou is a sagely lord of illustrious virtue; my father is a debauched, muddle-headed tyrant. How could I err and fail to live up to my master's instructions? Should I your apprentice do differently from what I have said, then I shall suffer [death] by a plough hoe" (老師之言差矣！周武明德聖君，吾父荒淫昏虐，豈得錯認，有辜師訓。弟子如改前言，當受犁鋤之厄).[156]

On his way to join Jiang Ziya, the leader of the Zhou forces, Yin Jiao happens upon a Daoist master named Shen Gongbao (申公豹) from Mount Kunlun (崑崙山), who convinces the prince it would be unbearably unfilial to attack his own father, a deed surely offensive to his ancestors. Moreover, the mighty prince would certainly be able to bring peace to the realm should he succeed his father as king. Yin Jiao gallantly resists, but Shen Gongbao persuades him by falsely claiming that Jiang Ziya killed his younger brother.

Yin Jiao takes up a vendetta against Jiang Ziya. Wielding his master's divine weapons with his fantastical body, Yin Jiao, who is at one point called an "evil deity" (*eshen* 惡神), proves to be an awesome warrior against the Zhou army.[157]

Finally, Jiang Ziya, aided by a group of transcendents, who include Yin Jiao's master Guangchengzi, secure divine weapons powerful enough to counter Yin Jiao and hunt him down. As he flees from the posse through a ravine toward a dead end, Yin Jiao desperately creates an escape route by hurling his Heaven-overturning seal at the mountain, splitting the mountain in two. Just as he is about to emerge from the crevice, one of his enemies magically closes up the mountain, trapping the prince's mighty body with only his heads sticking out. Recalling Yin Jiao's broken oath, Guangchengzi presents the promised plough hoe, which is used to decapitate him.

At the end of the novel, Yin Jiao's spirit joins all the spirits of the fallen on both sides of the conflict. Each is summoned by a banner, judged according to his good or bad deeds, and then canonized as deities serving various posts in the divine bureaucracy. Although it is acknowledged that Shen Gongbao deceived him, Yin Jiao is judged to have violated the will of Heaven by betraying his master Guangchengzi's instructions to support the Zhou conquest. He is then canonized as the god Great Year in charge of time deities holding jurisdiction over events during the year.

The Yin Jiao of *Canonization of the Gods* is strikingly different from the depiction of the god in any previous source. Although the novel places Yin Jiao in the familiar context of the Zhou conquest, and provides an etiology of how he acquired the kind of fantastical body visualized in a few earlier Daoist ritual manuals, here Yin Jiao begins a prince but becomes the model of an "evil deity." The Yin Jiao of *Canonization of the Gods* is neither loyal nor righteous. His sense of filial piety is perverted by the devious Daoist Shen Gongbao, who does not in the least resemble the saintly Shen the Realized One in canonical ritual texts, in *In Search of the Gods*, and in the hagiography preserved by Chen Diwen's lineage. In *Canonization of the Gods*, Yin Jiao begins as the loyal apprentice of the upstanding father figure Guangchengzi only to turn against him. Ironically, Yin Jiao misplaces his filial devotion on his amoral father King Zhou. Yin Jiao strikes something like an oath with his master and then willfully breaks it, which leads to the violent fulfillment of its stated consequence. At the conclusion of the novel, Yin Jiao's profound misdeeds are conspicuously recognized by the high gods before he is canonized the deity Great Year, which seems to provide an explanation for one image of that god as baleful.[158]

Narrative Choices

The depictions of Yin Jiao in the *Plain Tale*, in *Journey to the North*, and especially in *Canonization of the Gods* contrast markedly with the ritual texts and hagiographic literature that resonate most closely with the hagiography maintained by Chen Diwen's lineage. Recall that in Peng Yuantai's 1274 preface and 1290 colophon to the *Great Rite* ritual text, Yin Jiao is of extreme *yang qi* and directs the Earth Ministry as a lofty thunder god who comes from the Anterior Heaven and so wields boundless divine power and unfathomable numinous might. He enjoys the highest celestial rank of all the attendants of the Emperor of the North. The incantation in the Qingwei *Upper Clarity Great Rite* text lauds Yin Jiao as not only one who does not violate loyalty and filiality, but also as one who punishes those who rebel against those virtues. Yin Jiao's hagiography in *In Search of the Gods* specifies that he was nominally the son of King Zhou but was actually conceived when his mother trod on a giant footprint. Yin Jiao dutifully studies from his upright master, Shen the Realized One, and eventually fulfills his destiny by righteously joining the Zhou cause, renouncing his own claim to the Shang throne, and destroying Daji. The *Genealogical Investigation* maintained by Chen Diwen's lineage seems a direct descendant of the general narrative expressed in these texts.

Meulenbeld points out that episodes narrated in certain pieces of late imperial vernacular literature drew heavily on older Daoist ritual practices from the Song and Yuan periods. He shows also that vernacular works like the *Plain Tale, Journey to the North,* and *Canonization of the Gods* were more than fiction born solely from an author's creative mind. Instead, these "para-liturgies" were narrative accompaniments to ritual, analogous to commentaries on classical texts.[159] These sorts of late imperial novels functioned as counterparts to ritual just as we imagined the Yuan–Ming hagiography of Yin Jiao in *In Search of the Gods* functioned to ground ritual action in a particular story about the god, and just as we shall see Chen Diwen's knowledge of Yin Jiao's backstory preserved in his lineage's *Genealogical Investigation* is essential for efficacious performance of the Banner Rite.

However, Chen Diwen's lineage seems to have resisted conspicuous influence by the narratives about Yin Jiao in vernacular works. The Yin Jiao in the *Genealogical Investigation* hagiography, the Yin Jiao who participates in the Banner Rite, looks very different from the Yin Jiao in the *Plain Tale, Journey to the North,* or *Canonization of the Gods.* Recall that in the lineage's account Yin Jiao spends ten lifetimes as a crown prince, the last as the nominal son of King Zhou after he is divinely conceived by the Emperor of the North when his mother steps on his bootprint. The text emphasizes Yin Jiao's youth and adolescent lust for revenge for his slain mother until the upstanding Shen the Realized One turns him from the unfilial path of patricide toward the righteous path of Daoist practice. The text stresses Yin Jiao's loyalty, vigor, and righteousness in the detailed oaths Yin strikes with his master. After consuming a pellet of golden elixir given by Shen and practicing for three years in a cave, Yin Jiao apprehends truth without acquiring any kind of fantastical body. He is canonized with a title bequeathed by the Emperor of the North, which seems like a destined fulfillment of his original status as the son or manifestation of that high stellar god rather than any sort of domestication of an unruly spirit. The lineage's Yin Jiao is fierce not because he is an orphan spirit, but because he is a primordial celestial god who wields incredible power because of his close relationship with the Emperor of the North. This portrayal in the lineage resonates much more closely with the Yuan–Ming hagiography in *In Search of the Gods,* which seems to flesh out images of the god in the Qingwei *Upper Clarity Great Rite* text and in Peng Yuantai's late thirteenth-century account.

Chen Diwen's masters seem to have been aware of this gap between their image of Yin Jiao and that in *Canonization of the Gods.* When Jiang

Shenzhi was redacting the *Genealogical Investigation* in the early 1990s, he finished the piece by writing, "To see what happened to Yin Jiao after all this, one can consult *Canonization of the Gods* to inquire further" (以後殷郊之結果，可參考封神傳以探討之).[160] Unfortunately, Jiang Shenzhi died before I could ask him about this. His grandson and most ardent disciple, Jiang Yucheng, explains that masters in the lineage have known of the famous novel for quite a long time, but he doubts any of them, including Jiang Shenzhi, ever read it.[161] Jiang Shenzhi seems to have recognized that popular culture included stories about Yin Jiao, but felt there was no need to learn about them. It is the lineage's internal story that matters because it is that story that contextualizes crucial moments in the Banner Rite. The lineage's *Genealogical Investigation* does indeed work as a kind of paraliturgy augmenting the ritual, and that liturgical function seems to have privileged its telling of Yin Jiao's story over others.

Jiang Shenzhi's editorial move seems to echo those of his predecessors in the lineage. Little of the depictions of Yin Jiao in late imperial vernacular fiction has in fact influenced the lineage's hagiography or iconography. Most memorably, the Yin Jiao of *Canonization of the Gods*—an unruly, evil deity with a fantastically ferocious body who is in the end domesticated via canonization—is unrecognizable as the Yin Jiao in the lineage. The lineage seems to have willfully resisted overt influence by popular culture in favor of its own internal narrative, which we saw was rooted in an older narrative about Yin Jiao expressed in a certain hagiography and ritual texts from the Song and Yuan. Similar choices were constantly made by masters in the past. They used resources to promote their teachings and glorify their lineage's traditions while minimizing and even destroying resources that might jeopardize their teachings. Peng Yuantai is an example with which we have by now become very familiar. He angrily burned ritual texts he deemed heterodox resources that he felt hurt his lineage's authentic teaching and disparaged Marshal Yin Jiao's reputation.

Jiang Shenzhi did not disparage *Canonization of the Gods*. He deftly left space for a conciliatory relationship between his lineage's narrative of Yin Jiao and that in the popular novel. Other practitioners have been less generous. In Taiwan, the Palace of the Dragon and Phoenix of the Limitless Nine Heavens in Changzhi township (Changzhi wuji jiutian longfeng gong 長治無極九天龍鳳宮) has bristled at the widespread assumption that Yin Jiao the deity resembles his depiction in the novel. A caustic Facebook post dated January 15, 2017, is titled "The 'Misunderstanding' that *Canonization of the Gods* Has Brought to Celestial Lord Yin, Spirit General of the Thunder Bureau" (《封神演義》給雷部神將殷天君帶來的「誤會」). It states that "the Great Celestial Lord Yin, the [God of] Great Year and the Earth Ministry occupies a position of honor in Daoism; he is one of the thirty-six celestial generals of the Thunder Bureau" (地司太歲殷大天君在道教地位尊崇，是雷部三十六天將之一). Citing several of the visualized images of Yin Jiao in the Song and Yuan canonical texts, the lengthy post delineates the differences between the noble Yin Jiao who is to be venerated in Daoist practice, and the villainous Yin Jiao of *Canonization of the Gods*. The temple's Facebook friends are warned that "none of these novels tally with Daoist belief" (這些演義均不符合道教信仰). Armed with the Daoist canon, these practitioners use social media to resist what they consider the insidious influence of Ming vernacular fiction on Daoist practice (web figure 2.1).

Conclusion

Yin Jiao has been imagined in many ways. In the thirteenth century, Heart of Heaven master Peng Yuantai depicted him as a celestial deity from the Anterior Heaven who serves the Emperor of the North as his highest-ranking attendant in the heavenly court. From that lofty position, Yin Jiao holds jurisdiction over the terrestrial Earth Ministry, a paradox that seems to have invited varying interpretations. Peng argued vehemently that Yin Jiao ought not be confused with terrestrial spirits and demons from the Fengdu underworld, tacitly suggesting that such representations of the god were prevalent during the Southern Song. Instead, Yin Jiao and his trusty assistant general Jiang Rui display characteristics of Divine Empyrean thunder gods. They are fierce and speedy and can become powerful agents of a master should he succeed in forging a bond with them based on familiarity with their pedigrees and appearances. Peng's ritual text mentions that Yin Jiao was born an imperial prince in high antiquity who realized the Dao. A Pure Tenuity manual, the *Upper Clarity Great Rite,* includes an incantation extolling Yin Jiao as a loyal, filial crown prince born into ten lifetimes before realizing truth by ingesting a golden elixir and receiving a distinctive halberd and bell from the Emperor of the North.

As ritual use of Yin Jiao spread across almost all traditions of practice proliferating during the Southern Song, Yuan, and early Ming, his iconography also changed. In some ritual texts, including Peng Yuantai's *Great Rite,* Yin Jiao is to be visualized as a boyish prince in high antiquity whose yellow halberd, golden bell, and skull-necklace and headband exude martial prowess. In other ritual texts, he is to visualized as a full-grown warrior with his halberd, bell, and skull accessories. In yet other texts, especially Pure Tenuity manuals, he has a frightening, fantastical body, a ray-emitting third eye, and many arms—sometimes even protruding from his eyes. Another ritual text portrays Yin Jiao as a mild-mannered Daoist master.

These brief sketches of Yin Jiao's story and instructions for visualizing his appearance within traditions of practice made their way into literary culture during the Yuan and early Ming. Yin Jiao's hagiography in *In Search of the Gods* seems to have taken a select few of these sketches and images and fashioned them into a coherent narrative. Apparently building on depictions of Yin Jiao shared by Peng Yuantai and the Pure Tenuity *Upper Clarity Great Rite,* the hagiography situates Yin Jiao as the divinely conceived son of infamous King Zhou, a boy who is destined to overthrow his corrupt father and destroy the king's murderous concubine. The young, innocent prince Yin Jiao escapes certain death to train under Shen the Realized One, the wise and upright master who teaches him how to fulfill his destiny. Yin Jiao is depicted as a paragon of filial piety, loyalty, vigor, and righteousness within the story of the Zhou conquest of the Shang.

Longer works of Yuan and Ming vernacular literature paint different portraits. The Yuan *Plain Tale* places him in the thick of the Zhou conquest of the Shang, but lacks any story about his training with a master, and instead recounts the crown prince's facility with an enormous axe and his victories on the battlefield as he marches toward vengeance for his slain mother. The Ming novel *Canonization of the Gods* drew on this story to spin a nuanced tale that casts Yin Jiao as the aggrieved crown prince who trains with a righteous master to fight on the side of the Zhou forces, but after acquiring a terrifying body he is convinced by a deceitful master to turn on the Zhou army. As an "evil deity," he becomes a great villain of the story and ends up losing his several heads before being canonized as the god Great Year. *Journey to the North* tells an entirely different tale about how Yin Jiao recovered two of his spirit attendants and secured the thirteen skulls he wears around his neck while helping Zhenwu become the Dark Emperor.

Certain strands taken from these descriptions in liturgical manuals, and from these literary narratives—and, doubtless, from other sources lost to us—were selected and somehow woven together to produce the particular hagiography and iconography of Yin Jiao that have come down to Chen Diwen's lineage. Yin Jiao was born into his tenth lifetime as the son of wicked King Zhou after being divinely conceived by the Emperor of the North. Young and upright, Yin Jiao sought patricidal revenge for his slain mother until the righteous master Shen the Realized One turned him toward Daoist practice. Yin struck a series of oaths with his master, realized the Dao, and was canonized ruler of the Earth Ministry and god of the star Great Year in the Emperor of the North's court. Yin Jiao has a boyish face with forked buns of hair and a bare torso, wears a necklace of twelve skulls and a headband of one, and wields a great halberd and golden bell. Much of this story and iconography seem to have come down to the lineage from a particular source—Yin Jiao's hagiography included in the Yuan–Ming *In Search of the Gods,* which itself seems to have fleshed out earlier images of the god expressed in Peng Yuantai's *Great Rite* and in the Pure Tenuity *Upper Clarity Great Rite.* Chen Diwen's ancestral masters seem to have regarded their particular image of Yin Jiao as normative enough to have resisted different representations of him in other ritual traditions, and in Ming vernacular novels.

Yet, this image of Yin Jiao held dear by the lineage was not static. Somewhere along the line, Yin Jiao retained his boyish looks but began receiving blood offerings. Chen Diwen's masters note that Yin Jiao is attracted to bloody wine and meat, especially pork fat (web figure 2.2). In fact, Chen will offer him such treats during the Banner Rite. It might be tempting to interpret Yin Jiao's blood lust as a vestige of an ancient role in some local medium cult, but I prefer to read it according to the sources we have, which speak better to Yin's representation in Chen's lineage. Heart of Heaven master Peng Yuantai insisted that Yin Jiao is a celestial martial deity not to be confused with demonic spirits from the Fengdu underworld. No evidence indicates that Yin Jiao took blood offerings, which tallies with numerous Heart of Heaven prohibitions against blood for the Emperor of the North and his Four Saints. However, Peng Yuantai's image of Yin Jiao was likely influenced by Divine Empyrean notions of thunder gods. Marshals Deng, Xin, and Zhang, celestial thunder gods associated with the highest echelons of the heavenly bureaucracy, did take blood offerings. Perhaps Yin Jiao's earlier Heart of Heaven nature was increasingly influenced by Divine Empyrean notions of thunder gods as his image made its way down to Chen Diwen's lineage. We do not have the sources to know how this might have happened, but we do know that Chen's lineage comfortably holds together the image of Yin Jiao as divine child of the Emperor of the North and youthful prince of King Zhou, and as a bloodthirsty thunder god.

Barend ter Haar notes that although cultural resources tend to change while lending a sense of continuity as different layers of meaning come into being without eradicating those already there—processes of what Prasenjit Duara calls "superscription" and Paul Katz "cogeneration"—local communities select aspects of cultural resources according to locally established traditions and needs.[162] In our case, certain visual and literary depictions of Yin Jiao were chosen by ancestral masters of Chen Diwen's lineage based largely on a certain received theology and on their liturgical needs. Their changing yet seemingly continuous image of Yin Jiao as a halberd and bell-wielding boy sporting skulls won out over competing images. The lineage's evolving yet stable depiction meshed with their belief in the exorcistic power of the Emperor of the North as expressed in the world via thunder gods, a power they were committed to learning how to tap on behalf of their local communities.

Chen Diwen knew nothing of the provenance of his lineage's hagiography of Yin Jiao when he studied it during his training. He did not care about alternatives to the painted iconography of the god on the scroll that hung in altar spaces and on the god's paper image robe that hung from the rafters during liturgies. Chen did not worry that his liturgical ancestors must have made many choices about which stories and images of the god to incorporate into their liturgical tradition. But he was acutely aware that his mastery of Yin Jiao's narrative and iconography was crucial to successfully summon the god during the Banner Rite. "Indeed, the entire story is important because it gives an account of the genealogy [*chumai*] of Yin Jiao," Chen explains. "If you don't know that, how could you possibly move the main marshal [of the Banner Rite] when invoking him?" Like Bai Yuchan in the Southern Song, Chen Diwen understood that knowing about Yin Jiao's pedigree, including his great deeds and what he looks like, constituted ritual success.

The lineage's hagiography and iconography of Yin Jiao are, then, paraliturgies to the Banner Rite. They are accompaniments to the ritual that flesh out Yin Jiao's backstory, which, we shall see, will be directly invoked by Chen Diwen at crucial moments in the Banner Rite. Those accompaniments portray Yin Jiao as a subject. He has a rich narrative history marked by meaningful relationships that have shaped him. He is the divine son and dutiful attendant of the celestial Emperor of the North, and the loyal disciple of Shen the Realized One. And Yin Jiao possesses a certain agency in that he will play an active—and unpredictable—role in the Banner Rite.

The argument of this book is that the Banner Rite is a mode of communication between two subjects—a budding master and a martial deity—by which a relationship between them might be forged. Just as Chen Diwen is a subject with his own story in which he came to be defined by the long lineage of masters before him, so is Yin Jiao a subject with a story in which he was defined by his relationships with the Emperor of the North and with Shen the Realized One. We turn now to explore how both these subjects actively participate in the Banner Rite.

Interlude

By the autumn of 2003, Chen Diwen had been reading and rereading the *Genealogical Investigation* hagiography for some time. He had apprenticed at dozens of Buddhist funerals because demand for them was nearly constant. Although he had apprenticed at far fewer Daoist *jiao*, he felt he had mastered most of the flute parts and the chanted incantations. He observed that the logic and general contours of the various Daoist *jiao* were consistent across purposes, whether for ensuring good health and fortune by dispelling plague deities (*qingjiao* 清醮), for expressing gratitude for favor from a major deity like the Sagely Emperor of the Southern Marchmount or the Bodhisattva Guanyin (*xie'en jiao* 謝恩醮), for making rain (*qiuyu jiao* 求雨醮), for ridding crops of pests (*chonghuang jiao* 蟲蝗醮), for requesting good health or economic prosperity (*shoujiao* 壽醮), for absolving the effects of bad karma by confessing transgressions (*jieyuan jiao* 解冤醮), or for preparing the souls of a deceased person for a Buddhist funeral (*chaowang jiao* 超亡醮). Although Chen had not mastered all the intricacies of the lineage's entire ritual repertoire, he was allowed to officiate over particular rites from time to time during funerals and *jiao*, increasing his confidence through practice. Finally, he felt he had built a foundation strong enough to continue learning as an ordained Daoist-Buddhist master.

An apprentice is expected to approach his transmission master about ordination, so that any decision to be ordained is not foisted upon him. Jiang Yucheng explains:

If you feel things aren't working, that studying [the rites] just isn't for you, you can stop. This is absolutely all right. Your master will not decide for you. You can be ordained only if you yourself decide to do so because after you will bear the responsibility of giving people exorcisms to heal them and of presiding as the main officiant of an entire liturgy.

Masters have occasionally been known to become so frustrated with lazy apprentices that they refuse to continue training them, but that is rare. Typically, a master will train whomever he has agreed to train for as many years as it takes the apprentice to come to a decision. But if that decision is to be ordained, then the master must agree. The considerable pressure to perform the rites competently in public makes apprentices take the decision very seriously.

In December 2003, Chen Diwen approached Li Yezhen and asked to be ordained. Li recalled,

I saw that his flute playing, chanting, and memorization of things were pretty good. You don't have to be entirely proficient to be ordained. But, of course, the apprentice must first wish to be ordained and then his master must agree. Chen Diwen had studied for more than three years and only then requested that his master ordain him. I agreed the first time he asked.

Li then divined an auspicious day on which he would transmit to Chen the crucial esoteric teachings for proper performance of the Banner Rite. We examine the workings of that transmission in some detail in chapter 3.

After that day, Chen Diwen underwent a forty-nine-day retreat (*zhai* 齋), during which he fasted and abstained from sexual activity. He studied daily how to perform the Banner Rite, and with intensity. Finally, on the rainy afternoon of February 19, 2004, the *jiao* to ordain Chen Diwen commenced at his grandfather's hillside home on Mount Xiashan, where Chen had grown up. An altar space had been constructed in the foyer of the house (web figure interlude 1). The first ritual of the three-and-a-half-day ordination *jiao* was the Obeisance to the Family Letter Giving Advance Notice [to the Masters] (Bai yugao jiashu 拜預告家書). By reciting a "family letter" (*jiashu* 家書) and transmitting it to the celestial sphere by burning, Chen's transmission master Li Yezhen reverently alerted all the deceased masters of the lineage to the ordination *jiao* and invited them to the altar space to witness it. The document was addressed to four great realized ones (*si da zhenren* 四大真人)—Shen the Realized One, Sa Shoujian, Wang the Fire Master, and the thirtieth Celestial Master Zhang Jixian—whom the lineage recognizes as the four main ancestral masters or patriarchs of their Daoist tradition. Dozens of additional masters were invited, including several Song and Yuan-era figures discussed in chapter 2—Heart of Heaven patriarchs Tan Zixiao and Rao Dongtian; Divine Empyrean patriarchs Lin Lingsu, Wang Wenqing, and Bai Yuchan; and Peng Yuantai's ancestral master Liao Shouzhen. (Curiously, Peng himself seems to have dropped out of the lineage's memory.) And of course, the rite invited all the deceased masters discussed in chapter 1, who identify with the Daoist lineage poem that has organized the liturgical tradition for twenty generations.

As Li Yezhen called down each master by name, Chen Diwen waited nervously in the wings. All his training—indeed his whole life—would come down to his performance of the Banner Rite during the next hour and a half, in which he would attempt to summon Celestial Lord Yin Jiao so he could become the newest member of the lineage. The sophisticated sequences of the rite were in essence a nuanced mode of communication with Yin Jiao. At the heart of the rite, Chen would produce a talisman on a large blue cloth banner, which would be hoisted from a bamboo pole near the house. If Yin Jiao accepted the summons, he would knot the five streamers cut into the banner as a sign of his pledge to serve the budding master. No knot would mean Yin Jiao had rebuffed the summons and Chen would not be able to be ordained that day. A sloppy, loose knot would signal a less than enthusiastic response from the god. Anything but a well-knotted banner would surely be noticed by the village community, who were keen to discern Chen's liturgical power. His whole livelihood was at stake.

Chapters 3 and 4 ask how the Banner Rite works to compel Yin Jiao—or fails to work—in its own terms. The matter is not as simple as Chen Diwen's straightforwardly invoking the god. In performing the ritual, Chen will work to ensconce himself in a web of relationships around Yin Jiao. Through the power of visualization, Chen will attempt to transform his body and recover his true, primordial self, which can engage the celestial court of the Emperor of the North who directly commands his attendant Yin Jiao. Chen will have to secure from Yin's celestial superior an authoritative decree commanding the martial deity to form an alliance with him. In another crucial moment during the ritual, Chen will need to rely on the intercession of Shen the Realized One, the patriarch of his lineage who bonded with Yin Jiao so many centuries ago. Chen will call on Shen to remind Yin Jiao of the original oath of loyalty they swore, a bond that extends to all of Shen's liturgical progeny, including, hopefully, the lineage's newest prospective member.

This bond is possible only for bona fide members of the lineage. Chen Diwen's master Li Yezhen presented him to the lineage's entire retinue of deceased masters, which has deep and complicated roots in the region. The bond is also available only to those who are worthy. Chen will have to communicate successfully to Yin Jiao his knowledge about the nature and pedigree of the god. Chapter 2 makes it clear that that knowledge is rooted in particular images of Yin Jiao from Song and Yuan visualizations and incantations, as well as from a narrative expressed in a specific Yuan–Ming hagiography.

Implicit through the Banner Rite is a quintessentially Daoist theory accounting for why a mere mortal like Chen Diwen might be able to enter into this divine relationship. The two main subjects of the Banner Rite, as well as the Emperor of the North and Shen the Realized One with whom Chen will need to engage, ultimately originate in a common ancestor: the Dao. At their core, they each share the same undifferentiated stuff or *qi* that emanated from the Dao during the first stages of the cosmogony, and so each are ultimately variegated manifestations of primordial *qi* originating in the source of the world. A crucial moment in the Banner Rite consists of a method by which a practitioner like Chen Diwen can recover his primordial self composed of ancestral *qi*. Because that primordial self shares the same ontological ground as the deities with whom he wishes to communicate, the deep connection between them may be realized. It is their common ontology that allows for communication and relationship.

Our exploration of the Banner Rite will require that we rethink the category "talisman." The written talisman on the banner for which the Banner Rite is named is best understood not as a staid written text, nor even as the material product of the Banner Rite ritual. Instead, the talisman embodies all the ritual processes by which Chen Diwen enters into this particular web of divine relationships in order to forge a bond with Yin Jiao. The talisman is pregnant with all the invocations and visualizations by which Chen attempts to recover his primordial self in order to enter into the relationship between the Emperor of the North and Yin Jiao, and between Shen the Realized One and Yin Jiao. Imbued with the ontological weight of ritually cultivated ancestral *qi*, the talisman is the mode of communication by which Chen expresses his knowledge of Yin Jiao's pedigree in hopes of compelling the god to accept him as a legitimate member of the lineage and so worthy of a direct relationship. The talisman is the physical embodiment of the entire Banner Rite and its ritual goals.

Chapter Three

The Banner Rite

Recovering the Divine Self

> One must become a deity and only then can one communicate with deities.
>
> ——Master Jiang Yucheng (b. 1973)

> I use my primordially destined spirit to summon those spirits of the void emptiness; I use the *qi* of my fundamental body to accord with that *qi* of the void emptiness.
>
> ——Master Wang Wenqing (1093–1153)

At long last and after much preparation, the moment arrives for the Banner Rite to begin. In front of a gradually swelling crowd of extended family and villagers, Chen Diwen dons black robes and takes his place as head officiant facing south in front of the outer altar set up in the foyer of his grandfather's house. He is flanked on both sides by four masters whose rank as "officials of the Dao" (*daoguan*) he hopes to join. With nervous excitement, he takes a deep breath and opens the Banner Rite by bowing toward the five directions as he plays the courtly music that always inaugurates a Daoist rite (web video 3.1).

Then Chen Diwen follows the *Banner Rite* [*to Summon*] *Sire Yin* (*Yingong fanfa*) ritual manual laid out on the altar before him. In the name of his transmission master Li Yezhen, he announces the purpose of the entire ordination, formally called the *Jiao* Event of the Orthodox Teaching of Primordial *Yang* of the Anterior Heaven for [the Purpose of] Knotting the Banner, Manifesting the Dao, Presenting [an Ordinand] for Office, and Seeking a [Liturgical] Name [for Him] (Xiantian yuanyang zhengjiao jiefan xiandao zouzhi qiuming jiaoshi 先天元陽正教結旛顯道奏職求名醮事). Along with his guarantor master Jiang Yeqian on drum and cymbal, Chen invokes the full pantheon of gods recognized by the lineage, which number in the hundreds. They call down each and every deity and deceased master by singing his or her title, alternating between the two of them (web video 3.2). Flute music and reverent bowing follow each grouping of deity: high celestial gods; patriarchs and masters of the liturgical tradition beginning with the first Celestial Master, Zhang Daoling, and ending with the most recently deceased master; martial deities of the celestial Thunder Bureau (minus Yin Jiao); dragon deities and minor thunder deities; and tutelary gods in the realm of the living. Once assembled, Chen offers the large retinue tea and three glasses of wine.

Then Chen Diwen unfolds a document written on yellow paper that his transmission master Li Yezhen has prepared. Speaking for his master in whose voice the document was written, Chen recites the "Dispatch to Inform the Generals" (Baojiang die 報將牒) before the entire pantheon of gathered gods (web video 3.3). In the dialect of the region, he sings the contents of the yellow document, which addresses Yin Jiao and an impressive throng of thunder deities who march under his banner—including Marshals Deng, Xin, and Zhang.[1] Chen Diwen's father, mother, and grandmother kneel and prostrate themselves behind him. At one point during the announcement, Chen's presenting master, Jiang Yucheng, makes a correction in the text—accuracy is important.

Near the beginning of the document, Chen Diwen declares that the dispatch is directed to the "Thunder Department in the Limitless Capital of the Anterior Heaven for the sake of effecting and displaying the heavenly message, of inviting the generals, of knotting the banner, of manifesting the Dao, of presenting [the ordinand] for office, and of petitioning for rank" (先

天無極都雷府為效彰天信、請將、結旛、顯道、奏職、申銜事). The dispatch is Li Yezhen's formal introduction of his ordinand Chen Diwen to Marshal Yin Jiao and his entourage. It places Chen in the context of his lineage, identifying him as a recognized disciple of the Jiang-Li lineage branch. It clearly states that Chen is about to summon Yin Jiao and all the martial deities who march with him. Chen will "first draw [the talisman on] the thunder banner, and then wait for [Yin Jiao] to display his power by knotting [the banner on which will be inscribed] the talismanic graphs" (先畫雷旛，候彰靈於結篆). If that occurs, then the rest of the ordination *jiao* can continue. Chen's masters will present the ordinand's office and rank for recognition by the celestial bureaucracy, which will record them and keep them in their heavenly archives (web figure 3.1).[2]

After Chen reads the dispatch, his presenting master Jiang Yucheng takes it from him and places it in an envelope addressed to the General Governing Office of the Northern Extremity (Beiji zongshe si 北極總攝司), the celestial headquarters to which Yin Jiao belongs. A lay acolyte takes the document outside the altar space into the rain and burns it, transferring it to the celestial office. Meanwhile Chen's two auxiliary masters command officers of merit (*gongcao* 功曹) to carry the dispatch to its heavenly destination. They punctuate their commands by pounding a commanding tablet (*lingpai* 令牌)—a wooden block used to instruct spirits much like a judge uses a gavel—on the altar table and beating the drum.

Chen Diwen now prepares to undertake the heart of the Banner Rite—communication with Yin Jiao in hopes that the martial deity will respond and agree to provide his power to the aspiring young master. But communication with the martial god is complicated. Just as Chen exists in the context of a long lineage, Yin Jiao exists in a matrix of divine relationships. The martial god is bound up with ties of obligation to his celestial superior, the Emperor of the North, and to his own master Shen the Realized One. Cognizant of the polite protocols of the divine bureaucracy, Chen will have to engage both to communicate with Yin Jiao and compel him to reply.

As in any communication, a common ground or foundation must be established between participants for messages to be sent and received with the appropriate timbre. That common ground is ontological. This chapter explores the intricate visualizations and inner alchemical techniques the ordinand Chen Diwen will use to transform his body into a being ontologically capable of communicating with Yin Jiao and the deities associated with him. Chen does not use the visualizations and inner alchemical techniques merely to transform into a deity other than himself, as secondary scholarship has recognized in other liturgical contexts. Instead, Chen takes on divine bodies to recover and cultivate the divine core of his very self, which shares the same stuff, the same primordial *qi,* as the divine bodies of his celestial interlocutors. This primordial stuff emanated from the Dao as it gave birth to the fecund stillness of the first stages of the cosmogony, before patterned movement began to divide the stillness to bring forth the variegated, phenomenal world. As Poul Andersen points out, the theme common to a great many Daoist techniques is that they aim at re-creation through a return to the beginning.[3] Once Chen reunites with the cosmic ancestor, the Dao, and recovers his primordial self, he will be able to channel the primordial *qi* of which it is made to communicate personally first with the Emperor of the North and Yin Jiao's other celestial superiors via direct audience, and then with Shen the Realized One and Yin Jiao himself via talismanic language (chapter 4). It is this common ontology that allows for communication between divine subjects and makes possible the ultimate goal of the Banner Rite—a deep intersubjective relationship between Chen Diwen as his divine, primordial self and Celestial Lord Yin Jiao. Chen's mode of divine communication grounded in a common ontology strongly echoes particular strands of Heart of Heaven and Divine Empyrean ritual theory and practice from the Song and Yuan periods.

Calling upon the *Yuanchen*

After inviting the full pantheon of deities and masters and presenting the "Dispatch to Inform the Generals" document to the proper heavenly bureau, which took a full thirty-five minutes, Chen Diwen retreats from the outer altar and prostrates in front of the main altar in the innermost part of the consecrated space. His concerned master Li Yezhen stands behind him, lending silent support during a crucial visualization that will last almost two minutes. A lay acolyte stands to Chen Diwen's right waiting to collect the divination blocks needed at the end of the visualization (web figure 3.2).

Masters of the lineage refer to this visualization as "calling upon the *yuanchen*" (*kou yuanchen* 叩元辰). The term *yuanchen* here is difficult to translate. In the ritual manuals of Chen Diwen's lineage, as well as in manuals from cousin lineages in Hunan and in texts from the Song and Yuan, the term connotes one's true, primordial self—the deepest, most intimate part of oneself composed of "unified *qi* from the Anterior Heaven" (*Xiantian yiqi* 先天一炁) and so ontologically sharing in its source, the Dao. Chen's entire goal during the phase of the Banner Rite discussed in this chapter is first to call upon or recover (*kou*) his *yuanchen,* and second to mobilize (*yun* 運) and protect (*hu* 護) it so that it may travel to the lofty heavens in order to stand in audience before the high gods. There Chen in the form of his *yuanchen* might personally communicate with the gods to secure their divine decree that Yin Jiao descend and knot the banner.[4]

The "calling upon the *yuanchen*" visualization is the first step by which Chen Diwen attempts to recover his primordial self. The verb *kou,* literally "to knock" or "call upon," carries the senses of visiting, making an inquiry, and kowtowing. The masters of Chen's lineage explain that to call upon the *yuanchen* is to visualize the scene in which an apprentice like Chen Diwen undergoes the most intense moment of his training, when he receives from his transmission master the essential oral transmission (*kouchuan* 口傳)—the esoteric instructions for properly performing the Banner Rite. The masters of the lineage explain that the ordinand should take care to visualize four things: the physical conditions (*qingjing* 情景) in which he received the transmission from his master; the master's invoking the entire lineage of masters; the demeanor of the master when he was transmitting the esoteric instructions; and finally the particular sequence of divination blocks that sealed the transmission process. The masters call this entire scene "receiving the *yuanchen*" (*shou yuanchen* 受元辰). It is the climax of formal training, the point at which an apprentice moves from outer knowledge to inner knowledge, from how to perform the musical and incantatory parts of a given ritual and knowledge of

Yin Jiao's pedigree as per the lineage's *Genealogical Investigation* hagiography, to inner knowledge of how actually to summon and command Yin Jiao in ritual. It is the day on which an apprentice (*tudi* 徒弟) formally becomes an ordinand, a "disciple initially presented" (*chucheng dizi* 初承弟子, *xincheng dizi* 新承弟子) to the gods and ancestral masters for official acceptance into the lineage at an ordination *jiao* in the near future.

As Chen Diwen is prostrating in front of the main altar, he brings to his mind's eye the afternoon of January 7, 2004, when he received the secret oral transmission from Li Yezhen. First he visualizes the physical conditions of the event down to the lighting, temperature, and physical objects in the quiet room in his grandfather's house where just he and his transmission master were sitting. Then he imagines how his master, whispering, invited the entire lineage of ancestral masters down to the room to witness the solemn transmission. Chen takes care to recall the eight characters denoting the times of birth (*shengchen bazi* 生辰八字) of Li Yezhen's own immediate lineage of deceased masters—his transmission master (*dushi*) Li Shenming, that master's master (known as the master of the registry [*jishi* 籍師]) Li Feimao, and that master's master (known as the master of the canon [*jingshi* 經師]) Li Manjuan (see appendix). Jiang Yucheng explains that the ordinand recalls the times of birth of these three generations of his master's masters because they are his immediate links to the entire lineage, which has kept the esoteric teachings, the contents of the transmission, for centuries. That transmission consists of a "heart-to-heart conferral as oral transmission" (*kouchuan xinshou* 口傳心授) of ritual know-how from master to apprentice.

Continuing to prostrate himself in front of the main altar, Chen Diwen visualizes as best he can every detail about his master Li Yezhen's physical demeanor at the moment he transmitted the esoteric teachings. Chen imagines his master's facial expressions and tone of voice. The masters of the lineage explain that the entire oral transmission is far too rich to run through while an ordinand is prostrating and calling upon the *yuanchen,* so he visualizes his master's face and voice as symbols or manifestations of the whole of the esoteric teachings. The secret instructions received on the day of transmission actually consisted of Li Yezhen's slowly reading through the lineage's most precious theoretical text—the *Secret Transmission of Primordial Qi from the Anterior Heaven [as Revealed] by Patriarch Lü* (*Lüzu xiantian zuqi michuan* 呂祖先天祖炁密傳)—attributed to the purported late Tang or early Song transcendent Lü Dongbin (呂洞賓).[5] Li fleshed out crucial moments in the text by whispering to Chen oral instructions for actually performing the ritual sequences for taking on the bodies of various divine beings and for recovering and mobilizing the primordial self, both of which we shall examine below. Although Li did not confidently understand whole swaths of the theoretical text, he diligently explained to Chen how to do the series of visualizations, incantations, and hand mudras as his own master taught him.

Next, they worked through the *Banner Rite [to Summon] Sire Yin* manual. Again Li Yezhen augmented the lean text with oral instructions for ritual actions that should accompany the long written talisman with which to call Yin Jiao to service. And again without certain theoretical knowledge of every ritual moment, Li whispered how to augment the writing of particular talismanic graphs recorded in the text with incantations and visualizations his master had orally taught him. The masters of the lineage explain that simply performing the Banner Rite according to the ritual manual alone would not produce an efficacious result. One must supplement the *Banner Rite* text with the secret instructions orally transmitted by one's master. Like two halves of a whole, the oral instructions complete the ritual text and make viable the actual ritual performance.

Still prostrating in front of the main altar, Chen Diwen concludes by visualizing the particular sequence of divination blocks that marked the end of the transmission. He brings to mind how Li Yezhen, with whispered tones, had formally notified the entire lineage of witnessing masters, and especially the previous three generations of his own masters, that he had just transmitted the lineage's most precious ritual knowledge to his apprentice. He recalls how Li then prayed for their support. Jiang Yucheng explains, "The transmission master needs to ask that the ancestral masters will help the apprentice possess extremely efficacious *qi*. If the apprentice calls for the masters a thousand times, they will respond a thousand times; if he calls for them ten thousand times, they will quickly respond ten thousand times."

Jiang explains that an officiant never really practices a ritual alone. He is always supported by the entire lineage of deceased masters, whose witness is a sine qua non for ritual efficacy.

To garner their collective blessing of the transmission, Li Yezhen threw moon-shaped divination blocks (*cigua* 賜卦) three times (web figure 3.3). The masters explain that there is no better or worse combination of results. Two blocks facing up (*yanggua* 陽卦), two facing down (*yingua* 陰卦), and one up and one down (*shenggua* 勝卦) are all admissible. Each of the three results correlates with a congratulatory saying foretelling the general character of the future career of the apprentice. While prostrating in front of the altar, Chen Diwen remembers the three blocks that came up for him and their corresponding sayings. On the first toss, he received two blocks facing up, meaning "incense fires would pass through" (香火通行), that is, Chen's liturgical intentions would penetrate the celestial spheres and be heard by the gods. On the second toss, he received one block up and one down, which indicates that in liturgical affairs he would achieve "a hundred battles, a hundred victories" (百戰百勝). Finally, he received two blocks facing down, which means Chen would "be supported by [the deceased masters of the lineage in] the unseen world " (陰中扶助).[6] The masters in the lineage explain that one's particular sequence of divination blocks and their concomitant sayings constitute a kind of sworn allegiance. They are signs that the apprentice has promised to guard and responsibly practice the esoteric teachings he learned that day from his transmission master, and by extension from the entire lineage of deceased masters. The masters have in turn pledged to support the newest member of the lineage when he puts that secret knowledge into practice.

Still kneeling in front of the altar, Chen Diwen visualizes the last thing his master told him the day of the transmission. He vividly recalls how sternly Li Yezhen looked into his eyes as he said, "If you follow what I have taught you and do as I have said, if you remember the entire scene today and the divination blocks your master gave you, then you will be efficacious every time." Then Chen throws divination blocks on the floor in front of the altar to confirm that the ancestral masters continue to support him in his inaugural performance of the Banner Rite at his ordination *jiao*. He needs two blocks down (*yingua*) to signal confirmation. The first three tosses do not come up well. After each, Chen silently but intensely implores the deceased masters to support him. If the proper blocks fail to come up after several more tosses, Chen would have to redo the entire sequence of visualizations and throw the blocks again. Such an awkward delay would surely cast doubt on Chen's liturgical prowess among the sizable crowd gathered to witness his performance of the Banner Rite. Thankfully the right blocks come up on Chen's fourth toss. He and his master standing behind him are visibly relieved, and Chen returns to the outer altar to continue the ritual.

Esoteric Transmissions

It is not coincidental that the transmission process itself is shot through with secrecy. The intimate setting of just an apprentice and his master, the witness of the lineage's deceased masters, the emphasis on orality, the pledges of responsibility and support, and the highly guarded nature of the teachings themselves have all been hallmarks of the older liturgical traditions that shaped the living tradition Chen Diwen was trying to enter. Scholar Chang Ch'ao-jan has shown that already by the early medieval period, the Shangqing tradition—a source of inspiration for the Emperor of the North cults and Heart of Heaven traditions in which the Banner Rite is rooted—stressed that passing down teachings from masters to disciples ought to be "inner transmissions" (*neichuan* 內傳) consisting of oral teachings.[7] These operations were modeled on the divine transmissions to future Shangqing matriarch Wei Huacun, in which various realized ones (*zhenren*) descended to her private chamber and orally dictated scriptures to her. Later, the tradition established rules safeguarding secret transmission of teachings within the world. A master and disciple must "strike a covenant according to the regulations, make a vow, and only then hand over [the teachings]" (依科立盟，結誓而付). A disciple must swear not to leak the contents of the transmission to outsiders lest "he be born an inferior demon who will be tortured with daggers that cut like the wind" (身為下鬼，拷以風刀).[8] Chang

Ch'ao-jan supposes that Shangqing practitioners' insistence on the private nature and oral mode of passing on teachings, and their compulsion to strike binding oaths to safeguard those teachings, suggest that it was the experience of a close, personal relationship between master and disciple that made the transmissions "inner."[9]

The various liturgical traditions in the Song–Yuan period that have shaped the Banner Rite continued the Shangqing tradition's ethos of inner transmission. The "Preface to the Nine Essentials of Daoist Methods" (Daofa jiuyao xu 道法九要序), attributed to Bai Yuchan, asserts that the secrets of the Dao ultimately reside in masters' hearts and not in texts:

> Although the ancestral masters of high antiquity had trunks and crates full of numinous texts, they kept them [merely] to guide benighted commoners and to instruct future generations of students. [People] do not know that the hearts of masters possess the mystery of the utmost One, and [that masters] do not let people experience [it]. Even demons and deities do not know the crux of the matter. Employing the masters' mystery would certainly have resonance [efficacy].[10]

> 蓋上古祖師，雖有盈箱滿篋靈書，留之引導凡愚，開發後學。不知師心自有至一之妙，不教人見聞。鬼神亦不知其機。用之則有感通。

The essential mystery locked away in masters' hearts could only be orally taught by masters themselves. The *Hidden Texts of the Thunder Crystal of the Anterior Heaven,* a compilation of Southern Song and Yuan Divine Empyrean texts claiming association with Wang Wenqing, refers to a particular inner alchemical teaching as a "secret of heaven" (*tianji* 天機). "It cannot be transmitted by writing; [the teaching] resides in the wonder of mouth-to-mouth conferral from the heart, [it resides] in the truth of pointing it out to one's ears and telling it to one's face" (不可以文字而傳，在口口心授之妙，耳提面命之真).[11]

All this emphasis on face-to-face, heart-to-heart oral transmission created a taboo on writing the secret teachings. Song and Yuan ritual texts are rife with anxious explanations for why masters decided to break the taboo and commit the teachings to paper. Masters made clear to themselves, to readers, and to deceased masters that their good intentions should exempt them from heavenly punishment. For example, in a text included in the *Hidden Texts of the Thunder Crystal of the Anterior Heaven,* a master who went by Min Bin the Iron-Hearted Man of the Dao (Tiexin daoren Min Bin 鐵心道人閔霖) comments on why he decided to write the "usage of internal secrets" (*neimi yongfa* 內密用法):

> This method is of utmost secrecy and mystery; it is something scarcely seen in the world. . . . Now due to karmic causes conferred by Heaven I have secretly received [the secrets]. I professed over and over again that I would not lightly divulge them. Now I fear that over a long period of time [the secrets] will be forgotten and lost, and I worry that later disciples will not receive the transmission. So I write them down on paper. I record every detail of the mystery of the oral instructions and heart transmission, and attach them to the inner secrets. I give them to apprentices so the lineage bequeathed to them may be continued. The writings should be cherished and passed down; they should not be regarded as ordinary ritual methods. Keep them in secret! Keep them in secret! Should one lightly divulge, leak, or neglect them, not only will one fall into the earth prisons, but this misfortune will extend to seven generations of one's ancestors—an inevitable condemnation by Heaven![12]

> 此之一法至秘至玄，世所罕見……今霖天假因緣，得其密受，祝之再三，幸勿輕泄。今切恐其久而忘失，又應後學無傳。故筆之於書。備載口授心傳之玄而附于內秘之末，以授弟子，以續遺派。宜珍襲之，幸勿目以尋常之法。秘之秘之！輕泄漏慢，豈特身墮地獄，而禍及七祖翁，則天之譴者必然也。

This nervous master put his lineage's oral teachings to paper to safeguard the secrets over the vicissitudes of time. Jiang Shenzhi of Chen Diwen's lineage did the same thing. When redacting the *Banner Rite [to Summon] Sire Yin* in 1989, he made the decision to transcribe clearly the secret oral teachings that augment the text because almost all younger masters, including his grandson Jiang Yucheng, were spending so much time away from home working as migrant laborers. He feared the crucial oral component of the Banner Rite, traditionally transmitted during the process of receiving the *yuanchen,* would erode and so he took measures to codify it in text. We saw that Peng Yuantai decided to write down the *Great Rite* in 1274 for another reason. He felt he needed to create an orthodox Heart of Heaven text as a counter to heterodox texts floating about Hunan, which he charged were written by deluded "seeds of Fengdu" who blithely mistook Yin Jiao for a terrestrial deity. Although he had a righteous reason, Peng was still compelled to tell his readers that he "must certainly be exempted from the so-called offense of leaking" the contents of the ritual onto paper, which ran much greater risk of escaping the lineage's control than strictly oral teachings.

In the quoted passage, Min Bin the Iron-Hearted Man of the Dao stresses that the ritual texts he created should themselves be kept in secret and passed down within the lineage. In effect, he extends the taboo from divulging the oral transmission to divulging the texts recording those transmissions. The heavenly punishment for allowing the texts to leak to outsiders was harsh indeed—unfavorable rebirth in the earth prisons for oneself and for seven generations of one's ancestors. Passages like this suggest that the incredible proliferation of rituals during the Song–Yuan period must have intensified as oral transmissions were put to paper and inevitably made their way to those outside the hermeneutic control of lineages.

So we see masters work hard to reconnect ritual texts with their original oral transmissions residing in a master within a lineage that could trace itself back to a patriarch who received a revelation. Distinguishing his 1274 *Great Rite* ritual text from various others claiming to instruct how to summon Yin Jiao, Peng Yuantai asserts, "The mystery and wonder of this ritual method is that all of it is orally transmitted from master to master. It is in fact a treasure from the upper heavens, scarcely known by mortals" (是法之玄妙，皆師師口傳，實上天之寶，人所罕知).[13] Liu Yu, master of Divine Empyrean, Fengdu, and earth spirits rites, insists that an authentic ritual text be grounded in oral teachings gained through some initiation process within an established lineage. To operate without proper oral teachings not only renders the ritual text inefficacious, but also invites serious harm from demonic agents.

> Only from a source does [a stream] flow, so when practicing a ritual one must clarify its lineage. If the lineage is not authentic then the general [summoned] is unorthodox. What does "unorthodox" mean? If some itinerant practitioner of rituals accidentally happens upon a desperate situation [requiring a ritual

response], he might possess [a copy of] this text without first receiving [oral] instruction. He might say he has been recommended [by masters], has petitioned [high gods], and has received transmission, but in fact no general has been conferred [to him]. A demonic spirit might take advantage of this to steal [the general's] name and claim his position and so act as the general. The harm of this cannot be expressed in words, and the karmic consequences incurred could not be weightier![14]

有源斯流，行法須明派，派不真則將不正。何謂不正？假如江湖法友，偶墮窮途，雖有此文，元無撥受。名曰保明奏度，實則無將可傳。鬼神因而盜名竊位而為將，其害不可勝言，而招因果亦不勝其重。

These concerns with secrecy safeguarded by oral teachings within the confines of a specific lineage, so deeply rooted in Song and earlier traditions, have made their way down to Chen Diwen's lineage and into the very fabric of the Banner Rite. That the Banner Rite begins with an intense visualization of moments during the secret oral transmission of how to perform the Banner Rite itself is a remarkable moment of self-reflexivity. Performing the Banner Rite to communicate with Yin Jiao and the gods around him is the substantive core of this lineage's Daoist identity. It is the liturgical know-how that connects a master with the long line of masters in the past. Chen's performance of the recovering the *yuanchen* sequence connects his performance of the Banner Rite with all previous performances by the long lineage of liturgical ancestors before him. Chen repeatedly says, "Our masters support us" and "our liturgical power [*lingqi*] comes from our masters." Chen means that he does not practice the Banner Rite alone. He garners the support of all the masters who have ever practiced it. He taps into the reassurance generated by their collective practice as he begins to recover his primordial self and use it to communicate with Yin Jiao.

Transforming into a Divine Body

After calling upon the *yuanchen* and returning to the outer altar, Chen Diwen takes a deep breath to gather himself and then launches into an intense sequence called the "transformation into a divine body" (*bianshen*

變神／變身). Over the course of a little more than three minutes, Chen will visualize that he forms a fiery cocoon around him within which he completely destroys his mundane body with fire. From the ashes will emerge the-body of the first Celestial Master, Zhang Daoling. As the body of Zhang Daoling, Chen will then conceive, gestate, and give birth to an even loftier deity, the Dark Emperor Zhenwu, whose body will envelope his and thereby transform it into the rarified body of that high god. This transformation-of-the-body sequence is deeply grounded in Song–Yuan liturgical traditions, especially Heart of Heaven practice.

In the first minute of the sequence, one can observe the ritual trappings that frame Chen Diwen's work (web video 3.4). Conspicuous gong and cymbal music drones on in the background. There is no courtly flute music to please the gods and deceased masters as during the preliminary phases of the Banner Rite when Chen invited the entire pantheon to witness his performance. Instead only a monotonous, percussive rhythm accompanies the ritual action, which signals that the officiant must sustain a high level of concentration.[15] As Chen works through the sequence, his presenting master, Jiang Yucheng, busily prepares the pennants of the banner. Throughout the sequence, Jiang looks on to ensure that Chen does not commit any major gaffes. Although Chen spent forty-nine days memorizing and practicing the Banner Rite, the ritual manual remains open on the altar table in front of him. Notice that Jiang points to the liturgical manual when Chen seems to get stuck, and at one point orally reminds him how to conclude a ritual segment. The support of the masters extends even to the ordinand's actual performance of the Banner Rite in real time.

Golden Radiance

Chen Diwen begins the transformation of his body with an incantation, which is accompanied by his "walking along a guideline" (*bugang*) with his left thumb pressing on points in the palm of his left hand. He traces out a cosmic pattern while sotto voce chanting the incantation. The *Banner Rite* manual refers to this incantation as the *Palm Tracing of Golden Radiance* (*Jinguang zhang* 金光掌) (web video 3.4 [0:00 to 0:16]). Chen intones,

Mysterious ancestor of Heaven and Earth, fundamental root of variegated *qi,* [which exists] long and broad [over] vast *kalpas,* confirm my divine power.[16] Within and without the three realms only the Dao is honored. The body [of the Dao] possesses golden radiance, [which] covers and illumines my body. Neither visible to the eyes nor audible to the ears, [its] form envelopes Heaven and Earth and nourishes all living things. [I] sing [this hymn] one time and my body possesses radiant illumination. The Three Realms serve and guard me, the Five Emperors greet me, and the myriad deities salute me. [When I] employ the thunderclap, demons and sprites lose their gall, and [noxious] essences and sprites disappear. Within there is the thunderclap and the hidden names of thunder deities; cavernous wisdom penetrates and the five modes of *qi* soar and soar. Golden radiance, quickly appear! Cover and protect my body! [see figure 3.1][17]

天地玄宗子，萬氣本根丑，廣修浩劫寅，證吾神通卯。三界內外
辰，唯道獨尊巳。體有金光午，覆映吾身本命。視之不見丑，聽之
不聞未，包羅天地兌，養育群生子。持誦一篇離，身有光明午。
三界侍衛離，五帝司迎本命，萬神朝禮本命。役使雷霆震，鬼妖喪
膽艮，精怪亡形艮。內有霹靂震，雷神隱名震，洞慧交徹辰，五
炁騰騰巳。金光速現午，覆護吾身本命。

This incantation calling upon an invisible and inaudible manifestation of the Dao as golden radiance that envelopes the officiant's body appears widely in Song and Yuan rituals. One of the earliest, nominally datable texts that uses the incantation is the *Primordial Petition of the Thunder Crystal of the Nine Heavens* (*Jiutian leijing yuanzhang* 九天雷晶元章), a Divine Empyrean text from the Yuan or Southern Song. This text includes an *Incantation of the Smaller Golden Radiance* (*Xiao jinguang zhou* 小金光咒), which is nearly identical to that preserved by Chen Diwen's lineage.[18]

According to the oral teaching accompanying the Banner Rite, Chen Diwen touches with his thumb a specific joint on the fingers of his left hand as he utters each phrase of the incantation, which in the passage I indicate with characters in reduced type size. Pressing on his palm in this way—activating an oral instruction by literally "pinching the instruction" (*qiajue* 掐訣) with the fingers to form a hand gesture or mudra—is here a manual form of "walking along a guideline" (*bugang*), or taking a ritual walk or dance that traces cosmic patterns with the feet on the ground or with the thumb in the

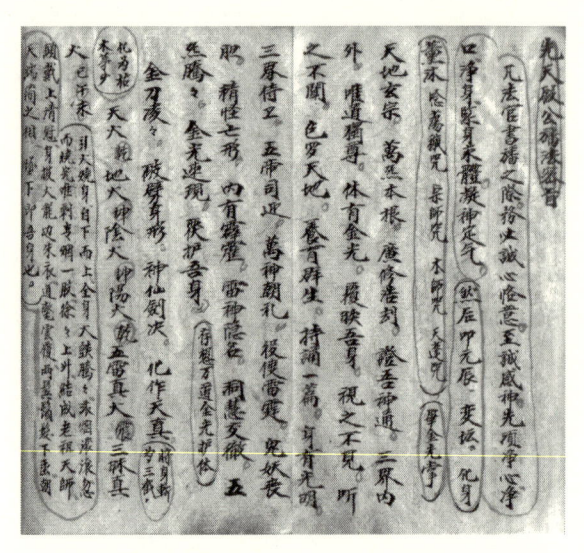

Figure. 3.1 Instructions and incantations for transforming into the divine body of Zhang Daoling in the *Banner Rite* manual, opened in front of Chen Diwen on the altar. Scan by the author.

palm of the hand. Often the thumb and foot move together synchronously, but at times, as in this case, the officiant uses only his left hand, which is why the ritual sequence is here called a "palm tracing" (*zhang* 掌) instead of a "walk" or "step" (*bu* 步).[19]

In the practice of tracing a pattern on the palm, Chen Diwen literally holds the cosmos in the palm of his hand. The points on the joints of his fingers correlate with the spatial organization of his body and the cosmos according to the terrestrial branches (*dizhi* 地支) and/or with the symbolic order of the eight trigrams (*bagua* 八卦) arrayed in their Posterior Heaven arrangement (web figure 3.4).[20] Chen activates energies associated with specific areas of his body and specific regions of the cosmos by touching points, called "palaces" (*gong* 宮), on his left hand with his left thumb. Other than touching the palace on the palm commonly associated with the content of the particular phrase in the incantation—such as touching the "thunder palace" (*zhengong* 震宮) on the middle joint of the index finger when mentioning thunder, or the "palace of fundamental destiny" (*benming gong* 本命宮) on the middle joint of the middle finger when mentioning his own body—I cannot discern a meaningful pattern—or more likely patterns—that Chen's walk along the guideline might trace. Nonetheless, as he presses each of the points on the palm of his hand during the "walk," he activates visualizations and breath circulations in his body that correspond with spatial and temporal points in the cosmos. Chen's walking the guideline activates forces within his body and in the cosmos that generate the golden radiance that eventually envelopes his body.[21]

The golden radiance invoked by the incantation and tracing on the palm is imagined as a luminous glow associated with the body of the Dao, here characterized as the ancient ancestor of heaven and earth, and the root of the myriad grades of *qi* that make up the phenomenal world. By intoning the incantation and tracing the guideline, Chen Diwen invokes the golden radiance of the body of the Dao to envelop his own body like a halo. Neither visible nor audible yet encompassing heaven and earth with its nourishing glow, the golden radiance imbues Chen's body with qualities of the divine. He gains the respect of celestial lords as he brandishes his potential to transform his mortal body into a divine body.[22]

On completing the incantation, Chen Diwen follows the instruction in the *Banner Rite* manual to "visualize that the ten thousand rays of golden radiance protect the body" (存想万道金光護體) (see figure 3.1).[23] From what might the body require protection? The Song–Yuan *Primordial Petition of the Thunder Crystal of the Nine Heavens* text lends some insight. After directing the practitioner to intone the *Incantation of the Smaller Golden Radiance*, that manual instructs him to "visualize his body within the golden radiance so that he might transform his spirit and become a true person" (存身在金光之內，變神為真人).[24] The golden radiance forms a cocoon of light within which the practitioner's mundane body will undergo the process of transforming into a divine body. Chen Diwen's body is about to undergo a violent transformation in which it will be incinerated and then arise from the ashes as a body of a divine being. The golden radiance Chen visualizes protecting his body forms a cocoon or womb of brilliant light within which his mortal body will undergo the transformation and be reborn reunited with the great ancestor, the Dao.

Incinerating the Mundane Body

Chen Diwen begins the radical transformation by destroying his mundane body (web video 3.4 [0:16–0:42]). Notice that Chen gets a bit lost here and his presenting master, Jiang Yucheng, points to the proper place in the manual where Chen should be. Regaining his focus, Chen raises the golden blade mudra (*jindao jue* 金刀訣)—the first two fingers of his left hand—under the sleeve of his robe and visualizes that he slices his body into parts as he incants,

> Golden blade be raised, break and split [my] physical form. Sword mudra of divine transcendents, transform [me] into a celestial true person! [see figure 3.1][25]
>
> 金刀凌凌，破劈身形。神仙劍決〔訣〕，化作天真。

With taps to his waist and abdomen with the golden blade as he incants, Chen visualizes that he hacks his body into three large pieces and then imagines them as dry as bundles of withered wood (*kumu* 枯木) and hay (*maocao* 茅草).[26]

Chen then activates flames associated with various parts of his own body and the cosmos and visualizes that he ignites his dry, withered body as one sparks kindling for a fire. He incants:

> Fire of heaven, fire of earth, fire of *yin,* fire of *yang,* true fire of the five thunders, true fire of *samādhi.*[27]
>
> 天火乾，地火坤，陰火坤，陽火乾，五雷真火震，三昧真火巳午未。

As he utters each phrase, Chen activates fire by using his left thumb to press on several "palaces" on his left palm. He activates the fire of heaven by activating the *qian* 乾 palace associated with heaven, and the fire of earth by activating the *kun* 坤 palace associated with earth. He does the same for the fire of *yin* and *yang.* He touches the *zhen* 震 palace, associated with thunder, to activate the fire of the five thunders, and the *si* 巳, *wu* 午, and *wei* 未 palaces, each associated with the heart and the element of fire, to activate the fire of *samādhi* concentration (web figure 3.4).

The details of this visualization—using a sword mudra to hack apart the officiant's body as if it were bundles of wood and hay and then incinerating them—were hallmarks of both Heart of Heaven and Divine Empyrean practice. We saw in chapter 2 that the Heart of Heaven tradition emphasized several inner cultivations, such as the daily imbibing of *qi* emanating from the Three Radiants—the sun, moon, and stars of the Northern Dipper. Among those cultivations, rites to transform the body into that of a deity (*bianshen*) were crucial liturgical ways to request that the Emperor of the North in his stellar Palace of Purple Tenuity dispatch the mighty general Tianpeng and the rest of the Four Saints from their headquarters in the Department of Exorcism of the Northern Extremity. The process of transforming the body included the imaginative incineration of the practitioner's mundane body. In his *Correct Rites of the Heart of Heaven of the Shangqing Tradition,* Deng Yougong instructs the practitioner to burn incense, chant incantations to purify the altar, and then "visualize his body as a withered tree" (存本身如枯樹). He should "draw fire from the heart, which burns from the heart toward the crown of the head" (引心火，自心前燒至頂門), and then "visualize the fire burning his body" (存火燒身). Finally, he should blow breath from his mouth while "visualizing the ashes being completely cleared away" (存灰燼蕩盡).[28]

A similar practice is found in the *Preface to the Abstruse Directives of the Thunderclap from Wang the Fire Master,* a foundational Divine Empyrean text. As discussed in chapter 2, the text claims to record teachings transmitted to Wang Wenqing by Wang the Fire Master. The text was annotated by Zhu Zhizhong in 1104, who likely studied from Wang Wenqing himself, and then Bai Yuchan wrote an introduction to the text in the late twelfth or early thirteenth century. In the text, Wang the Fire Master gives the following instructions:

> Visualize with your eyes and heart while intoning the true incantation. Hold in your hands a party of thunder deities without allowing delay [from any of them]. Transform into a deity and summon the generals just as was done in the past. In the void [in front of you] draw a talismanic order to lay the foundation of [inner] alchemy.

目想心存念真咒，手握雷局無令遲。變神召將一如故，虛書符命下
丹基。

Zhu Zhizhong offers an annotation to this instruction: "[To perform]
the method of transforming into a deity, first [visualize that] the flying
Dipper asterism covers your body. Then form the transforming-into-a-deity
mudra by pressing fingers into the palm, and visualize that one's own body
transforms into withered wood" (變神之法，先飛斗一座蓋身，次掐變神
訣，存己身變成枯木). After breathing in *qi* and generating internal sparks,
the practitioner should then "emit fire and completely reduce [the wood] to
ashes and cinder" (發火徧燒為灰燼). Then the practitioner should press the
xun palace on his palm to "raise wind from the *xun* direction, which comes
from the southeast and blows away the ashes and cinder" (起巽風，自東南來
吹蕩灰燼).[29]

This sort of visualization practice to incinerate the body penetrated
various liturgical traditions due to the pervasive influence of Heart of Heaven
and Divine Empyrean ritual during the Southern Song, Yuan, and early
Ming periods. For example, similar instructions are given in the *Secret Ritual
Method [to Summon] Marshal Zhao of the Mysterious Altar of Orthodox Unity*—
a Zhengyi ritual method designed to call Marshal Zhao Gongming, who was
said to serve the first Celestial Master, Zhang Daoling. "Visualize your own
body as a thousand-year-old withered tree or tens-of-thousands-of-years-old
withered wood" (存自身為千年枯樹萬年枯木). Then the practitioner ought to
employ the "five fires mudra" (*wuhuo jue* 五火訣) and "visualize that the five
fires burn the body to ashes, and then raise wind from the *xun* direction to
blow away the ashes" (存五火燒身，化為灰，起巽風吹過其灰).[30]

Much as these Heart of Heaven, Divine Empyrean, and Zhengyi ritual
sequences do, Chen Diwen visualizes that he internally generates fire by
touching his thumb to certain points on his left palm and then allows the
conflagration to burn away his desiccated body. According to the logic of the
Banner Rite, the annihilation of Chen's mundane body is a precondition for
his acquiring a divine body during the next steps of the transformation of the
body sequence. Like a dying tree, the body must be reduced to ashes so that
one's primordial spirit—one's *yuanchen*—might be recovered and manifest as
a new, divine body capable of communicating with high gods.[31]

Transformation into the Body of Zhang Daoling

Having sparked multiple internal fires, Chen Diwen rolls his eyes back into his head as he visualizes images according to the instructions given in the *Banner Rite* manual (web video 3.4 [0:42–end]):

> Draw the fire to incinerate the body. From bottom to top, flames from the entire body rise and rise, and dense smoke billows and billows. Suddenly [the flames] burn out and only one puff of azure smoke remains. Slowly, slowly [it] rises upward and congeals into the Celestial Master, the Old Patriarch. [see figure 3.1][32]

> 引火燒身，自下而上，全身火燄騰騰，濃煙滾滾，忽而燒完，唯剩青煙一股，徐徐上升，結成老祖天師。

Out of the smoke of Chen's consumed body emerges the second-century patriarch of the Zhengyi tradition with which Chen's lineage identifies, Zhang Daoling. Following the manual, Chen visualizes the precise appearance of the first Celestial Master:

> [His] head dons the crown of Upper Clarity, [his] body is clad in a vermillion robe bordered by a fiery dragon, [and] a Daoist robe with feather trimmings and cloud shoes [i.e., shoes curled like clouds at their tips]. Two sideburns, a beard, and hair hang down and [he has] the appearance of one who holds a tablet in an audience with Heaven. [His body] descends and is my body.[33]

> 頭戴上清冠，身披火龍邊朱衣，道氅雲履，兩鬢鬚髮下垂，朝天端簡之相，墜下即吾身也。

In startling detail, Chen Diwen visualizes Zhang Daoling emerge from the conflagration of his own body and then descend downward again to take the place of his original body. To ordinary eyes, Chen remains in the altar space, neither in trance nor noticeably altered. But to extraordinary eyes, Chen has, within the safety of the halo of golden radiance enveloping him, destroyed his mundane form and replaced it with the body of a notable deity. This divine body is composed of *qi* far more resonant with the ultra-rarified ancestral *qi* generated by the Dao at the origin of the cosmos. Chen has just moved one step closer to the Dao, and therefore one step closer to access to the high celestial palace where he hopes to have an audience before high gods and present his petition that the Celestial Lord Yin Jiao be ordered to descend to the ordination *jiao.*

That Chen Diwen takes on the specific body of Zhang Daoling is significant here. Andersen has noticed that both in Song-era Heart of Heaven texts and in present-day ritual in Tainan, the deity impersonated by the officiant is very often the first patriarch of the lineage's ritual tradition or the deity who is thought to have transmitted those rituals to the world.[34] Li Zhihong notes that since the Song liturgical traditions have regarded a particular deity as the initiator of a tradition and later generations of patriarchs as transmitters of that initial teaching. Practitioners often activated points on the palm of their hand while intoning incantations and visualizing that they transform their own bodies into those patriarchs. By morphing an ordinary body into the extraordinary body of a patriarch, practitioners relied on the authority of the patriarch to conduct a ritual that summoned and deployed both demons and deities.[35]

We saw in chapter 2 that the Heart of Heaven tradition claimed to have originally been transmitted by the first Celestial Master, Zhang Daoling. Its practices are peppered with vivid instructions for taking on the body of that patriarch. One of the more vivid instructions appears in the *Secret Essentials of the Most High for Assembling the Realized Ones for Assisting the Country and Saving Its People,* in which Miao Yuanzhong instructs the practitioner to "visualize that one's own body becomes the Commissioner of the Department of Exorcism of the Northern Extremity [Zhang Daoling], whose left hand holds the official seal of the great ritual methods of all the heavens, and whose right hand brandishes the fire-bell sword of *samādhi.* [The Commissioner] appears in the regalia of the Realized One of the Orthodox Unity of the Three Heavens, with a crown of interpenetrating tranquility, a fish-finned robe, and red boots with black toes" (存己身為北極驅邪院使 左手執都天大法主印，右手仗三昧火鈴劍，如三天正一真人服飾 交泰冠，魚鬣服，烏爪朱履).[36]

It is not surprising that Zhang Daoling plays a conspicuous role in the transformation of the body ritual sequence in Chen Diwen's lineage. As discussed chapter 2, the lineage seems to have inherited much of the liturgical tradition articulated by Peng Yuantai's 1274 *Great Rite* text, which saw itself belonging to a Heart of Heaven lineage descending from Liao Shouzhen in the late twelfth or early thirteenth century, and ultimately from the mysterious Shen the Realized One before that. Given the Heart of Heaven tradition's insistence that its origin lies in Zhang Daoling, it makes sense that Chen's lineage has also viewed Zhang Daoling as an early patriarch and so visualizes taking on his body during the transformation of the body sequence.

Another accounting for the prevalence of Zhang Daoling here is possible. As discussed in chapter 1, a nineteenth-century manual preserved by Chen Diwen's lineage claims their Daoist tradition descended from the Celestial Masters in Jiangxi who established the Jade Void Palace in Xinhua county, which then branched out to six houses throughout Hunan. As the Zhengyi tradition led by the Celestial Masters headquartered on Mount Longhu in Jiangxi gained political prominence during the late Southern Song, Yuan, and into the Ming dynasties, they wielded mighty influence throughout south China. Whether the lineage's text is historically accurate that Celestial Masters actually came to Xinhua to establish a temple, or whether it is an anachronistic tale seeking official legitimation by practitioners of a local cult, the Celestial Masters and their patriarch Zhang Daoling have loomed large in Daoist practice across south China, including that of Chen's lineage. Whatever the reason, the lineage identifies Zhang Daoling as the first patriarch of its ritual tradition and so it makes liturgical sense that officiants take on the body of the first Celestial Master.

Transformation into the Body of the Dark Emperor

Chen Diwen-cum-Zhang Daoling proceeds to engage in an inner alchemical procedure that will transform his already deified body into the body of an even more ethereal deity, the Dark Emperor (Xuandi 玄帝), also known as Zhenwu 真武, the True Warrior (web video 3.5 [0:00–0:57]). Following his liturgical manual, Chen forms the "jade trace" (*yuwen* 玉文) mudra with his two hands in front of his chest and, using his "celestial eye" (*tianmu* 天目)

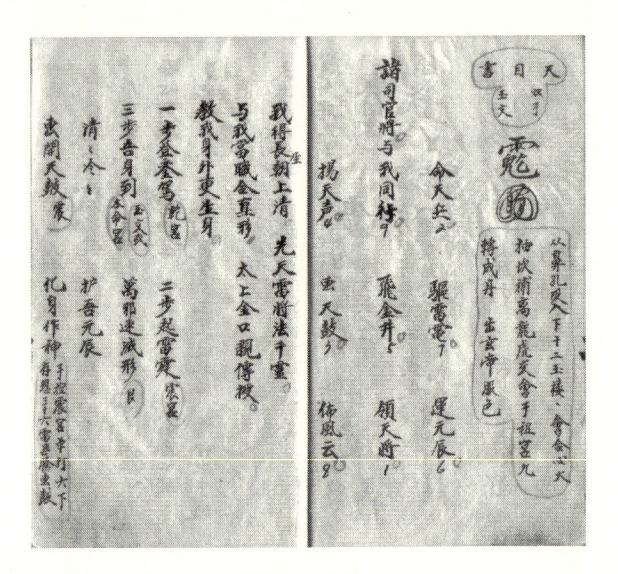

Figure. 3.2 . Instructions and incantations for transforming into the divine body of
Zhenwu and ascending to the celestial court in the *Banner Rite* manual.
Scan by the author.

—the third eye imagined to be located slightly above the eyebrows on his
celestial body—he inscribes in the air the taboo name (*hui* 諱) for the Dark
Emperor (see figure 3.2).

The masters of Chen Diwen's lineage regard the unpronounceable
graph on the top right of the manual, underneath the instructions circled
in red, as a secret name for Zhenwu. Written in celestial script, the graph
signals that the following inner alchemical process is designed to transform
Chen's celestial body of Zhang Daoling into to the more rarified body of
the Dark Emperor. Some evidence indicates that the character *qi* 乞, which
makes up the most distinctive component of the graph, has been regarded as
a taboo character in relation to Zhenwu. Shin-yi Chao has uncovered a set
of precepts (*jie* 戒) buried in a liturgical manual from the Southern Song or
Yuan that scripts a *jiao* for Zhenwu called the Grand Offering Liturgy for
the Numinous Response of Zhenwu (Zhenwu lingying dajiao yi 真武靈應
大醮儀). The fourth precept states, "On days the Perfected Lord [Zhenwu]
descends, do not write taboo words such as 'to tell' (*gao* 告) or 'to beg' (*qi* 乞)

in petitions" (真君降日，不得奏章之內有犯諱字，謂告乞字).[37] It seems the character *qi* has been appropriated by the ritual tradition that has come down to Chen and now constitutes part of Zhenwu's taboo graph. Chen's masters explain that within the context of the Banner Rite the celestial graph is designed to call forth the Dark Emperor.

Chen Diwen continues by inscribing in the air with his celestial eye a graph called the golden radiance taboo (*jinguang hui* 金光諱), which is noted immediately below the taboo graph for the Dark Emperor in the manual (see figure 3.2). The imperceptible golden radiance that continues to envelope Chen's deified body provides the spark that begins an inner alchemical reaction that will produce the Dark Emperor from within Chen's own body. Chen takes one beam (*yilun* 一輪) of the golden light and is instructed as follows:

> Breathe [it] in through the nostrils, let it descend through the twelve jade mansions [the esophagus], and combine [it] with the spark in the heart. Extract [the central *yao*-line from the trigram] *kan* and replenish [the central *yao*-line in the trigram] *li*. The dragon and the tiger copulate. Circulate [this embryo] nine times in the Ancestral Palace [the lower cinnabar field] to form the elixir. Exteriorize the Dark Emperor in full regalia.[38]

> 從鼻孔吸入，下十二玉樓，會合心火，抽坎補離，龍虎交會，于祖宮九轉成丹，出玄帝服色。

To explain this entire process, which the masters call "mobilizing ancestral *qi*" (*yundong zuqi* 運動祖氣), they augment their verbal interpretations with the theoretical tract called the *Secret Transmission of Ancestral Qi from the Anterior Heaven [as Revealed] by Patriarch Lü* (*Lüzu xiantian zuqi michuan*, or *Secret Transmission*), which is, along with the *Banner Rite*, the most precious esoteric text preserved in the lineage's cache. Recall that both texts were orally taught to Chen Diwen by his master Li Yezhen during the process of Chen's receiving the *yuanchen*. The *Secret Transmission* text describes this moment in the ritual as an inner alchemical operation by which the officiant refines primal essence (*yuanjing* 元精) into primal *qi* (*yuanqi* 元氣), and primal *qi* into primal spirit (*yuanshen* 元神).

Chen Diwen forms a "jade trace" mudra and with it "pinches" a single, round beam of the golden radiance that wreathes his numinous body. From the cupped hands of the mudra he inhales the golden light deep down into his heart. The masters regard this fiery, rarified *qi* originating from outside the body as the primal essence, the first ingredient in the alchemical operation. This primal essence mixes with the fire associated with the heart to produce primal *qi*.[39]

Chen further refines this primal *qi* by means of a well-established inner alchemical operation for melding the opposite trigrams *kan* 坎 and *li* 離. Clarke Hudson characterizes this symbolic language of trigrams from the ancient *Book of Changes* as expressing an effort by the adept to reverse a cosmogonic devolution, and the *Secret Transmission* text held by these masters concurs.[40] The text explains that before the cosmos as we know it came into being, a state of primal unity reigned in which pure *yang qi* 陽氣, symbolized as the trigram *qian* 乾, existed in pristine motionlessness full of creative potential. As this Anterior Heaven (Xiantian) began to differentiate, producing the regular movements of the Posterior Heaven (Houtian 後天) of phenomenal form according to the patterns of the five phases and eight trigrams, primal *qian* ☰ lost its central *yao*-line 爻 and exchanged it with the central *yao*-line of primal *kun* 坤 ☷ to form the trigrams *li* 離 ☲ and *kan* 坎 ☵. In the cycle of generation, decay, and regeneration that characterizes the Posterior Heaven, the trigrams *kan* and *li* reside as opposites whose melding is imagined as the method to reacquire the lost state of pristine *yang* cosmic unity.[41]

The human body is imagined as a microcosm of this cosmic devolution. At conception in the womb, a person comes into being as a product of the father's essence as semen (*jing* 精), and the mother's essence as blood. The resulting fetus is composed of ancestral *qi*, the "correct and harmonious *qi*" (*zhonghe zhi qi* 中和之氣) of the Anterior Heaven, and is described as a still, pristine body of pure *yang qi* symbolized by the trigram *qian*. Emotions associated with human existence in this world—delight, anger, grief, and joy (*xi nu ai le* 喜怒哀樂)—have not yet stirred. At birth, the fetus breaks into the world with its first cry, a sign that the correct and harmonious pure *yang* of ancestral *qi* that composes the child is being disrupted. In the imagery of the trigrams, the pristine *qian* ☰ trigram loses its central *yao*-line, takes on the central *yao*-line of the trigram *kun* ☷, and becomes the trigram *li* ☲. The wandering *yao*-line of *qian* becomes lodged within the trigram *kun* ☷ to create the trigram *kan* ☵. The constant, contentious transformations of *qi* in the pattern of the five phases and eight trigrams, which will regulate the human's body for the rest of his or her mortal life, have begun. In this sense, a newborn loses the still, harmonious nature of the Anterior Heaven and takes on the nature of contending *qi* in the Posterior Heaven. The goal of Chen Diwen's inner alchemical procedure is to reverse this natural devolution and recover the pristine *yang* body associated with an unborn fetus.[42]

Chen seeks to create the primal body of a fetus by "extracting from *kan* in order to replenish *li*" (*choukan buli* 抽坎補離). The *Secret Transmission* text explains:

> As for the *yang* [*yao*-line] within the *qian* [trigram] that was lost from the Anterior Heaven, seek it by digging into the earth of the *kan* [trigram] in the Northern Sea. Pry open the two *yin* [upper and lower *yao*-lines of the *kan* trigram] and there gather the central, single *yang yao*-line. The *yin* [*yao*-line displaced from the *li* trigram] descends and the *yang* [*yao*-line gathered from the *kan* trigram] rises, restoring the original body of the *qian* and *kun* [trigrams].[43]
>
> 將先天所失乾中之陽，在北海坎地掘尋。撥開二陰，取那中爻一陽。陰降陽升，復還乾坤本體。

Chen visualizes that the *kan* trigram, associated with the water of the urogenital organ located in the north of the body between the kidneys, here called the Northern Sea, and the *li* trigram, associated with the fire of the heart located in the south of the body, meld. In his mind's eye, Chen recovers the central *yang yao*-line from the *kan* trigram ☵ and uses it to replace the central *yin* line in the *li* trigram ☲, thereby transforming *li* back to its original pure *yang* state, the prenatal and pre-cosmic *qi* of the Anterior Heaven symbolized by the *qian* trigram ☰. These masters refer to this pristine *yang qi* as primordial spirit (*yuanshen*).[44]

The instructions Chen Diwen follows in the *Banner Rite* manual euphemistically refer to this same operation as "copulation between the dragon and the tiger" (*longhu jiaohui* 龍虎交會). The masters point to their *Secret Transmission* text for language to explain these terms.

> The saliva of the defeated dragon and the spittle of the subdued tiger congeal into one entity. Like quicksilver in a basin, [when it] scatters there are a hundred thousand [beads], when it unites there is one. This is the primordial spirit.[45]
>
> 降龍之涎，伏虎之沫，凝聚一團。如水銀在盆，散則百千，合而為一，此元神也。

In this scheme, the dragon represents the trigram *li*—*yin* within *yang* ☲— and the tiger points to *kan*—*yang* within *yin* ☵. The reaction between *yin* within *yang* and *yang* within *yin* is here imagined as a melding of saliva or quicksilver into a single elixir, the primordial spirit.

Chen Diwen then visualizes that this primordial spirit descends to the Ancestral Palace—the lower cinnabar field located three inches below the navel. In a circular motion, he rubs his belly with his right hand nine times to produce in the womb of the cinnabar field an elixir. He visualizes that the elixir, like a fetus, gestates into the form of a tiny Zhenwu. It grows until it bursts forth from the lower cinnabar field and travels slowly up through three passes along the dorsal tract of the spine—the coccygeal pass, the spinal pass, and the occipital pass.[46]

Then with a great "whoosh" sound Chen Diwen exteriorizes the Dark Emperor in full regalia through the middle eye in his forehead. Chen visualizes that the Dark Emperor Zhenwu floats up and stands on wisps of incense smoke emanating from the altar table. Another of the lineage's ritual manuals that scripts this same ritual sequence articulates the vision:

> The Emperor wears [long] hair and he brandishes a sword. His left hand clasps the seal of the Dark Warrior. [He has] bare arms and his feet tread on a tortoise and a snake. In front and behind [him stand] the six *jia* and six *ding* [spirits]. In a powerful air [about him] that inspires awe, he descends.[47]
>
> 帝披髮仗劍，左手扣玄武印，赤膊，足踏龜蛇，前后六甲六丁，威風凜凜而下。

Chen visualizes that he exteriorizes the Dark Emperor in all his glory with his retinue of attending spirits. The Dark Emperor then descends onto Chen's body, sheathing it like a bamboo envelop (*zhao* 罩), just as Zhang Daoling did. It is at this point that the masters of the lineage speak of "transforming into" (*biancheng* 變成) the Dark Emperor, who possesses an even more ethereal body than the Celestial Master Zhang Daoling.[48]

Divine Identities

The masters of the lineage call this entire sequence of intense visualizations "transforming into a divine body" (*bianshen* 變身), or more simply "transforming into a deity" (*bianshen* 變神). Chen Diwen visualizes that a womb of golden radiance surrounds him within which he completely incinerates his mortal body, takes on the body of the first Celestial Master, Zhang Daoling, and then continues to conceive, gestate, and give birth to the Dark Emperor, whose ethereal body then envelops Chen's already divinized body and saturates it, thereby transforming it into the rarified body of a high celestial god. In his *Correct Rites of the Heart of Heaven of the Shangqing Tradition,* Song-period master Deng Yougong also described this sort of bodily transformation in alchemical terms. The practitioner literally engages in a "great transformation by internal refining" (*neilian dabian* 內鍊大變). The sense of "refining" here draws on the fundamental meaning of *lian* as "smelting"—burning away impurities from ore to extract the essential metal within. Likewise, Chen's mortal body is refined by intense heat. As Deng Yougong put it, the practitioner "visualizes that his own body becomes [that of] the Celestial Master, or of Tianpeng or Zhenwu according to his intention" (自身存為天師，或天蓬真武任意).[49]

The historical texts drawn on to help interpret Chen Diwen's visualization make it clear that this sequence of his lineage's ritual practice closely resembles the "transforming into a deity" or "visualized transformation" (*cunbian* 存變) practices developed by practitioners of Song and Yuan liturgical traditions, especially the Heart of Heaven tradition. Scholar Li Zhihong shows that Heart of Heaven practices of bodily transformation were based on an older Shangqing visualization method called the "blending of circulating winds" (*huifeng hunhe* 回風混合). The Shangqing practitioner would, via the *qi* of the breath, mix his body with those of various deities in an attempt to hold those deities inside his body for as long as possible, which would facilitate his attempt to achieve the body of a true being (*zhenren*). During the Song and Yuan periods, new liturgical traditions like the Heart of Heaven often imagined those deities as the divine revealers of their own traditions or as patriarchs who transmitted those teachings. Through visualization, incantation, and employing mudras, a practitioner transformed his own ordinary body (*fanshen* 凡身) into the extraordinary body (*feifan zhi shen* 非凡之身) of the very god or patriarch responsible for revealing or transmitting the ritual. That god or patriarch himself—not the practitioner—would in effect perform the ritual. By shifting identity in this way, the practitioner would rely on divine authority to execute the ritual, including rituals designed to summon and deploy martial deities.[50]

Reading the same Heart of Heaven sources, especially Deng Yougong's *Correct Rites of the Heart of Heaven of the Shangqing Tradition,* scholar Chang Ch'ao-jan asks further how Heart of Heaven practitioners, whom he calls "ritual masters of exorcism" (*quxie fashi* 驅邪法師), actually used their divine bodies once they acquired them. He stresses that the ritual master-cum-deity wielded his divine authority to command various martial deities to carry out the exorcistic goal of the ritual, or even battled demons himself. In one way or another, the master-cum-deity himself always participated in the exorcistic work of the ritual.

Chang Ch'ao-jan takes the argument a step further. He asks what, if anything, makes the masters of exorcism of the new Song liturgical movements different from those of the "classic" (*jingdian* 經典) Daoist traditions—Celestial Master, Shangqing, and Lingbao—of the medieval period. He argues that "dignitaries of the Dao" (*daoshi*), or Daoists, of the earlier period executed a liturgical task like exorcism by civil (*wen* 文) means. They wrote, recited, and transmitted petitions to various cosmological bureaus in order to beseech high divinities to dispatch martial deities to accomplish exorcistic goals. Daoists functioned as messengers interacting with the highest levels of the divine hierarchy on behalf of people. Daoists were rather removed from any actual exorcistic work. But a ritual master of exorcism working in a new liturgical tradition like Heart of Heaven turned himself into a specific high deity and relied on that authority to summon divine generals and soldiers and command them, and sometimes even to take on demons himself. In this sense, Song ritual masters were personally much more involved in the actual work of the ritual. They themselves directly participated in the martial (*wu* 武) aspects of the exorcism. For Chang, these different self-identities (*ziwo shenfen* 自我身分) taken on by the practitioner during the ritual—civil dignitary of the Dao on the one hand, martial master of exorcism on the other—are what distinguish classic Daoist priests of the medieval period from the ritual masters of the Song liturgical movements.[51]

Given the latest scholarship, it is tempting to conclude that the transformation of the body sequence in the Banner Rite has indeed derived from typical Heart of Heaven practice from the Song period, in which the role of the practitioner was distinct from that of classic medieval Daoist practice. Yet, a close look at the logic running through the Banner Rite reveals that the transformation of the body sequence does not aim to transform Chen Diwen's mundane body into that of Zhang Daoling and then into the Dark Emperor so that Chen might rely on the authority of one or both to execute the "martial" goal of the entire Banner Rite—to summon and command Celestial Lord Yin Jiao. Instead, the transformation of the body sequence here is an intermediary step toward a loftier goal that more closely resembles the "civil" character of classic Daoist practice. Chen's transformations into divine bodies are steps toward recovering his divine true self, the *yuanchen* that shares the ancestral *qi* emanating from the primordial Dao. It is that *yuanchen* in its ontological unity with the Dao that actually has the authority to approach the highest gods of the cosmos and to request that they command the martial deity Yin Jiao and his minions to respond to Chen's summons. This ritual logic is deeply rooted in certain strands of Divine Empyrean and Pure Tenuity thunder ritual, which resonate with classic medieval Daoist practice much more than we might expect.

Mobilizing the Primordial Self and Ascent to Heaven

Having taken on the rarified body of the Dark Emperor, Chen Diwen steadies himself and launches into the next phase of the Banner Rite, in which he visualizes a journey to the lofty Upper Clarity (Shangqing) heaven in order to present to the high gods his case that Celestial Lord Yin Jiao ought to obey his summons (web video 3.5 [0:57–1:09]).

Chen prepares for the ascent by walking a guideline (*bugang*) simultaneously with his left palm and with the heel of his left foot as he incants in a loud and authoritative voice,

> [I] control the celestial generals; [I] command the celestial armies; [I] beat the celestial drum; [I] broadcast Heaven's voice; [I] fly out from the golden well; [I] mobilize the *yuanchen;* [I] drive forward thunder and lightning; [I] deploy the wind and clouds. Officials and generals of the various bureaus accord with my movements! I have attained everlasting life and have an audience in [the heaven of] Upper Clarity. [see figure 3.2][52]

> 領天將1坎，命天兵2坤，擊天鼓3震，揚天聲4巽，飛金井5本命，運元辰6乾，驅雷電7兌，佈風雲8艮。諸司官將與我同行9離。我得長生朝上清。

This short ritual sequence would seem straightforward were it not for the puzzling line "[I] mobilize the *yuanchen*" (*yun yuanchen* 運元辰). We saw earlier that Chen Diwen began the heart of the Banner Rite by calling on the *yuanchen* (*kou yuanchen*). In that visualization, Chen recalled how his transmission master Li Yezhen taught him the Banner Rite during the afternoon he "received the *yuanchen*" (*shou yuanchen*), a metaphor for receiving instructions to recover one's true, primordial self. This line "[I] mobilize the *yuanchen*" and its echo of the earlier visualization calling on the *yuanchen* puzzles Chen and his masters. It is unclear to them who actually makes the ascent and stands in audience before the stellar gods.

Several of the most intellectually engaged masters—including the redactor of the *Banner Rite* text Jiang Shenzhi, his grandson Jiang Yucheng, and the former village head Li Yeshi—grappled with my questions about this one afternoon while watching the film of Chen's performance of the

Banner Rite. After more than an hour of debate, they came to the uneasy conclusion that it was Chen Diwen as the Dark Emperor who actually made the trip, citing the passage from the *Banner Rite* manual quoted. Directly after Chen transforms into the body of the Dark Emperor, the text instructs the officiant to use his divine power to deploy martial forces in preparation for the ascent, capped by the declaration that "I have attained long life and have an audience in [the heaven of] Upper Clarity." For the masters, Chen Diwen-cum-the Dark Emperor was the "I" (*wo* 我) who ascended to the stellar realm. It was Chen merged with the Dark Emperor who had the godly ability and authority to approach the celestial throne. Chen literally took on the Dark Emperor's rarified, divine body to act as the god does and roam to the highest echelons of the cosmos.

The masters admitted they were unsure about any possible relationship between the mobilization of the *yuanchen* (*yun yuanchen*) here in the ritual and the prior sequence recalling the *yuanchen* (*kou yuanchen*). As in many moments in the rituals bequeathed to them, they are not entirely sure about the theory or logic assumed by the instructions. The lineage's intellectual leaders, especially Jiang Shenzhi, do their best to make liturgical sense of their heirlooms with the texts and oral teachings available to them.

The next section presses on my question of who exactly ascends to the celestial sphere. Comparing the lineage's *Banner Rite* text with a remarkably similar nineteenth-century text from a cousin lineage in central Hunan reveals a recognizable ritual logic for the transformation of the body sequences that both sublineages share. The final goal of the transformation of the body is not to transmute the mundane body of an officiant like Chen Diwen into that of a powerful deity like Zhang Daoling or the Dark Emperor, in whose guise the officiant does ritual work. Instead, those moments in the transformation of the body are necessary steps in a larger process by which the officiant reveals and reconnects with his own *yuanchen*—his primordial self, the true "I" always and already within him and according with the cosmic reality of the Dao. It is his true self, his *yuanchen,* that travels to the celestial sphere, has audience with the high gods, and receives permission from them to summon and deploy the martial deity Yin Jiao.

A Missing Piece—Mobilizing the Yuanchen from the Formless Void

The masters of Chen Diwen's lineage struggled with my question because the piece of the Banner Rite ritual explaining the role of the *yuanchen* in this ritual sequence likely dropped from their textual or oral tradition during the vicissitudes of ritual transmission. We do not know when the lacuna may have occurred or why. We only know that the lineage's intellectual leader Jiang Shenzhi, ordained in 1946, last redacted the *Banner Rite* text in 1989 from sources that do not survive.

Fortunately, the likely missing step in Jiang Shenzhi's textual or oral tradition can be found in older ritual manuscripts that were used by cousin lineages in central Hunan. Recall from chapter 1 that the Jiang-Li lineage Chen Diwen entered has dominated the area around Fuqing for more than two hundred years. It is one of many cousin lineage branches in the Daxiong Mountains of northern Xinhua and Anhua counties, all of which trace their ancestry to the Jade Void Palace in Xinhua. We do not know whether some version of the Banner Rite to summon Marshal Yin was practiced at the Jade Void Palace or at its six branch temples during the Ming dynasty. But we do have Qing-era texts scripting remarkably similar versions of the Banner Rite from all over Hunan, even beyond the Daxiong Mountains.[53] Clearly, the Banner Rite to summon Yin Jiao was widely practiced among historically related lineages claiming a common source in the Jade Void Palace. This is almost certainly the reason ritual manuals scripting the Banner Rite are so similar. On these grounds, we are able to read the ritual manual maintained by Chen's lineage up against similar manuals from around central Hunan with a good deal of confidence. This comparative reading enables us to piece together a fuller picture of the ritual claims about the *yuanchen* and its function animating this moment in Chen's performance of the Banner Rite, which seem to have dropped out of his lineage's memory.

Among the various Banner Rite manuscripts I have examined, one text collected by Patrice Fava stands out for its exceptionally robust scripting of the ritual. The *Banner Rite [to Summon] Sire Yin of the Anterior Heaven* (*Xiantian Yingong fanfa yizong* 先天殷公旛法一宗) was produced by a certain Luo

Congyao (羅從堯) (b. 1813) for his ordination ceremony sometime during the Xianfeng (咸豐) era (1851–1861). Likely from central Hunan, the manuscript instructs the ordinand—Luo Congyao himself—to call lineage patriarchs associated with the Jade Void Palace to witness the ordination.

A close reading of Luo's nineteenth-century manual against the *Banner Rite* used by Chen Diwen demonstrates that both share a similar ritual structure and logic, and often identical content. Luo's *Banner Rite* text begins with the same preliminary practices as Chen's. Luo the ordinand then encases his body in a cocoon of protective golden radiance by the same incantation and palm tracing, hacks his mortal body into pieces with a sword mudra, and then incinerates them.

Then Luo Congyao's *Banner Rite* instructs how to transform into a divine body by an inner alchemical procedure that maintains the same ritual logic as the sequence performed by Chen Diwen, though several details depart. In Luo's text, the practitioner conceives and gestates an infant (*ying'er* 嬰兒) who matures into the first Celestial Master, Zhang Daoling. A protective layer of golden radiance shines about this figure, who then transforms into something more abstract—the "ancestor of the yellow courtyard" (*huangting zhi zu* 黃庭之祖). The ancestor here seems to be a metaphor for ancestral *qi* brought forth by the Dao in the stillness of the Anterior Heaven during the early stages of the cosmogony. In the human body, ancestral *qi* resides in the center mass of the body in a space called the yellow courtyard. Having mobilized the ancestral *qi* deep inside the body, the *Incantation of the Golden Radiance* and palm tracing are performed once again. Then the text instructs Luo to

> visualize that ten thousand rays of golden radiance descend from the heavens, shine upon the body, and fill up the entire room. Clack the teeth three/six [nine or eighteen or thirty-six] times while the god of moats and walls and local god of the soil line up on either side. Visualize the true person of primordial destiny [*yuanming zhenren* 元命真人] within the formless. Only after a short while does it seem the [true person of primordial destiny] consents to come [out from the formless]. Clothed in divine radiance, it emits from [the ordinand's] two eyes and disperses to

fill up the empty void. Golden radiance from the Gate of Heaven connects with the Earth Door, and thunderous radiance surges upward. The three [radiances of heaven, earth, and thunder] merge into one. My body stands in the middle as the Lord of Transformations who summons the ten thousand gods. They descend from the heavens and gush up from the earth. They all have great bodies that brace the heavens above and the earth below, and their powerful radiance dazzles. They stand respectfully with hands clasped listening for my command, and then they are dispatched according to that command. [see figure 3.3][54]

存萬道金光，自天而下，交射一身，沖滿一室。叩齒三六通，城隍土地佈列左右。想元命真人身入無形之內，少柱便刻，纔若應到，便着神光，自兩眼中出，散滿虛空。天門金光下接地戶，雷光上沖，三合為一。我身立於其中，為造化之主，呼召萬神。從天下降，自地湧出，皆為大身，上柱天，下柱地，威光赫奕，拱立聽令，隨令驅遣。

The passage is striking. Luo Congyao recovers his true person of primordial destiny, which resides in the formless, cosmic void. Various manuscripts scripting the Banner Rite from Hunan use the term "true person of

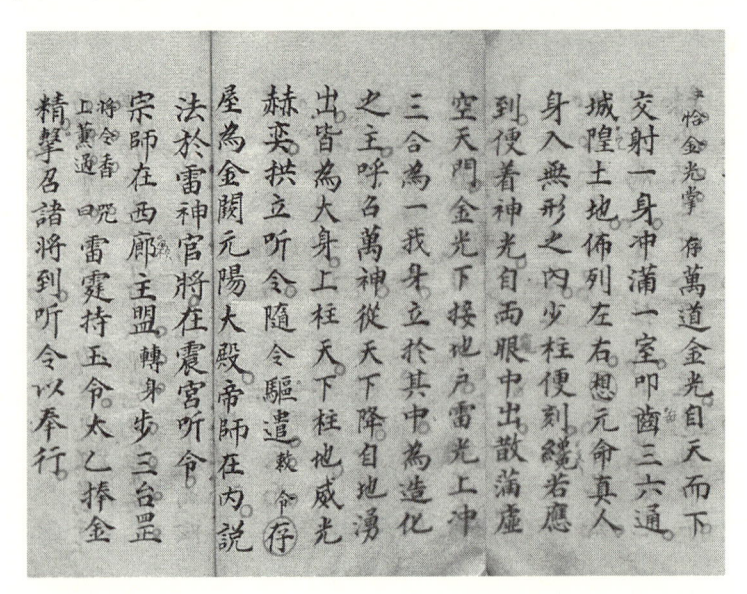

Figure. 3.3 Luo Congyao's *Banner Rite* manual. Text courtesy of Patrice Fava. Photograph by the author.

primordial destiny" interchangeably with "primordial spirit" (*yuanshen*) and "primordial destiny" (*yuanming* 元命) to mean one's true "self" (*wo* 我), true "heart" (*xin* 心), or true "spirit" (*shen* 神). These terms all denote the deepest, most intimate self composed of the unified *qi* of the formless void, the Anterior Heaven, which directly emanated from the Dao during the early stages of the cosmogony. This intimate self was "primordially destined or assigned" (*yuanming*)—bequeathed by the Dao at the moment of birth, but normally remaining hidden in the formless void of the Anterior Heaven.

In this sequence, Luo Congyao actively calls forth or recovers the secluded true self naturally in accord with the Dao in the formless void. That true self is then emitted from Luo's body and manifests in the world as dazzling radiance filling up the space between heaven and earth. Luo does not look to acquire the rarified body of another deity such as Zhang Daoling or the Dark Emperor and then act as that deity. Instead he looks inward and brings forth from the primordial void his true self, always already the Lord of Transformations merged with the Dao and so able to summon and command all the gods of the universe. Power is not ultimately defined as some divinity outside one's innate nature into which one transforms, but instead as one's true self rooted in the primordium.

This profound claim echoes a theme running through inner alchemical teachings on thunder rites in Divine Empyrean and Pure Tenuity traditions from the Southern Song, Yuan, and early Ming. In the *Lineage Talks by Court Attendant Wang, Master of Penetrating Mystery of the Hollow Void* (*Chongxu tongmiao shichen Wang xiansheng jiahua* 沖虛通妙侍宸王先生家話), a record of Wang Wenqing's teachings collated by his disciples likely during the mid-twelfth century, Wang equates one's "primordial spirit" (*yuanshen*) with the power of the cosmogony itself. "The indestructible primordial spirit of the Anterior Heaven is what we today revere as primordial commencement" 先天不壞之元神，即今所尊元始也.[55] The sense here is not that the practitioner transforms into the actual Celestial Worthy of Primordial Commencement, but that the primordial spirit at the core of the practitioner embodies the same cosmic power as the deity associated with the emergence of the Anterior Heaven during the cosmogony. In another text attributed to Wang Wenqing, the *Great Rite of the Five Thunders for Interrogation and Execution in the [Office of the] Jade Pivot in the Divine Empyrean on High*, the master insists that it is the "primordially destined or assigned spirit" (*yuanming zhi shen* 元命之神) that has the power to summon and command deities. "[I] use my primordially destined spirit to summon those gods of the void emptiness; [I] use the *qi* of my fundamental body to accord with that *qi* of the void emptiness" (以我元命之神，召彼虛無之神，以我本身之炁，合彼虛無之炁).[56] As in Luo Congyao's manual, it is the practitioner's primordial spirit, the fundamental core of his body assigned at birth, that shares in the ultimate cosmogonic power of the Dao and uses it to manipulate the deities of the universe.

In a collection of Bai Yuchan's sayings, *True Words by which to Cultivate the Dao* (*Xiudao zhenyan* 修道真言), that Divine Empyrean and Southern Lineage of the Golden Elixir master is said to have taught that everything at root possesses primordial *qi* from the Dao. To identify that primordial spirit and mobilize it is to experience oneself as united with the Dao, which is to experience oneself as united with all other selves in the cosmos. "My body is heaven and earth, and heaven and earth are my body. All people under heaven are me, and I am all people under heaven" (吾一身即天地，天地即吾一身，天下之人即吾，吾即天下之人).[57] The singularity of one's mundane self gives way to a primordial self that shares in the nature of the Dao and so is ontologically connected to all things. Zhao Yizhen, a major codifier of the Pure Tenuity tradition, defines the crux of the transformation into the divine in a similar way. His *Pivot of the Methods of the Dao of the Qingwei [Tradition]* (*Qingwei daofa shuniu* 清微道法樞紐) reads,

> Someone asked, "What is the way of transforming into the divine?" The master replied, "During the original *kalpa* of primordial commencement, unified *qi* divided reality. I am primordial commencement; primordial commencement is me. This is what is called transforming into the divine."[58]
>
> 或問：「變神之道如何？」師曰：「元始祖劫，一炁分真。我即元始，元始即我。此即謂之變神。」

For this great Pure Tenuity master, there is no division between the practitioner's true self (*wo*) and the latent power of unified *qi* prior to its division into the variegated world of phenomena. To transform into the divine is not ultimately to transform one's mortal body into the body of Zhang Daoling, the Dark Emperor, or some other deity. Instead, it is to recover within oneself the ontological wholeness of primordial unity. These theories seem baked into Luo Congyao's manual. The point of transforming into the divine is to recover within oneself the primordially assigned true person residing in the formless void of the primordium. That primordial spirit fills the entire space between heaven and earth with its brilliant radiance, connected to all primordial spirits of the myriad gods.

Even a modest glance at these Divine Empyrean and Pure Tenuity teachings, heavily inspired by inner alchemical theory and practice, suggests that the concept "transformation into the divine" itself transformed from earlier Heart of Heaven theories and practices from the Northern Song. Recall that scholar Li Zhihong points out that in typical Heart of Heaven practice the practitioner strove to transform into another deity in order to rely on that deity's power to engage in the actual exorcistic work of the ritual. By transforming into a specific deity, the practitioner, Li writes, comes "to possess [divine] authority to carry out the ritual, so he can carry out the matter of summoning and deploying demons and deities."[59] Heart of Heaven practice assumes a deep divide between the power of the mortal practitioner and the power of a deity. Transforming into the divine aims to bridge that divide. The lowly practitioner transforms into a deity to commandeer that deity's greater power and use it to summon and command martial gods or even to exorcise demons himself.

The inner alchemical theories running through later Divine Empyrean and Pure Tenuity thunder rites in the Southern Song, Yuan, and early Ming periods break down this divide in a different way. Instead of transforming into some powerful deity outside himself to appropriate its power, the practitioner looks inward to recover his primordial spirit, his true self composed of ancestral *qi* emanating from the Dao. By returning to or recovering his ontological core, the practitioner exists as a manifestation of the same ancestral *qi* that manifests as deities. That ontological commonality provides the resonance allowing the practitioner himself to communicate with deities, either to command thunder gods to work or to approach high deities in audience. The practitioner does not rely on the authority of deities such as Zhang Daoling or the Dark Emperor as intermediaries, but instead on the power of the primordial Dao.[60] In Zhao Yizhen's language, the practitioner is primordial commencement. In Luo Congyao's text, he is the Lord of Transformations.

After having drawn from the void his true person of primordial destiny or true self, Luo Congyao then ascends to the high heavens. Either with his foot or palm or both, he walks a guideline while incanting,

> [I] control the celestial generals; [I] command the celestial armies; [I] beat the celestial drum; [I] broadcast heavenly divinity; [I] stir up the golden well; [I] set in motion my *yuanchen;* [I] drive forward thunder and lightning; [I] deploy the wind and clouds. Every bureau, official, and general accords with [my] movements! Guard my *yuanchen* to have an audience in [the heaven of] Grand Clarity.[61]

> 領天將子，命天兵申，擊天鼓卯，揚天神巳，揮金井中，運元辰亥，驅雷電酉，佈風雲艮。諸司將午，與同行。護我元辰朝泰清巳。

Luo brandishes his primordial power with every phrase and corresponding step on the heavenly guideline. The pattern of the guideline is a magic square arranged according to the organization of the eight trigrams in the Posterior Heaven. Poul Andersen notices that in southern Taiwan this particular *bugang* pattern is commonly referred to as the Guideline for Summoning Generals (zhaojiang gang 召將罡). On sending up a petition or personally traveling to a celestial palace to deliver a document, the officiant walks this guideline to dispatch a spirit army to ensure safe passage.[62] Likewise, Luo Congyao seems to surround himself with protective martial forces to journey to Grand Clarity, one of the loftiest celestial realms, to have an audience with the high gods whose taboo names (*hui*) he is then instructed to inscribe—the Jade Emperor (Yuhuang 玉皇), the Celestial Emperor (Tianhuang 天皇), Ziwei (Emperor of the North), Great Yang (Taiyang 太陽), and Great Yin (Taiyin 太陰). In the context of Luo's ritual manual, the meanings of "I set in motion my *yuanchen*" and of "Guard my *yuanchen* to have an audience in Grand Clarity" are clear. Luo drew his *yuanchen*—his primordially destined or assigned true self—from the empty void and it is that true self that journeys under divine protection to the heavens for an audience with the high gods.

This guideline and incantation mirrors Chen Diwen's performance in 2004, with which we began this section. Recall that Chen walks the same magic square guideline with his left palm and with the heel of his left foot as he incants a nearly identical incantation (see page 198). As did Luo Congyao, Chen surrounds himself with martial forces in order to journey safely to the celestial sphere where he will stand in audience. As did his liturgical relative, Chen also declares "I mobilize the *yuanchen*" (see figure 3.4). Chen's text does not state as unequivocally as Luo's that it is indeed the *yuanchen* that is guarded in order to have an audience with the high gods. However, the shared logic of the entire sequence is too cognate to ignore the strong suggestion that Chen's manual also assumes that it is the officiant's *yuanchen,* his primordial self, that is mobilized (*yun*) from the empty void of the Anterior Heaven and then guarded or protected (*hu*) by divine generals and soldiers upon its ascent to a heavenly audience before the high gods. It is not that the practitioner takes on the divine body of Zhang Daoling or the Dark Emperor

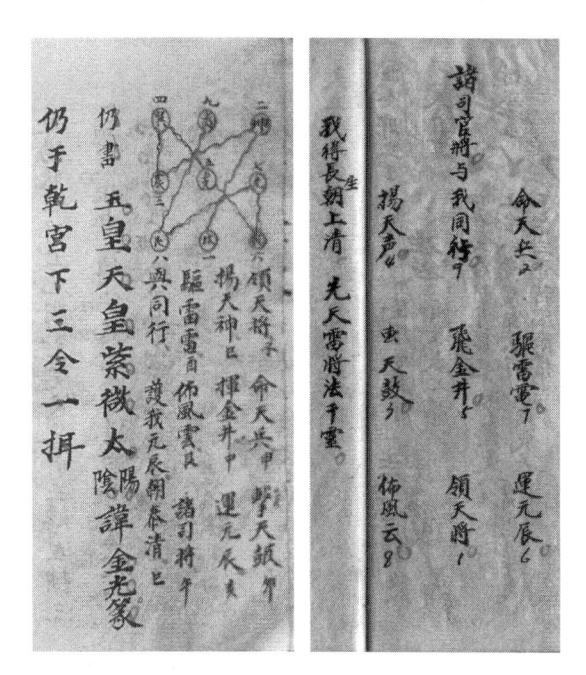

Figure. 3.4 Journey to the celestial sphere in Luo Congyao's *Banner Rite* manual (left) and Jiang Shenzhi's *Banner Rite* manual used by Chen Diwen (right). Luo text courtesy of Patrice Fava. Photograph and scan by the author.

and as that transformed body ascends to the celestial sphere. Instead, it is the *yuanchen* that traverses the cosmos and contacts its supreme gods.

The cryptic allusions to the term *yuanchen* in Chen Diwen's *Banner Rite* manual point to the important status of the *yuanchen* concept that the masters of his lineage struggle to articulate. When their *Banner Rite* text is read against cognate texts from central Hunan, especially a very full text like Luo Congyao's, we realize it is likely that the ritual sequence by which the practitioner recovers his *yuanchen* from the void of the Anterior Heaven has somehow fallen out of practice in Chen's lineage. A vestige of a prior age, the term *yuanchen* remains in the lineage's *Banner Rite* manual, but it has lost its conspicuousness. So, as do theologians everywhere, the masters of Chen's lineage do their best to make sense of what has come down to them. Following their ritual manual, they suppose it is the officiant as the rarified body of the Dark Emperor who ascends to the celestial court. Such interpretive thinking according to what is given is the nature of manuscript culture.

Images of the Yuanchen

This reading of the central role of the *yuanchen* in the Banner Rite is bolstered by interpretations of the concept in thunder rites and inner alchemical texts from the Southern Song and Yuan periods. Zhang Shanyuan (張善淵), a second-generation disciple of famed Divine Empyrean master Mo Yueding (莫月鼎, also known as Mo Qiyan 莫起炎)(1226–1294), sought to synthesize the key issues across the great variety of rites of his day.[63] In his *Penetrating Discourse on the Myriad Methods* (*Wanfa tonglun* 萬法通論), Zhang instructs that a master must first visualize "one point of bright numinousness in the Anterior Heaven" (先天一點明靈), and then "form three flowers on the crown of the head, and concentrate one's two eyes on the point between the eyebrows" (結三花於頂上，攢兩曜於眉間). Then the practitioner should "focus his eyes and emit radiant light which forms a circular shape" (注睛迸光，作一圓象). This circle of light is "the great Dao, the unified *qi* of the Anterior Heaven" (此大道也，先天一炁也). When located inside the body, it is called "the essence of *yang*, one's own *yuanchen*" (此陽精也，自己元辰也).[64]

For Zhang Shanyuan, the *yuanchen* is the great Dao within the human body. In ontological terms, it is the aspect of the body composed of the pure, unified *yang qi* of the primordial Anterior Heaven. This primordial *qi*, this expression of Dao, is "limitlessly radiant, filling up the entire universe" (晃曜無邊，充塞宇宙). By definition, one's *yuanchen* shares that radiance and expansiveness, and so "there is nowhere [the practitioner] cannot reach and nothing he cannot bring about" (無所不通，無施不可). For a practitioner who can recover his *yuanchen*, "deploying thunder and lightning, or subduing demons and deities, are but easy things" (至於驅役雷電，制伏鬼神，抑其容易事也).[65] Foreshadowing Luo Congyao's manual, Zhang insists that to grasp one's *yuanchen* is to "become the Lord of Transformations who summons and gathers the myriad gods" (為造化之主，召集萬神).[66] Visualizing the Dao as primordial, unified *qi* within oneself—visualizing one's *yuanchen*—is the key to liturgical power shared by all reputable ritual methods.

The concept of *yuanchen* as the great Dao within the body, the essence of *yang qi* from the Anterior Heaven that is one's primordial self, also permeated the Zhengyi tradition on Mount Longhu down to the twentieth century. In 2010, scholar Lee Fong-mao co-wrote an article with a prominent Zhengyi Daoist named Zhang Zhixiong (張智雄), a disciple of and personal assistant to the sixty-third Celestial Master, Zhang Enpu (張恩溥) (1904–1969), who fled the mainland to Taiwan in 1949. Lee insists that what he learnt from Zhang Zhixiong should be considered the authentic esoteric teaching of the Zhengyi tradition passed down via oral transmission through generations on Mount Longhu.

One particular hymn taught to Zhang Zhixiong by the sixty-third Celestial Master himself, called the *Key for Penetrating Heaven with the Thunderclap* (*Leiting tongtian qiao* 雷霆通天竅), references the term *yuanchen* in three of its verses: "For ritual methods, employ [*qi* from the] Anterior Heaven and illumine the great Dao; for [commanding] generals, use the *yuanchen* that is merely one's self" (法行先天明大道，將用元辰只自己); "Divine generals are what my *yuanchen* is; inscribing talismans without the key is [to invite] deceptions from demons and spirits" (神將即我元辰是，書符無竅鬼神欺); and "Using this *qi* from primordial commencement, my body moves all the sages and worthies of the various heavens" (我身以此元始炁，感動諸天諸聖賢).[67]

Lee Fong-mao and Zhang Zhixiong interpret the hymn as eulogizing a visualization by which a Zhengyi practitioner "refines" (*lianhua* 煉化, *lianyang* 煉養) the *yuanchen* within the body, thereby calling forth (*zhaochu* 召出) the *yuanchen* and uniting with it, which enables the practitioner to move the deities of the various heavens. Several of Lee and Zhang's insights resonate. First, they equate the *yuanchen* with the "true person of primordial destiny" (*yuanming zhenren*). Both terms refer to the divine aspect of the self which was assigned at birth according to the heavenly stems and earthly branches system marking time of birth. The practitioner must learn to identify this primordially assigned true self via visualization. Second, this recovery of the primordial self enables the practitioner to inscribe talismans by which to summon and employ divine generals. Without this key visualization, talismans would lack efficacy. And third, it is the masters of the lineage who teach the practitioner how to recover his true self in order to summon and employ martial deities via talismans. These transmitted instructions are in fact a prerequisite for ordination into the lineage. Therefore, the visualization is bound up with honoring the ancestral masters and the oaths taken on receiving liturgical office and a register (*lu* 錄) during ordination. For Lee and Zhang, the goal of such admission into the lineage, reception of the *lu* register, and attainment of the teaching is to "confirm one's true person of primordial destiny" (目的就是確定自己的元命真人).[68]

This last insight sheds light on why Chen Diwen's lineage puts a great deal of emphasis on two interrelated practices: calling upon the *yuanchen* (*kou yuanchen*) and receiving the *yuanchen* (*shou yuanchen*). Recall that, near the beginning of the Banner Rite, Chen prostrated in front of the main altar and "called upon the *yuanchen*." He visualized the scene weeks before the ordination in which he had received from his master the transmission of oral instructions for how to perform the Banner Rite. He visualized his master's demeanor while teaching and the birth times of the three generations of masters directly above his master as a way to connect himself with the entire lineage of ancestral masters who had been invited to witness the transmission. He recalled the sequence of divination blocks that had sealed the transmission. Chen's lineage refers to the entire transmission as "receiving the *yuanchen.*" The term *yuanchen* here is understood as a kind of general label designating the entire content of the oral teachings from one's master, and by extension from the long lineage. Grounded in the prerequisite of "receiving the *yuanchen,*" Chen the ordinand may execute the teaching transmitted to him and successfully "call upon the *yuanchen*" during the Banner Rite.

Lee and Zhang's explanation of Zhengyi practices helps us speculate that the "receiving the *yuanchen*" practice in Chen's lineage functions like various prerequisite activities in the Zhengyi tradition, which serve to teach the young Daoist how to identify and recover his primordial self so that he can use it to communicate with high gods during the performance of a ritual. In Chen's tradition, "receiving the *yuanchen*" seems to denote the esoteric instructions for recovering one's primordial self. "Calling upon the *yuanchen*" seems to signify the actual recovery of one's primordial self via visualization for execution of the Banner Rite. In both cases, the term *yuanchen* refers to the primordially assigned true self bequeathed at birth but normally hidden in the void of the Anterior Heaven, whence it needs to be actively recovered by means of visualization for ritual use. It is this concept of *yuanchen* as primordial self that is more or less clearly articulated in cognate Banner Rite manuals from central Hunan and in ritual programs from the past.

Although this meaning of *yuanchen* and the visualization instructions by which to recover it have fallen out of the collective memory of the masters of Chen Diwen's lineage, their *Banner Rite* manual continues to assume that the officiant's *yuanchen* is the primordial self that communicates with high deities in hopes of securing their authoritative decree that Yin Jiao obey the officiant's summons.

Ascent, Heavenly Audience, and Celestial Appointment

Having made clear what the term *yuanchen* means in the Banner Rite, we can continue our exploration of Chen Diwen's performance of it (web video 3.5 [1:09–1:29]). Chen incants in a loud voice,

The thunder generals of the Anterior Heaven transform into a thousand numinous [beings]. [I] accord with [their] true forms according to the office I hold. These golden words from most high have faithfully been passed down, teaching me how to generate bodies beyond this [mundane] body. [see figure 3.2][69]

先天雷將法〔化〕千靈，與我當職合真形。太上金口親傳授，教我身外更生身。

Thunder gods, bound to duty by virtue of the liturgical office the officiant holds, manifest to protect Chen's *yuanchen* as it prepares to ascend to the heavens. The incantation seems to punctuate the conclusion of the entire transformation process. Chen has generated a series of divine bodies beyond his mortal body, those of Zhang Daoling and the Dark Emperor, which has somehow revealed his primordial self now preparing to ascend through the cosmos. That true self accords with thunder gods, who constitute a divine entourage.

This incantation has roots in the early Divine Empyrean tradition developed by Wang Wenqing. We find a nearly identical line in the *Preface to the Abstruse Directives of the Thunderclap from Wang the Fire Master,* which, as discussed in chapter 2, claims to be a text revealed by Wang the Fire Master to Wang Wenqing. In 1104, the text was annotated by a certain Zhu Zhizhong, who seems to have studied with Wang Wenqing, and then Bai Yuchan added an introduction about a century later. A line from one of Wang the Fire Master's poems reads, "The divine generals of the Five Thunders transform into a thousand true persons, and I instruct my disciples to accord with their true forms. These golden words from most high have been passed down, teaching me how to generate bodies beyond this [mundane] body" (五雷神將化千真，吾令弟子合真形。太上金口相傳授，教吾身外更生身).[70] Zhu Zhizhong indicates that the poem in which this line occurs was used as an incantation during the process of transforming into the divine.[71] A nearly identical incantation is also found in another early Divine Empyrean text, the *Great Rite of the Five Thunders for Interrogation and Execution in the [Office of the] Jade Pivot in the Divine Empyrean on High,* which was also attributed to Wang the Fire Master and prefaced—and perhaps written—by

Wang Wenqing.[72] Somehow this snippet of early Divine Empyrean practice for transforming into the divine has made its way down to the Banner Rite to summon Celestial General Yin.

Chen Diwen's *yuanchen* finally makes its way up to the high heavens. He traces a guideline on his left hand while incanting,

> With one step [I] mount the imperial carriage, with the second step [I] raise the thunderclap, with the third step my body arrives and the myriad deviant [spirits] quickly dissipate. [see figure 3.2][73]

一步登鑾駕乾宮，二步起雷霆震宮，三步吾身到玉文或本命宮，萬邪速滅形艮。

As Chen activates the *qian* point on his palm associated with heaven, he visualizes that he rides an opulent celestial carriage upward. As he activates the *zhen* point associated with thunder, he imagines the great vehicle is protected on all sides by a retinue of thunder gods. As he activates the center of his palm associated with his primordial self—the "jade writ" or "palace of primordial destiny"—he arrives at his destination, which is purified of malevolent spirits as he activates the *gen* point on his palm associated with demons.

Then Chen Diwen proclaims loudly,

> Pure and cold! Guard my *yuanchen*! Beat the heavenly drums for I have transformed my body into the divine! [see figure 3.2][74]

清清冷冷，護吾元辰。擊開天鼓震，化身作神。

As Chen arrives at the gate of the pure and pristine heavens, he calls out for the protection of his *yuanchen* as it stands on the brink of the celestial realm. Following the manual's instructions, he taps the *zhen* point on both palms six times as he traces six counterclockwise circles about his ears while making a low, thunder-like sound deep in his throat. As he does so, he visualizes the thirty-six thunder generals in his entourage flying up to bang drums alerting the denizens of the celestial realm that he has arrived.

The centrality of the primordial self in this crucial moment in the Banner Rite is put in sharp relief when this passage is compared with nearly identical passages in Qing-era manuals for summoning Yin Jiao from around the empire. The oldest manuscript I have so far collected is dated 1728 and titled the *Pure Tenuity [Practices] for Combined Refinement and Summons* (*Qingwei hunlian zhaohe* 清微混煉召合). A preface by a certain master called Wu Keheng 吳科亨 (fl. 1688–1728), likely from Jiangsu, states that during the late seventeenth century he studied on Mount Longhu where he received teachings directly from the fifty-fourth Celestial Master, Zhang Jizong 張繼宗 (1666–1715). Wu Keheng's manuscript compiles various rituals from different liturgical traditions all designed to summon and deploy marshal deities, including Yin Jiao. Each ritual includes a common sequence in which the practitioner visualizes the birth of an infant within the body. The infant then transforms into "the true person of primordial destiny, my primordial spirit" (我元神元命真人). After the primordial self emerges wearing a golden crown and Daoist robe, the practitioner incants, "Pure and quiet. Guard my primordial spirit. Beat the heavenly drums for I have transformed my body into the divine. Quickly in accordance with the statutes and commands" (清寧清寧，護我元神。擊開天鼓，化身作神。急急如律令).[75] When we read Chen Diwen's *Banner Rite* manual against this ritual text with such congruent ritual logic, it becomes even clearer that Chen's *yuanchen* seeking protection before the celestial realm is indeed his primordial spirit, his primordially assigned true self.

Then the Banner Rite leaps to a moment right after Chen Diwen's primordial self has had an audience with the high gods. We see in chapter 4 that the ritual logic implies that Chen did indeed stand in audience before the high gods where he requested from the Emperor of the North himself— Yin Jiao's celestial superior—an imperial edict commanding Yin to comply with Chen's summons. Here the Banner Rite picks up the action after the audience, when Chen has clearly secured the imperial decree (web video 3.5 [1:29–end]). Following the manual, Chen proclaims in an authoritative voice,

> I am a Celestial Master libationer who carries the favor of the Celestial Emperor. [My] head is crowned with the Three Terraces, [my] body is clad in the Northern Dipper, and my back bears the Kuigang [asterism]. To the

left [I] command the lords of the Azure Dragon [of the east]; to the right [I] command the spirits of the White Tiger [of the west]; in front there are the generals of the Vermillion Bird [of the south]; and behind there are the soldiers of the Dark Warrior [of the north]. [Whether] my body moves, sits, or reclines, three hundred and sixty thousand imperial guardsmen follow the directives of my heart. Wind, fire, thunder and lightning [I] bring forth and flashes of lightning [I] cast out from dark thunder [such that] it shakes Mount Tai, causing it to collapse. [My] hand grasps the *qi* of the Nine Heavens and my body straddles the back of the fiery dragon. [In] the Northern Extremity ruled by the Three Emperors, the myriad deities clasp their hands in salutation and follow [me]. [see figure 3.5][76]

吾為天師祭酒，當承天帝所賜。頭頂三台巳午未，身披北斗，背負魁罡。左命青龍君卯，右命白虎神酉，前有朱鵲將午，后有玄武兵子。吾身行坐臥，侍衛三十六萬兵，隨吾心所指。風火雷電生，電火擲陰雷，震動泰山傾，手把九天氣，身跨火龍背，三皇統北極，萬神拱手隨。

As Chen Diwen makes this proclamation, notice the resolve in his eyes and force in his voice. His primordial self declares to all celestial denizens that he has assumed the position of Celestial Master libationer, a term that echoes the parish leaders of the ancient Celestial Master community but here denotes a position in the celestial bureaucracy. In this position, Chen's *yuanchen* takes on cosmic proportions. His body is adorned with celestial asterisms, and he activates one of them, the Three Terraces (Santai 三台), by touching the *si, wu,* and *wei* points located on the tips of the first three fingers of his left hand. He is flanked by spirit armies of the four cardinal directions, and commands them by touching the points on his palm associated with each: *mao* for the east, *you* for the west, *wu* for the south, and *zi* for the north (web figure 3.4). Chen wields atmospheric forces and celestial *qi,* and the deities of the Northern Extremity salute him in deference. Chen's primordial self has become a powerful deity within the celestial bureaucracy after a personal audience with the high gods. He then punctuates the lengthy transformation into the divine sequence by declaring that it was all done "urgently in accordance with the statutes and commands having to do with the transformation into the divine [issued by] the Great Celestial Worthy, the

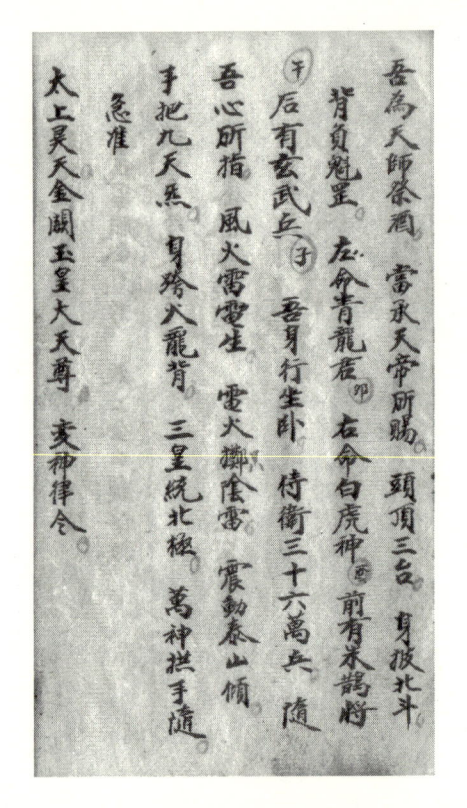

Figure 3.5 Proclamation by the *yuanchen* of the officiant in the *Banner Rite* manual. Scan by the author.

Jade Emperor of the Golden Portal of the Most High Vast Heavens" (急准太上昊天金闕玉皇大天尊變神律令).[77]

It is with the heavenly authority from this celestial position that Chen Diwen will commence to summon Yin Jiao.

Chapter Four

The Banner Rite

Inscription of the Talisman

Today I plead with you in hopes that you will appear and generously bestow thunder power to provide support for the rite.

——*Yin Jiao Incantation* intoned by Chen Diwen

Within, one must refine the elixir of return to one's true self; without, one can then cut down demons and cure illness.

——Master Bai Yuchan (fl. 1194–1229)

Chen Diwen had become a god. After transforming his body into various deities, he had recouped the vestige of cosmogonic power latent within and recovered his primordial self. As his true self, Chen acquired divine position as a Celestial Master libationer in the heavenly bureaucracy and was able to communicate directly with the gods. He stood in audience in front of Yin Jiao's superior, the Emperor of the North, and other high gods. Now Chen Diwen was ready to communicate directly with Yin Jiao.

The technology by which Chen would do so involves inscribing on a blue banner a long talisman comprising hundreds of written graphs, some in legible Chinese script and others illegible to all but the gods. The process of drawing the inscription would require more than half an hour and was far more complicated than simply writing out a series of graphs on a large piece of cloth. Chen explains:

> While inscribing the talisman, I got rid of all distracting thoughts and sincerely drew each and every talismanic graph. As I inscribed each graph, I visualized a certain something and incanted a certain something. I didn't go off and pay attention to something else. And I did not doubt myself, since I had already practiced the Banner Rite for forty-nine days and really knew it. But I wasn't certain whether the banner would knot. I could only rely on Marshal Yin and on all the gods, including my own three masters— my transmission master, my master of the registry, and my master of the canon.[1]

For this sort of talisman, inscription is bound up with simultaneous incantation and visualization in a complicated ritual amalgam meant to communicate with the celestial sphere and move a particular martial deity to respond, all with the support of the invited pantheon of gods and masters. This was an intense moment, and to face it Chen had to muster all the confidence gained from nearly two months of dedicated study of the Banner Rite.

Chen Diwen noted that the notion of talisman here is wider and more dynamic than simple inscription. The talisman to summon Marshal Yin encompasses ritual performance fundamentally concerned with the ontological status of the inscriber's body. The efficacy of talismanic script is inextricably bound up with the body in relation to the cosmic ancestor and the celestial hierarchy. The necessary first step of inscribing a talisman is the transformation of the inscriber's body and recovery of his primordial self. The inscriber cultivates his latent ancestral *qi* from the primordium and recovers his true nature united with the cosmic ancestor, the Dao. He then channels that potent ancestral *qi* into the very talisman itself. Chen will saturate the brush and ink with ancestral *qi* from his divinized body and imbue every stroke of every graph comprising the talisman with ancestral *qi* via breathy incantation and thick visualization. It is that ontological resonance with Yin Jiao and the gods that allows both the legible and illegible graphs of the talisman to penetrate (*tong*) the celestial sphere and garner a divine response. Talismanic script is not simply signification. It is more than a grammar of strange signs used to send written messages to deities. Talismanic script is also *material*. It is an expression of ancestral *qi,* the primordial stuff from the

Dao. Messages inscribed with that ancestral *qi* can resonate with deities who share in that reality.

Several months before Chen Diwen's ordination, I noticed how deep this assumption about talismans really is among masters of the lineage. While participating in a large *jiao* on behalf of several village communities thanking the Sagely Emperor of the Southern Marchmount for his blessings, I was struck by how unguarded Chen's masters were when writing out talismans during various rituals. Inevitably, a few outside the lineage would closely observe and even copy the talismans that were being written in front of them and, I learned, later try to sell them for profit, to my mind creating local competition for ritual services. Chen's masters were not concerned. Jiang Yucheng explained dryly that a talisman is inefficacious, literally "without numinous *qi*" (*meiyou lingqi* 沒有靈氣), if the inscriber does not first learn how to transform his body into the divine and stir ancestral *qi*. Without its ontological foundation, a talisman is simply a piece of cloth or paper with writing on it.[2]

A few moments in the ritual illustrate exceptionally well how signification charged with material power works to put the subject Chen Diwen in communication with the subject Yin Jiao. Defined by his history and his lineage, Chen will attempt to use terse celestial language to establish an intimate relationship with Yin Jiao. First, Chen will imbue brush and ink with his rarified breath so that their mundane bodies of wood and liquid transform into deified bodies of dragons and fire capable of conducting ancestral *qi*. In wielding these extensions of his deified body, Chen will communicate directly with Yin Jiao via the divine language of the talisman. He will remind the martial deity of his duty to his celestial superior by presenting Yin Jiao with the Emperor of the North's decree that Yin ought to respond to the summons, which Chen secured while in audience with the high gods. In another moment, Chen will evoke, in strikingly personal terms, Yin Jiao's obligation to honor the oath sworn to serve Shen the Realized One and his liturgical progeny, which ought rightfully to include Chen. By trafficking in this ontologically grounded mode of communication, Chen will attempt to remind Yin Jiao of the divine relationships that have formed who he is, and of the responsibilities they carry. As discussed in chapter 2, those relationships were fleshed out in certain Song and Yuan liturgical and hagiographical sources associated with Heart of Heaven, Emperor of the North, Divine Empyrean, and Pure Tenuity traditions. Those sources echo in the very fabric of the talisman. Finally, close reading of this talisman prompts us to rethink prevailing scholarly notions about the nature of talismans.

Transmogrification of Ritual Implements

Before Chen Diwen can begin to inscribe the talisman, he must transform the implements with which to inscribe it. The brush and ink must be made instruments capable of conducting the ancestral *qi* that gives the graphs potency in the celestial sphere (web video 4.1).

As Chen Diwen grasps the brush, he purifies the part of the altar in which the ritual implements will be transformed. He breathes in deeply a bit of the imperceptibly subtle Golden Radiance enveloping his divinized body and focuses on the front of the altar table, where the brush and ink will be transformed. Then he exhales it with an audible "*xi*" sound, literally blowing away any stale *qi* that might be lingering. The space thus purified, Chen soaks the brush with incense smoke (*xunmu* 熏沐) as he incants,

> Divine brush so numinous, fiery essence of the south, inscribe the talisman [in order to] knot the banner. Quickly implement it! [see figure 4.1][3]
>
> 神筆靈靈，南方火精，書符結旛，火速奉行。

No longer simply a mundane writing utensil, the brush takes on a divine aura of its own. Chen's incantation imbues it with ancestral *qi* from his body. The incense smoke—also a form of rarified *qi* and a purifying agent—infuses the brush with its celestial stuff that naturally rises upward toward the heavens. Next, Chen swirls the brush in a well of ink that sits on the altar. The manual instructs him to visualize that the brush transforms into a fiery dragon and the ink well transforms into a sea of fire (筆化為火龍一條，盒化為火海).[4] The infusion of rarified *qi* in Chen's incantation causes the long, tapered brush to transmogrify into the winding form of a fiery dragon, and

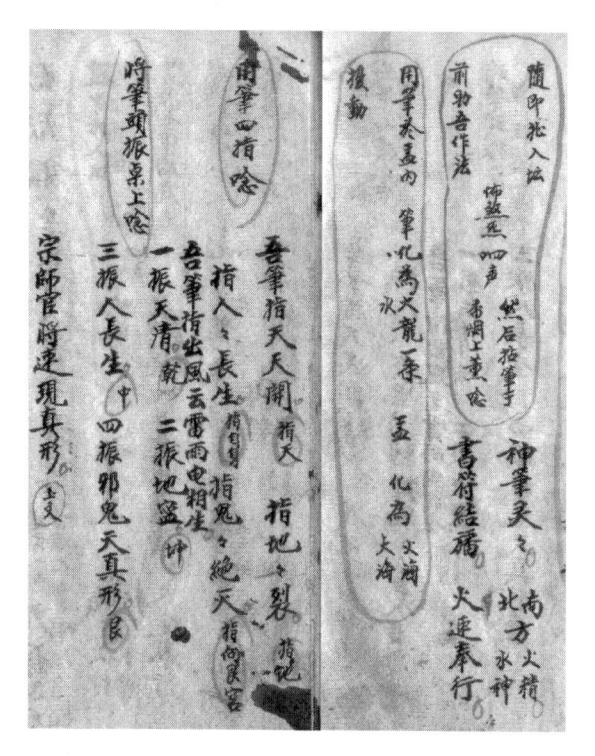

Figure 4.1 Instructions and incantations for the transmogrification of ritual implements in the *Banner Rite* manual. Scan by the author.

the bowl of ink into the fiery sea in which the dragon swims. Just as Chen's body was refined and transformed into the divine, so do the brush and ink transmogrify into divine tools capable of producing an efficacious talisman.[5]

Next, Chen Diwen extols the numinous power that emanates from the brush and ink. He incants loudly,

> When my brush points to heaven, heaven opens; when [it] points to the earth, the earth splits open; when [it] points to people, they gain long life; and when [it] points to demons, they are cut down and dissipate. [Wherever] my brush points, wind, clouds, thunder, rain, and lightning are generated. [see figure 4.1][6]

吾筆指天天開指天，指地地裂指地，筆指人人長生指自身，指鬼鬼絕滅指向艮宮。吾筆指出，風雲雷雨電相生。

As Chen voices each line, he points the brush in the appropriate direction: toward the heavens, toward the earth, toward himself, and toward the *gen* palace on his left hand, the place in the northeast called the "gate of demons." Imbued with the rarified *qi* from Chen's deified body, the transmogrified brush and ink become instruments of considerable power. They become the utensils by which Chen communicates with or "penetrates" the realms of heaven, earth, humans, and demons.

Chen Diwen continues to celebrate this rather bureaucratic expression of his cosmogonic power. He taps the altar table in front of him with the end of the brush while activating with his thumb the points corresponding to heaven, earth, humanity, and the demon gate on his left palm while incanting,

> [When I] raise [my brush] the first time, Heaven becomes clear; [when I] raise [it] the second time, Earth is pacified; [when I] raise [it] the third time, people gain long life; and [when I] raise [my brush] the fourth time, deviant demons are obliterated and [revert to] their true forms, [while] lineage masters, officials, and generals immediately manifest their true forms. [see figure 4.1][7]
>
> 一振天清乾，二振地寧坤，三振人長生中，四振邪鬼滅真形艮，宗師官將速現真形玉文。

Armed with the transmogrified implements, Chen is ready to begin inscribing the talisman. The brush and ink are ontological extensions of his deified body, conductors through which primordial *qi* flows into the written form of the talisman inscribed on the cloth of the banner.

What I find so striking about this ritual sequence is that the writing tools—the brush and ink—undergo a transformation of *their* mundane bodies, so to speak, just as the ordinand's body was refined and reunified with the primordial power of the Dao. Incense smoke purifies the brush and ink, and Chen Diwen's incantations imbue them with ancestral *qi* by which the mundane utensils transform into fiery, celestial implements. Body, ink, and brush are all transformed into divine things capable of channeling cosmogonic power. Paul Copp's notion of "material efficacy" to describe medieval Chinese Buddhist spells (*dhāraṇī, tuoluoni* 陀羅尼, *zongchi* 總持)

comes to mind. Physical objects like amulets worn on the body, reliquaries inscribed with spells, and stone pillars take on the power of those words and pass it along to those who touch them. The sound of spells infuses writing, which infuses the object inscribed, which infuses things that come in contact with that inscribed object. Spells become material things that have material effects on things in the world. Although Copp is careful to make a distinction between medieval Buddhist imagery of the transformative words of the Buddha, his body, and spells and the kind of monist worldview embraced by Daoist practitioners in which *qi* substantiates all phenomenal things in the cosmos, Copp's attention to ways in which material things are imbued with power is instructive.[8] In the case of the Banner Rite, the breathy incantations emanating from Chen Diwen's divinized body carry ancestral *qi* to ink and brush, which will then conduct that charged substance to the graphs composing the talisman. Power flows from Dao to body to ink and brush, and finally to language itself.

The Initial Sequence of the Talisman

Chen Diwen begins the actual inscription of the talisman by producing a circular graph referred to as the ancestral *qi* of the primordial chaos (*hundun zuqi* 混沌祖氣), also called the ancestral *qi* of the Anterior Heaven (*Xiantian zuqi* 先天祖氣). The graph signals that the entire talisman to come is itself an expression of ancestral *qi* flowing from the primordial stillness of the Anterior Heaven, which was tapped by Chen when he recovered his primordial self (see figure 4.2, web video 4.2 [0:00–0:24]).

To explain this graph, Chen Diwen's masters turn to the lineage's main theoretical text, the *Secret Transmission*, which, recall, was taught to Chen by his transmission master the day he received the *yuanchen*. That text defines ancestral *qi* as follows:

Figure 4.2
Talismanic graph
for the ancestral
qi of the primordial
chaos.

Ancestral means incipience or beginning. *Qi* means numinosity of the void; it does not mean the breath that is exhaled and inhaled. Ancestral *qi* emerged from the time prior to the undifferentiated state, from the beginning of the great ultimate. Were Heaven to lack this unified *qi,* then the sun and moon would not shine. Were the earth to lack this unified *qi,* then plants and trees would not grow. Were human beings to lack this unified *qi,* then their minds and intentions would lack a master.[9]

祖者，初也，始也。氣者，虛靈也，非吹噓之氣也。祖氣出於混沌之前，太極之始。天無此一氣則日月不明。地無此一氣則草木不生，人無此一氣則心意無主。

In his early 1990s commentary on the *Secret Transmission*, Jiang Shenzhi comments on this passage:

The ancestral *qi* of the Anterior Heaven is the process of transformation of the myriad things. This is to say that at present there exist heaven and earth, and within the world there exist the myriad things. None of them would have been formed outside the progressing transformations of ancestral *qi* from the Anterior Heaven.[10]

先天祖氣是萬物之變化過程。若現在之有天地，世間之有萬物，皆不外乎先天祖氣演變而成之。

Ancestral *qi* is the numinous power (*ling*) of creative potency that existed in the void, before the undifferentiated, murky chaos emerged, which the great ultimate divided into *yin* and *yang*—dark and light, turbid and rarified *qi*—which constituted the first patterned movements stirring the birth of the cosmos. In the subsequent phenomenal world, everything retains a vestige of this numinous, creative power in its nature (*xing* 性). Ancestral *qi* is the potency by which things in the world flourish. The sun and moon shine in the heavens, the vegetation of the earth grows, and human beings have the capacity for reasoned thought and emotion. Ancestral *qi* remains as the remnant of creative capacity from the primordium, the impulse that drives the patterned movements by which things are generated and maintained.

As we have seen, ancestral *qi* is the fundamental power that Chen Diwen recouped when he recovered his primordial self after destroying his mundane body and taking on the bodies of several deities. It is that entire process of identification with cosmogonic power to which this first graph refers. Chen first draws the circular frame of the graph and then uses the brush to inscribe one strong calligraphic stroke within it. In one of the lineage's manuals scripting a truncated version of this talisman used in minor exorcistic rites, the officiant is instructed to draw this graph while simultaneously incanting, "One point [within] the sphere of radiance gathers the myriad deities" (圓光一點，統集萬神). Further along in the manual, the officiant is directed to draw the graph again while visualizing the appearance of Yin Jiao and intoning, "One point [within] the sphere of radiance and the Marshal appears" (圓光一點，元帥現形).[11] It seems that the spherical shape of the graph denotes the primordial chaos itself, a radiant void within which a single point of numinous power emerges ready to spark the transformations desired in the ritual.

Some historical corroboration can be found in Zhao Yizhen's *Pivot of the Methods of the Dao of the Qingwei [Tradition]*: "In rites these days, when inscribing a talisman one must first draw the image of a circle. This is the

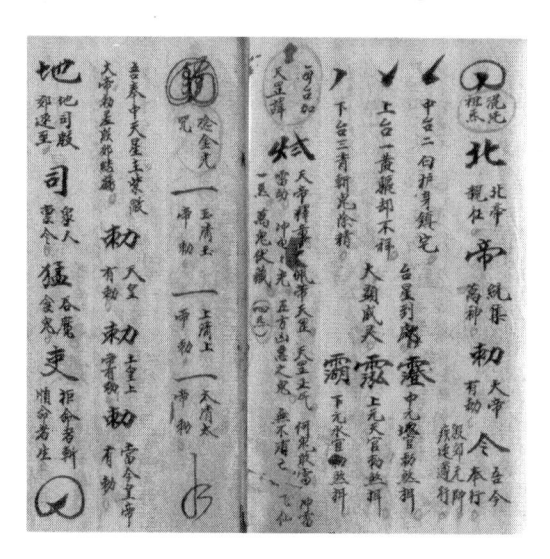

Figure 4.3 The dispersed form of the beginning sequences of the talisman to summon General Yin in the *Banner Rite* manual. Scan by the author.

[image of] creative transformation that can then be seen" (今法書符必先畫一圓象，其為造化便可見矣).[12] Zhao's instruction for drawing a circle at the head of a talisman seems to resonate with the teachings of Zhang Shanyuan. That master taught practitioners to visualize one point of bright light in the Anterior Heaven, which is emitted through the eyes in the form of radiant light that forms a circle. This circle, Zhang explained, is the great Dao, the primordial *qi* of the Ancestral Heaven; when located in the body it is one's primordial self.[13]

Chen Diwen's inscription of the talisman's initial graph seems to echo the teachings of these Song and Yuan masters. The graph itself is an externalization of the ancestral *qi* emanating from his primordial self. As the first graph in the talisman, it marks off the ensuing script as special writing. As Chen inscribes each graph to follow, he will simultaneously voice an incantation or engage in a visualization memorized from the *Banner Rite* manual (see figure 4.3). A kind of synthesis is produced between written word, speech, and mental image. All are intermingling expressions of ancestral *qi* flowing from Chen's primordial self. His voice and mental imagery not only convey meaning to Yin Jiao but also imbue the graphs with ancestral *qi* via the brush and ink enabled to conduct such powerful stuff after their transmogrification. The entire talisman is charged with cosmogonic power certain to penetrate the celestial sphere and resonate with the martial deity.

Chen Diwen continues the talisman by inscribing four graphs. Unlike many of the graphs that make up the talisman, they are written in mundane Chinese, comprehensible to all. The four characters read: "The Emperor of the North decrees" (*Beidi chiling* 北帝勅令). They identify the entire talisman as a mandate from the Emperor of the North telling Yin Jiao to obey the summons (see figure 4.4, web video 4.2 [0:24–1:06]).

As Chen inscribes the four characters, he intones sotto voce an accompanying incantation. He utters one verse of the incantation with each character and adds a fifth verse at the end. Altogether the incantation states,

> The Emperor of the North himself raises [celestial troops]; he musters the myriad spirits. The great Emperor has a decree that today I implement. Marshal Yin Jiao, quickly comply! [see figure 4.3][14]

北帝親征，統集萬神。大帝有敕，吾今奉行。
殷郊元帥，疾速遵行。

In chapter 3, we saw that Chen Diwen's primordial self traveled to the celestial sphere with a protective retinue of thunder deities and had an audience with the high gods. Here we see that Chen has secured an official decree from the Emperor of the North and now boldly proclaims that he is implementing the imperial mandate that Yin Jiao comply with Chen's summons. The talisman plays on the hierarchical relationship between Yin Jiao and the Emperor of the North. Recall from the end of the lineage's *Genealogical Investigation* hagiography that the Emperor of the North descended from Purple Tenuity and conferred on Yin Jiao a title stating his allegiance to the throne of the Emperor of the Northern Extremity. In fact, references to Yin Jiao's position as directly subordinate to the Emperor of the North are shot through the lineage's texts. One manual for summoning Yin identifies him as belonging to the Governing Office of the Northern Extremity (Beiji zongshe si) ruled by the Emperor.[15] In an audience ritual to the Emperor of the North (Chao Beidi ke 朝北帝科), typically performed on the second day of any *jiao*,

Figure 4.4
Talismanic graphs
for the "Emperor of
the North decrees."

Marshal Yin is employed to guard the delivery of the memorial from the officiant's altar to the Emperor's administrative seat, the Palace of the Stellar River (the Milky Way) of the Northern Extremity (Beiji xinghan gong 北極星漢宮).[16] Various rites to summon Yin Jiao by sublimation (*zhaolian* 召煉) end by beseeching Yin to reply "quickly in accordance with the statutes and commands of the Great Emperor of Purple Tenuity, Lord of the Stars of the Central Heaven of the Northern Extremity" (急准北帝中天星主紫微大帝律令).[17] Marshal Yin is clearly a functionary of the Emperor of the North's celestial administration.[18]

We saw in chapter 2 that this bureaucratic relationship has been recognized since at least the late twelfth or thirteenth century. Peng Yuantai insisted that Yin Jiao is the most esteemed attendant of the Emperor of the North. Like the Four Saints—Tianpeng, Heisha, Xuanwu, and Tianyou—of Heart of Heaven and older Emperor of the North traditions, Yin Jiao serves the Emperor as a heavenly martial deity who deals with demons but is resolutely not of the Fengdu underworld. Peng Yuantai's *Great Rite* instructs the officiant to chant the *Incantation for Communicating with Purple Tenuity (Ziwei chongzhou)*. One line states, "When the Emperor on High has a mandate, [Yin Jiao] quickly descends" (上帝有命，疾速降臨).[19] That Emperor on High is clearly the Emperor of the North, given that the incantation ends with "quickly, quickly in accordance with the statutes and commands of the Great Emperor of Purple Tenuity of the Northern Extremity, which decree that Yin, Marshal of Great Power, Great Year of the Earth Ministry quickly descend" (急急如北極紫微大帝律令，勅召地司太歲大威力元帥殷某速降).[20] The Pure Tenuity *Upper Clarity Great Rite* includes an incantation ending with a similar exhortation.[21] Chen Diwen's four-character inscription and incantation draws on this old bureaucratic relationship to compel Yin Jiao to respond to the summons.

The hagiography of Yin Jiao preserved by Chen's lineage gives this bureaucratic relationship the intimacy of kinship. Recall that Yin Jiao's mother was impregnated by the *qi* of the Emperor of the North as he descended on horseback from the celestial realm to the depths of Fengdu.[22] After Yin Jiao attained the Dao under the tutelage of Shen the Realized One, the Emperor of the North again descended, this time riding a whirlwind carriage, to confer on Yin a divine title designating him as a servant before the throne of the Northern Extremity.[23] The shape of the story suggests that the Emperor of the North welcomed his divine son home to serve as his personal aide, seemingly echoing Peng Yuantai's thirteenth-century accolade: "His merits are the greatest and his position is the highest [of all the gods who attend the Emperor]."[24]

When read in the context of the larger Banner Rite, these four graphs of the talisman hang together in a discernible ritual syntax. Chen Diwen's inscription of the graphs with the accompanying incantation is a bold declaration to Yin Jiao that Chen ascended to the heavenly court and has secured proper authority from the Emperor of the North himself to summon the martial deity. The declaration aims to compel Yin Jiao to recognize his administrative duty to his celestial superior. When read with the lineage's hagiography, the talismanic declaration is imbued with the more intimate responsibilities of kinship. These graphs exude a sense that the Emperor of the North, Yin Jiao, and Chen Diwen are bound together in a nexus of both bureaucratic and personal responsibility. The talisman that Chen has learned to wield is itself a manifestation of the divine power of the Emperor of the North to activate Yin Jiao and unleash his exorcistic might.

Chen Diwen continues working on the banner by inscribing three checkmark-like graphs under the watchful eye of his presenting master, Jiang Yucheng (see figure 4.5, web video 4.2 [1:06–2:16]). Beginning at the center, he inks the cloth with a standard calligraphic stroke, first pressing down on the brush and then lightly upward and to the right while intoning an incantation under his breath. Then on top of the thick, teardrop part of the graph he inscribes two more celestial graphs, each accompanied by an incantation. The latter two

Figure 4.5
Talismanic graphs for the Three Terraces, Three Officers, and Celestial Guideline.

graphs remain obscure to all but Marshal Yin and the deities witnessing the ritual. Chen continues the same sequence on the right side of the banner. First the checkmark-like graph, this time created with a different calligraphic stroke, followed by two more graphs on top, all accompanied by incantations. He does the same on the left side of the banner. In all, the three visible marks on the banner are actually nine graphs and incantations.

The graphs, made of ancestral *qi* channeled through the media of ink and sound, invoke the apotropaic powers of stellar deities known as the Three Terraces, the Three Officers (Sanguan 三官), and the Celestial Guideline (Tiangang 天罡). The cluster of deities is called upon to purify the talisman, to rid it of meddlesome demons and noxious *qi* attracted to the divine activity. These deities ensure that demonic forces do not interfere with Chen's production of the talisman and encumber communication of its message to Yin Jiao.

As Chen Diwen inscribes each of the first three graphs, he intones the following incantations:

 Upper Terrace, first and yellow, expels inauspiciousness.
上台一黃，驅卻不祥。

 The Officer of Heaven of the Upper Prime decrees that killer [*qi*] be bound!
上元天官敕煞攝。

 The Celestial Emperor disperses the insignia [of the Celestial Guideline] and [I] wear it about my waist. What demon can stand before the orthodox *qi* of the Celestial Guideline? It pours out thunder [and so] thunder rumbles; it pours out lightning [and so] lightning strikes. In the five directions, all the demons of inauspiciousness and evil perish. Myriad demons lie in hiding when the flying transcendent [the officiant] unifies *qi*.

天帝釋章，佩帶天罡。天罡正氣，何鬼敢當。沖雷雷動，沖電電光。五方凶惡之鬼，無不消亡。飛仙一氣，萬鬼伏藏。

Chen continues to inscribe the right side of the banner, incanting, "Middle Terrace, second and white, protect [my] body and guard [this] household. The Officer of Earth of the Middle Prime decrees that killer [*qi*] be bound!" (中台二白，護身鎮宅。中元地官敕煞攝). Chen finishes the sequence with the same incantation to the Celestial Guideline. Last, he inscribes the left side of the banner as he incants, "Lower Terrace, third and azure, beheads demons and expels sprites. The Officer of Water of the Lower Prime decrees that killer [*qi*] be bound!" (下台三青，斬鬼除精。下元水官敕煞攝). Chen then repeats the incantation to the Celestial Guideline and finishes the sequence by intoning, "Wherever Terrace stars arrive, they manifest their great power and might!" (台星到處，大顯威靈) (see figure 4.3).[25]

The Three Terraces Chen Diwen invokes are deities associated with the three pairs of stars located below the Big Dipper. This cluster of stellar deities has often been associated with the practice of walking a guideline to ascend to the heavens when an officiant visualizes he personally delivers a petition to the celestial court.[26] But here Chen invokes each of the Three Terraces with breath and brush and exhorts them to lend their protective power over the talisman itself. Each of the Three Terraces is imagined to emit ancestral *qi* that separated into three modes of primal *qi*—yellow, white, and azure—during the cosmogony.[27] These modes, potent with exorcistic power, charge the talisman and protect it from demonic disruption. The practice of calling on the deities of the Three Terraces to imbue an object with exorcistic *qi* was in wide use by the Song. When producing talismans, ritual officiants routinely "drew through the nose" (*biyin* 鼻引) or "gathered up" (*qu* 取) the chromatic luminous breaths emitting from the Three Terraces and "infused" or "poured" (*guanzhu* 灌注) them into lustral water or the brush used to inscribe a talisman.[28] Something along these lines is going on here. Chen appeals to the deities of the Three Terraces to imbue the talisman with their apotropaic, primal light to purify it.

The graphs inscribed inside each of the check-like marks function in a similar way. Chen Diwen produces the taboo names of the Three Officers of Heaven, Earth, and Water.[29] In the early Celestial Master movement, the Three Officers were the high gods to which practitioners wrote out petitions in triplicate, placing one copy on a mountain, burying one in the ground, and tossing one in a body of water. The Three Primes referred to the three modes of *qi*—dark (*xuan* 玄), primal (*yuan* 元), and commencing (*shi* 始)—into which unified, primordial *qi* divided during the cosmogony.[30] By the Song, the Three Officers were explicitly associated with the cosmogonic breaths of the Three Primes. The titles Officer of Heaven of the Upper Prime (Shangyuan tianguan 上元天官), Officer of Earth of the Middle Prime (Zhongyuan diguan 中元地官), and Officer of Water of the Lower Prime (Xiayuan shuiguan 下元水官) are common in sources from Song and Yuan traditions. These titles seem to cast each of the Three Officers as purveyors of these three primal breaths, just as the deities of the Three Terraces emanate tripartite cosmogonic power. By the Song period, the taboo names of the Three Officers were often invoked during rituals for inscribing talismans. For example, the *Jade Mirror of the Numinous Treasure* (*Lingbao yujian* 靈寶玉鑑) instructs the officiant to "inscribe these three characters one on top of the next at the bottom. With the eyes, pour the three [modes of] *qi*—azure, yellow, and white—[into a brush]. Combine the [*qi* of the] Three Officers and transfer it to the brush for use" (疊書此三字于下，目注青、黃、白三氣。三官混合，運筆作用).[31] Just as the practitioner following this text employs the Three Officers to purify the stylus used to inscribe a talisman, so Chen Diwen invokes the Three Officers to marshal the chromatic, cosmogonic modes of *qi* associated with the Three Primes and use them to contain noxious *qi,* thereby purifying the talisman.

The last graph and incantation included within each checkmark continues the theme of apotropaic protection. The masters of Chen's lineage and their texts define the graph as the taboo name of the Celestial Guideline. The Celestial Guideline is here an appellation that refers to the deities of the Big Dipper asterism, but it has also been specifically identified with the lord of the seventh star of the Dipper, Pojun (破軍), the star that points out from the bowl. The Dipper has been called the Celestial Guideline because it rotates throughout the year from its fixed point near the Northern Extremity to trace the circumference of heaven, like the sphere of a compass.[32] In Song sources, the invocation of the Celestial Guideline commonly follows the invocation of the Three Terraces during the production of talismans. The *Correct Rites of the Heart of Heaven of the Shangqing Tradition* provides vivid imagery:

> Great Sage Celestial Guideline, Stellar Lord Pojun, [I] request that [your] jade-like radiance descend and [your] true *qi* infuse my heart, my five viscera, my six organs, [my] three hundred and sixty joints and bones, and [my] eighty-four thousand pores. Expel diseased *qi* and demonic *qi*.[33]

> 天罡大聖，破軍星君，願降瑤光，真氣灌注臣身心、五臟、六腑、三百六十骨節之內、八萬四千毫竅之中。驅逐病氣鬼氣。

The Heart of Heaven practitioner visualizes that he pours filaments of divine, exorcistic *qi* from the Terrace stars and the Celestial Guideline into his body. According to the *Secret Essentials of the Most High for Assembling the Realized Ones for Assisting the Country and Saving Its People*, he may then "draw the orthodox *qi* of each [of those deities] into a talisman" (各取正氣入符中).[34]

Similarly, Chen Diwen "unifies the *qi*" of these stellar deities; that is, he absorbs it into his body. Then each of the three times he inscribes the taboo name while intoning the incantation, he disperses their orthodox *qi* into the talisman. While he inscribes the last upward stroke of the graph, he forces breath out of his mouth into the talisman by making a pronounced

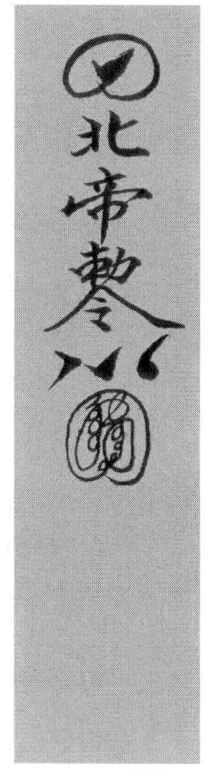

Figure 4.6
Talismanic graph for
Golden Radiance.

"*xi*" sound (see figure 4.3). The cluster of stellar deities invoked by this ritual sequence all issue primal *qi* generated during the cosmogony. Chen directs this *qi* into the talisman to cleanse it of stale breaths and demonic forces that might disrupt the ability of the talisman to penetrate the celestial sphere. The primordial self that Chen recovered during his transformation into the divine enables him to wield such powerful, cosmic forces.

Next Chen Diwen inscribes the circular graph for the Golden Radiance while intoning the same *Incantation of the Golden Radiance* that we examined at the beginning of the transformation into a divine body sequence in chapter 3 (see figure 4.6, video 4.2 [2:16–2:39]). Instead of casting a fiery net around his body and sparking the inner alchemical reaction necessary to transform it, Chen invokes the Golden Radiance to wreath the talisman. The masters speak of the Golden Radiance here as functioning like an "opening of the eyes" (*kaiguang* 開光) ritual in which a master dots the eyes of an image of a deity with charged ink and breath to activate it (web figure 4.1). The talisman, having been imbued with ancestral *qi* from stellar deities, is imagined to emit a radiant glow that protects it from demonic influences.

Figure 4.6
Talismanic graph for
Golden Radiance.

Figure 4.7
Talismanic graph
denoting decrees
by high gods.

In the next sequence, Chen Diwen invokes the authoritative mandates of several high deities in the pantheon (see figure 4.7, web video 4.2 [2:39–end]). Chen first makes three horizontal strokes, each associated with one of the Three Pure Ones, pure emanations of the Dao and lofty gods in the pantheon. Then he makes a vertical stroke that represents the Emperor of Purple Tenuity (the Emperor of the North). With each stroke, Chen intones a verse of an incantation:

> The Jade Emperor of Jade Purity decrees; the Upper Emperor of Upper Purity decrees; and the Great Emperor of Great Purity decrees. I serve the Great Emperor of Purple Tenuity, the Stellar Lord of the Central Heaven, [who] decrees that Yin Jiao be dispatched to knot the banner.[35]

> 玉清玉帝敕，上清上帝敕，太清太帝敕。吾奉中天星主紫微大帝，敕差殷郊結旛。

Below the vertical stroke, Chen begins inscribing graphs one on top of the other. They will eventually bleed into one another to form a thick inkblot of graphs on the bottom of the banner. Chen begins a talismanic sequence that continues to invoke the mandates of other high deities in the pantheon. As he inscribes, "Decree, decree, decree the fierce clerk of the Earth Ministry" (敕敕敕地司猛吏), Chen incants the following, one verse per character:

> The Emperor of Heaven has made a decree; the Upper Emperor of the Earth has made a decree; and the reigning emperor has made a decree that Yin Jiao of the Earth Ministry quickly arrive. Everybody, take these orders to swallow fiends and devour demons! Those who resist the mandate will be decapitated; those who accord with it will live. [see figure 4.3][36]

> 天皇有敕，土皇上帝有敕，當今皇帝有敕，地司殷郊速至。眾人稟令，吞魔食鬼。拒命者斬，順命者生。

We saw in the beginning sequence of the talisman that Chen's primordial self traveled to the celestial court and garnered the decree from the Emperor of the North. The language here implies Chen also secured other decrees. He announces to Yin Jiao in ink and voice that he wields the mandates of several of the most exalted deities in the pantheon. Chen's masters remind that Yin Jiao himself is ferocious and wild. He needs strong incentive to comply with the summons.

The Heart Seal

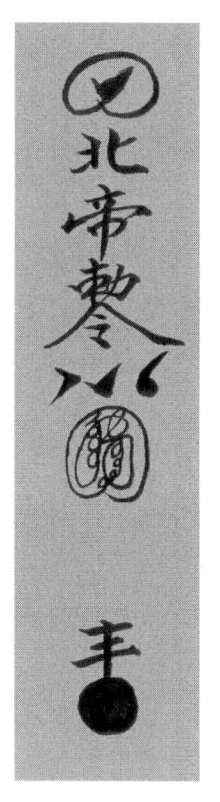

Figure 4.8
Ink blot formed by
dozens of graphs.

On the bottom of the banner, Chen Diwen continues to inscribe over a hundred graphs while intoning their accompanying incantations, one on top of the other, to form a thick ball of charged ink (see figure 4.8, web video 4.3). Groups of graphs and incantations hang together in discernible sequences, as if they have been stitched together into one great talisman. They constitute a storehouse of all the talismanic content related to Yin Jiao that has come down through the lineage. In fact, the talisman in the Banner Rite is the mother talisman of two truncated versions—one very short and the other a little longer—used in minor exorcistic rites.[37] Just as with the entire Banner Rite, Chen and his masters do not understand everything about how the long talisman has been knitted together, nor can they explain the meaning of every graph and incantation. They trust that the writings and intonations work to communicate to Yin Jiao that he ought to comply with the summons. Doing the ritual writing is more important than understanding it. Yet Chen and his masters do focus on several moments in the inscription of the talisman, which provide a fascinating window into one way in which the talisman works to compel Yin Jiao to obey the summons. In one of those moments, Chen inscribes and incants Yin Jiao's "heart seal" (*xinyin* 心印).

Masters of the lineage explain that a heart seal is a kind of taboo name (*hui*) derived from one's Daoist name to which a spoken incantation is added. Recall that Chen Diwen's master, Li Yezhen, chose for him two liturgical names—one Daoist and one Buddhist—that he will, if the Banner Rite is successful, formally submit to the celestial bureaucracy for inclusion in the heavenly archives. Chen's Daoist name, Chen Yude (陳玉得), consists of three characters: his surname, a generational character, and a personal character. As we saw in chapter 1, Chen's generational character, *yu,* was taken from the poem used to mark his lineage's Daoist generations. The final character, *de,* is his personal character and was chosen by his transmission master.

The personal character and an accompanying incantation constitute Chen Diwen's heart seal. When he conferred on Chen his Daoist name, Li Yezhen broke the character *de* 得 into its four orthographic components (*chi* 彳, *ri* 日, *yi* 一, and *cun* 寸) and used them to compose a poetic incantation:

The five phases of a doubled man rise	双人五行起
To the sun, moon, and the three-flower stars.	日月三花星
One-point-three inches [below the navel] recycle [the divine embryo] nine times,	一寸三九轉
It attains the Dao in the Palace of the Muddy Pellet [the upper cinnabar field in the head].	得道泥元[丸]宮
As quickly as this heart seal is brought forth	心印火速到
Generals and marshals arrive at the altar space.	將帥赴壇中

After he dies, Chen will be able to ascend to the celestial office assigned to him later in the ordination. His heart seal will become a talisman. When any future disciple invokes the deceased Chen Diwen, the disciple will use his mind's eye to visualize writing each component of the character *de* while incanting the corresponding line of the poem. Visualizing and incanting Chen's heart seal will be the mechanism by which his disciples invoke him to witness their performances of the ritual procedures he taught them. Likewise,

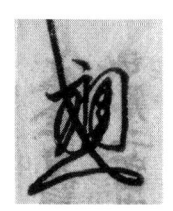  

Figure 4.9 The heart seal of Yin Jiao derived from the character *jiao* 郊 (left), of Wang Lingguan derived from *ling* 靈 (center), and of Zhang Jue derived from *jue* 珏 (right). Scans by the author. Taken respectively from *Yingong fanfa*, 12b; *Wangshuai zhaolian*, 2a; *Zhangshuai zhaolian*, 9b.

Chen will employ his master Li Yezhen's heart seal to invoke him after his passing. Every time he employs his master's heart seal, an officiant not only calls on his master to support him in the performance of a rite, but also is reminded from whom he acquired the esoteric knowledge from which ritual efficacy flows. Memory, knowledge, gratitude, and obligation inhere in a touching moment of connection between disciple and master.[38]

Not only masters have personal heart seals. Martial deities do as well. Yin Jiao's heart seal is a highly stylized derivation of his name, *jiao* 郊. The *Yin Jiao Incantation* is usually chanted while composing it. Chen's lineage also recognizes heart seals of other martial deities. For example, Wang Lingguan's heart seal derives from the *ling* character in his name, and that of Zhang Jue from the *jue* character in his name (see figure 4.9).[39] Just as talismanic graphs used to summon masters derive from their names, so do graphs for invoking martial deities derive from theirs. Chen Diwen's knowledge of Yin Jiao's esoteric name identifies Chen as a member of the lineage to which Yin Jiao belongs. It is a marker of a legitimate relationship between the two, and so should garner the attention of the fickle martial deity.

The concept of heart seal at play here is pregnant with multiple meanings that have made their way to Chen Diwen's lineage. In inner alchemical texts, the term generally connotes reception of precious teachings within an authentic lineage. That is, the true teachings of the Dao have been legitimately transmitted from master to disciple down the generations of an orthodox lineage. In his early Ming annotation of the *Wondrous Scripture on the Heart Seal of the Jade Emperor on High (Gaoshang Yuhuang xinyin miao-*

jing 高上玉皇心印妙經), likely a Southern Song text, Quanzhen master Zhou Xuanzhen (周玄貞) notes,

> This [heart seal] means that the Jade Emperor transmitted [the teaching] by heart, and generations of sages have passed it on by imprinting one heart upon another. Awakened realization and thorough comprehension both follow from this instruction, which none of the Three Teachings [Daoism, Buddhism, and Confucianism] violate. Therefore it is called "heart seal."[40]
>
> 此玉帝傳心，聖聖相承，以心印心，明悟了證，皆宗此旨，三教莫違，故云心印。

Here the term "heart seal" connotes the essential inner alchemical teaching from one of the most august deities in the pantheon, which is then passed from master to disciple down the generations without variation, like a seal impressing an identical imprint on one heart or mind after another.

This metaphor of a seal or stamp imprinting one true, primordial teaching on a series of practitioners to form a lineage echoes earlier Chan Buddhist images of mind-to-mind transmission. The action of the mind of the Chan master—the awakening experience itself—imprinting itself on the mind of a disciple is captured by the image of an inked stamp pressing on an absorbent surface. The experience of awakening is perfectly duplicated, connecting the disciple, his master, and all previous masters in a line back to the Buddha.[41] In inner alchemical practice, the metaphor of the heart seal implied that the esoteric knowledge passed down heart to heart, mouth to mouth (*kouchuan xinshou* 口傳心授) within a lineage was far superior to receiving scriptures and other written texts. In his commentary on Zhang Boduan's (張伯端) (987?–1028) inner alchemical classic *Folios on Awakening to Truth* (*Wuzhen pian* 悟真篇), Southern Lineage of the Golden Elixir master Weng Baoguang (翁葆光) (fl. 1173) wrote:

> The thousands of scriptures and tens of thousands of treatises are merely branches spreading [from the main trunk of the teaching]. The utmost Dao is not complicated; it is transmitted solely through the heart seal. If one has not yet met a true master, whatever has been said is in vain![42]
>
> 千經萬論，惟布枝條。至道不繁，獨傳心印。未遇真師，徒勞口耳。

These inner alchemical notions of heart seal stressed the idea of authenticity. Masters' transmitting a single essential teaching to disciples by other than written text asserted that that teaching emanated from the Dao. The notion of heart seal both safeguarded the absolute esoteric nature of teaching and defined the boundaries of a lineage.

This connotation of heart seal was complicated by another meaning. In Song and Yuan ritual performance, heart seals functioned as a kind of marker of an officiant's personal identity. In the *Great Incantatory Rite for Assembling the True Ones* (*Zongzhen dazhou fa* 總真大咒法), included in Deng Yougong's *Correct Rites of the Heart of Heaven of the Shangqing Tradition,* a seventy-seven-character incantation is presented for recitation in several rites, including those for rainmaking and exorcising demons. The incantation ends with the line, "Whether I walk, stand, sit or recline, I orally declare [my] heart seal. Quickly, quickly in accordance with the statutes and commands!" (行住坐臥，口述心印。急急如律令).[43] Like a signature at the end of a declaration, the officiant discloses his identity to the realms of both deities and demons after he communicates to them his liturgical intent. Similarly, in the *Great Rite of the Thunderclap of the Jade Pivot of Cavernous Mystery* (*Dongxuan yushu leiting dafa* 洞玄玉樞雷霆大法), a Divine Empyrean text recognizing Bai Yuchan as a patriarch, the officiant is instructed to inscribe his heart seal at the end of any petition he presents, including that for requesting promotion to a higher celestial office.[44] The heart seal functions as a traditional seal used for signatures. It identifies the sender of the petition to the divine bureaucracy, thereby authenticating the document.

Texts in another collection, the *Great Rite of the Five Thunders of the Fiery Court of Taiyi* (*Taiyi huofu wulei dafa* 太乙火府五雷大法), refer to heart seals as "flower signatures" (*huaya zi* 花押字) or simply as "signatures" (*ya* 押).[45] The term *flower signature* echoes a practice from calligraphic culture. From at least the Period of Disunion, officials might use excessively ornate cursive script (*caoshu* 草書) or a symbol derived from a specific character to sign official documents, especially contracts. Calligraphers and artists also created artistic scripts to display their personal identities. They often created flower signatures by isolating and embellishing individual strokes that together comprise a character. For example, Emperor Song Huizong famously created such a signature by disassembling and embellishing each stroke of the character *tian* 天, "Heaven," to imply the phrase *Tianxia yiren* (天下一人), "One man under Heaven."[46] It seems that during the Tang–Song period, the pursuit of individual expression in calligraphy had permeated the use of heart seals in religious practice.

Just as a ritual officiant might use a heart seal to mark his personal identity, he might also proffer the heart seal of a martial deity. The *Esoteric Rite [to Summon] Marshal Wang Lingguan of the Fiery Chariot of the Three and Five of the Thunderclap* (*Leiting sanwu huoche lingguan Wang yuanshuai bifa* 雷霆三五火車靈官王元帥祕法) features Divine Empyrean master Sa Shoujian, who subdued the demon-turned-thunder deity Wang Lingguan. In an instruction for producing a talisman to summon and deploy one of Wang's associates, Marshal Qiu (邱元帥), the practitioner is directed to "blow [my] worthy *qi* toward the *kui* asterism in the Big Dipper, and inscribe [the deity's] heart seal to draw [him] out from the *kui* asterism" (吹賢炁魁斗，塗書心印，出魁).[47] Here the marshal's heart seal is identified with an esoteric talisman that, when imbued with rarified astral *qi,* gets the deity's attention and draws him down to service. This case reveals two underlying assumptions: the martial deity must have already established a relationship with the practitioner's lineage and revealed his heart seal to it, and the practitioner must have learned how to produce this talismanic heart seal from a master in his lineage.

In yet other cases, a practitioner might produce the heart seal of a patriarch of the lineage, and by that authority press a martial deity into service. For example, the *Esoteric Rite [to Summon] Marshal Zhao of the Mysterious Altar of Orthodox Unity* (*Zhengyi xuantan Zhao yuanshuai bifa* 正一玄壇趙元帥祕法) instructs how to employ Marshal Zhao Gongming, who serves the first Celestial Master, Zhang Daoling.[48] The practitioner is first directed to visualize Marshal Zhao, who is "utterly fierce, mighty, and frightening" (大怒威猛可畏), and seemingly resistant to summons. Then the practitioner should "immediately illumine this heart seal of the Celestial Master, our revered ancestor, and then visualize that the might of the Marshal has been restrained" (急將老祖天師心印照之，想元帥威收却) (web figure 4.2). The practitioner should then breathe the martial deity into his own body and perform an inner alchemical visualization by which the god "mixes and becomes one with the mysterious altar of [the practitioner's] own palace [the central cinnabar field near the lungs]" (與本宮玄壇混合為一).[49] Here the practitioner harnesses the ferocity and might of Marshal Zhao by producing Zhang Daoling's heart seal, thereby invoking the authority of the deity's master. The officiant can then form an intimate relationship with Marshal Zhao, in this case by literally uniting with him in his body. In this ritual, the heart seal functions not only as a marker of the patriarch's identity, but also as a kind of credential. It is an authentication of the practitioner's membership in the patriarch's lineage, and a password allowing the practitioner to form a relationship with the patriarch's divine functionary. This kind of heart seal displays a hierarchical yet close relationship between practitioner, patriarch, and martial deity.[50]

These two major meanings evoked by the image of the heart seal—the impression of precious teachings received within a lineage and a personal marker of identity or authentication in ritual events—both hang together. We see this in, for example, the *Hymn by Celestial Master Xujing to Excise [Ritual] Impropriety* (*Xujing tianshi powang zhang* 虛靖天師破妄章), a text attributed to the thirtieth Celestial Master, Zhang Jixian, but likely compiled by later members of the Celestial Master lineage during the Southern Song, Yuan, or early Ming. In the voice of Zhang Jixian, the text declares that "seals ought to be heart seals" (印須心印) and then comments with a poem:

The heart seal is transmitted to those who are destined.	心印相傳付有緣
People today carve wood without understanding the mystery [of the heart seal].	今人刊木不知玄
Where [one's heart seal] is shared with the heart seals of ancestral masters,	祖師心印相同處

> Pearls of radiant light pervade the Nine Heavens.[51]   顆顆光明徹九天

Far from simply a ritual implement made of carved wood, the heart seal is the mysterious, essential teaching that is passed down the generations. Its profundity is available only to those who have been destined to become members of the lineage. The poem then implies that ancestral masters, and therefore all members of the lineage, possess their own heart seals. When shared or shown to one another in ritual moments, the intention of the ritual is successfully communicated to the celestial sphere.

The one truth of the heart seal as essential teaching is impressed on individual masters and disciples—and, as discussed, martial deities as well. In ritual, that one teaching is embodied and expressed by those individuals, binding them together into a lineage defined by its reception of truth. A quintessential Daoist logic is at play here. The teaching emanating from the one Dao manifests as creative impulse in the variegated world expressed by ritual action. Individual heart seals reflect and illumine the ultimate heart seal. Recognition of others' heart seals, then, is recognition of this shared teaching about the reality on which ritual turns.

The heart seals produced in the Banner Rite reverberate with many of these meanings from the Song, Yuan, and early Ming. Chen Diwen's masters explain that the poem accompanying Chen's heart seal is included on every document submitted to the heavens during the ordination *jiao,* including the Dispatch to Inform the Generals sent off at the beginning of the Banner Rite. It is the seal of authentication that Chen has been initiated into the core esoteric teaching of the lineage—how to perform the Banner Rite—which he received from his transmission master, who had received it from his, and so on back to the patriarchs of the lineage, especially, it is implied, Shen the Realized One. "Only when the heart seal is submitted up to the heavens will it be useful," Jiang Yucheng explains, "only then can it become a talisman [for invoking the master after he has passed on to his next lifetime]." Similarly, when Chen produces Yin Jiao's heart seal, he displays that he, as an initiate into the lineage, knows the martial deity's secret name. Yin Jiao's heart seal is a talisman, a calling card designed to get Yin's attention, to "press him a little," as Jiang Yucheng says. Yin Jiao's heart seal is one more way to achieve the goal of the Banner Rite—to communicate with Yin Jiao and compel him to comply with the summons and form a collaborative relationship with the ordinand Chen Diwen.

Evocation of a Past Oath

Now that we understand something of the thick meanings implied by the lineage's usage of heart seals, let us return to the Banner Rite. Armed with the decree that Yin Jiao obey the summons from the Emperor of the North, as well as decrees from other high gods, Chen Diwen produces Yin Jiao's heart seal (web video 4.3 [0:00–0:12]). Chen demonstrates his knowledge of the martial deity's heart seal, which was transmitted to Chen by his master within the lineage. But here the heart seal conveys more. It evokes the memory of Yin Jiao's relationship with his own master during his tenth lifetime as crown prince of the Shang dynasty. Recall from the lineage's hagiography that Yin Jiao studied the Dao with Shen the Realized One after he abandoned his quest to avenge his slain mother. Yin Jiao swore an oath to serve as Shen's martial functionary, attained the Dao, and was rewarded with title and office in the celestial bureaucracy by the Emperor of the North, his divine father. Yin Jiao's heart seal is imbued with the memory of the young man's oath to his master. [52]

Chen Diwen and his masters read the heart seal together with the several graphs immediately following it (see large graphs in figure 4.10). Jiang Yucheng explains, "When Yin Jiao left Shen the Realized One after having acquired his [exorcistic] skills, Shen gave Yin Jiao these graphs." We shall see that the heart seal and ensuing graphs work together to remind Yin Jiao of his eternal obligation to serve his master. As Shen's legitimate liturgical heir, Chen Diwen produces the graphs to pique Yin Jiao's sense of duty and convince the fickle martial deity to obey Chen's summons. As patriarch

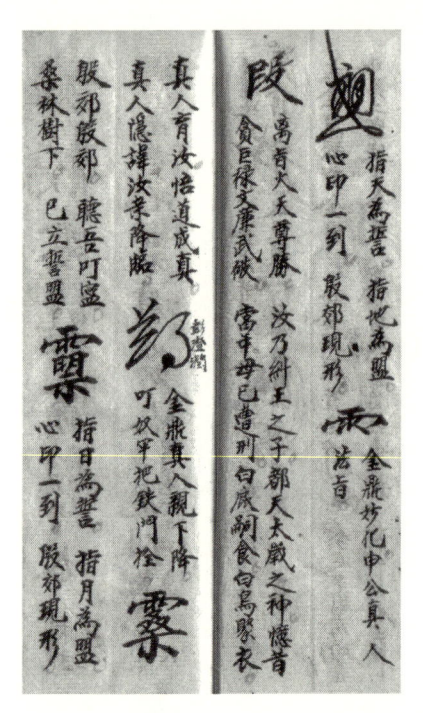

Figure 4.10 Yin Jiao's heart seal followed by graphs and incantations evoking his oath to Shen the Realized One in the *Banner Rite* manual. Scan by the author.

of the lineage and Yin Jiao's master, Shen is the link between the ordinand and the martial deity, and Chen uses the talismanic language from Shen to convince Yin Jiao to serve him as he serves his master.

As Chen Diwen inscribes Yin Jiao's heart seal, he incants the following: "[You, Yin Jiao,] pointed to Heaven and pledged an oath; [you] pointed to Earth and made a covenant. As soon as [this] heart seal is brought forth, Yin Jiao will appear" (指天為誓，指地為盟，心印一到，殷郊現行) (see figure 4.10).[53] The language of the incantation directly evokes the oath Yin Jiao made to his master as recorded in the lineage's hagiography. Recall from chapter 2 that Yin Jiao took incense in his hands, looked up, and declared to the gods and masters:

> Your disciple Yin Jiao is the crown prince of King Zhou and the Queen. I was born their son on behalf of Heaven, and zealously intended to keep peace in the country. But it happened that my father the King was without

morals. He abandoned me to the great wild and relegated my mother to the chilly palace. Fortunately, I encountered the general Marquis Yin, who rescued me and nurtured me in my hapless life. When I was eighteen years old, my heart harbored hatred for my father and I wished to find strong military men to take revenge. When I met my master, he exhorted me to realize this action would be a great crime against Heaven. I have already turned my heart toward goodness. I have vowed to obey my master's instructions and to the end will not be of two minds. Should I violate this oath, I will be willing to suffer Heaven's punishment.[54]

Chen Diwen's inscription of Yin Jiao's heart seal and the accompanying incantation calls on Yin to remember the oath he made to his master before heaven and earth. Implicit is the idea of the heart seal as a marker of identity given to a disciple by his master. Chen knows Yin Jiao's secret heart seal, which Chen and his masters regard as given to Yin by Shen the Realized One. Just as Bai Yuchan knew the pedigrees of the thunder deities he summoned several hundred years before, Chen knows the story about Yin Jiao to which the heart seal and its incantation allude. Chen displays that he is an insider, Shen's liturgical heir. Just as Yin Jiao struck an oath to serve Shen, so should he strike an oath to serve Chen. The heart seal resounds with the filial obligation Yin Jiao has for the master who turned him toward the Dao.

This evocation of Yin Jiao's obligation to his master continues through the following series of talismanic graphs (web video 4.3 [0:12–end]). The next three graphs invoke the authority and beckon the presence of Shen the Realized One (see figure 4.10). The first is a rain radical that constitutes, along with the second graph on the top of the page, the dispersed form of one of the names associated with Shen. Peng Yuantai's thirteenth-century *Great Rite* text helps us. We saw in chapter 2 that Peng lists Shen's full title as Shen Xia the Realized One, Executor of the Rite amid the Wondrous Transformations of the Golden Tripod (Jinding miaohua zhifa Shen zhenren Xia 金鼎妙化執法申真人霞).[55] The moniker "Chromatic Cloud," Xia (霞), printed in smaller font in the text, seems to be a personal name, or perhaps a taboo name. It has come down to Chen's lineage as a taboo name for Master Shen.

As Chen Diwen inscribes the rain radical of the taboo name, he intones, "The ritual instructions of the Realized One Sire Shen of the Wondrous

Transformation of the Golden Cauldron" (金鼎妙化申公真人法旨). Then Chen continues on to the phonetic of Shen's taboo name and its incantation:

> *Li, zhi, huo, tian, zun, sheng. Tan, ju, lu, wen, lian, wu, po.* You [Yin Jiao] are the son of King Zhou, the god of [the star] Great Year Who Governs the Heavens. Recall the past. Your mother had already suffered her punishment, a white dear suckled you and white birds clothed you, the Realized One raised you, and [you] were awakened to the Dao and apprehended true reality. [Upon seeing] the Realized One's secret taboo name, you yourself [Yin Jiao] will descend![56]

> 離旨火天尊勝。貪巨祿文廉武破。汝乃紂王之子，都天太歲之神。憶昔當年，母已遭刑，白鹿嗣食，白鳥聚衣，真人育汝，悟道成真。真人隱諱，汝親降臨。

The masters of the lineage explain that Chen relies on the authority (*quanli* 權力) of Shen to summon Yin Jiao. That influence flows from Yin Jiao's gratitude to his master for raising him and making him into the deity he became.

What I find so arresting is that Chen brazenly pulls on Yin Jiao's heart-strings. Chen reminds Yin of his intimate relationship with his old master, of what Shen had done for the wayward prince. It seems that Chen compels Yin Jiao to respond to the summons by appealing to his sense of filial devotion, which is and has been one of Yin Jiao's great virtues according to the lineage's hagiography and the Yuan–Ming hagiography on which it is in part based. I am not certain why abbreviated names of the six stars of the Southern Dipper and the seven stars of the Northern Dipper are included in the incantation. Perhaps they are called upon to witness Chen's enactment of Shen's ritual instructions. What is clear is that Chen's ability to produce Shen's taboo name and this strikingly intimate incantation display yet again that he is truly an insider, a legitimate heir of Shen's lineage and so a rightful recipient of Yin Jiao's loyalty.

This liturgical logic continues as Chen Diwen inscribes the next large, free-flowing graph and incants: "The Realized One of the Golden Tripod himself descends. Dingnao, hold fast to the bolt of the iron gate" (金鼎真人親下降，叮奴〔呶〕牢把鐵門栓) (see figure 4.10).[57] Chen and his masters regard this graph as the heart seal of Peng Chengrun 彭澄潤, as the manual notes, and it seems to be a highly stylized rendering of the character *peng* 彭. Recall from chapter 2 that the lineage's hagiography identifies Peng Chengrun as the personal name of Shen the Realized One before he apprehended truth and acquired his taboo name Shen Xia.[58] When Chen produces this heart seal, Yin Jiao's master descends to the altar space. He, or perhaps Chen himself, intimately addresses Yin by his nursing name, Dingnao. Evoked again is a strong sense of the filial relationship between disciple and master. Although nothing about an iron gate appears in the lineage's hagiography— or in any other hagiography or piece of iconography I have seen—images of Yin Jiao's vulnerable boyhood seem to be conjured by the usage of his nursing name.[59] Shen was responsible for making him into the god he is today from precarious beginnings, and now Yin Jiao ought to listen to his plea to reply to the summons.

Producing the heart seal of a patriarch to press a martial deity to duty is not a new practice. We saw that Song and Yuan masters summoned martial deities, such as Zhao Gongming, by generating the heart seals of their masters, such as Zhang Daoling, who were recognized as patriarchs of the master's lineage. Akin to practitioners from centuries ago, Chen Diwen produces the heart seal and taboo name of the patriarch of his lineage to rely on the ancient master's authority to convince his martial functionary to comply with Chen's summons.

Chen Diwen continues. As he inscribes the graph of a stylized mulberry tree (*sang* 桑), he incants,

> Yin Jiao, Yin Jiao! Hear me urge [you] over and over again! Underneath the tree in the mulberry grove, [you] already struck a covenant!
>
> 殷郊殷郊，聽吾叮盦〔嚀〕。桑林樹下，已立誓盟。

Chen continues to the next graph, the components of which can literally be read as "the sun and moon bear witness" (*riyue shi* 日月示).

> [You] pointed to the sun and pledged an oath; [you] pointed to the moon and made a covenant. As soon as [this] heart seal is brought forth, Yin Jiao will appear! (see figure 4.10)[60]
>
> 指日為誓，指月為盟。心印一到，殷郊現行。

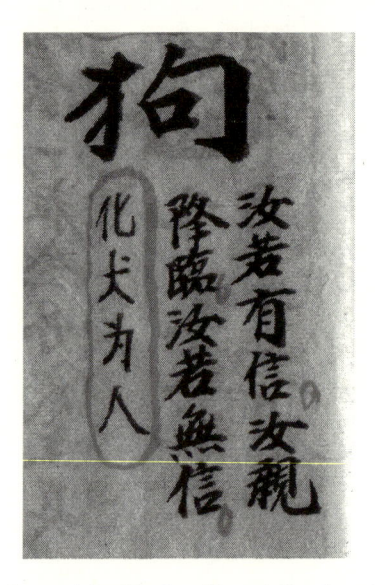

Figure 4.11 Talismanic graph for "dog" and incantation threatening Yin Jiao in the *Banner Rite* manual. Scan by the author.

A little further on in the manual, Chen inscribes the graph for "dog" (*gou* 狗), which echoes the malediction Yin Jiao swore to his master. As Chen draws, he incants, "If [you] keep your pledge, you yourself will descend. If [you] do not keep your pledge, [you] will turn into a dog for the next lifetime" (汝若有信，汝親降臨。汝若無信，化犬為人) (see figure 4.11).[61] The last phrase of the incantation is encircled in red ink in the text. The masters explain that it is an instruction to the officiant that he should visualize a dog instead of uttering the terrible verse.

These three graphs evoke the actual scene in which Yin Jiao made his oath to Shen the Realized One. Recall from chapter 2 that Yin Jiao pledged loyalty to his master under a mulberry tree. With the sun and moon as witnesses, he vowed eternal fealty on pain of cosmic punishment. The lineage's hagiography narrates the event:

> Master [Shen] then opened a great golden well [that is, he drew the graph for well (*jing*) on the ground]. Yin Jiao stood in the center of it, as did the master. Yin Jiao then loudly announced an oath: "I bow to the Realized One as my master and till the end of my days I shall not forget. I untie my silk waistband and divide it for each of us. I hold the silk and swear to

Heaven: Should I break the covenant and back out of my oath then I shall certainly spend my next lifetime as a dog." Therefore the talismanic symbol of "the dog" [in the manual].[62]

師即大開金井，郊立井中，師立井中。郊乃大發誓願：「自拜真人為師，歿世不忘。解下絲繰，各分一半。郊以絲繰向天立誓，如有背盟悔誓，吾來世永為犬也。」故有狗字符號。

Chen Diwen calls on Yin Jiao to remember the crucial moment he submitted himself to his master and then struck the solemn oath to serve him. By inscribing these esoteric graphs and intoning these words, Chen makes Yin Jiao relive his past in another attempt to pique the god's sense of obligation to his master and, by extension, to his master's liturgical descendant. Chen's silently calling to mind the malediction in Yin's oath is striking. The ordinand audaciously reminds the martial god of the dire consequences should he fail to honor his vow. Given that Yin Jiao was born a crown prince in his previous ten lifetimes, rebirth as a lowly dog would be a harsh punishment indeed.

This remarkable sequence of talismanic graphs conjoins to remind Yin Jiao of his duty to his master, the patriarch of the lineage to which the ordinand Chen Diwen belongs. Chen displays that membership by producing the esoteric heart seals and taboo names associated with Yin Jiao and Shen the Realized One, which Chen learned when he received the *yuanchen* from his transmission master. Chen knows Yin Jiao's pedigree and story in which the graphs and incantations are rooted. The lineage's hagiography functions as a rich paraliturgy. It supplies the narrative assumed by this sequence of talismanic graphs. By enacting that narrative with talismanic language, Chen communicates Yin Jiao's own history and words back to him, hoping to evoke the emotions that might spur the unruly god to action. Those emotions progress throughout the sequence. Yin Jiao is first invited to reminisce about his intimate relationship with the master who saved him from calamity and led him to awaken to the Dao. The graphs and incantations tug at Yin Jiao's sense of filial piety and moral duty, gently shaming him to respond to the summons. The sequence ends with a threat. Yin Jiao is reminded of the terrible consequences of refusal to comply in terms so harsh the ordinand is instructed not to utter them. The graphs and incantations attempt to coerce Yin Jiao into doing what is right under pain of karmic penalty.

The talismanic language here does not summon Yin Jiao with certainty. Simply knowing Yin's heart seal—and the heart seal and taboo name of his master—is not enough to compel the god to do what he is supposed to do. Many scholars have noted the power of secret names to summon, employ, or bind deities and demons. To know the taboo or personal name of a spirit is to know its intrinsic nature and thus to claim influence over that spirit. In her classic study of Shangqing texts, Isabelle Robinet put it memorably:

> To name, *ming* 名, is both to order, *ming* 命, and to give life, *ming* 命. He who knows the names has power over what he names. In this way, the deities who reveal their names give the adept power over them. They give a pledge that obligates them. Knowledge of the deities' names is by itself the proof of a contract and is equivalent to a password. To meditate on these names insures divine protection.[63]

In the Banner Rite, the esoteric names of Yin Jiao and Shen the Realized One are not so straightforward. We saw that their heart seals do indeed function as a kind of credential. Chen Diwen's knowing their secret names displays his membership in Shen's lineage which enjoys a relationship with Yin Jiao. And the esoteric names do echo Yin Jiao's pledge to his master, which obliges him to serve Chen. However, the Banner Rite offers no assurance that Yin Jiao will comply with his obligation. Indeed, the entire ritual takes very seriously the possibility that he may not. The talismanic names and incantations in this sequence are therefore designed to persuade, induce, cajole, and even threaten the martial deity. The mood of the entire ritual sequence is subjunctive. Chen hopes to move Yin Jiao to do his duty. The talismanic language here has a perlocutionary quality: it affects the feelings, thoughts, or actions of the recipient. The graphs and incantations are not, as Robinet implies, illocutionary. They do not act in their inscribing and intoning to make Yin Jiao appear.[64] Instead, the outcome of these graphs and intonations is far from certain. As the sequence unfolds, the sense of uncertainty seems to increase as the talismanic language moves from gentle persuasion to outright threat.[65]

The use of perlocutionary ritual language to persuade and even threaten martial deities has a long history. During the Song and Yuan periods, Divine Empyrean masters frequently cajoled thunder gods during summoning rites to get them to do their part in a ritual. What stands out in many of those rites is the harshness of the maledictions threatening thunder gods should they fail to cooperate. Well beyond earnestly urging them to comply, these curses often use downright vituperative language to coerce, browbeat, and shame thunder gods to assent to the ritual work.

The *Hidden Texts of the Thunder Crystal of the Anterior Heaven,* which as noted was likely a Yuan collection of Divine Empyrean rites from the Southern Song, provides a vivid example. The practitioner is instructed to visualize that Marshal Zhang appears before the altar space. The practitioner solemnly declares these ominous words:

> I know your name; I know your surname. I am your elder brother; you are my younger brother. Should you not implement [the rite], I shall curse nine generations of your ancestors. Should I turn on you my younger brother, I shall sink to the underworld forever. I shall make your name known to all under Heaven.[66]

> 吾知汝名，吾知汝姓。吾為汝兄，汝為吾弟。汝若不至，罵汝九祖。吾負汝弟，永墮幽冥。吾叫汝名天下知。

The practitioner speaks directly to Marshal Zhang, straightaway telling the deity he knows exactly who he is. Taking advantage of his slightly superior position in the cosmic hierarchy, the master curses several generations of the thunder deity's ancestors should the god fail to work for the rite to which he has been summoned. Here the verb "to curse" (*ma* 罵) carries the sense of scolding or rebuking by using threatening language meant to humiliate or subject to indignity. That the practitioner, somewhat audaciously, curses the deity's ancestors implies that the god would bear great shame for causing his kin harm. Such coercive language aims to elicit a favorable response when Marshal Zhang's compliance is anything but certain.[67]

Echoing his Divine Empyrean forebears, Chen Diwen gently shames and then harshly threatens Yin Jiao in hopes that the martial deity might be moved to respond to the summons. In Chen's inscription and incantation of the heart seals and taboo names of Yin Jiao and his master, we can discern a theology of Yin Jiao. That is, we can see something of his nature. He is a filial martial deity bound by an ancient oath to his master and yet fickle and unruly enough to be capable of refusing to honor it for members of his master's lineage. Yin Jiao is indeed a subject whose history and formative relationships Chen evokes with ritual language. Although Chen has had no hand in crafting those symbols and their intonations, which have been passed down to him through the generations of his lineage, they still express his status as a legitimate member of the lineage who knows Yin's story and has received the lineage's esoteric teachings for summoning him. Chen beckons the subject Yin Jiao to participate in the Banner Rite and tries to compel him not to ignore it.

Raising the Banner

Chen Diwen carries on his task inscribing and incanting graphs, one on top of the other, memorized from several more pages of the *Banner Rite* manual. The ink stain on the bottom of the banner becomes so thick it bleeds through the fabric. Chen also produces a sequence of graphs on the backside of the banner, and on the ends of five streamers cut into the bottom end of the cloth.

At last, Chen draws and intones the final graph—Yin Jiao's heart seal once again—in a conspicuous spot on the front of the banner that has been saved for this moment (see figure 4.12, web video 4.4 [0:00–0:16]). The final heart seal punctuates the talisman, marking it as finished and ready to be presented to Yin Jiao in its "assembled form" (*juxing* 聚形). As he inscribes, Chen incants the *Yin Jiao Incantation,* which closely matches the incantation included in the Pure Tenuity *Upper Clarity Great Rite* text from the Song or Yuan discussed in chapter 2. The intonation extols Yin Jiao's great deeds and beseeches the god to respond to the summons:

With sincere heart [I] take refuge in the mandated ceremony. [I] respectfully plead to the Top General Yin of the Earth Ministry, the Great General of the Orthodox Prime Who Kills Demons. [You] practiced ten lifetimes as crown prince and apprehended orthodox truth after [consuming] one pellet of golden elixir. [Gods of] heavenly stars and earthly lights converge under your banner. The Emperor of the Earth and [demons of] pestilence submit under your whip. You do not violate loyalty and filiality, and follow the commands and directives. The Emperor [of the North] bestowed upon you a yellow halberd with which to vanquish sprites and fiends. As for those [demons] who dare not comply with my words, [you] will first cut off their heads and only later report [their offenses] to the Emperor. Today I plead [with you] in hopes that you will appear and generously bestow thunder power to provide support [for the rites].[68]

志心皈命禮。仰啟地司殷上將，正元殺鬼大將軍，十世修行為太子，一粒金丹成至真，天星地曜歸麾下，土皇瘟疫伏驅馳，忠孝不違法令旨，帝賜黃鉞斬妖精，敢有不順吾道者，先斬人頭后奏帝。吾今啟請望來臨，大賜雷威加擁護。

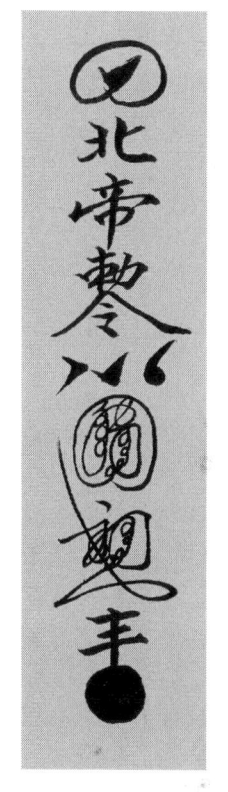

Figure 4.12 Yin Jiao's heart seal (second graph from bottom) added to complete the talisman.

After Chen Diwen produces the heart seal, he continues to draw a few quick graphs in the ink blot before relinquishing his brush (web video 4.4 [0:16–0:42]). He explains that he inscribed and incanted four graphs not called for in the manual—his own heart seal, that of his transmission master Li Yezhen, that of his master of the registry, and that of his master of the canon.[69] On completing the talisman, Chen throws divination blocks on the ground until he gets two sides down (yin'gao 陰筶), which signals that the deceased masters witnessing the event agree that the talisman is ready to go.

Chen Diwen and several masters then parade the banner up the slope from the Chen family home as a lay villager sets off firecrackers to clear

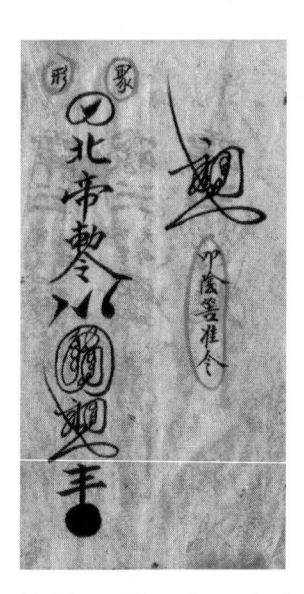

Figure 4.13 The assembled form of the talisman in the *Banner Rite* manual.
Scan by the author.

the path of any noxious spirits (web video 4.4 [0:42–end]). Under steadily falling rain on a terraced rice paddy, Chen's guarantor master, Jiang Yeqian, works to attach the banner to a ten-meter bamboo pole (web figure 4.3). Meanwhile, Chen's presenting master, Jiang Yucheng, performs a short ritual alerting both celestial gods and local tutelary deities that the soil is about to be dug into in order to anchor the banner. Jiang inscribes several talismans in the air with his wooden command placard while intoning their accompanying incantations. He includes the graph for "well" (*jing* 井), which creates a temporary prison in which to trap any lurking demonic agents that might disrupt the invocation (web figure 4.4).

After the pole has been duly prepared, a team of seven villagers strain to erect the great mast and the banner takes flight. Following the last section of the *Banner Rite* manual he has memorized, Chen Diwen faces the banner and gnashes his teeth three times. Then he flails his robe-covered arms in a circular motion for about ten seconds, doing what the manual calls a "dance to carry [the talisman] upward in flight" (*feiyang juanwu* 飛揚捲舞) while he

Figure 4.14 Raising the banner. Photograph courtesy of Doug Kanter.

intones the *Incantation of the Vermillion Crow* (*Chiya zhou* 赤鴉咒), designed to summon the emissary Marshal Zhang to ferry the intention of the talisman to Yin Jiao's celestial office.[70] Chen looks on with hope and apprehension as the banner and its streamers flutter in the wind. Then he and his masters return to the house to wait.

Conclusion

The long talisman Chen Diwen produced invites much more exploration. As mentioned, it is a storehouse of smaller talismans and segments of talismans that have somehow accreted over the centuries. Unfortunately, an attempt to make sense of every moment of the talisman would be both Herculean and foolhardy. Herculean because a study of more than a hundred talismanic graphs would require several volumes of relentless analysis. Such is the incredibly dense nature of ritual. Foolhardy because neither the masters with their experience and oral tradition nor I with my corroborations with earlier sources have been able to gain much purchase on large swaths of the Banner Rite. Like Chen and his masters, we must remain humble in our inquiry. When Jiang Shenzhi redacted the *Banner Rite* manual in 1989, most of his disciples were living elsewhere as migrant laborers. He added to the text many directives traditionally taught orally. But he could add nothing to numerous moments in the text. He simply did not know and so respectfully kept them in the ritual without comment. Similarly, we must recognize that the staggeringly multivalent nature of ritual always exceeds our ken.

What stands out about Chen Diwen's production of the talisman is the Banner Rite's preoccupation with the act of writing, a concern shared by other religious traditions. In his analysis of the ancient Greek Magical Papyri, Jonathan Z. Smith writes,

> If one reads through the entire corpus with an eye toward ritual activities, it is not purification, nor incubation, nor even sacrifice that predominates. Rather, the chief ritual activity within the Greek Magical Papyri appears to be *the act of writing itself*. The vocabulary of inscription constitutes one of the larger groups. Alongside the evident concern for the accurate transmission of a professional literature marked, among other features, by scribal glosses and annotations, is an overwhelming belief in the efficacy of writing, especially in the recipes that focus on the fashioning of amulets and phylacteries—themselves, miniaturized, portable, powerful written texts of papyrus, metal, stone, and bone.[71]

What I find insightful about Smith's observation is that writing is considered a ritual activity. This might seem an obvious point to make about inscriptions described within the context of ritual texts, but it warrants close attention. In the Greek Magical Papyri, inscriptions were, according to Smith, not simply products of ritual activity, the intellectual and material fruit of ritual work. Rather, writing itself *was* the ritual activity. It was an enterprise in which the inscribers seem to have expended a great deal of energy to ensure it was correctly executed. It seems the "overwhelming belief in the efficacy of writing" by Greek magicians had to do with the proper ritual procedure for the act of writing itself at least as much as with what the writing actually said or purported to do.

We saw in Chen Diwen's production of the talisman a comparable concern with the actual writing of the talisman. Chen and his masters worried about how accurately and concentratedly he drew each graph, intoned each incantation, and performed each visualization. How the talismanic script was produced was as crucial as the inscribed object that was produced. The process was as important as the product. Implied here is a notion of talisman as something that embodies all the ritual processes that went into its making. Chen's notification of Yin Jiao by reciting and sending off the Dispatch to Inform the Generals, his garnering support from his lineage of deceased masters while calling upon the *yuanchen*, his burning away of his mundane body and taking on divine bodies, his recovery of his primordial self, his ascent to the heavens and audience with the high gods, and his stirring potent ancestral *qi* within himself and imbuing each graph with charged ink, voice, and intention—all of it was baked into the inked cloth of the talisman itself. The scripted cloth produced by the Banner Rite was inseparable from the entire ritual process of the Banner Rite.[72]

Scholars working on the ancient and medieval periods in China have recognized that talismans are efficacious because they have an intrinsic power that allows influence over the things named or portrayed, like people, gods, and even nature itself.[73] Ge Hong and the practitioners of the emerging Shangqing and Lingbao traditions thought that strange talismanic writing was a facsimile of illegible "celestial patterns" (*tianwen* 天文) that arose spontaneously. Those patterns composed of rarified *qi* were directly generated from the primordial creative process and so were intrinsically imbued with that creative power. The efficacy of a talisman depended on how precisely one copied that primordial form in inscription. What was important about a talisman was not whether it was legible, but how well it captured the original form of the celestial pattern. Efficacy inheres in graphic form.

But the Banner Rite and its masters account for efficacy in a slightly different way. The efficaciousness of the talisman has less to do with the intrinsic power of the graphs themselves and more to do with the precise way they are produced. It is true that the graphs are believed to have been revealed from the heavens to the realm of the living, though no one in the lineage knows which deity might have done so, or when. Recall that Peng Yuantai implies that his fourth-generation master, Liao Shouzhen, received a talisman for summoning Yin Jiao, a few of the graphs and incantations of which have made their way into Chen Diwen's lineage. Peng does not flesh out exactly how the transmission of the talisman to Liao occurred, however. It is also true that the graphs in the Banner Rite talisman are believed to be wholly composed of ancestral *qi,* the primordial stuff close to the source of all power, the Dao. The talisman, though, is not powerful because it faithfully mimics a celestial template. Instead, its efficacy flows from how well the practitioner can harness powerful ancestral *qi* by inner alchemical procedures, channel it through his body, and then express it in the form of writing, incantation, and visualization. The talismanic writing in itself is not efficacious. The primordial *qi* that composes it is what makes it efficacious, and that *qi* can only be accessed and wielded by a competent practitioner of the Banner Rite. Again, that is why masters of Chen's lineage are not terribly concerned that people outside the lineage might copy the written form of their talismans. Any forms inscribed, even with extreme precision and in good faith, are powerless without the ritual process. In this sense, efficacy is produced—or, better, tapped—by ritual rather than intrinsic to the written form of a talisman itself.

When properly produced, the talisman carries immense ontological weight. It is that weight that allows the talisman to signify, or make meaning, in the world. A logic of identity is implied here. The ancestral *qi* out of which the talisman is made resonates with the rarified *qi* of the celestial realm and its denizens. It is this material basis that allows the talismanic language to penetrate (*tong*) the celestial realm, to communicate with deities. In semiotic terms, the talisman is an iconic sign; it shares in the reality to which it refers, which is the reality of rarified ancestral *qi.* Imbued with the ontological weight of ritually cultivated ancestral *qi,* the talisman is the medium by which Chen Diwen sends messages to Yin Jiao.

Scholarly discussion has been considerable as to whether the strange, seemingly illegible scripts of different kinds of talismans might actually be intelligible, and if so how. Working on archaeological materials from the Eastern Han (27–220), Wang Yucheng argues against the somewhat prevalent notion that talismans are largely gibberish, incomprehensible signs designed to impress users by simulating some imagined celestial language. He shows that some talismanic scripts were actually derived from pre-Qin seal-script or highly stylized common graphs in regular use. Others were fantastical representations of animals or people. Or, a seemingly illegible talismanic script might imaginatively express in emblematic form the semantic content of an accompanying inscription. Talismans and incantations express similar meanings in different forms, and so can be read as mutually explicable.[74] Thinking on the cloud-like forms used in the talismans in early medieval Daoist movements, Gil Raz suggests that they were recognizable rather than fully comprehensible. The strange writing pointed to the actual primordial *qi* that first generated their forms during the cosmogony while not meaning in any conventional way. Any messages these signs might carry remained incomprehensible, but the talismans themselves were recognizable as emanations of the Dao. Along these same lines, other kinds of written talismans revealed the "true form" (*zhenxing* 真形) or "true name" (*zhenming* 真名) of things in the world such as mountains and deities. Talismans expressed the true and real aspects inherent to things, which normally remain hidden. Such talismans were forms of the ethereal *qi* that is the ultimate shape and name of the place or deity. Talismans signify not in any ordinary way, but by pointing to the very primordial *qi* that forms them.[75]

When we read the talisman in the Banner Rite in the context of the ritual procedure by which it is produced, we see that the talisman does signify, but again in a way different from these accounts of talismans from earlier periods. The talisman as a whole is not an incomprehensible yet still recognizable sign pointing to the mysteries of the primordial first expressions of the Dao, although a few graphs, such as the circular one expressing the stirring of the ancestral *qi* that initiates the talisman, do seem to embody that idea. The talisman as a whole is a mode of direct communication from an officiant to Yin Jiao. The different forms of writing, incantation, and visualization hang together—in a way Wang Yucheng would appreciate—to form comprehensible signs pointing to recognizable referents, which are often moments in the Banner Rite itself, or moments in Yin Jiao's life as articulated in the lineage's hagiography and represented in his iconography.

In the initial sequence, the graphs signifying the Emperor of the North's edict are written straightforwardly in mundane Chinese. Even the semantic value of the cryptic straight lines signifying the decrees of other high gods are defined when read with their accompanying incantations. Those graphs point to moments earlier in the ritual performance itself when Chen Diwen recovered his primordial self, journeyed to the celestial court, and acquired heavenly legitimation to summon Yin Jiao. Directed at Yin, these talismanic commands vouch for Chen as an agent of heaven's will, an official whose authority is grounded in his relationship with the high gods, especially with Yin Jiao's direct superior. Accompanying incantations explain the strange taboo names of the Three Officers of the Three Primes and the deities of the Celestial Guideline. Each beseeches these high gods to grace the talisman itself with their potent *qi* to cleanse it and protect its integrity, lending the entire talisman the glow of the Golden Radiance and protecting its ability to communicate. Even the strange heart seals of Yin Jiao and Shen the Realized One make sense. Like the heart seals of masters, they are highly stylized names of those deities known only to insiders of the lineage. The heart seals and other slightly stylized signs hanging with them point directly to Yin Jiao's pedigree and episodes in his history, especially to his oath to serve the patriarch of the lineage and his descendants, thereby legitimizing Chen as an authentic practitioner in the lineage to which Yin swore fealty. These talismanic signs are not incomprehensible or only vaguely recognizable as ethereal forms of the Dao's first expressions. They are laden with meanings comprehensible both to the gods and to initiated lineage members who know the Banner Rite and Yin Jiao's hagiography and iconography.

Each part of the talisman, then, communicates information to Yin Jiao, and information about the officiant himself. That Chen Diwen has learned how to produce the various graphs of the talisman conveys that he has the knowledge necessary to deal with Yin Jiao through the proper channels. Chen is a legitimate recipient of the lineage's esoteric knowledge and so ought to be privy to Yin Jiao's services. Chen communicates to Yin Jiao that he knows all about the god's pedigree and history, and by piquing Yin's senses of duty, fear, and shame, he reminds the god of his obligations to the lineage. The communication is clear and repeated yet tempered with a sense of entreaty. This talismanic language, even Yin Jiao's esoteric heart seal, does not function to control the deity like the true names in medieval practice. Instead, it can only persuade—and at times cajole and threaten—Yin Jiao to comply. The mode of ritual communication in the talisman of the Banner Rite assumes that Yin Jiao, like Chen Diwen, is not a puppet to be manipulated with talismanic technology, but a subject who actively participates in the ritual.

Postlude

Yin Jiao will heed the command and follow the directives of the officiant whenever he produces his heart seal. The General ought not to be reckless, wild, or indolent; his numinous power ought to manifest as soon as requested.

——Chen Diwen's ordination certificate

Chen Diwen sat on his stool under the awning of his grandfather's house, just out of the rain. He smoked his cigarettes while his masters, family, and dozens of villagers ate a lunch prepared by his grandmother, wife, and female relatives. Chen could not eat. He sat quietly alone and tried not to look up the hill every minute. Plenty of people would let him know the moment the banner knotted. One of them, a lay acolyte, sat at the foot of the pole offering incense and burning paper money next to a makeshift altar with tea, wine, and a bowl of pork fat—Yin Jiao's favorite (web figure post.1). On the outer altar where Chen had performed the Banner Rite, other lay acolytes kept incense burning in front of the cardboard tablets listing the names of the high gods, including those whose decrees Chen sought.

"After finishing the Banner Rite I didn't think of anything other than hoping that the banner would knot up quickly. Of course I was anxious! I really didn't know whether the inscribed banner would knot. If it didn't, I would lose so much face!" Chen Diwen's budding career as a master hung in the balance for all to see. He worried whether he adequately performed the Banner Rite. Perhaps he did not sincerely enough visualize the private scene in which his master taught him how to perform the ritual. Perhaps he did not concentrate hard enough to transform into divine bodies and tap ancestral *qi*. Perhaps he did not inscribe each graph, intone its incantation, or perform its visualization well enough to communicate with Yin Jiao. Perhaps he was not able to convey to the general that the summons was by the authority of the Emperor of the North and the highest gods, or to induce Yin Jiao to remember his oath to Shen the Realized One and recognize Chen as his legitimate liturgical heir. Perhaps Chen Diwen even performed the Banner Rite admirably, but the martial deity would simply choose not to respond to the summons. "After all, Yin Jiao *is* a god," Jiang Yucheng observes, "and he is a little bit unruly."

If the banner remained unknotted into the night, and especially into the next day, something of a crisis would ensue. Some masters of the lineage argue that it would be best not to continue the ordination *jiao*. Chen Diwen would have to spend another forty-nine days relearning the entire Banner Rite and then try again. Others take the position that it would be too much trouble and expense to organize another *jiao*, especially for the hosts, Chen's family. The ordination might go on, but Chen would have to invest another forty-nine days of secluded study and try the Banner Rite again before he could officiate over any ritual.[1] In either case, the social consequences of a failed Banner Rite would be undeniable. An unknotted banner would certainly shake the community's confidence in Chen's liturgical powers and dissuade them from hiring him in the future. "All I could do is rely on all the gods and on Marshal Yin, and on my own transmission master, master of the registry, and master of the canon." Chen could do nothing except trust—in the esoteric teachings handed down to him by the lineage, in his training, in the sincerity with which he performed the Banner Rite, in the power of the high gods, and in Yin Jiao himself. It helped that the sporadic rain was driven by a decent wind.

After almost two packs of cigarettes, Chen Diwen heard someone yell, "The banner has knotted! The banner has knotted!" Although it seemed much longer, only an hour and fifteen minutes passed since they had raised the banner—an auspicious sign that Yin Jiao enthusiastically agreed to bond with Chen. The ordinand, several of his masters, and a group of villagers rushed up the hill to collect the banner. Chen could not contain his joy as his presenting master and guarantor master worked to detach the banner from the bamboo mast. "I was so excited! I had practiced the Banner Rite for over a month and in the end it was successful. [The banner] would from there on out be a sign that I could practice as a head officiant" [web figure post.2].

The knot was the clear sign that Yin Jiao had agreed to serve as Chen Diwen's martial functionary. A tight, robust knot signals a firmer pledge than a loose, sagging knot. Two particular shapes are especially auspicious. Local scholar Zhang Shihong reports that a "lion banner" (*shizi fan* 獅子旛) features a knot resembling the head and four legs of a lion, whereas the knot of a "prince banner" (*taizi fan* 太子旛) resembles the head and limbs of a person, which has the look of the character *da* 大, "great," and so etymologically lends itself to the moniker "prince" (*taizi* 太子).[2] Both kinds of knots inspire enthusiastic confidence from the community. The knot of Chen Diwen's banner did not resemble these two shapes, but he and everyone else were exceedingly happy with the outcome. "My banner knotted quickly and knotted well—full and round," Chen boasts, "proof that my practice would be prosperous!"[3]

Chen Diwen carefully furled the sopping banner and proudly carried it down the hill back to the house, preceded and followed by lay acolytes setting off strings of firecrackers. His transmission master Li Yezhen, his wife, his parents and grandparents, and onlookers from area hamlets beamed with joy as he strode past. Chen placed the knotted banner in the center of the main altar table for the duration of the ordination *jiao* (see figure post.1). "This is Marshal Yin's banner, Marshal Yin's sign (*biaozhi* 標誌)," Jiang Yucheng explains. "The banner successfully knotted, which indicates that Chen Diwen and Marshal Yin can communicate. During future rites, whenever Chen invokes Marshal Yin, he will come." Displayed for all to see, the knotted banner was the sign of the relationship struck between Chen and Yin Jiao. The talisman produced on the banner with ink, voice, and imagination was both the way Chen communicated with Yin Jiao and the material vestige of successful communication.

Figure Post.1 The knotted blue banner on the main altar, hanging above the wooden statue of Yang Faqing wrapped in red cloth. Photograph by the author.

The medium on which the talisman was produced matters. The banner itself is the mode of communication from Yin Jiao back to Chen Diwen, and to everyone around him. That the streamers knotted indicates that Yin Jiao heard the summons and heeded it, but the quality of the knot indicates something about the quality of the relationship the banner expresses. Here, again, subtle theological light is cast on the figure Yin Jiao. He is indeed a subject who actively participates in the ritual. He does so by conveying not only a message of consent, but also his level of enthusiasm for that consent. The communication reveals something of the tenor of Yin Jiao's relationship with Chen. Just as we saw that the written aspect of this kind of talisman cannot be separated from the ritual that produced it, here we see that the talisman cannot be separated from its medium. To do so would write Yin Jiao's role out of the ritual, to portray him as a flat character in a ritual play. But Yin is not a passive figure over which the officiant exerts brute force. Yin Jiao is a subject who acts, and he acts with style.

With Yin Jiao's consent to serve the young ordinand, Chen Diwen could go on to be ordained. On the fourth and final day of the *jiao,* Li Yezhen conferred upon Chen his Daoist liturgical name, Chen Yude, and his Buddhist name, Chen Changde (陳常得), both following their respective poems. Chen received the articles of investiture he would need for his practice, among them liturgical robes, implements, and newly copied ritual manuals, including the *Banner Rite* and *Secret Transmission.*

The bond with Yin Jiao made during the Banner Rite reverberated through the essential moments of the rite of passage. Chen and Li Yezhen simultaneously transformed their bodies into divine ones and exteriorized Yin Jiao from within them. On behalf of his ordinand, Li concluded a formal blood covenant with Yin Jiao in which he swore to venerate him in return for his exorcistic power when called upon.[4] Then Li installed Yin Jiao, his minions, and all the thunder generals and their spirit armies at Chen's thunder altar (*leitan* 雷壇), his personal altar in his home.

Finally, Li Yezhen presented Chen with his official ordination certificate stating his credentials as a full-fledged master. Again, the bond with Yin Jiao took center stage. At the heart of the ordination certificate, Li had produced a shortened version of the talisman to summon General Yin. That talisman was rent in two and one half inserted into the *yin* version of the ordination certificate (*yinping* 陰憑), the other into the *yang* version (*yangping* 陽憑) (see figure post.2). Li burned the *yin* certificate and transmitted it to the celestial office to which Chen Diwen had been assigned. Chen would keep and treasure the *yang* certificate until the end of his days. When Chen passes from this life, his disciples will immediately burn it. When he arrives at his celestial office, heavenly bureaucrats will match the tallies and he will be allowed to begin his new role as a deceased master, ready to respond whenever his disciples invoke him by his heart seal. For Chen and his lineage, the relationship first forged with Yin Jiao in the Banner Rite is the sine qua non for a career as a liturgical master in this life and the next.[5]

We began this study by noting that every ritual is itself a theory of ritual writ large. The symbols of a ritual, strung together in a particular way in performed action, give a subtle accounting of the nature of ritual itself. The theory running through the Banner Rite is the idea that ritual performance itself is first and foremost a kind of communication. The interlocutors are subjects thick with their histories, formative relationships, and ability to participate in the ritual activity itself in a more or less engaged way—or not to participate at all. All of that thickness comes to bear in the Banner Rite. Ritual as communication demands stunning self-transformation, fantastic engagement with a host of divine figures, and sincere execution of the difficult technology of a talisman—all in hopes of convincing a god

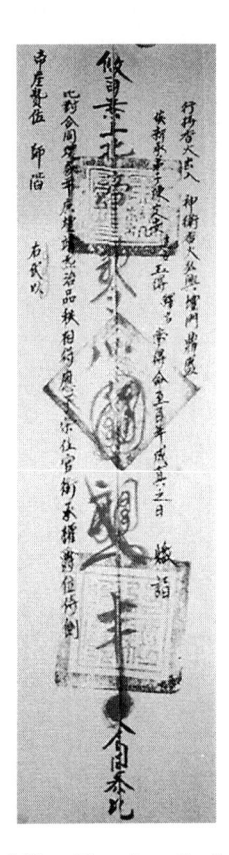

Figure Post.2 The two halves of Chen Diwen's ordination certificate sharing the talisman for summoning Yin Jiao. Photograph by the author.

that he should do what he is supposed to do. The Banner Rite begins with a sense of hierarchy in which the ordinand cautiously approaches the deity. If successful, the hierarchy is reversed and the deity takes his place as functionary of the new master. Yet at every turn, the Banner Rite resists easy characterization as a simple expression of hierarchy. A close reading of the ritual in real time and in its social and historical contexts reveals that the ritual is actually a site in which subjects behave as subjects within hierarchies that shift rather than rigidly impose. Ritual efficacy depends on the relationships forged by those subjects' interactions.

The masters who perform the Banner Rite are aware of all of this and express it in their terms. At every turn, Chen Diwen and his masters use the word "communication" (*goutong*) to characterize the ritual. They recognize that it is a highly technical "method" (*fa* 法) by which an ordinand can interact with divine beings, and that that method is powered by a "way" or "teaching" (*dao* 道) for achieving ontological transformation via the power of visualization. This recognition is the foundation of the living practice of Chen Diwen's lineage just as it is for lineages all over south China that have descended from the great liturgical movements of the Song and Yuan.

After Chen Diwen's ordination concluded, as the congratulatory guests were heading home, a villager from a neighboring hamlet approached him. The villager's daughter-in-law was six months pregnant, and he asked Chen to protect her, her unborn child, and her entire household from demonic attack. To help the villager, Chen would have to call upon Yin Jiao, the thunder generals under his banner, and their spirit armies to set up a perimeter around her body and the entire house. "Because my banner knotted well, people thought I was all right," Chen remembers with a smile. "The evening after my ordination, I went to perform a minor rite as an officiant."

The Daoist Lineage of the Daxiong Mountain Region

Generation			Identified Lineage Members		
1	*dao* 道				
2	*de* 德		The lineage and the lineage poem likely started in the sixteenth century		
3	*liu* 流				
4	*lai* 來		No reliable identifications can be made for the first five generations		
5	*yuan* 遠				
6	*tong* 通		伍通靈, 伍通真		
7	*zhen* 真		伍真霆, 吳真莫		
8	*xuan* 玄	陳玄真, 陳玄道, 陳玄機, 陳玄慧	吳玄真, 張玄真, **李玄明 (d. 1731)**, **謝玄應**, 謝玄清, 謝玄道[1]		
9	*miao* 妙	陳妙法, 陳妙生, 陳妙行, 陳妙元, 陳妙相	羅妙色	龔妙靈; 袁妙發[2]	張妙臨; 李妙靈

Generation	Identified Lineage Members						
10 *shen* 深	陳深密, 陳深識	羅深澤, 羅深德, **羅深惠**				方深智	
11 *san* 三	陳三元, 陳三正, 陳三智, 陳三道, 陳三級, 陳三教, 陳三微, 陳三福	羅三福, 羅三善		**蔣三祿**		**龔三教**, 龔三清[3]	方三振, 方三靜
12 *qian* 千	陳千真, 陳千澤, 陳千聖, 陳千春, 陳千才, 陳千元	羅千意, 羅千照, 羅千煇, 羅千志[4]		**蔣千靈, 蔣千珍, 蔣千和**		**龔千神,**[5] **龔千煇,**[6] 龔千金	方千習, **方千明**[7]
13 *gong* 功	陳功就, 陳功克, 陳功悟, 汪功學	羅功吉, 羅功善		**蔣功傅 (b. 1804), 蔣功清, 蔣功禪**[8]	李功員		**扶功玉, 扶功昭**
14 *xing* 行	方行成, 方行修, 胡行義	羅行憲 (1839–1891),[9] 羅行靜; 李行裕 (1814–1885)		**蔣行時 (b. 1832), 蔣行運 (b. 1829)**[10]	李行春, 李行章 (b. 1816)[11]		扶行明, 扶行閱, 扶行時; 蕭行祥
15 *man* 滿	胡滿真, 伍滿明	羅滿意 (fl. 1890), 李滿傳 (1854–1917)		**蔣滿鋥,** 蔣滿鋁, 蔣滿錫, 蔣滿吉, 蔣滿桔 (fl. 1889), 蔣滿銓[12]	**李滿銷 (b. 1860),** 李滿星, 李滿洗, 李滿揚[13]		
16 *fei* 飛	胡飛斗, 陳飛諱 (b. 1890)	張飛悟 (fl. 1875)	李飛靈 (1892–1971)	**蔣飛清 (1888–1971),** 蔣飛法, 蔣飛章	**李飛茂,** 李飛明, 李飛江	龔飛悟	

Generation		Identified Lineage Members					
17	*shen* 身 / *sheng* 昇	胡身慧, 陳身令 (b. 1906)	張昇真 (b. 1915)	李昇級 (1917–2010)	蔣身恒, 蔣身臨, 蔣身朝, **蔣身志 (1928–2018)**	**李身銘,** 李身鎮, 李身悟, 李身浩, 李身福	龔昇桓	
18	*ye* 謁		張謁恩, 張謁惠		**李謁詩 (b. 1948), 蔣謁謙 (b. 1950)**	**李謁真 (1933—2007)**	龔謁聖, 龔謁丹	
19	*yu* 玉		張玉垣		**蔣玉誠 (b. 1973)**	**陳玉得 (Chen Diwen, b. 1976)**		
20	*jing* 京	陳京妙	張京碧					
Prominent Clan		❼ Chen and Hu	❻ Luo and Zhang	❺ Luo and Li	❶ Jiang	❷ Li	❸ Gong	❹ Fang and Fu
Region		Zhenshang	Meicheng	Meicheng	Fuqing	Fuqing	Fuqing	Fuqing
		Central Daxiong Mountains	Southeastern Daxiong Mountains					

Source: Author's tabulation based on ritual manuals in the author's personal collection, which mention members from clans ❶❷❸❹❺❻; various articles in Chen and Arrault, *Xiangzhong zongjiao yu xiangtu shehui diaocha baogao,* which mention genealogical information about the clans in ❼; Lui and Li, *Shi Dao heyi*; Les statuettes religieuses du Hunan database, which supplies biographical information from consecration certificates hidden within wooden statues dedicated to several masters (http://hunan.efeo.fr).

Notes: Names of masters in boldface are mentioned in chapter 1.

Clans ❶❷❺❻ all stem from the Luo clan, active during the eighteenth and nineteenth centuries.
The Jiang clan ❶ has flourished since the late eighteenth century. Sources show that masters of the Jiang clan have historically collaborated with

masters of clans ❷❸❹❺❻ who have lived in the southeastern Daxiong Mountains. Sources also show that members of the Jiang and Gong ❸ clans intermarried.

The Li clan ❷ learned ritual practices from the Jiang ❶ clan and likely joined the lineage in the early nineteenth century. Since then, members of the Jiang and Li clans have often intermarried, and men in those clans have apprenticed together.

Not every master, past and present, whose Daoist name follows this generational poem, was included. In the interest of space, masters of several other clans who were trained by masters from these seven prominent clans were excluded.

[1]   Les statuettes religieuses du Hunan (cote no. T0328).
[2]   Ibid. (cote nos. T0801, T0772). These two consecration certificates show intermarriage between the Gong and Yuan clans.
[3]   Ibid. (cote no. T0277).
[4]   Ibid. (cote no. FS-0202).
[5]   Ibid. (cote nos. Y.1122019, Y.1122067).
[6]   Ibid. (cote no. T0118).
[7]   Ibid. (cote no. T0190).
[8]   Ibid. (cote no. Y.1122019).
[9]   Ibid. (cote no. FS-0004).
[10] Ibid. (cote nos. Y.1122013, Y.1122142, Y.1122015).
[11] Ibid. (cote no. Y.1122012).
[12] Ibid. (cote no. FS-0164).
[13] Ibid. (cote no. Y.1122011).

Notes

Prelude

1 Chen Diwen's name has been altered.

2 A *jiao* 醮 (offering) is a large-scale religious ceremony in which a local community or a household hires a troupe of Daoist masters to perform a sequence of rites in which they offer petitions to the pantheon of gods on behalf of the patrons. *Jiao* as performed by Chen Diwen's lineage usually last from one to five days, depending on the amount of money raised for the event.

3 I choose to translate the term *zhenren* 真人 as "realized one" or "realized person" rather than as the more common "perfected." For an extended argument for this interpretation of the concept *zhen*, see Andersen, *Paradox of Being*, 67–114.

4 We shall explore the dual Daoist-Buddhist identity of Chen Diwen's lineage in chapter 1.

5 These masters pronounce the term *mizhi* (esoteric instruction) rather than *bizhi*. I use "exorcism" here broadly to mean both apotropaic ritual designed to avert demonic effects like social discord, economic woe, and bodily illness, and therapeutic ritual designed to purge demonic entities from unhealthy places or bodies.

6 I leave untranslated the foundational term *qi* 氣/炁. In the Chinese monist cosmos, *qi* is the stuff of all existence. All matter and energy consist of different grades of *qi*. More solid things—earth, stones, bones, and so on—are composed of more turbid *qi*. More ethereal things—air, energy, thoughts, spirits, and so on—are composed of more rarified *qi*.

7   Lawrence Sullivan made this point in a lecture for his course "How to Understand Religion: Theory from Max Müller to Catherine Bell" (Harvard University, Cambridge, MA, October 15, 2001). See also Sullivan, "Sound and Senses."

8   Schipper, *Taoist Body*, 72. Schipper often uses the term *ke* (ritual or liturgy) to denote the power of an entire program of ritual action to integrate and order the world. "The classification of beings, not only human beings and gods, but, in principle, all the things of the world according to their 'fundamental destiny' (*benming* 本命), their merit and their function, is the work of the [Daoist] masters. It is their work, their liturgy, called, in Chinese, *ke*: to class, to divide, and also degree, promotion, exam, or competition for an official position in the imperial administration. . . . The liturgy thus aims at integration and order, and moreover to 'pass' all beings to a higher level in one vast movement, so that the whole world may obtain the natural, spontaneous order of the heavens, and be at one with the cosmological system" (65–66).

9   Schipper, "Outline of Taoist Ritual," 114.

10   For Schipper's full argument, see "Outline of Taoist Ritual," in which he draws inspiration from the scholar of Vedic ritual Frits Staal. For a concise articulation of Frits Staal's approach to ritual as formal syntax, see his "Meaninglessness of Ritual."

11   Schipper, *The Taoist Body*, 45–46.

12   Ibid., 53; see also Schipper, "Vernacular and Classical Ritual in Taoism," 27–32.

13   Schipper, *The Taoist Body*, 69.

14   Andersen, "Concepts of Meaning in Chinese Ritual," especially 162–163.

15   My working definition of "subject" implies two intertwined aspects of being in the world. On one hand, subjects are constructed in that they are formed by relationships with others, which can be articulated in narratives. Subjects are molded by the very experiences in which they are situated. On the other hand, subjects are active in that they choose how to participate in certain moments in those narratives and can even configure them. Chapter 3 explores another mode of being that transcends this notion of subject, which I generally call the "true self" and ritual manuals refer to by various names.

16   For Bakhtin's theory of utterance, see Vološinov, *Marxism*, 65–113; and Bakhtin, "Problem of Speech Genres." A strong argument holds that Bakhtin himself wrote all or part of the text attributed to his friend Vološinov. For that controversy, see Clark and Holquist, *Mikhail Bakhtin*, 146–170. Reliable guides for reading Bakhtin are Holquist, *Dialogism*; and Todorov, *Mikhail Bakhtin*.

17 See Meulenbeld, *Demonic Warfare*, 1–23, 60–97.

18 See LaMothe, *Between Dancing and Writing*, 129–158.

19 For the kind of phenomenology of religion that informs this book, see Carman, *Majesty and Meekness*; Patton, *Religion of the Gods*; and LaMothe, *Between Dancing and Writing*.

Chapter One: The Ordinand

Epigraphs. Master Jiang Yucheng, communication to the author. Master Liu Yu, DZ 1220:253.5b2–3.

1 For the religious statuary of Hunan, see Arrault, *History of Cultic Images*; and Arrault, "Analytic Essay."

2 *Anhua xianzhi*, 530–531.

3 Already in the eighteenth century, black tea from Anhua was attracting merchants from Guizhou, Sichuan, Fujian, Guangdong, Guangxi, Jiangsu, Zhejiang, Shaanxi, and Henan. Perdue, *Exhausting the Earth*, 100.

4 *Anhua xianzhi*, 530–531.

5 For a journalistic account of the lives of migrant workers, see, among others, Pai and Benton, *Scattered Sand*. For the experiences of women migrant laborers, see Ngai, *Made in China*; and Chang, *Factory Girls*. For a sociological study of how returning wealth affected rural society in the interior of China in the 1990s, see Murphy, *How Migrant Labor Is Changing Rural China*.

6 Throughout this study, I refer to all masters by their Daoist names (*daoming* 道名) bequeathed to them at ordination. Those names are used only within the confines of their esoteric Daoist rituals and are not generally known outside the lineage.

7 This paragraph and the next draw on Mozina, "Daubing Lips with Blood," 274.

8 The musical instruments used are bamboo flute, drum (*gu* 鼓), handheld drum (*biangu* 邊鼓), handheld gong (*zhengzi* 鉦子), hand cymbal with hammer (*nao* 鐃), small cymbal (*xiaoba* 小鈸), large cymbal (*daba* 大鈸), "wooden fish" (*muyu* 木魚), chime bell (*qing* 磬), and conch (*haijiao* 海角). A gong (*luo* 鑼) is usually played by a layman.

9 This language is also used by other masters in central Hunan and in Fujian. See Liu Tiefeng, "Meishan wenhua zhong daojiao"; Chen Yisong, "Daxiongshan zhong de Huizhen leitan"; Ye Mingsheng, "Fujian Taining de Pu'anjiao"; and Lagerwey, "Popular Ritual Specialists."

10 The term "ritual master" (*fashi* 法師) shifts depending on who uses the term and how. In the Le'an region, the term is used generically by locals to refer to any liturgical master, regardless of whether he identifies as a practitioner of Daoist, Buddhist, or Yuanhuang rites. It is also used, however, by some masters to specify practitioners of Yuanhuang rites, though other masters insist that the term *fashi* is only used by uninitiated locals and not by Yuanhuang practitioners themselves.

11 For studies on Yuanhuang rites and how they coexist with Daoist rites within lineages in central Hunan, see Lui and Li, *Shi Dao heyi*; Li Xinwu, "Lengshuijiang Yangyuan Zhangtan shigong yu daoshi de yitong bijiao"; Fava, *Aux portes du ciel*; Meulenbeld, "Dancing with the Gods"; Meulenbeld, "The Dark Emperor's Law"; and Meulenbeld, "Classifying a Local Cult in Hunan."

12 This paragraph and the next draw largely on von Glahn, *The Country of Streams and Grottoes*, 295–359; Wu Xinfu, *Hunan tongshi*, 391–401; Zhang Shihong, *Meishan wenhua*, 15–21, 22–60; Guo Zhaoxiang, *Zhongguo Meishan wenhua*, 12–31; Lui and Li, *Shi Dao heyi*, 27–34; and Perdue, *Exhausting the Earth*, 93–110. For a general survey of the history of central Hunan (Xiangzhong 湘中) and its Daoist and Buddhist traditions, see Robson, "Among Mountains and between Rivers."

13 *Daojiao gepai paixushi*, 1b.

14 All the Daoist masters I have personally encountered around Le'an township and Meicheng township (梅城鎮) to its east identify with this lineage poem. Local scholar Liu Tiefeng reports that masters in Songshan village (松山村) in Zhenshang township (圳上鎮), which lies to the west of Le'an deeper in the Daxiong Mountains in northern Xinhua, also use the poem. Chen Yisong, a working master in the Zhenshang area, reports that his lineage identifies with the poem as well. See Liu Tiefeng, "Meishan wenhua zhong daojiao"; and Chen Yisong, "Daxiongshan zhong de Huizhen leitan." The masters Patrice Fava works with further south in Xinhua, and the ones Mark Meulenbeld, Lui Wing Sing, and Li Xinwu work with near Lengshuijiang (冷水江), identify with different poems, indicating they and their liturgical ancestors have belonged to different lineages these past many generations.

15 Liu Tiefeng, "Meishan wenhua zhong daojiao," 184.

16 The text indicates the geographical region of central Hunan in Qing administrative terms. Created in 1376, the provincial administration commissions (*chengxuan*

buzhengsi 承宣布政司) were the principle Ming governmental agencies charged with directing routine administrative business and handling communication between the central government and regional and local administrative units. The Qing maintained this administrative system. In 1664, the Qing divided the old Ming Huguang province (湖廣省) into Hubei and Hunan provinces. Hunan was organized into four administrative circuits (*dao* 道), of which the Changbao circuit (Changbao dao 長寶道) encompassed Changsha prefecture (長沙府), which administered Anhua county, and Baoqing prefecture (寶慶府), which administered Xinhua county. Hucker, *Dictionary of Official Titles*, 127.

17 *Dongyuan sanmei*, 29a–30a. The first and last character of the title of this manuscript are obscured.

18 The following information on Zeng Rushou and the Jade Void Palace is taken from Li Xinwu, "Lengshuijiang Yangyuan Zhangtan shigong," 290–292; Lui and Li, *Shi Dao heyi*, 48–52, 56; Zeng Di, "Xinhuaxian daojiao yuanliu," 204–208; Liu Weishun, "Xinshaoxian Wenxianguan diaocha baogao," 76–94; Luo, "Xinhua maochang leitan," 455–460; Fava and Wan Yilin, "Hunan daojiao diaocha yanjiu," 34–35; Fava, *Aux portes du ciel*, 37–38; and Meulenbeld, "The Dark Emperor's Law," 13–20.

19 Local scholar Liu Weishun speculates it is possible that Zhang Jinghua feigned blood relationship with the Celestial Masters to claim their prestige. Liu, "Xinshaoxian Wenxianguan diaocha baogao," 77.

20 The first of those students, Deng Yuanshou (鄧元壽), spread the tradition farther south in Hunan to Shaoyang (邵陽). The second, Li Zhizhen (李志真), founded, along with his disciples, Daoist temples on twenty-eight mountains across Xinhua.

21 Lui and Li, *Shi Dao heyi*, 189–190. Meulenbeld argues that the Office of the Daoist Association governed all the Daoist institutions in the Xinhua region, which worshiped the same gods as the Jade Void Temple and paid fees to maintain affiliation. See Meulenbeld, "The Dark Emperor's Law," 78–85. On the Office of the Daoist Association, see Goossaert, "Bureaucratic Charisma," 127–128.

22 A certain Li Shaozhen (李紹珍) was associated with a temple called Daotang Abbey (道堂觀); Wang Shaoxuan (汪紹瑄) with Dongyang Abbey (洞陽觀); Zeng Shaocong (曾紹琮) with Miaotian Abbey (苗田觀); Wang Shaoqiong (王紹瓊) with Longxing Abbey (龍興觀); Qu Shaoling (屈紹玲) with Huilong

Abbey (回龍觀); and Duan Shaolin (段紹琳) with Chongyang Abbey (崇陽觀). Luo, "Xinhua maochang leitan," 456; and Lui and Li, *Shi Dao heyi*, 51.

23   Other temples chose to be affiliated with the prominent Jade Void Palace, for example, a Chongde Abbey (崇德觀) (mentioned in Li Xinwu, "Lengshuijiang Yangyuan Zhangtan," 288–292; and Meulenbeld, "The Dark Emperor's Law," 18–19), and a Lingjiu Abbey (靈鷲觀) (mentioned in Meulenbeld, "The Dark Emperor's Law," 19–20, 29–32). It is reasonable to surmise that, as the Jade Void Palace gained prominence in the region, some small, local religious entities originally not associated with the Jade Void Temple would prefer to establish a relationship with it by becoming its affiliates.

24   For example, Master Luo Jieyong (羅傑勇) of Luguan township (爐觀鎮) in Xinhua claims that his lineage descends from the Jade Void Palace through the Chongyang Abbey. Luo, "Xinhua maochang leitan," 456. Lui and Li report that masters in the region around the upper reaches of the Zi River—from the Xinhua county seat, southeast to Lengshuijiang, and farther south to Xinshao county (新邵縣)—all trace their lineages to the six houses. Lui and Li, *Shi Dao heyi*, 51.

25   Liu Tiefeng, "Meishan wenhua zhong daojiao," 188.

26   Robson, "Among Mountains and between Rivers," 21.

27   Esposito, "Longmen School," 621–622, 629–630, 654; and Goossaert, "Quanzhen Clergy," 702–703.

28   After the liturgical ancestors of Master Zou Shengyun (鄒昇雲) of Shuiche exhausted the last *ran* 然 character of the Zhengyi poem attributed to Zhang Jinhua (桂志以繼道，玄洞漢妙元，高明惟再弘，成真守自然), they adopted the Quanzhen Longmen poem (道德通玄靜，真常守太清，一〔元〕陽來復本，合教〔寬恕〕永元明). Lui and Liu, *Shi Dao heyi*, 50–52.

29   Li Xinwu speculates that the Zhang clan began using characters in the Quanzhen Longmen poem after 1567. See Li, "Lengshuijiang Yangyuan Zhangtan shigong," 292; and Lui and Li, *Shi Dao heyi*, 51.

30   Luo, "Xinhua maochang leitan," 455–457.

31   Fava and Wan, "Hunan daojiao diaocha yanjiu," 34–35.

32   Esposito, "Longmen School," 621–622; and Goossaert, "Quanzhen Clergy," 725.

33   See Liu Tiefeng, "Meishan wenhua zhong daojiao"; and Chen Yisong, "Daxiongshan zhong de Huizhen leitan."

34 *Hetong yinshu shi*, 46b.

35 The text was composed in the early 1990s by Jiang Shenzhi, at the time the most senior living master in the lineage, who wrote out dozens of secret instructions that had previously been taught only as oral transmissions.

36 See Ye Mingsheng, "Min xibei Pu'an qingwei"; Ye, "Fujian Taining"; Tam Wai Lun, "Zhongguo dongnanbu jiaoyi"; Tam, "Cong Yuebei Yingde de 'nanwu' jiaoyi"; multiple chapters in Tam Wai Lun, *Minjian fojiao yanjiu*; and Lui and Li, *Shi Dao heyi*, 140–142.

37 Ye Mingsheng, "Fujian Taining," 246, drawing on a Yuan source, the *Xinbian lianxiang soushen guangji*, 82–84.

38 Wang and Zhou, *Pu'an chanshi quanji,* 371. Tam Wai Lun reports that the *Pu'an zushi lingyan ji* is also included in a large compilation of Pu'an-related texts collected by John Lagerwey in Pu'an's hometown of Yichun in northwestern Jiangxi. Tam, "Yinsu Pu'an (1115–1169) zushi de yanjiu zhi chutan," 227n1.

39 See Ye, "Min xibei Pu'an qingwei," 386–392; and Lagerwey, "Popular Ritual Specialists," 476–481, 490–492, 498.

40 See Tam, "Zhongguo dongnanbu jiaoyi"; and Tam, "Cong Yuebei Yingde de 'nanwu' jiaoyi."

41 *Xiantian bodu jian Puzu chuandu ke*, 29a, 32b.

42 Tam Wai Lun also reports that lineages he has worked with in Guangdong and Jiangxi are also rather clear about the boundaries. See "Zhongguo dongnanbu jiaoyi," 131–156; "Yinsu Pu'an," 215–225; and "Cong Yuebei Yingde de 'nanwu' jiaoyi," 100, 106–108.

43 Although lineages like Chen Diwen's are clear about these boundaries, exactly how Pu'an Buddhist, Daoist, and local *shi* traditions have historically come to influence and shape one another in places like Anhua is an important question that demands a monograph-length response.

44 The copyist of this text (or one of the copyists of a previous text on which it is based) mistakenly wrote "Xuandou prefecture" (玄都府) for "Yuanzhou prefecture" (袁州府). The pronunciations of these two words are similar in the local dialect.

45 *Fojiao banshe ke*, 39a–39b.

46 Hucker, *Dictionary of Official Titles*, 404–405.

47 Tam, "Yinsu Pu'an," 234, drawing on Deng Cihuang, *Tianxia da Cihua*, 5–6.

The 1806 genealogy, titled *Chici Nanquanshan zongpu* (敕賜南泉山宗譜), was originally collected by local scholar Deng Cihuang in the 1980s. For that story, see Yang Yongjun, "Nanquan Puzu menxia," 200n1; and Wang Shuigen, "Cihuasi jiqi Pu'an zushi shulun."

48 *Fojiao ciri chaoke*, 90b. Ye Mingsheng notes that another Southern Spring Shrine (Nanquan'an 南泉庵) was founded in the Chenghua era in Ninghua county (寧化縣) in northwestern Fujian, suggesting that this period was a time of active temple-building by monks from Pu'an's Monastery of Compassionate Transformation. Ye, "Fujian Taining de Pu'anjiao," 247.

49 Li Wuhan, "Daxiongshan jingnei sishijiu," 69; Lui and Li, *Shi Dao heyi*, 140; and Liu Guoqiang, *Hunan fojiao siyuan zhi*, 365.

50 Tam, "Yinsu Pu'an," 234–235.

51 Li Wuhan, "Daxiongshan jingnei sishijiu," 69.

52 Chen Yisong, "Daxiongshan zhong de Huizhen leitan," 454. Lui and Li, who draw on Chen Yisong, claim that in an eastern hall (*dongdian* 東殿) of the Western Spring Monastery was a thunder altar for Daoist and local *shi* traditions, while a western hall housed Buddhist ritual spaces. Lui and Li, *Shi Dao heyi*, 140.

53 *Fojiao ciri chaoke*, 90b.

54 Ibid.

55 Chen Yisong, "Daxiongshan zhong de Huizhen leitan," 454; Liu Tiefeng, "Meishan wenhua zhong daojiao," 177.

56 Li Wuhan reports the Universal Transformation Monastery was built during the Ming dynasty, destroyed in 1958, and rebuilt beginning in the late 1980s and early 1990s. Li, "Daxiongshan jingnei shishijiu," 70, 74.

57 *Fojiao banshe ke*, 39b–40a.

58 The modest Guanyin Temple was built at the mouth of Guanyin Cave (Guanyindong 觀音洞), which encloses the Bamboo Grove Shrine (Zhulin'an 竹林庵). For details of the temple, see Liu Guoqiang, *Hunan fojiao siyuan zhi*, 310–311.

59 *Fojiao ciri chaoke*, 87a.

60 Ibid.

61 *Chici Nanquan zongpu*, 6a–6b. Many thanks to Tam Wai Lun for sharing these pages with me.

62 *Buxu gaoseng zhuan*, X77, no. 1524, 474c17–475c8. See also *Zhongnanshan tianlong huiji zimen shipu*, X86, no. 1603, 484c24–485a1. Tam Wai Lun recounts

a legend he heard in northwestern Jiangxi that elaborates this story. Before Zhu Yuanzhang became the Hongwu emperor, he was counseled by aides to seek out Jin Bifeng. Zhu found him but was irked by the monk's unwillingness to break his meditation to greet him. Zhu angrily brandished his sword and yelled, "Have you never before seen a murderous general?" Jin Bifeng angrily yelled back, "Have you never before seen a monk who does not fear death?" Zhu promptly offered the monk gifts, which were reciprocated. Jin Bifeng told his new friend, "Jiankang [Nanjing] is a place you may rule." After Zhu unified the empire and ascended the throne, he decreed Bifeng Monastery to be the monk's residence and bestowed upon him a Buddhist chasuble and an alms bowl made of precious jade. Tam, "Yinsu Pu'an," 233–234.

63 Chen Yisong, "Daxiongshan zhong de Huizhen leitan," 451–452.

64 The text introduces him as "Xie Xuanying, a servant of a branch lineage of the Great Chan Monastery of Compassionate Transformation, Decreed as Protector of the State out of Vast Compassion, on Mount Nanquan, the Prefectural Buddhist Registry of Yuanzhou prefecture [under the jurisdiction] of the Provincial Administrative Commission of Jiangxi Province in the Great Qing Dynasty" (大清國江西省承宣佈政使司袁州府僧綱司南泉山敕賜廣慈護國大慈化禪寺演派臣謝玄應). Lui and Li, *Shi Dao heyi*, 142.

65 Account given by Li Yeshi (李謁詩), July 9, 2010.

66 *Zhaolian qingsheng ke*, 18b–21b.

67 Zhidao renmin tuanti zhuzhi zongbaogaobiao (指導人民團體組織總報告表), May 1, 1942, Minguo Anhuaxian minzhengke, 1943, box 505, folder 428, Anhua County Archives.

68 The following quotations from Jiang Shenzhi are taken from a long interview with the author on July 24, 2010, as well as from several subsequent conversations in 2010 and 2014.

69 This Cultural Revolution slogan heralded the destruction and replacement of old thinking, old culture, old customs, and old habits (*jiu sixiang, jiu wenhua, jiu fengsu, jiu xiguan* 舊思想, 舊文化, 舊風俗, 舊習慣).

70 Zhang Shihong, "Anhua daojiao de diaocha baogao," 32–33. This piece also appears in Zhang Shihong, *Meishan wenhua*, 154–240.

71 An abbreviation for branch secretary of the Party in a village (*cundangzhibu shuji* 村黨支部書記).

72 This quotation and the next are taken from a discussion between Li Yeshi and the author on July 9, 2010.

73 The demonstrators demanded the release of Falun gong members who had been arrested during a protest two weeks prior in Tianjin, an assurance of the freedom to practice Falun gong cultivation, and the permission to publish Falun gong literature.

74 For nuanced analyses of this event in the context of twentieth-century religious and political history, see Ownby, *Falun Gong*, especially 161–227; and Palmer, *Qigong Fever*, especially 219–277.

75 Li Yeshi's points unwittingly parallel those that have been made since the 1999 Falun gong demonstration by organizations like the China Buddhist Association (Zhongguo fojiao xiehui 中國佛教協會) and academic authorities on college campuses. See Ownby, *Falun Gong*, 180–182; and Palmer, *Qigong Fever*, 262–263.

Chapter Two: The Deity

Epigraphs. Marshal Yin Jiao, *Yin Jiao chumai*, 6b; Master Bai Yuchan, DZ 1220:82.29b2–3.

1 See, for example, Kleeman, *God's Own Tale;* Katz, *Demon Hordes*; Shahar, *Oedipal God*; and ter Haar, *Guan Yu.*

2 The *Genealogical Investigation* is referred to by its shortened title, *Yin Jiao chumai* (殷郊出脈), in the notes.

3 Jiang Shenzhi mostly based his redaction of the *Genealogical Investigation* on an undated and anonymous hagiography titled *Yin Jiao xueben* (殷郊血本). He also drew on the ritual manuals *Xiantian fufa michuan* (先天符法秘傳), *Xiao Yingong fufa* (小殷公符法), *Da Yingong fufa* (大殷公符法), and *Xiantian Yinlei xueying mizhi* (先天殷雷削影秘旨), in addition to the *Banner Rite.*

4 *Yin Jiao chumai*, 1a.

5 According to the text, the third lifetime was spent as son of Zhang □ (張□); the fourth lifetime as son of Li □ (李□); the fifth as son of Yugong Ting (余公挺); the sixth as son of Zhan Xia (旃轄); the seventh as son of □ Zhuan (□轉); the eighth as son of Huituo Liuming (迴脫流明); and the ninth as son of Xun Du (訊都). *Yin Jiao chumai*, 1b.

6 *Yin Jiao chumai*, 2a.

7 Ibid., 2a–2b.

8 The text states, 殷郊與蔣銳遊訪天下，至青城山，洞有彭澄潤之徒，諱名霞，號一玄，字守真. *Yin Jiao chumai*, 3a. The character *tu* 徒 here could mean either

"disciple" or simply "fellow," so the line could be read as talking about the disciple of Peng Chengrun or the man himself. I choose to translate *tu* as "fellow" and so read the line as talking about Peng Chengrun himself because that is the way the Banner Rite refers to him.

9   For readers familiar with Ming–Qing vernacular novels, Shuilian Cave is also the name of the grotto in which Sun Wukong (孫悟空), the Monkey King, dwells in the *Journey to the West* (*Xiyou ji* 西遊記). That Shuilian Cave does not seem to bear any obvious relation to the Shuilian Cave here.

10   *Yin Jiao chumai,* 4b.

11   Ibid., 5a.

12   Ibid., 5a–5b.

13   This is evidence of a seam in the story. Before, the text states Shen studied on Mount Qingcheng, here it is Mount Heming. It seems the first half of the story about Yin Jiao's early life and travels was stitched to the story of his oath with Shen the Realized One.

14   *Yin Jiao chumai,* 5b.

15   Ibid., 6a. The mention here that Yin Jiao learned of his father's evil deeds at age eighteen, as opposed to age twelve, is another seam in the text, which the redactor Jiang Shenzhi decided to keep rather than reconcile.

16   Ibid., 6a–6b.

17   Ibid., 6b.

18   Ibid., 7b–8a. Shen was created the Realized One of the Court of Upper Clarity (上清院真人). General Magpie Wang Huaiyu was styled Assistant General Who Decapitates Demons with His Great Blade, Shoots Sprites and Restrains Demons without Tenderness, Universally Aids the Great Transformations, and Administers the Bureau of the Earth Ministry (副將掌地司府普濟弘化攝魔無佞收鬼大刀斬鬼將軍).

19   *Yingong fanfa,* 24a.

20   Hucker, *Dictionary of Official Titles,* 131. On the relationship between the Jixianyuan and the Yuan dynasty's administration of Daoist affairs, see Lin Qiaowei, "Shilun Yuandai Jixianyuan."

21   DZ 1220:246.3b3. The title also appears in another canonical text summoning Yin Jiao, DZ 1166:44.1a4. The title is always used by Chen Diwen's lineage when invoking Liao Shouzhen, for example, in *Daojiao qishi chaoke,* 42a; and *Zhaolian qingsheng ke,* 18a. Another canonical text for wielding Yin Jiao refers to Liao by the title Ancestral Master Liao Shouzhen, Realized One of Great

Clarity, Master of the Numinous Gem (祖師靈寶先生太清真人廖守真), but this title is not recognized by Chen's lineage. See DZ 1220:247.1a5.

22 Liao Shouzhen transmitted the rite to a certain Xiao Anguo (蕭安國), who transmitted it to his son Xiao Daoyi (蕭道一), who served as Peng Yuantai's transmission master and passed on the rite shortly before he died (DZ 1220: 246.2a5–8).

23 DZ 1220:246.3b1–2. Recall that the lineage's hagiography introduces Shen as the Realized One of the Wondrous Transformations of the Golden Tripod (Jinding miaohua Shengong zhenren). The lineage's manuals all include the phrase "Wondrous Transformations of the Golden Tripod" in various versions of his title: Ancestral Master Shen the Realized One of the Wondrous Rites (Transformations) of the Golden Tripod of Shuilian Cavern Heaven, Patriarch of the Heart of Heaven (祖師天心教主水濂洞天金鼎妙法〔化〕申真人); and Sire Shen the Realized One, Directing Dignitary and Autumn Hermit of the Wondrous Rites (Transformations) of the Golden Tripod of Shuilian Cavern-Heaven (水濂洞天金鼎妙法〔化〕秋隱執士申公真人). Because they are homonyms in the local dialect, the word *hua* 化 (transformations) is often confused for *fa* 法 (rites) in the lineage's manuals (*Daojiao qishi chaoke*, 41a; and *Zhaolian qingsheng ke*, 18a).

24 Chen Diwen's lineage preserves a text stating that a certain "Huang Fu the Realized One of Mount Qingcheng was originally Shen the Realized One" (青城山黃甫真人原是申真人) (*Xiantian Yinlei xueying mizhi*, 21a). It is remotely possible this cryptic line refers to the well-known Southern Song master Huang Futan (皇甫坦) (d. 1178), who traveled widely but spent significant time on Mount Qingcheng in Sichuan and at a temple called the Abbey of Manifest Response (Xianyingguan 顯應觀) in western Hunan. It is tempting to surmise that, given Huang Futan's dates, he might have served as Liao Shouzhen's master in Sichuan (see DZ 297:3.9b4–17a7). Another remote possibility is that Shen the Realized One might have been a distant patriarch of Liao Shouzhen's lineage in Sichuan. A prominent Daoist named Shen Xun (申迅) was associated with Mount Qingcheng during the late Tang and Five Dynasties (see Hu Fuchen, *Zhonghua daojiao dacidian*, 110).

In his collection of Daoist ritual texts, Lee Fong-mao includes an undated text of unknown provenance that describes Shen the Realized One as personally transmitting ritual instructions for invoking Yin Jiao to Liao Shouzhen. During the ritual, the officiant recites, "I invoke Ancestral Master and Great Patriarch of the Teaching Shen the Realized One of the Wondrous Transformations of the Golden Tripod, who admired [the Dao] and practiced on a mountaintop in western Sichuan. After cultivating the golden elixir nine times he achieved awakening and then personally transmitted the ritual instructions to Master Liao" (啟請祖師大教主，金鼎妙化申真人，西蜀山上慕修行，九轉金丹成正覺，親授廖師傳法旨). This passage identifies Shen the Realized One as a personal master of Liao Shouzhen, although it is ambiguous whether Shen was human or a deity (DFHH 20:424).

In other places in his collection, Lee asserts that Shen the Realized One was actually Huang Shunshen (黃舜申) (1224–after 1286), a Fujian native and early codifier of the Qingwei liturgical tradition. Unfortunately, Lee does not argue for this assertion. Given that Shen is listed as senior to Liao Shouzhen in both the *Great Rite* and in the ritual text included in Lee's compendium, and that the *Great Rite* implies that Liao would have been active during the late twelfth or early thirteenth century, it is highly unlikely Shen the Realized One was indeed Huang Shunshen, who was active during the mid- to late thirteenth century (see DFHH 1:108, 218).

25 On the popularity of the *Scripture of Salvation* during the Song, see Strickmann, "Longest Taoist Scripture"; von Glahn, *Sinister Way,* 156–157; and Boltz, *Survey of Taoist Literature,* 206–211. For Great Cavern Practices, see Chang Ch'ao-jan, "Xipu, jiaofa jiqi zhenghe," 41–44, 225–247.

26 DZ 1220:246.1b2–8.

27 Liu Yu, courtesy name Qingqing (清卿), who originally went by Liu Shi (劉世) and studied with the notable master of Divine Empyrean, Fengdu, and Earth Spirits rites Lu Ye (盧埜), is not to be confused with another Liu Yu (劉玉) (1257–1308) of Jiangxi who founded the Pure and Bright Way of Loyalty and Filiality (Zhongxiao jingming dao 忠孝淨明道) devoted to the transcendent Xu Xun (許遜) (trad. 239–374). See Boltz, *Survey of Taoist Literature,* 264–265n59; and Skar, "Ritual Movements," 428, 448. A biography of Liu Yu (Liu Shi) by his disciple Huang Gongjin (黃公瑾) (fl. 1274) is available in DZ 1220:253.10a7–12a3.

28 DZ 1220:253.1b8–2a1. Different meanings have been associated with terms for altar spaces such as "gate of Heaven" (*tianmen* 天門) and "Earth door" (*dihu* 地戶). Following the standard configuration of the eight trigrams in the

Posterior Heaven (Houtian 後天), the gate of Heaven here likely corresponds to the trigram *qian* ☰ denoting the northwest corner of the altar space and the direction of the heavens beyond. The Earth door likely corresponds to the trigram *kun* ☷ denoting the southwest corner of the altar and the direction of the Earth. The trigram *xun* ☴ denotes the southeast direction, which is often associated with the summoning of thunder gods in Divine Empyrean texts. See, for example, DZ 1220:56.6b3–6, 7a8–7b9.

29   The trigram *kun* ☷ symbolizes Earth.

30   DZ 1220:246.1a4-b2.

31   For the significance of the trigram *kan* in Daoist ritual, see Lagerwey, *Taoist Ritual*, 14. For discussions of the *locus classicus* of the concept *kan* in the *Yijing* (易經), see Zhou Zhenfu, *Zhouyi yizhu*, 281.

32   DZ 1220:246.10a5–6.

33   See Li Yuanguo, "Ziwei dadi xiaokao," 62–65; Hsiao Teng-fu, *Taisui yuanshen*, 286–313; and Hsiao, "Shilun Ziwei dadi shen'ge," 790–819.

34   DZ 1016:10.11a1.

35   For studies on Tianpeng, see Liu Zhiwan, "Tenhōshin to tenhōju ni tsuite"; and Li Yuanguo and Wang Jiayou, "Tianpeng yuanshuai kaobian." For a partial translation of the *Tianpeng Incantation*, see Strickmann, "History, Anthropology, and Chinese Religion," 228. On the Six Heavens and the six palaces, see Bokenkamp, *Early Daoist Scriptures*, 188–194; Robinet, *La révélation du Shangqing*, 2:163–169; and Mollier, "La méthode de l'Empereur du Nord," 336–340, 359–361.

36   This paragraph relies on Li Yuanguo, *Shenxiao leifa*, 10–15.

37   DZ 1248:4.10b1–7.

38   DZ 296:32.7a3–7b3.

39   DZ 1:37.3a6–10.

40   DZ 1412:1.1a3–8a10. See also Andersen, "*Taishang Yuanshi tianzun shuo Beidi fumo shenzhou miaojing.*"

41   DZ 1412:3.24b8–10.

42   My account of the origin story, texts, and main tenets of the Heart of Heaven tradition in the following several paragraphs relies on Li Zhihong, *Daojiao tianxin zhengfa yanjiu*; Andersen's analyses of Heart of Heaven texts in Schipper and Verellen, *Taoist Canon*, 2:1056–1074, 1074–1080; Andersen, "Taoist Talismans"; Hymes, *Way and Byway*, 26–46; Davis, *Society and the Supernatural*, 21–24; and Boltz, *Survey of Taoist Literature*, 33–38.

43 The dating of these texts has been the subject of some debate. Poul Andersen has argued that Deng Yougong's preface for DZ 566 *Shangqing tianxin zhengfa* was likely written before 1075 and that the rest of the text was composed by him sometime toward the end of the eleventh century. The extant text preserved in the Ming Daoist canon is likely an expanded, mid-twelfth-century or later version of the earlier text by Deng Yougong. Andersen dates DZ 461 *Shangqing gusui lingwen guilü* to no later than 1116. Judith Boltz argued earlier that Deng Yougong likely lived from 1210 to 1279 and that these two texts were written in the late Southern Song. Robert Hymes painstakingly fleshed out the discrepancy between Boltz and Andersen and independently concluded Andersen's dates are correct, which I follow here. See Andersen, "*Shangqing tianxin zhengfa*"; Andersen, "*Shangqing gusui lingwen guilü*"; Andersen, "Taoist Ritual Texts," 81–83, 89–90; Boltz, *Survey of Taoist Literature*, 265–266n65; and Hymes, *Way and Byway*, 271–277.

44 DZ 1227:1.1a5–8.

45 Sometimes the Northern Dipper asterism was considered to include two more hidden stars to total nine stars. For the role of the Northern Dipper in regulating individual fate, see Hou, *Monnaies d'offrande*.

46 On these four deities and their relationship with the Emperor of the North, see Davis, *Society and the Supernatural*, 67–86; Lagerwey, *Taoist Ritual*, 257–258; Chao Shin-yi, *Daoist Ritual*, 21–28; Li Yuanguo, "Ziwei dadi xiaokao"; Li and Wang, "Tianpeng yuanshuai kaobian"; and Hsiao, "Shilun Ziwei dadi shen'ge."

47 Poul Andersen points out that one of the core Tianxin texts assigns this title to Rao Dongtian instead of Zhang Daoling. See "*Taishang zhuguo jiumin zongzhen biyao*," 1058.

48 Li Zhihong, *Daojiao tianxin zhengfa yanjiu*, 152–157.

49 This paragraph relies on Li Zhihong, *Daojiao tianxin zhengfa yanjiu*, 16–35; and Poul Andersen's contributions in Schipper and Verellen, *Taoist Canon*, 2:1056–1074, 1074–1080.

50 DZ 1227:1.1a7–10.

51 DZ 567:1a2–7; and Li Zhihong, *Daojiao tianxin zhengfa yanjiu*, 32.

52 For a detailed study of biographic information on the thirtieth Celestial Master, Zhang Jixian, see Kao Chen-hung, "Xujing tianshi chuanshuo yanjiu."

53 See Liu Zhongyu, *Daojiao shoulu zhidu yanjiu*, 149–165; and Goossaert, "Jindai Zhongguo de tianshi shoulu xitong."

54   See Andersen, "*Shangqing gusui lingwen guilü*," 1061; and Li Zhihong, *Daojiao tianxin zhengfa yanjiu,* 21–32.

55   DZ 220:21.1a3–5. The Master in the quotation refers, according to a colophon to the text, to the Heavenly Lord Great Founder of the Teaching (Da jiaozhu tianjun 大教主天君), the deity who revealed a host of these "model sayings" (*geyan* 格言) interspersed throughout the text. See also Andersen, "*Wushang xuanyuan santian yutang dafa*," 1070–1071.

56   For examples of offerings, see DZ 566:6.4a5–4b9; and DZ 1227:2.13b1, 2.17a7–9, 3.13a5–9, 6.33a4–7.

57   DZ 1227:2.9a9–9b2.

58   DZ 1220:246.2b5–10. The line about Zhou Jiu appears to have been a vernacular saying in the Southern Song dynasty. I have not found corroboration.

59   DZ 1220:246.2b10–3a5.

60   DZ 1220:246.10b5. For masters of the new ritual traditions of the Song who worked with mediums, see Davis, *Society and the Supernatural.*

61   In his preface and colophon, Peng Yuantai does not explain Yin Jiao's association with the asterism Great Year. The term "Great Year" shows up only in Yin Jiao's title—Marshal Yin Jiao of Great Might and Utmost Virtue, Ferocious Great Year of the Earth Ministry who Assists in the Rite by Cutting off Ears of Sprites as Trophies and Vanquishing Demons, who Embodies the Dao and Manifests Efficacious Power before the Emperor of the Northern Extremity (北極御前顯 靈體道助法馘精滅魔地司猛吏太歲大威力至德元帥殷郊). DZ 1220:246.3b5–6. By the Song period, the asterism Great Year was often seen as a baleful star associated with fundamental destiny (*benming* 本命) and illnesses caused by illicitly disrupting the earth. In the Song ritual manuals examined in this chapter, Yin Jiao came to be seen as the lord of Great Year. It seems Peng Yuantai is criticizing those who falsely regard that association as indicating Yin Jiao himself is baleful. It is notable that for Peng, as well as for Chen Diwen's lineage, Yin Jiao's status as the god Great Year is not central to his persona. For detailed analyses of the history of Great Year, see Ch'en Chun-Chih, "Taisui de xinyang suyuan," especially 19–38, 97–135; Hsiao, *Taisui yuanshen,* especially 258–285; and Hsiao, "Zailun Taisui yuanqi."

62   It is possible Peng Yuantai is specifically talking about his own lineage descended from Liao Shouzhen of Sichuan.

63   My account of Fengdu and its cults in the following paragraphs relies on Kao Chen-hung, "Song–Yuan–Ming daojiao fengyuefa yanjiu"; Mollier, "La

méthode de l'Empereur du Nord du Mont Fengdu"; and Chenivesse, "Fengdu:
Cité l'abondance, cité de la male mort."

64   DZ 1307:1.3b7–10.

65   Scant sources make it difficult to date this lineage precisely. In one hagiographic
      snippet, Lu Ye practiced on Mount Qingcheng in Sichuan, and is said to have
      studied from the famous thirtieth Celestial Master Zhang Jixian (fl. 1092–
      1126). Given that another source mentions that the notable Jiangxi master
      Liu Yu (otherwise known as Liu Shi [fl. 1258]) was Lu Ye's disciple, it seems
      likely that Lu Ye was active during the early to mid-thirteenth century and
      that his encounters with Zhang Jixian in Sichuan were with one of the many
      reported manifestations of the renowned Celestial Master after he died. See DZ
      1220:253.10a7–12a3.

66   DZ 1220:265:14a2–3.

67   DZ 1220:265.2b9–3a3. The entire story of the Emperor of the North's
      conquest of Fengdu is found on 265.1a5–3a3, and echoes the story in DZ
      1412:1.1a3–8a10.

68   See DZ 1220:265.4a8–4b4; and DZ 1220:267.18a7–9.

69   DZ 1220:265.4b5–9.

70   DZ 1220:265.2a10–2b1.

71   DZ 1220:265.1b6–7.

72   Upon returning to the Northern Extremity after defeating the forces of
      Fengdu, the lords of the Northern Dipper extol the Emperor of the North as
      the Lord who Administers the Myriad Ritual Methods, the Great Emperor of
      the Northern Extremity and Ancestral Master (祖師北極大帝為萬法之主). DZ
      1220:265.1b4.

73   DZ 1220:267.1a5–8.

74   DZ 1220:265.10a10–10b2.

75   DZ 1220:246.10b4–6.

76   DZ 1220:246.10b2–3. Lowell Skar notes that masters in the Song partial to
      older, classical Daoist traditions claimed their superiority derived from the
      simplicity of their ancient rites. Heart of Heaven texts were simple in that they
      were based on only three talismans and two seals. Skar, "Ritual Movements,"
      457.

77   DZ 1220:246.3a5–9.

78   DZ 1220:246.1a6.

79   DZ 1220:246.1b8–2a4.

80　This section relies on Li Yuanguo, *Shenxiao leifa*, especially 30–55, 153–211; Liu Zhongyu, "Wulei zhengfa yuanyuan kaolun"; Li Zhihong, *Daojiao tianxin zhengfa yanjiu*, 88–109; Strickmann, "Longest Taoist Scripture"; Strickmann, "Sōdai no raigi"; Skar, "Administering Thunder"; Skar, "Ritual Movements"; Chao, "Huizong and the Divine Empyrean Palace"; Matsumoto, "Sōdai no raihō"; Davis, *Society and the Supernatural*, 24–29; Boltz, *Survey of Taoist Literature*, 26–30; Boltz, "Not by the Seal"; Hymes, *Way and Byway*, 116–121; Meulenbeld, "Civilized Demons," 44–168; and Liu Zhiwan, "Raijin shinkō to raihō no tenkai."

81　Michel Strickmann showed that the first scripture in Song Huizong's Daoist canon, the *Wondrous Scripture of the Upper Chapters on Limitless Salvation from the Numinous Gem [Corpus]* (*Lingbao wuliang duren shangpin miaojing* 靈寶無量度人上品妙經), which comprises sixty chapters of Divine Empyrean commentary on the medieval *Scripture of Salvation* of the Lingbao corpus, was willfully placed at the head of the Cavern of Truth (Dongzhen 洞真) section, which housed scriptures associated with the medieval Shangqing tradition, the most exalted in the canon. The text retained its preeminent position in the Ming canon published in 1445. See Strickmann, "Longest Taoist Scripture," 331–339.

82　See DZ 1220:76.3a9–8a1.

83　DZ 1250:1.1a2–2a6.

84　For example, in the colophon to the *Preface to the Abstruse Directives of the Thunderclap from Wang the Fire Master* (*Wang huoshi leiting aozhi xu* 汪火師雷霆奧旨序) compiled in 1104, Daoist Zhu Zhizhong (朱執中) tells the story how he too encountered Wang the Fire Master and received the revelation of a thunder book. However, the main body of the text claims that the *Abstruse Directives* from the Fire Master was transmitted by Wang Wenqing to Zhu and then annotated by him. This discrepancy indicates the central role Wang Wenqing played in teaching the Divine Empyrean thunder rites that were attributed to the Fire Master. See DZ 1220:76.3a6–8, 41a1–42a9.

85　DZ 1220:56.1a3–3b5. For introductory discussions on Wang Wenqing's vision of the Divine Empyrean and theory of thunder, and how they draw on other texts attributed to Wang, see Reiter, "Discourse on the Thunders"; and Reiter, "Preliminary Study."

86　Celestial thunder gods respond to large-scale disasters and should only be petitioned by rulers in the realm of the living. Divine thunder gods move easily between all three realms — the heavens, the realm of the living, and the underworld — and deal with all sorts of crises such as natural disasters, unjust behavior by individuals, and karmic debts. Dragon thunder gods serve the Dragon Lord to regulate rainfall and protect divine scriptures. Water thunder gods work in the lower realms to respond to draughts and floods.

87 DZ 1220:56.13a1–14b8.

88 DZ 1220:56.2a1–5a1.

89 DZ 297:4.1a3–3a3.

90 DZ 1220:76.1a2–3a3.

91 DZ 1220:56.15a5–9.

92 DZ 1220:56.15b2–3. On Deng Bowen, see also Meulenbeld, "Civilized Demons," 109–120.

93 Hsieh Shu-wei believes the text, which spans chapters 83–87 of the *Daofa huiyuan*, was begun during the Southern Song period and then reorganized with additions during the Yuan. See Hsieh, "Zaoqi Doumu," 216–224.

94 DZ 1220:83.5b2–4.

95 DZ 1220:61.7a4–5.

96 DZ 1220:56.14b10; and *Hanyu dacidian* (漢語大詞典), s.v. "欻."

97 The piece is included at the end of a ritual manual entitled the *Great Rite of Prayer to the Fiery Thunder God Emissary Zhang of the One Qi of the Anterior Heaven* (*Xiantian yiqi huolei Zhang shizhe qidao dafa* 先天一炁火雷張使者祈禱大法). See DZ 1220:82.23b2–29b8.

98 The Three Sovereigns and the Five Emperors (*Sanhuang wudi* 三皇五帝) were believed to be the ancient sage kings who invented various aspects of civilization before and during the prehistoric Xia dynasty (c. 2070–c. 1600 BCE).

99 DZ 1220:82.28a8.

100 DZ 1220:82.29a2–10.

101 DZ 1220:82.29b2–3.

102 Li Zhihong, *Daojiao tianxin zhengfa yanjiu,* 82, 116–118.

103 DZ 1220:246.4a2–10. Seventy-two *hou* 候 and twenty-four *qi* 炁 refer to deities having to do with time. One *hou* equals five days, and one *qi* equals three *hou,* or fifteen days. So, one year comprises seventy-two *hou* or twenty-four *qi* (see *Hanyu dacidian,* s.v. "侯").

104 DZ 1220:246.11a4–5.

105 For studies lending a feel for this religious fervor, see Davis, *Society and the Supernatural*; and Hymes, *Way and Byway.* For an overview of the diffusion of

the Heart of Heaven tradition, see Li Zhihong, *Daojiao tianxin zhengfa yanjiu*, 82–125.

106 The first of the two manuals dedicated to Yin Jiao seems as if it might have been of the same general liturgical tradition as Peng Yuantai's 1274 *Great Rite*. Both recognize Liao the Realized One as an ancestral master, both clearly label Yin Jiao an attendant to the Emperor of the North, and both recognize Jiang Rui as Yin Jiao's assistant general and include similar talismans to summon him (see DZ 1166:44.1a2–18b3). The second of the two manuals dedicated to Yin Jiao does not leave clues of its provenance. Based on Yin Jiao's similar iconography in all three, I believe that it is of the same liturgical tradition as the first manual and Peng's *Great Rite* (see DZ 1166:44.18b4–24a1). Following these, the two Divine Empyrean–style manuals—one including talismans related to thunder gods like Marshals Deng, Xin, and Zhang, and the other featuring the True King Jade Clarity—are available in DZ 1166:44.24a2–34b3.

107 For example, Yin Jiao shows up in a roster of gods invoked in the *Hidden Texts of the Thunder Crystal of the Anterior Heaven*, a Divine Empyrean text associated with Wang Wenqing and Bai Yuchan (see DZ 1220:86.5a2).

108 The label Loyalty and Filiality refers to a liturgical tradition that emerged by the Tang dynasty and spawned a mode of practice called the Pure and Bright Rites (Jingming fa 淨明法). Often associated with the Lingbao tradition, these ritual traditions were devoted to Xu Xun (許遜 (trad. 239–374). In the late Southern Song, Liu Yu (劉玉 [1257–1308], not to be confused with Lu Ye's disciple Liu Yu [fl. 1258] who practiced Fengdu and Divine Empyrean rites) developed a version of these rites known as the Pure and Bright Way of Loyalty and Filiality (Jingming zhongxiao dao 淨明忠孝道). See Boltz, *Survey of Taoist Literature*, 70–78; and Huang Xiaoshi, *Jingmingdao yanjiu*.

109 DZ 508:52.25a1, 19a1–3.

110 DZ 1413.12b6. For the dating of this text, see Andersen, "*Beidi fumo jingfa jiantan yi*," 1192.

111 For an introduction to the Pure Tenuity tradition, see Boltz, *Survey of Taoist Literature*, 38–41.

112 DZ 1220:37. The scholarly consensus is that the first fifty-five chapters of the *Daofa huiyuan* are Pure Tenuity texts. See van der Loon, "Taoist Collection"; Schipper and Yuan, "*Daofa huiyuan*," 1106; and Schipper, "Master Chao I-chen."

113 Yin Jiao is simply listed within larger pantheons in DZ 1220:30.29a7, 41.9b4, 44.2a6, 47.2b1, 48.2a10, 49.3a8.

114 DZ 1220:246.3b6–8.

115 DZ 1166:44.1a8–1b1.

116 DZ 1166:44.18b7–8.

117 Some scholars would interpret Yin Jiao's childlike, seminude, barefooted features as clues that he began as a spirit that possesses mediums in the vernacular cults of local communities. See, for example, Meulenbeld, *Demonic Warfare,* 70–73. Although this interpretation is plausible, I can find no evidence that Yin Jiao was ever imagined as such a spirit. It is important to note that from at least the Southern Song, Yin Jiao's boyish features and bare skin hung together comfortably with his image as a high celestial deity. Most important for our study, it was that depiction that made its way down to Chen Diwen's lineage.

118 DZ 1166:30.3b6–7.

119 DZ 1220:37.1a7–9.

120 DZ 1220:247.1a9–1b1.

121 My thanks to Poul Andersen for this connection.

122 DZ 1166:35.1a5–9.

123 DZ 1220:111.1a5–9.

124 DZ 1220:112.18a5.

125 Judith Boltz notes, "In their autocratic manner of establishing hierarchies of diverse scriptural legacies, the Celestial Masters often obscured, if not completely obliterated, the local origins of some of the most creative textual traditions. Assimilation of these vast corpuses of revealed literature by the Zhengyi heritage meant their implicit subordination to it" (*Survey of Taoist Literature,* 17).

126 Nikaidō, *Dōkyō, minkan shinkō,* 180.

127 Ch'en, "Taisui de xinyang," 77–81, especially n216. See also Lee, "Cong xuannü dao jiutian xuannü."

128 Kao, "Song-Yuan-Ming," 294–295.

129 Tao, "Qin'an yizhen," especially 74–75.

130 *Tianlei wuwang Yin da yuanshuai,* 18b.

131 Dating Yin Jiao's hagiography is tricky. The modern version of the *In Search of the Gods* collection I am using, the *Huitu sanjiao yuanliu soushen daquan* (繪圖三教源流搜神大全) (Shanghai: Shanghai guji chubanshe, 1990), includes

three distinct texts: the *Chongkan huitu sanjiao yuanliu soushen daquan* printed by the renowned scholar and book collector Ye Dehui (葉德輝) (1864–1927) during the late Qing; the *Soushen ji* (搜神記) associated with Gan Bao (干寶) (fl. 317–322) and added to the 1607 supplement to the Daoist canon (*Xu daozang* 續道藏) by the fiftieth Celestial Master, Zhang Guoxiang (張國祥) (d. 1611); and the *Xinbian lianxiang soushen guangji* (新編連相搜神廣記) compiled by Qin Zijin (秦子晉) during the Yuan dynasty. Yin Jiao's hagiography shows up only in Ye Dehui's Qing printing. However, circumstantial evidence indicates that the hagiography is much older. Ye explains that one day in the market he happened upon an undated woodblock text called the *Soushen guangji* (搜神廣記). Judging from its design, style, woodblocks, and printing technique, he dated it to the Yuan dynasty. Later, he discovered another text titled *Huitu sanjiao yuanliu soushen daquan* (繪圖三教源流搜神大全) that indicated it was from the Ming dynasty. He noticed this Ming text was essentially the same as the *Soushen guangji* he believed to be from the Yuan. The Ming text simply updated official titles granted to deities by early Ming emperors, and added couplets hung in various temples and shrines. For Ye, the text he printed in the late Qing, which includes Yin Jiao's hagiography, was originally from the Yuan. So, I cautiously take Ye's judgment and, without other sources to corroborate it, think it safe to loosely date Yin Jiao's hagiography to the Yuan–Ming period. For the story of Ye's dating his collection, see his preface to the *Chongkan huitu sanjiao yuanliu soushen daquan*, 3–4. For a general assessment of the relationship between Ye Dehui's reprinting and Qin Zijin's compilation, see Liu Yonghai, *Yuandai daojiao shiji yanjiu*, 56–57, 235.

132 See Campany, *To Live As Long*, 98–117; and *Making Transcendents*, 8–11. See also Judith Boltz's discussion on the evolution and significance of hagiography in *Survey of Taoist Literature*, 54–56.

133 DZ 1220:82.23b2–29b8.

134 Campany, *Making Transcendents*, 217.

135 DZ 1220:37.2a9–2b2.

136 The image of a seahorse as Yin Jiao's vehicle found its way into an undated ritual manual summoning Yin Jiao, the *Disi gaodou xuanke* (地司告斗玄科), which was collected by Lee Fong-mao. See DFHH 20:400.

137 "Taisui Yin yuanshuai."

138 Even Yin Jiao's names in the lineage's *Genealogical Investigation* are derived from the same narrative articulated in *In Search of the Gods*. In the Yuan–Ming

text, Shen the Realized One names the boy Jin Nezha (唵哪吒), whereas the lineage's hagiography lists his ritual name as Jin Nezha (金哪吒). Likewise, the Yuan–Ming text mentions the boy's Daoist name as Jin Dingnu (唵叮奴), and the lineage's hagiography as Jin Dingnao (金叮呶).

139 Campany, *To Live As Long,* 101.

140 Meulenbeld, *Demonic Warfare,* 67–73.

141 *Quanxiang pinghua Wuwang.* For an English translation, see Liu, *Buddhist and Taoist Influence,* 6–75.

142 Here I follow Wilt Idema's argument against the received scholarly view that plain tales were prompt-books produced for professional storytellers to aid their oral performances of these fictionalized historical episodes. See Idema, "Remarks and Speculations," especially 121–141, 168–172.

143 The *Plain Tale* was printed in a collection of five plain tales, the *Quanxiang pinghua wuzhong* (全相平話五種), an original copy of which is preserved in the National Archive (Kokuritsu Kōbunshokan 国立公文書館) in Tokyo. Idema, "Remarks and Speculations," 125.

144 This reading follows Liu Ts'un-yan, who fills in minor corruptions of the text with his own interpretation. The text reads "姜皇后降生一太子，名囗囗景明，王號為殷〔郊〕。只因王打囗囗囗降此人，此人便是太歲也。" See *Quanxiang pinghua Wuwang,* 5; and Liu, *Buddhist and Taoist Influences,* 16.

145 *Quanxiang pinghua Wuwang,* 20.

146 Liu Ts'un-yan, who discovered the text in the British Library, infers the 1602 date from internal evidence against received scholarly opinion that Yu Xiangdou authored the text. Liu notes that the 1602 edition of the text includes several poems by a certain Mr. Yu (余氏) that are clearly interpolations into an older text. If the Mr. Yu was indeed Yu Xiangdou, this suggests that he received an older text rather than creating it himself. See Ts'un-yan Liu, "*Siyou ji* de Ming keben," 436; and Liu, *Chinese Popular Fiction,* 4–5; see also Seaman, *Journey to the North,* 6–9.

147 In ancient China, the term *taibao* denoted a very high official in the imperial court charged with protecting the emperor. By the Song and Yuan periods, the term referred both to attendants tending to the incense and candles in local temples and to unorthodox mediums (*wushi* 巫師), as well as to bandits in the wild. It seems all these connotations of *taibao* are at play in the story. See *Hanyu dacidian,* s.v. "太保"; and Hucker, *Dictionary of Official Titles,* 480.

148 *Beiyou ji,* 255 (translation modified from Seaman, *Journey to the North,* 186).

149 Ibid. (modified from Seaman, *Journey to the North,* 187).

150 See DZ 1166:35.1a5–9; and DZ 1166:44.1a8–1b1.

151 Yin Jiao is described with twelve skulls hanging from his neck in DZ 1166:30.3b6–7; DZ 1166:44.1a8–1b1, 18b7–8; and 1220:247.1a9–1b1. In DZ 1220:37.1a7–9, he is imagined as wearing a single skull on his head and nine skulls around his neck.

152 Recall that the hagiography in *In Search of the Gods* was drawing on a narrative expressed in Peng Yuantai's 1274 *Great Rite* ritual text (DZ 1220:246) and in the roughly contemporaneous Qingwei *Upper Clarity Great Rite* (DZ 1220:37).

153 Recall the fearsome visualized images of Yin Jiao in the likely Qingwei texts DZ 1220:247:1a9–1b1 and DZ 1166:35.1a5–9. It is interesting that an image of Yin Jiao with three faces and six arms made its way into a frontispiece of a 1716 edition of DZ 10 *Gaoshang Yuhuang benxing jijing* (高上玉皇本行集經), reproduced in Fava, *Aux portes du ciel,* 59.

154 Meulenbeld, *Demonic Warfare,* 65–66. Meulenbeld notes that the first position was taken by many traditional scholars, including Lu Xun (魯迅) (1881–1936); the second was put forth by Liu Ts'un-yen in the 1960s; and the third by PRC scholar Zhang Peiheng (章培恆) in the 1990s.

155 *Fengshen yanyi,* 627.

156 Ibid.

157 Ibid., 654.

158 Recall that Great Year was often seen as a baleful star associated with illnesses caused by illicitly disrupting the earth.

159 Meulenbeld, *Demonic Warfare,* 67–73.

160 *Yin Jiao chumai,* 8a.

161 A thirty-six-episode, televised version of *Fengshen yanyi* titled *Fengshen bang* and directed by Guo Xinling (郭信玲) had begun being broadcast in 1990 by the Shanghai branch of the China Teleplay Production Center (Zhongguo Shanghai dianshiju zhizuo zhongxin 中國上海電視劇製作中心), but Jiang Yucheng says that his grandfather did not own a television at that time and so definitely was not influenced by it.

162 Ter Haar, *Guan Yu,* 250–251. See also Duara, "Superscribing Symbols," 779–780; and Katz, *Demon Hordes,* 114.

Chapter Three: The Banner Rite

Epigraphs. Master Jiang Yucheng, communication to the author. Master Wang Wenqing, DZ 1220:61.1b5–6.

1   According to these masters and their "Dispatch to Inform the Generals," Yin Jiao is a kind of first among thunder deities. By invoking him and forming a personal relationship with him, an officiant implicitly enlists several other well-known thunder generals who are also understood to serve under Yin Jiao's command—Wang Shan (王善, also known as Wang Lingguan), Ma Sheng (馬勝), Zhao Gongming (趙公明), Wen Qiong (溫瓊), Yang Gengfang (楊耿方), Zhu Yan (朱彥), Gao Diao (高刁), and Kang Ning (康佞). Following them are the Sire of Thunder (Leigong 雷公), the Mother of Lightning (Dianmu 電母), the Earl of Winds (Fengbo 風伯), the Master of Rain (Yushi 雨師), the Clerk of Clouds (Yunli 雲吏), thirty-six gods of the thunderclap, seventy-two assistant generals, and local tutelary gods—the God of Moats and Walls (Chenghuang, the city god), the God of the Soil (Lishe 里社), and the Director of Destinies (Siming 司命). *Zouzhi quanbu shushi,* 21a–21b.

2   The template for the "Dispatch to Inform the Generals" is found in *Zouzhi quanbu shushi,* 19b–22b.

3   Andersen, *Method of Holding,* 24. For a philosophical investigation of this claim, see Andersen, *Paradox of Being.*

4   This inner alchemical usage of the term *yuanchen* seems to have emerged with Song inner alchemical sources. This sense of the term seems to be rather distinct from better known usages denoting an ambivalent stellar god, bound up with one's moment of birth, which manages one's destiny along with one's god of personal destiny (*benming shen* 本命神). This latter sense of *yuanchen* was prevalent in Celestial Master practice already by the early medieval period. This sense continued to flourish with the popularity of the medieval *Scripture of the Northern Dipper (Beidou jing* 北斗經) through the late imperial period up to today. I suspect a deep theoretical connection since the Song era between the senses of the term *yuanchen* as a deity of personal destiny and as one's true "self" composed of primordial *qi*, but much more research is necessary to tease it out. The lineage's *Banner Rite* manual, cousin manuals from Hunan, and certain canonical texts from the Song and Yuan periods all make clear that the word *yuanchen* carries the inner alchemical sense of primordial self. For a preliminary study on the history of the term *yuanchen,* see Liu Changdong, "Benming

xinyang kao." For early Celestial Master rituals dealing with fundamental destiny, see Verellen, "Tianshidao shangzhang keyi." For the classic study on fundamental destiny in late imperial and present-day China, see Hou, *Monnaies d'offrande.*

5   For a detailed analysis of this theoretical treatise, see Mozina, "Living Redactions."

6   Divination blocks accompanied by these sayings will again be cast three times for Chen Diwen by his transmission master and two witnessing masters during the formal Rite of Transmission on the last day of the ordination *jiao.* Those three blocks and their concomitant sayings mark the happy occasion of a concluded ordination but are not cherished nearly as much as these blocks conferred while receiving the *yuanchen.* For a description of the casting of divination blocks during the Rite of Transmission, see Mozina, "Daubing Lips with Blood," 281.

7   Chang Ch'ao-jan, "Xipu, jiaofa jiqi zhenghe," 173.

8   Ibid., 187–188, 204, 275–278.

9   Ibid., 312.

10 DZ 1220:1.17b9–18a2.

11 DZ 1220:84.20a4–5.

12 DZ 1220:85.13b1–14a3.

13 DZ 1220:246.2a8–9.

14 DZ 1220:253.5b2–6.

15 The traces of flute music audible in the background at points during the ritual emanate from another young apprentice practicing his craft. It is not part of the ritual.

16 The term *shentong* 神通, which I translate as "divine power," is also the traditional term used to translate the Buddhist notion of *abhijñā,* the preternatural powers attained through meditation by the Buddha, bodhisattvas, and arhats. The concept of *abhijñā* may very well be echoed in this incantation. See Buswell and Lopez, *Princeton Dictionary of Buddhism,* 8–9.

17 *Yingong fanfa,* 7a–7b.

18 DZ 1220:89.2a2–2b1. Hsieh Shu-wei notes that this text hangs together with the *Xiantian leijing yinshu* (DZ 1220:83–87), which he suggests is a Yuan collection of Southern Song texts. See Hsieh, "Zaoqi Doumu," 218.

19 This discussion of Chen Diwen's walking along the guideline draws heavily on Poul Andersen, who has traced the origin of *bugang* to the ancient "steps of Yu"

(*Yubu* 禹步) and has interpreted the indigenous cosmological concepts that have informed variations of the practice from the Period of Disunion (220–589 CE) to present day Taiwan. See Andersen, "Practice of *Bugang*"; and "Guideline of the Eight Trigrams."

20 For an exposition of the basic Daoist cosmology assumed in this practice, see Lagerwey, *Taoist Ritual,* 3–17, especially 16–17.

21 The best explanation I have come across that explains the function of touching points on the hand with the thumb has been found by Poul Andersen. He quotes Lu Shizhong, founder of the Great Rites of the Jade Hall ritual tradition in the 1120s: "Between heaven and earth man is the most numinous of all things. Therefore, whenever he points in his hand or walks with his feet, he is united with Perfection (*zhen* 真). The method of *bugang* arises from this. To perform *bugang* is to fly along the essences of heaven, to tread the numinae of earth, and to set the perfection of man in motion. Through it the Three Powers (*sancai* 三才, the three cosmic planes [of heaven, earth, and humanity]) unite their virtues, the nine breaths are aligned, and demons and spirits spin" (DZ 220:19.1b5–9, translated in Andersen, "Practice of *Bugang*," 28).

22 Interpreting an almost identical version of the incantation performed by Master Chen Rongsheng's (陳榮盛) lineage in Tainan (台南), John Lagerwey follows the early thirteenth-century *Lingbao wuliang duren shangjing dafa* (靈寶無量度人上經大法) to interpret the "Golden Light" as issuing from the Heavenly Worthy of Primordial Commencement, the most august of the Three Pure Ones. By merging this Golden Light of the Heavenly Worthy with light generated from the lower cinnabar field within the body, the practitioner "achieves the 'universal wisdom' (*donghui* 洞慧) that will protect him from the stellar winds as he goes on the 'distant journey' to heaven's gates." See Lagerwey, *Taoist Ritual,* 86–87; and Ōfuchi, *Chūgokujin no shūkyō girei,* 248b.

23 *Yingong fanfa,* 7b.

24 DZ 1220:89.2b2.

25 *Yingong fanfa,* 7b.

26 Images of the body as withered wood has a long pedigree in literature that mentions sacrifice and meditation practices that involve visualized incineration or trance, especially in the *Zhuangzi* (莊子). In the *Huainanzi* (淮南子), Isabelle Robinet points to the Jingshen xun (精神訓) chapter: "The body like dry wood and the heart like dead ashes, he forgets his five internal organs, he thins his

body" (形若槁木，心若死灰，忘其五藏，損其形骸). Robinet, *Taoist Meditation*, 43. For a broad historical sketch of these images, see Meulenbeld, "From 'Withered Wood' to 'Dead Ashes.'"

27 *Yingong fanfa*, 7b.

28 DZ 566:2.1a8–1b3.

29 DZ 1220:76.11a1–11b9.

30 DZ 1220:232.20a3–8.

31 The ritual logic here differs from Poul Andersen's analysis of a transformation of the body ritual sequence in Taiwan. Drawing on the ritual performances of masters in Tainan and on liturgical manuals from Xinzhu (新竹) collected by Michael Saso, Andersen points out that an important component of the transformation of the body in those traditions includes avoiding danger by depositing one's souls in a department of heaven. Meulenbeld gives another interpretation. Looking at the transformation of the body as performed by masters in Xinhua county in Hunan, he posits that the brilliant glow of the golden radiance enables the officiant to abandon the world. He discards his persona and his identity becomes abstract. As will become clear, the ritual logic driving the Banner Rite is that the mundane body must be completely destroyed so that one's primordial spirit might be recovered from the void of the Dao. See Andersen, "Transformation of the Body," 196–201; and Meulenbeld, "From 'Withered Wood' to 'Dead Ashes,'" 229–234.

32 *Yingong fanfa*, 7b.

33 Ibid.

34 Andersen, "Transformation of the Body," 195–196.

35 Li Zhihong, *Daojiao tianxin zhengfa yanjiu*, 221–223. Judith Boltz writes, "No longer was mere visualization or actualization (*ts'un* 存) sufficient for the purposes of these multifarious therapeutic rites. Instead, this new generation of adepts was instructed to 'envision yourself as' (*ts'un tzu-shen wei* 存自身為) or 'metamorphose yourself into' (*pien wei* 變為). With the aid of the appropriate incantations and talismans, the Ritual Masters thus came to embody the very deity whose role it was to convey the prescribed remedies. By achieving such a transformation, a practitioner was perceived not merely as a manipulator of divine forces but as the agent through whom they took charge" (Boltz, *Survey of Taoist Literature*, 24–25).

36 DZ 1227:2.1b7–9. For other examples of instructions to Heart of Heaven practitioners for transforming into the body of Zhang Daoling, see DZ 566:2a8–9, 567:3a8.

37 DZ 1225:63.5b10–6a1, translated in Chao, "Zhenwu," 102. For debates over the dating of this manual, see 92–93.

38 *Yingong fanfa,* 8b.

39 *Lüzu xiantian zuqi michuan,* 20a.

40 See Hudson, "Spreading the Dao," 322–323, 331–333. For a comprehensive exposition of the various symbolic schemes that have been used by inner alchemists, see 210–366.

41 *Lüzu xiantian zuqi michuan,* 11b–12b.

42 Ibid., 14a–14b.

43 Ibid., 14b.

44 Ibid., 20a–20b.

45 Ibid., 20a.

46 Respectively referred to as the Tail Gate Pass (Weilü guan 尾閭關), the Spinal-Straights Pass (Jiaji guan 夾脊關), and the Jade Pillow Pass (Yuzhen guan 玉枕關). *Lüzu xiantian zuqi michuan,* 20b. For a general explanation of these passes along the dorsal tract of the body in inner alchemy, see Hudson, "Spreading the Dao," 288–291.

47 *Zhaolian qingsheng ke,* 31a.

48 Slightly different versions of this inner alchemical operation are discussed in Mozina, "Living Redactions," 43–50; and "Daubing Lips with Blood," 286–287.

49 DZ 566:2.2a8–9.

50 Li Zhihong, *Daojiao tianxin zhengfa yanjiu,* 221–223.

51 Chang Ch'ao-jan, "Ziwo shenfen."

52 *Yingong fanfa,* 8b.

53 Many thanks to Patrice Fava and Mark Meulenbeld for sharing with me relevant manuscripts they collected.

54 *Xiantian Yingong fanfa yizong,* 27a–27b. This passage is not an invention in nineteenth-century central Hunan. A very similar passage can be found in a major theoretical treatise of the Pure Tenuity tradition, the *Qingwei zongzhi* (清微宗旨), composed by Zhao Yizhen (趙宜真) (d. 1382) in the late Yuan or early Ming. See DZ 1220:4.11a2–9.

55 DZ 1250.4b8–9.

56 DZ 1220:61.1b5–6.

57 ZWDS 23:806.7a7–8.

58 DZ 1220:1.5b1–2.

59 Li Zhihong, *Daojiao tianxin zhengfa,* 221.

60 Poul Andersen reaches a similar conclusion: "The divine body, or *fashen* (法身), 'dharma-body,' is not merely the body of specific gods, but the body of anyone who has realized his or her divine potential." Andersen, "Essence and Function," 19; see also "Transformation of the Body," especially 193. Andersen develops these ideas in conversation with western existential philosophy in *Paradox of Being*.

61 *Xiantian Yingong fanfa yizong*, 31a.

62 Andersen, "Guideline of the Eight Trigrams," 15; see also Lagerwey, *Taoist Ritual*, 84–85; and Ōfuchi, *Chūgokujin no shūkyō girei*, 250a. Andersen also shows that the nine steps of the *bugang* movement according to the magic square was in the Eastern Han dynasty patterned after the creative movement of Taiyi (太乙), the celestial deity who resided in the Northern Extremity. Often imagined as the personification of primordial *qi* (*yuanqi* 元氣), Taiyi's life-producing breath radiates from the center of heaven and flows through the universe by means of the eight trigrams. It seems entirely possible that something of this meaning is also resonating in Luo Congyao's walking of the guideline. See Andersen, "Guideline of the Eight Trigrams," 23; and *Paradox of Being*, 171–188. For an introduction to the concept of the magic square, see Cammann, "Magic Square of Three."

63 For the relationship between Mo Yueding and Zhang Shanyuan, see Li Yuanguo, *Shenxiao leifa*, 108–112.

64 DZ 1220:67.7a9–7b10.

65 DZ 1220:67.7b10–8a5.

66 DZ 1220:67.9a5.

67 Lee and Zhang, "Shufu yu fuhao," 337–338.

68 Ibid., 338.

69 *Yingong fanfa*, 9a. I read 化 for 法 here, following the emendation of Jiang Yucheng. In the local dialect, the two words are homophones. This emendation is also supported by the fact that the same incantation in another of the lineage's manuals records 化. *Zhaolian qingsheng ke*, 31b.

70 DZ 1220:76.12a2–3.

71 DZ 1220:76.12a2.

72 DZ 1220:61.12b6–8.

73 *Yingong fanfa*, 9b.

74 Ibid.

75 *Qingwei hunlian zhaohe*, 18a2–3. Here the expression "pure and quiet" (*qingning qingning* 清寧清寧) may be an allusion to *Daode jing* (道德經) 39: "Heaven attains the One and thereby purity, earth attains the One and thereby tranquility" (天得一以清，地得一以寧). The phrase "pure and chilly" (*qingqing lengleng* 清清冷冷) in Chen Diwen's Banner Rite manual may be some sort of copy error, perhaps due to dialect, when compared with the passage as expressed in Wu Keheng's text.

76 *Yingong fanfa*, 9b.

77 Ibid., 9b.

Chapter Four: The Banner Rite

Epigraphs. Yin Jiao Incantation preserved by Chen Diwen's lineage, in *Yingong fanfa*, 1a. Master Bai Yuchan, DZ 1220:76.2a4–5.

1 Recall that the master of the registry (*jishi*) is the master of one's transmission master (*dushi*), and the master of the canon (*jingshi*) is that master's master. The three generations of masters through whom one receives the ritual teachings are a personal connection to the entire lineage.

2 The masters of Chen Diwen's lineage did not feel threatened by those who would seem to undercut their business. Jiang Yucheng explains that the masters of the Jiang and Li clans are so established in the area that they trust residents of the various local hamlets not to hire anyone else to meet their ritual needs. It seems such peace of mind is a pleasant consequence of two hundred years of local liturgical dominance.

3 *Yingong fanfa*, 10a. The same instructions are given in another of the lineage's manuals (*Xiantian fufa qianchuan mizhi*, 12a).

4 *Yingong fanfa*, 10a.

5 The masters explain that when preparing to inscribe talismans used to make rain (*ranghai* 讓海) or prevent floods (*shuijin* 水禁), they visualize that the brush be associated with the "watery spirit of the north" (*beifang shuishen* 北方水神), and that the brush transforms into a "watery dragon" (*shuilong* 水龍) and the inkwell into "the great sea" (*dahai* 大海) (see figure 4.1).

6 *Yingong fanfa*, 10b.

7 Ibid.

8 Copp, *Body Incantatory*, especially 141–196.

9   *Lüzu xiantian zuqi michuan,* 12b.

10 *Xiantian zuqi zailun,* 21b.

11 *Xiao Yingong fufa,* 12b, 13b.

12 DZ 1220:1.8a7–8, translation modified from Andersen, "Essence and Function (*ti* and *yong*)," 16. Also, John Lagerwey asserts that Daoists have historically referred to primordial *qi* (*yuanqi* 元氣)—what Chen Diwen's lineage calls ancestral *qi* (*zuqi*)—as a kind of gem, "a single pearl in the midst of a boundless ocean" (*Taoist Ritual,* 8).

13 DZ 1220:67.7a9–7b10. Song and Yuan masters had many different interpretations of the relationship between the Dao, ancestral *qi,* and one's primordial self. Poul Andersen notices that many masters, including Bai Yuchan and Wang Weiyi (王惟一), make a sharp distinction between the Dao and ancestral *qi.* See *Paradox of Being,* 67–114, 196–198.

14 *Yingong fanfa,* 11a.

15 *Yinshuai zhaolian,* 12a.

16 *Zouzhi quanbu shushi,* 1a.

17 *Yinshuai zhaolian,* 13b, 15a.

18 In the lineage's texts, other marshal deities are associated with other high gods. For example, Wang Lingguan is affiliated with the administration of the Ancestor of the Dao, the Upper Emperor of Primal *Yang* (Daozu yuanyang shangdi 道祖元陽上帝); Xin Hanchen with the Thunder Ancestor (Leizu 雷祖); and Wen Qiong with the Jade Emperor. *Zouzhi quanbu shushi,* 1a–1b.

19 DZ 1220:246.4a6.

20 Ibid., 4a8–10.

21 DZ 1220:37.2b4–6.

22 *Yin Jiao chumai,* 2b.

23 Recall that the alternative name for the entire Banner Rite is the Banner Rite of Celestial Lord Yin Jiao in which Purple Tenuity Mounts his Horse.

24 DZ 1220:246.1a10–1b1.

25 *Yingong fanfa,* 11a. For a slightly different translation of the incantation invoking the Three Terraces as performed by Master Chen Rongsheng's lineage in Tainan, see Lagerwey, *Taoist Ritual,* 73; and Ōfuchi, *Chūgokujin no shūkyō girei,* 706a. The sense of Lagerwey's translation and my own is the same.

26 See Andersen, "Practice of *Bugang,*" 30.

27 Poul Andersen reports that Master Chen Rongsheng likewise interpreted the three checkmark symbols to represent the scattering of primal breath into three in the cosmogony (personal communication with the author, February 2006).

28 For two of many examples, see DZ 547:7.15a–15b; and DZ 1227:2.10a–10b.

29 For a detailed study of the Three Officers and their visual representations, see Lee Fong-mao, "Sanguan chuxun," 104–111.

30 The Three Primes also referred to the festivals of the Three Primes held on the fifteenth day of the first, seventh, and tenth lunar months. For discussions of the Three Primes and Three Officers, see Robinet, Miura, and Yamada, "*Sanyuan* 三元, Three Primes, Three Origins"; Kleeman, "*Sanguan* 三官, Three Offices"; and Lai, "Tian di shui sanguan xinyang."

31 DZ 547:7.16b10. The dating and authorship of this text are difficult to determine, but it seems to adopt methods from the Great Rites of the Lingbao, Heart of Heaven, and Divine Empyrean traditions. See Lagerwey, "*Lingbao yujian.*"

The three graphs here associated with the Three Officers have often been interpreted as the taboo names for the Three Pure Ones. Lee Fong-mao and Zhang Zhixiong mention this has been the case for the Zhengyi tradition on Mount Longhu. Lagerwey reports that Master Chen Rongsheng's lineage in Tainan does the same, as does Patrice Fava for the masters with whom he works in Xinhua county in Hunan. See Lee and Zhang, "Shufu yu fuhao," 350–351; Lagerwey, *Taoist Ritual,* 54; and Fava, *Aux portes du ciel,* 68–69.

32 Andersen, "Practice of *Bugang,*" 25. In thunder ritual, the Celestial Guideline has been said to control the rise and fall of thunder and, on the microcosmic level, has been associated with the heart. For more on the Celestial Guideline (Tiangang), see Hu, *Zhonghua daojiao dacidian,* 1165, 585.

33 DZ 566:1.3a10–3b2.

34 DZ 1227:2.11b10.

35 *Yingong fanfa,* 11b.

36 *Yingong fanfa,* 11b. Very similar, in places identical, sequences of graphs and incantations are found in DZ 1220:246.5a, 247.1b; and DZ 1166:30.4a, 35.4b, 44.3a.

37 The Shorter Talismanic Method for [Summoning] Sire Yin (Xiao Yingong fufa) and the Longer Talismanic Method for [Summoning] Sire Yin (Da Yingong fufa) are scripted in *Xiantian fufa qianchuan mizhi,* 12b–20a.

38 Chen Diwen's lineage is not unique in composing a poem from the components of the characters of Daoist names, which are included in ordination documents. Patrice Fava has found that the masters with whom he works in Yangxi township in Xinhua also confer "flower signatures" (*huaya* 花押) on initiates, though they include both the generational character and personal character and do not appear to regard the characters and poem as a talisman to be used by

future disciples to summon their deceased master. See Fava, *Aux portes du ciel*, 202.

39 Patrice Fava reports that lineages in Xinhua also associate Yin Jiao and Wang Lingguan with these same graphs. Another working master in Xinhua, Qin Guorong, attests that his lineage also uses these heart seals for Yin Jiao and Wang Lingguan, but explains them a little differently from Chen Diwen's masters. Qin explains that they are actually eccentric forms of the seal-script renditions of martial deities' surnames rather than their forenames. In either interpretation, the notion remains that the heart seal is a stylized written name of a martial deity accompanied by an incantation. See Fava, *Aux portes du ciel*, 40; and Qin, "Guangchangong changyong benjing," 167.

40 DZ 1440:10.31a1.

41 For a pithy discussion of "mind-to-mind transmission" in the early Chan tradition, see Wright, *Philosophical Meditations,* 140–142, which interprets the teachings of Huangbo Xiyun 黃檗希運 (d. 855).

42 DZ 141:6.19a1–2. For sketches of Weng Baoguang and his inner alchemical theories, see Tuan, "Shilun Weng Baoguang"; Kong, *Song–Ming daojiao sixiang yanjiu*, 151–155; and Baldrain-Hussein, "Weng Baoguang."

43 DZ 566:2.7a10–10b1.

44 DZ 1220:153.5a8.

45 For example, see DZ 1220:193.1b8–2a3.

46 Maggie Bickford calls this signature Emperor Huizong's "personal cipher." Bickford, "Huizong's Paintings," 456. Given Huizong's dedication to Daoism, it is tempting to surmise that this seal script might have meant more than an artistic signature by him. Perhaps it also functioned as something like the emperor's own heart seal.

47 DZ 1220:241.7b1–4. The *kui* asterism refers to either the four stars making up the bowl of the Northern Dipper or the star at the tip of the bowl.

48 An accounting of this relationship is given the beginning of the text. See DZ 1220:232.1a3–2b3.

49 DZ 1220:232.8a1–7.

50 Sa Shoujian's heart seal is similarly used to summon Marshal Wang Lingguan. In the *Esoteric Rite [to Summon] Marshal Wang Lingguan of the Fiery Chariot of the Three and Five of the Thunderclap* examined above, the practitioner is instructed to "employ the Patriarch [Sa Shoujian's] heart seal to send [Marshal Wang] away under escort" (用祖師心印押發). DZ 1220:241.5b9–6a3.

51 DZ 1220:71.4a3–5.

52 An earlier version of this section was published as Mozina, "Summoning the Exorcist."

53 *Yingong fanfa*, 12b.

54 *Yin Jiao chumai*, 6a.

55 DZ 1220:246.3b2.

56 *Yingong fanfa*, 12b–13a.

57 Ibid., 13a.

58 *Yin Jiao chumai*, 3a.

59 Chen's masters are also stumped as to what the phrase "the bolt of the iron gate" might mean and so leave it in the ritual. I can only surmise that it echoes a strand of Yin Jiao's hagiography that has fallen out of their text. I have found that the two lines of this short incantation show up, cryptically, in most Yin Jiao ritual manuals collected by me or others in Hunan and beyond, suggesting they originate in some older source and have been widely used in rituals summoning Yin. For instance, the lines appear in a ritual text called the *Golden Banner Talismanic Rite for Manifesting the Dao of the Five Thunders* (*Wulei xiandao jinfan fufa* 五雷顯道金旛符法), which was copied between 1861 and 1875 by a master named Biyun (碧雲) in the Changde (常德) region in northern Hunan. See DFHH 13:132.

60 *Yingong fanfa*, 13a.

61 Ibid., 16a.

62 *Yin Jiao chumai*, 6b.

63 Robinet, *Taoist Meditation*, 27.

64 A classic example of an illocutionary speech act is a certified minister's uttering "I pronounce you man and wife." The words themselves do the work of bringing about what they say.

65 John Austin's philosophical investigation of illocutionary and perlocutionary speech acts in *How to Do Things with Words* has inspired generations of scholars working on ritual. Here, I am thinking with Tambiah, "Magical Power" and "Form and Meaning"; Sullivan, "Sound and Senses"; and Faraone, *Talismans and Trojan Horses*, 117–122.

In other places in her study on Shangqing texts, Robinet does hint that talismans might exhibit what Austin and his heirs have called a perlocutionary quality.

> The formulas, like the talismans, *coerce* the deities that are summoned, described, and named. They demonstrate the adept's knowledge which he takes advantage of so that the deities will grant his desires. They *remind* the deity of its obligation to recompense the service of the faithful. In later rituals, these formulas are followed by the imperative expression: "Hurry! Hurry! So that the order is executed!" (*jiji ru lüling*).

Robinet, *Taoist Meditation*, 36–37, emphasis added. However, Robinet does not develop this insight. The Banner Rite demands that we do so.

66 DZ 1220:83.5a8–10.

67 For a fuller discussion of the role of coercion in Divine Empyrean rites and its roots in cosmology and inner alchemical practice, see Mozina, "Oaths and Curses."

68 *Yingong fanfa*, 1a. For the version of the incantation in the *Upper Clarity Great Rite*, see DZ 1220:37.2a9-b2, translated in chapter 2.

69 While reviewing this film, Jiang Yucheng recalled being a little dismayed that Chen added these extra graphs on his own. Jiang felt there was no reason to add them here—a moment of disagreement between practitioners.

70 Chen Diwen's masters are not certain why they do this part of the ritual. Jiang Yucheng surmises that gnashing the teeth points to the conveyance of Chen's primordial self (*yuanchen*) into the banner as it is raised toward the heavens, and his gesticulating arms in a kind of circular dance might somehow aid the wind. As we have seen all along, masters are humble about what the ritual might mean, but are careful to perform the ritual as written and orally taught.

The *Incantation of the Vermillion Crow* is as follows:

> Vermillion Crow, Vermillion Crow, fire chariot of the wind and thunder, black rabbit within thunder, *yakṣa* beyond the clouds, accept this order from the Emperor of the North, receive this command from Danxia. Come quickly! Respond quickly! [I] call the *yakṣa* of the wind: [the officiant intones a mantra of transliterated Sanskrit and pseudo-Sanskrit syllables]. Kang Min, Zihua. Son of Emperor Ku, grandson of Zhuan Xu, I summon you now. Quickly come out from your thunder abode! (*Yingong fanfa*, 17a).
>
> 赤鴉赤鴉，風雷火車，雷中烏兔，雲外夜叉，受命北帝，稟令丹霞，急來急應，呼風鴉叉：鴉鴉□□，咖咖鴉鴉，鴉鴉□□，唵唵□□。康旻，子華。帝嚳之子，顓頊之孫，吾今召爾，速出雷家。

The Vermillion Crow is a moniker for Marshal Zhang Jue. According to the *Hidden Texts of the Thunder Crystal of the Anterior Heaven*, he sports a vermillion, winged body with a phoenix's beak, huge eyes, vermillion hair, fleshy horns, and dragon's talons. In his left hand he holds an edict from the Emperor of Heaven, and in his right a black flag with the imperial order to summon the thunder deities. He is often referred to as the Emissary (Shizhe). DZ 1220:83.2b6–3a2. It seems that Marshal Zhang's role as an emissary able to summon other thunder gods is likely the reason Chen Diwen invokes him at this point in the Banner Rite. For analyses on the role of emissaries in delivering talismans (*fushi* 符使), see Drexler, *Daoistische Schriftmagie*, 110–112; and Andersen, "Taoist Talismans," 142–143.

Note also that the incantation cryptically connects Zhang Jue with Kang Min, a name for the goddess Molizhitian (摩利支天, Skt. Mārīcī), the Mother of the Dipper (Doumu 斗母). Zhang Jue is also linked to Wang Zihua the Fire Master, and with two of the Five Emperors of antiquity—Emperor Ku and Zhuan Xu. Very similar versions of the *Incantation of the Vermillion Crow* show up in Divine Empyrean texts. See DZ 1220:85.12b10–13a5; and DZ 1220:76.28b10–29a5. For an account of Zhang Jue's relationship with Kang Min/Molizhitian, see the *Zhupin lingzhang leijun bizhi* (諸品靈章雷君秘旨), in ZWDS 29:14b8–15a2. For a preliminary study of Molizhitian in Song and Yuan practice, see Hsieh Shu-wei, "Zaoqi Doumu Molizhitian wenben tantao."

71 Smith, "Trading Places," 226, emphasis in the original. This article, and especially this quotation, has been somewhat of a catalyst for scholarship on magical writing and talismans. The essay appeared originally as the first piece in a significant edited volume on notions of magic and ritual in Greek, Roman, ancient Near Eastern, and late antique traditions. See Meyer and Mirecki, *Ancient Magic and Ritual Power*. James Robson uses the quotation to launch his exploration of Buddhist talismanic writing through a literature review of scholarship on Daoist talismans. See Robson, "Signs of Power," 131.

72 In his work on talismans, especially talismans during the Song and late imperial periods, Liu Zhongyu similarly urges us to pay close attention to the process of writing talismans. See Liu, *Fulu pinghua*, 95–96. Only when we look beyond the inscribed object of the talisman to its process might we discern the subtle meanings obscured within the writing itself, like the dozens of graphs and thick layers of meaning obscured by the ink blot at the bottom of Chen Diwen's talisman.

73 The literature on talismans that informs this discussion is sizable. For useful categorizations of the different notions of talisman in ancient and medieval

political, military, and religious practice, see Hsieh, "Writing from Heaven," especially 1–108; Bumbacher, *Empowered Writing*, 1–80; Despeux, "Talismans and Diagrams"; and Li Yuanguo, "Lun daojiao fulu de fenlei." The following paragraphs draw especially on several influential works on ancient, early medieval, and middle-period talismans: Raz, *Emergence of Daoism*, 127–176; Lewis, *Writing and Authority*, 13–51, 241–286; Seidel, "Imperial Treasures"; Seidel, "Traces of Han Religion"; Kaltenmark, "*Ling-pao*"; Stein, "Aspects de la foi jurée"; Campany, *To Live as Long*, 60–69; Lagerwey, "Oral and the Written"; Lagerwey, *Taoist Ritual*, 152–166; Hsieh, "Zhenxing, shentu yu lingfu"; Verellen, "Dynamic Design"; Mollier, "Talismans"; des Rotours, "Les insignes en deux parties"; and Drexler, *Daoistische Schriftmagie*.

74 See Wang Yucheng, "Donghan daofu shili," "Tang–Song daojiao mizhuanwen shili," "Wenwu suojian Zhongguo gudai daofu shulun," and "Zhongguo gudai daojiao qiyi fuming kaolun."

75 See Raz, *Emergence of Daoism*, 127–176. See also Hsieh, "Zhenxing, shentu yu lingfu"; Hsieh, "Writing from Heaven"; and Schipper, "True Form."

Postlude

1 Master Qin Guorong of Xinhua reports that if the banner fails to knot at an ordination *jiao* in his lineage, the ordinand is consigned for the rest of his life to serve as an acolyte and may not become a full-fledged priest. Qin, "Guangchangong changyong," 162.

2 Zhang Shihong, "Anhua daojiao de diaocha baogao," 50–51; see also *Meishan wenhua*, 206.

3 Patrice Fava reports that masters in Xinhua also attribute divinatory significance to the shape of knots in banners used in cognate banner rites performed during ordinations. Furthermore, he acquired a fascinating Qing-dynasty text, *Cloud Seal Scripts of Imperial Banners* (*Huangfan yunzhuan* 皇旛雲篆), printed from woodblocks in the Abbey of Two Immortals (Erxian'an 二仙菴) in Chengdu in 1916. That text identifies auspicious seal-script characters that could be deciphered from some 265 shapes of knots in banners tied by various martial deities. See Fava, *Aux portes du ciel*, 197–198.

    Yin Jiao shows up in five of those entries. For example, one entry interprets a knot to read "seventeen radiances." It explains,

This banner is a sign that the Celestial Worthy of Pervading Vacuity saw that the hearts of believers were radiant, and so he dispatched Marshal Yin along with his emissary the Earl of Wind to come to the altar and skillfully tie [a knot to read] "seventeen radiances." [It is a sign that] all the affairs of those who promote goodness will go smoothly, and that the clans of those who give alms will be auspicious and their wives and children will be at peace (此旛迺冲虛天君見信人心地光明，差殷元帥同功曹風伯來壇，巧結「十七光明」，建善者百事亨通，修齋者家門清吉，人眷平安之兆). *Huangfan yunzhuan,* 90b (web figure post.3).

Many thanks to Patrice Fava for sharing this text with me.

4   For an exploration of the roots of oaths with martial deities in Song and Yuan Divine Empyrean practice, see Mozina, "Oaths and Curses."

5   For a full articulation of Yin Jiao's role during the final day of Chen Diwen's ordination *jiao,* see Mozina, "Daubing Lips with Blood."

Bibliography

Abbreviations

DFHH *Daofa haihan diyiji* 道法海涵第一輯. Edited by Lee Fong-mao 李豐楙. 20 vols. Taipei: Xinwenfeng chuban gongsi, 2014.

DZ *Zhengtong daozang* 正統道藏. 60 vols. Taipei: Xinwenfeng chuban gongsi, 1977. Numbered according to Schipper and Verellen, *The Taoist Canon* (see Secondary Sources).

X *Shinsan dainihon zokuzōkyō* 卍新纂大日本續藏經. Edited by Watanabe Kōshō 河村孝照. 90 vols. Tokyo: Kokusho kankōkai, 1975–1989. Chinese Buddhist Electronic Text Association version, www.cbeta.org.

ZWDS *Zangwai daoshu* 藏外道書. Edited by Hu Daojing 胡道靜, Chen Yaoting 陳耀庭, Duan Wengui 段文桂, and Lin Wanqing 林萬清. 36 vols. Chengdu: Bashu shushe, 1992–1994.

Primary Sources

Anhua xianzhi 安化縣志 1986–2000. Compiled by Hunansheng Anhuaxian difangzhi bianzuan weiyuanhui 湖南省安化縣地方誌編纂委員會. Beijing: Fangzhi chubanshe, 2005.

Bai yugao jiashu 拜預告家書. Liturgical document prepared by Jiang Shenzhi 蔣身志 for Chen Diwen's 陳迪文 ordination, 2004. Template in *Zouzhi quanbu shushi* 奏職全部疏式, 36a–38b. Manuscript copied by Jiang Shenzhi, early 1990s. Anhua county, Hunan. Collected by the author.

Baojiang diewen 報將牒文. Liturgical document prepared by Jiang Shenzhi for Chen Diwen's ordination, 2004. Template in *Zouzhi quanbu shushi* 奏職全部疏式,

19b–22b. Manuscript copied by Jiang Shenzhi, early 1990s. Anhua county, Hunan. Collected by the author.

Beiyou ji 北遊記. In *Huitu dong nan xi bei youji* 繪圖東南西北遊記, 205–263. Taipei: Fenghuang chubanshe, 1974.

Buxu gaoseng zhuan 補續高僧傳. X77, no. 1524, 474c17–475c8.

Chici Nanquan zongpu 敕賜南泉宗譜, 1806. Reprinted by Jiangxisheng Yichunshi Yuanzhouqu dang'anguan 江西省宜春市袁州區檔案館, Yichun, Jiangxi, 2015.

Chongkan huitu sanjiao yuanliu soushen daquan 重刊繪圖三教源流搜神大全. Compiled by Ye Dehui 葉德輝, 1909. Reprinted in *Huitu sanjiao yuanliu soushen daquan* 繪圖三教源流搜神大全, 3–354. Shanghai: Shanghai guji chubanshe, 1990.

Da Yingong fufa 大殷公符法. In *Xiantian fufa qianchuan mizhi* 先天符法遣船祕旨, 15b–20a. Manuscript copied by Jiang Shenzhi, early 1990s. Anhua county, Hunan. Collected by the author.

Daojiao gepai paixushi 道教各派派序詩. In *Daojiao gepai paixushi, Zhang yuanshuai maikao, Jiwei zhenren maikao, Sa zhenren yu Wang yuanshuai* 道教各派派序詩, 張元帥脈考, 幾位真人脈考, 薩真人與王元帥, 1a–2b. Manuscript copied by Jiang Shenzhi, early 1990s. Anhua county, Hunan. Collected by the author.

Daojiao qishi chaoke 道教啟師朝科. In *Xiantian churi kefan* 先天初日科範, 36a–50b. Manuscript copied by Jiang Shenzhi, early 1990s. Anhua county, Hunan. Collected by the author.

Disi gaodou xuanke 地司告斗玄科. In DFHH 20:385–468.

Dongyuan sanmei 洞淵三昧. Manuscript copied by Fu Gongyu 扶功玉, early to mid-nineteenth century. Anhua county, Hunan. Collected by the author.

Fengshen yanyi 封神演義. Edited by Yang Zongying 楊宗瑩 and Miao Tianhua 繆天華. Taipei: Sanmin shuju, 2004.

Fo Dao michuan ji kuanshi 佛道秘傳及款式. Manuscript copied by Jiang Shenzhi, early 1990s. Anhua county, Hunan. Collected by the author.

Fojiao banshe ke 佛教頒赦科. In *Fojiao ciri chaoke* 佛教次日朝科, 30a–43b. Manuscript copied by Jiang Shenzhi, early 1990s. Anhua county, Hunan. Collected by the author.

Fojiao ciri chaoke 佛教次日朝科. Manuscript copied by Jiang Shenzhi, early 1990s. Anhua county, Hunan. Collected by the author.

Hetong yinshu shi 合同陰疏式. In *Zouzhi quanbu shushi* 奏職全部疏式, 42b–46a. Manuscript copied by Jiang Shenzhi, early 1990s. Anhua county, Hunan. Collected by the author.

Heyun zhuojian keyi 和允酌餞科儀. Zhengyi tianshi keshu ji 正一天師科書集 13, edited by Zhang Jintao 張金濤. Jiangxi: Longhushan sihan tianshifu, 2006.

Huainanzi jishi 淮南子集釋. Compiled by He Ning 何寧. 3 vols. Beijing: Zhonghua shuju, 1998.

Huangfan yunzhuan 皇旛雲篆. Woodblock print from Erxian'an 二仙菴, 1916. Chengdu, Sichuan. Collected by Patrice Fava.

Jiutian yingyuan leisheng Puhua tianzun shuo yushu baojing 九天應元雷聲普化天尊説玉樞寶經. Color illustrated manuscript, 1527. National Tenri Library, Tenri, Japan. Accessed by Poul Andersen.

Laozi jiaoshi 老子校釋. Compiled by Zhu Qianzhi 朱謙之. Beijing: Zhonghua shuju, 2000.

Les Statuettes religieuses du Hunan database 湖南神像資料庫. Edited by Alain Arrault. Paris: Ecole Française d'Extrême-Orient; accessed May–June 2017. http://hunan.efeo.fr.

Lüzu xiantian zuqi michuan 呂祖先天祖炁密傳. In *Zuqi michuan, Yin Jiao chumai* 祖炁秘傳, 殷郊出脈, 9a–20b. Manuscript copied by Jiang Shenzhi, early 1990s. Anhua county, Hunan. Collected by the author.

Pu'an zushi lingyan ji 普庵祖師靈驗記. In *Pu'an chanshi quanji* 普庵禪師全集, edited by Wang Zhengshi 王徵士 and Zhou Xunnan 周勳男, 358–385. Taipei: Dasheng jingshe yinjinghui, 1990.

Qingwei hunlian zhaohe 清微混煉召合. Manuscript signed by Wu Keheng 吳科亨 (fl. 1688–1728). Likely Jiangsu. Collected by the author.

Quanxiang pinghua Wuwang fa Zhou shu 全相平話武王伐紂書. In *Yuankan quanxiang pinghua wuzhong jiaozhu* 元刊全相平話五種校注, annotated by Zhong Zhaohua 鐘兆華, 1–97. Chengdu: Bashu shushe, 1989.

"Taisui Yin yuanshuai 太歲殷元帥." In *Chongkan huitu sanjiao yuanliu soushen daquan*, 234–236.

Tianlei wuwang Yin dayuanshuai shuo hutan guigen zhenjing 天雷无妄殷大元帥説護壇歸根真經. In *Wang Ma Yin Wen hudao zhenjing* 王馬殷溫護道真經, 17a–21a. Woodblock text printed by Tongqingtang 同慶堂, 1891. Collected by the author.

Wang Ma Yin Wen hudao zhenjing 王馬殷溫護道真經. Woodblock text printed by Tongqingtang 同慶堂, 1891. Collected by the author.

Wang Zhengshi 王徵士, and Zhou Xunnan 周勳男, eds. *Pu'an chanshi quanji* 普庵禪師全集. Taipei: Dasheng jingshe yinjinghui, 1990.

Wangshuai zhaolian 王帥召煉. In *Wang Zhang Yin zhaolian ke* 王張殷召煉科, 1a–6b. Manuscript copied by Jiang Shenzhi, early 1990s. Anhua county, Hunan. Collected by the author.

Wulei xiandao jinfan fufa 五雷顯道金旛符法. Manuscript copied by Biyun 碧雲, between 1861 and 1875. Changde, Hunan. In DFHH 13:123–186.

Xiantian bodu jian Puzu chuandu ke 先天撥度兼普祖傳度科. Manuscript copied by Jiang Shenzhi, early 1990s. Collected by the author.

Xiantian fufa michuan 先天符法秘傳. In *Xiantian fufa qianchuan mizhi* 先天符法遣船祕旨, 1a–12a. Manuscript copied by Jiang Shenzhi, early 1990s. Anhua county, Hunan. Collected by the author.

Xiantian fufa qianchuan mizhi 先天符法遣船祕旨. Manuscript copied by Jiang Shenzhi, early 1990s. Anhua county, Hunan. Collected by the author.

Xiantian Yingong fanfa yizong 先天殷公旛法一宗. Manuscript signed by Luo Congyao 羅從堯 (b. 1813). Xinhua country, Hunan. Collected by Patrice Fava.

Xiantian Yinlei xueying mizhi 先天殷雷削影秘旨. In *Xiantian Wang Yin lei xueying mizhi, Leibu tianzhang michuan, Longhushan geshi, Shou leishi michuan* 先天王殷雷削影秘旨, 雷部天章秘傳, 龍虎山格式, 收雷屍秘傳, 6a–12b. Manuscript copied by Jiang Shenzhi, early 1990s. Anhua county, Hunan. Collected by the author.

Xiantian zuqi zailun 先天祖氣再論. In *Zuqi michuan, Yin Jiao chumai* 祖炁秘傳, 殷郊出脈, 21a–23b. Manuscript composed by Jiang Shenzhi, early 1990s. Anhua county, Hunan. Collected by the author.

Xiao Yingong fufa 小殷公符法. In *Xiantian fufa qianchuan mizhi* 先天符法遣船祕旨, 12b–15a. Manuscript copied by Jiang Shenzhi, early 1990s. Anhua county, Hunan. Collected by the author.

Xinbian lianxiang soushen guangji 新編連相搜神廣記. Compiled by Qin Zijin 秦子晉 (fl. 13th–14th century). Zhongguo minjian xinyang ziliao huibian, diyiji 2 中國民間信仰資料彙編, 第一輯 2, edited by Lee Fong-mao 李豐楙 and Wang Ch'iu-kuei 王秋桂. Taipei: Taiwan xuesheng shuju, 1989.

Xiudao zhenyan 修道真言. In ZWDS 23:798–802.

Yangping 陽憑. Ordination certificate prepared by Li Yezhen 李謁真 for Chen Diwen's ordination, 2004. Template in *Zouzhi quanbu shushi* 奏職全部疏式,

42b–48a. Manuscript copied by Jiang Shenzhi, early 1990s. Anhua county, Hunan. Collected by the author.

Yin Jiao chumai 殷郊出脈 (*Disi tongsha taisui Yin Jiao tianjun shishi xiuxing maikao* 地司統煞太歲殷郊天君十世修行脈考). In *Zuqi michuan, Yin Jiao chumai* 祖炁秘傳, 殷郊出脈, 1a–8a. Manuscript copied by Jiang Shenzhi, early 1990s. Anhua county, Hunan. Collected by the author.

Yin Jiao xueben 殷郊血本. Manuscript by unknown author, undated. Anhua county, Hunan. Collected by the author.

Yingong fanfa 殷公旛法. Manuscript copied by Jiang Shenzhi, 1989. Anhua county, Hunan. Collected by the author.

Yinping 陰憑. Ordination certificate prepared by Li Yezhen for Chen Diwen's ordination, 2004. Template in *Zouzhi quanbu shushi* 奏職全部疏式, 42b–46a. Manuscript copied by Jiang Shenzhi, early 1990s. Anhua county, Hunan. Collected by the author.

Yinshuai zhaolian 殷帥召煉. In *Wang Zhang Yin zhaolian ke* 王張殷召煉科, 12a–15b. Manuscript copied by Jiang Shenzhi, early 1990s. Anhua county, Hunan. Collected by the author.

Zhangshuai zhaolian 張帥召煉. In *Wang Zhang Yin zhaolian ke* 王張殷召煉科, 7a–11a. Manuscript copied by Jiang Shenzhi, early 1990s. Anhua county, Hunan. Collected by the author.

Zhaolian qingsheng ke 召煉請聖科. Manuscript copied by Jiang Shenzhi, early 1990s. Anhua county, Hunan. Collected by the author.

Zhidao renmin tuanti zuzhi zongbaogaobiao 指導人民團體組織總報告表, May 1, 1942. Minguo Anhuaxian minzhengke, shengfu xianfu guanyu baohu sichan siseng foxiang jingdian, jingzhi waidao jishen liancai, fenhui gaizu xuanju qingli sichan banxiao shaozhen simiao dengji daojiao huiyuan mingce deng cailiao 民國安化縣民政科, 省府縣府關於保護寺產寺僧佛像經典、禁止外道笈神斂財、分會改組選舉清理寺產辦校詔診寺廟登記道教會員名冊等材料, 1943. Anhua County Archives, Dongping, Hunan.

Zhongnanshan tianlong huiji zimen shipu 終南山天龍會集緇門世譜. In X86, no. 1603, 484c24–485a1.

Zhou Zhenfu 周振甫, ed. *Zhouyi yizhu* 周易譯注. Beijing: Zhonghua shuju, 1991.

Zhupin lingzhang leijun bizhi 諸品靈章雷君秘旨. In ZWDS 29:9–17.

Zouzhi quanbu shushi 奏職全部疏式. Manuscript copied by Jiang Shenzhi, early 1990s. Anhua county, Hunan. Collected by the author.

Sources from the Daoist Canon *(Zhengtong daozang)*

DZ 1   *Lingbao wuliang duren shangpin miaojing* 靈寶無量度人上品妙經

DZ 10   *Gaoshang Yuhuang benxing jijing* 高上玉皇本行集經

DZ 16   *Jiutian yingyuan leisheng puhua tianzun yushu baojing* 九天應元雷聲普化天尊玉樞寶經

DZ 141 *Ziyang zhenren Wuzhenpian zhushu* 紫陽真人悟真篇註疏

DZ 219 *Lingbao wuliang duren shangjing dafa* 靈寶無量度人上經大法

DZ 220 *Wushang xuanyuan santian yutang dafa* 無上玄元三天玉堂大法

DZ 296 *Lishi zhenxian tidao tongjian* 歷世真仙體道通鑑

DZ 297 *Lishi zhenxian tidao tongjian xupian* 歷世真仙體道通鑑續篇

DZ 461 *Shangqing gusui lingwen guilü* 上清骨髓靈文鬼律

DZ 508 *Wushang huanglu dazhai licheng yi* 無上黃籙大齋立成儀

DZ 547 *Lingbao yujian* 靈寶玉鑑

DZ 566 *Shangqing tianxin zhengfa* 上清天心正法

DZ 567 *Shangqing beiji tianxin zhengfa* 上清北極天心正法

DZ 1016 *Zhen'gao* 真誥

DZ 1166 *Fahai yizhu* 法海遺珠

     30 *Taisui bifa* 太歲祕法

     35 *Taisui wuchun leifa* 太歲武春雷法

     44 *Jiucha disi Yin shuai dafa* 糾察地司殷帥大法

DZ 1220 *Daofa huiyuan* 道法會元

     1 *Qingwei daofa shuniu* 清微道法樞紐

     4 *Qingwei zongzhi* 清微宗旨

     30 *Ziji xuanshu zougao dafa* 紫極玄樞奏告大法

     37 *Shangqing wuchun lielei dafa* 上清武春烈雷大法

     41 *Qingwei yangong wenjian* 清微言功文檢

     44 *Qingwei rangyi wenjian* 清微禳疫文檢

     47 *Shenjie wulei qidao jian* 神捷五雷祈禱檢

     48–49 *Shenjie wulei qidao jianshi* 神捷五雷祈禱檢式

     56 *Shangqing yufu wulei dafa yushu lingwen* 上清玉府五雷大法玉樞靈文

     61 *Gaoshang shenxiao yushu zhankan wulei dafa* 高上神霄玉樞斬勘五雷大法

     67 *Leiting xuanlun* 雷霆玄論

     71 *Xujing tianshi powang zhang* 虛靖天師破妄章

     76 *Wang huoshi leiting aozhi xu* 汪火師雷霆奧旨序

     82 *Xiantian yiqi huolei Zhang shizhe qidao dafa* 先天一炁火雷張使者祈禱大法

     83–87 *Xiantian leijing yinshu* 先天雷晶隱書

     89 *Xiantian leijing yuanzhang* 先天雷晶元章

111–112 *Diling baozhu wulei qidao dafa* 帝令寶珠五雷祈禱大法

153 *Dongxuan yushu leiting dafa* 洞玄玉樞雷霆大法

188–190 *Taiyi huofu wulei dafa* 太乙火府五雷大法

193 *Taiyi huofu neizhi* 太乙火府內旨

232 *Zhengyi xuantan Zhao yuanshuai bifa* 正一玄壇趙元帥祕法

241 *Leiting sanwu huoche lingguan Wang yuanshuai bifa* 雷霆三五火車
靈官王元帥祕法

246 *Tianxin disi dafa* 天心地司大法

247 *Beidi disi Yin yuanshuai bifa* 北帝地司殷元帥祕法

253 *Diqi fa* 地祇法

265 *Beiyin fengdu taixuan zhimo helü lingshu* 北陰酆都太玄制魔黑律靈書

267 *Taixuan fengdu heilü yige* 泰玄酆都黑律儀格

DZ 1225 *Zhenwu lingying dajiao yi* 真武靈應大醮儀

DZ 1227 *Taishang zhuguo jiumin zongzhen biyao* 太上助國救民總真祕要

DZ 1248 *Sandong qunxian lu* 三洞群仙錄

DZ 1250 *Chongxu tongmiao shichen Wang xiansheng jiahua* 沖虛通妙侍宸王先生
家話

DZ 1307 *Haiqiong Bai zhenren yulu* 海瓊白真人語錄

DZ 1412 *Taishang Yuanshi tianzun shuo Beidi fumo shenzhou miaojing* 太上元始
天尊說北帝伏魔神咒妙經

DZ 1413 *Beidi fumo jingfa jiantan yi* 北帝伏魔經法建壇儀

DZ 1440 *Gaoshang Yuhuang benxing jijing zhu* 高上玉皇本行集經註

Secondary Sources

Andersen, Poul. "*Beidi fumo jingfa jiantan yi* 北帝伏魔經法建壇儀." In Schipper
and Verellen, *Taoist Canon*, vol. 2, 1191–1192.

———. "Concepts of Meaning in Chinese Ritual." *Cahiers d'Extrême-Orient* 12
(2001): 155–183.

———. "Essence and Function (*ti* and *yong*): A Daoist Theory of Ritual." Paper
presented at the conference "Ritual Dynamics and the Science of Ritual,"
University of Heidelberg, September 29–October 2, 2008.

———. "Guideline of the Eight Trigrams." *East Asian Institute Occasional Papers* 6
(1990): 13–30.

———. *The Method of Holding the Three Ones: A Taoist Manual of Meditation of the
Fourth Century A.D.* London: Curzon Press, 1980.

———. *The Paradox of Being.* Cambridge, MA: Harvard University Asia Center, 2019.

———. "The Practice of *Bugang*." *Cahiers d'Extrême-Asie* 5 (1989–1990): 15–53.

———. "*Shangqing gusui lingwen guilü* 上清骨髓靈文鬼律." In Schipper and Verellen, *Taoist Canon*, vol. 2, 1060–1062.

———. "*Shangqing tianxin zhengfa* 上清天心正法." In Schipper and Verellen, *Taoist Canon*, vol. 2, 1064–1067.

———. "*Taishang Yuanshi tianzun shuo Beidi fumo shenzhou miaojing* 太上元始天尊說北帝伏魔神咒妙經." In Schipper and Verellen, *Taoist Canon*, vol. 2, 1189–1191.

———. "*Taishang zhuguo jiumin zongzhen biyao* 太上助國救民總真祕要." In Schipper and Verellen, *Taoist Canon*, vol. 2, 1057–1060.

———. "Taoist Ritual Texts and Traditions with Special Reference to *Bugang*, the Cosmic Dance." PhD diss., University of Copenhagen, 1991.

———. "Taoist Talismans and the History of the Tianxin Tradition." *Acta Orientalia* 57 (1996): 141–152.

———. "The Transformation of the Body in Taoist Ritual." In *Religious Reflections on the Human Body*, edited by James Marie Law, 186–208. Bloomington: Indiana University Press, 1995.

———. "*Wushang xuanyuan santian yutang dafa* 無上玄元三天玉堂大法." In Schipper and Verellen, *Taoist Canon*, vol. 2, 1070–1073.

Arrault, Alain. "Analytic Essay on the Domestic Statuary of Central Hunan: The Cult to Divinities, Parents and Masters." *Journal of Chinese Religions* 36 (2008): 1–53.

———. *A History of Cultic Images in China: The Domestic Statuary of Hunan*. Hong Kong: The Chinese University of Hong Kong Press, 2020.

Austin, John L. *How to Do Things with Words*. Cambridge, MA: Harvard University Press, 1962.

Bakhtin, Mikhail. "The Problem of Speech Genres." In *Speech Genres and Other Late Essays*, edited by Caryl Emerson and Michael Holquist, translated by Vern W. McGee, 60–102. Austin: University of Texas Press, 1986.

Baldrain-Hussein, Fareen. "Weng Baoguang 翁葆光." In Pregadio, *Encyclopedia of Taoism*, vol. 2, 1036–1037.

Bickford, Maggie. "Huizong's Paintings: Art and the Art of Emperorship." In Ebrey and Bickford, *Emperor Huizong and Late Northern Song China*, 453–516.

Bokenkamp, Stephen R. *Early Daoist Scriptures, with a Contribution by Peter Nickerson*. Berkeley: University of California Press, 1997.

Boltz, Judith M. "Not by the Seal of Office Alone: New Weapons in Battles with the Supernatural." In *Religion and Society in T'ang and Sung China,* edited by Patricia Buckley Ebrey and Peter N. Gregory, 241–305. Honolulu: University of Hawai'i Press, 1993.

———. *A Survey of Taoist Literature: Tenth to Seventeenth Centuries.* Berkeley, CA: Institute of East Asian Studies, 1987.

Bumbacher, Stephan Peter. *Empowered Writing: Exorcistic and Apotropaic Rituals in Medieval China.* St. Petersburg, FL: Three Pines Press, 2012.

Buswell, Robert E., Jr., and Donald Lopez Jr. *The Princeton Dictionary of Buddhism.* Princeton, NJ: Princeton University Press, 2014.

Cammann, Schuyler. "The Magic Square of Three in Old Chinese Philosophy and Religion." *History of Religions* 1, no. 1 (1961): 37–80.

Campany, Robert Ford. *Making Transcendents: Ascetics and Social Memory in Early Medieval China.* Honolulu: University of Hawai'i Press, 2009.

———. *To Live as Long as Heaven and Earth: A Translation and Study of Ge Hong's Traditions of Divine Transcendents.* Berkeley: University of California Press, 2002.

Capitanio, Joshua. "Sanskrit and Pseudo-Sanskrit Incantations in Daoist Ritual Texts." *History of Religion* 57, no. 4 (2018): 348–405.

Carman, John B. *Majesty and Meekness: A Comparative Study of Contrast and Harmony in the Concept of God.* Grand Rapids, MI: William B. Eerdmans, 1994.

Chang Ch'ao-jan 張超然. "Tang–Song daojiao zhaiyi zhong de 'lishi cunnian' jiqi yuanliu kaolun: Jianlun daojiao zhaitan tuxiang de yunyong 唐宋道教齋儀中的「禮師存念」及其源流考論：兼論道教齋壇圖像的運用." *Qinghua xuebao* 清華學報 45, no. 3 (2015): 381–413.

———. "Xipu, jiaofa jiqi zhenghe: Dongjin–Nanchao daojiao shangqing jingpai de jichu yanjiu 系譜、教法及其整合：東晉南朝道教上清經派的基礎研究." PhD diss., National Chengchi University, 2008.

———. "Ziwo shenfen, lunli xingge yu shehui xiangzheng: Dao yu fa de genben chayi yu fuhe xianxiang 自我身分、倫理性格與社會象徵：道與法的根本差異與複合現象." *Huaren zongjiao yanjiu* 華人宗教研究 8 (2016): 33–64.

Chang, Leslie T. *Factory Girls: From Village to City in a Changing China.* New York: Spiegel & Grau, 2009.

Chao, Shin-yi. *Daoist Ritual, State Religion and Popular Practices: Zhenwu Worship from Song to Ming (960–1644).* New York: Routledge, 2011.

———. "Huizong and the Divine Empyrean Palace 神霄宮 Temple Network." In Ebrey and Bickford, *Emperor Huizong and Late Northern Song China*, 324–358.

———. "Zhenwu: The Cult of a Chinese Warrior Deity from the Song to the Ming Dynasties (960–1644)." PhD diss., University of British Columbia, 2002.

Ch'en Chun-chih 陳峻誌. "Taisui de xinyang suyuan yu jisi kongjian: Yi Taiwan weizhu de taolun 太歲的信仰溯源與祭祀空間：以臺灣為主的討論." PhD diss., National Chung Hsing University, 2014.

Chen Yisong 陳益松. "Daxiongshan zhong de Huizhen leitan 大熊山中的會真雷壇." In Chen and Arrault, *Xiangzhong zongjiao yu xiangtu shehui diaocha baogao ji*, vol. 1, 451–455.

Chen Zi'ai 陳子艾, and Alain Arrault (Hua Lan 華瀾), eds. *Xiangzhong zongjiao yu xiangtu shehui diaocha baogao ji* 湘中宗教与鄉土社會調查報告集. 2 vols. Beijing: Wenhui shuma yinzhi zhongxin, 2006.

Chenivesse, Sandrine. "Fengdu: Cité l'abondance, cité de la male mort." *Cahiers d'Extrême-Asie* 10 (1998): 287–339.

Clark, Katerina, and Michael Holquist. *Mikhail Bakhtin*. Cambridge, MA: Harvard University Press, 1984.

Copp, Paul F. *The Body Incantatory: Spells and the Ritual Imagination in Medieval Chinese Buddhism*. New York: Columbia University Press, 2014.

Davis, Edward L. *Society and the Supernatural in Song China*. Honolulu: University of Hawai'i Press, 2001.

Deng Cihuang 鄧慈煌. *Tianxia da Cihua* 天下大慈化. Yichun: Yichun shuju yinshuachang, 1993.

Despeux, Catherine. "Talismans and Diagrams." In Kohn, *Daoism Handbook*, 498–540.

des Rotours, Robert. "Les insignes en deux parties (*fou* 符) sous la dynastie des T'ang (618–907)." *T'oung Pao* XVI, no. 1–3 (1952): 1–148.

Drexler, Monika. *Daoistische Schriftmagie: Interpretationenen zu den Schriftamuletten Fu im Daozang*. Stuttgart: Franz Steiner Verlag, 1994.

Duara, Prasenjit. "Superscribing Symbols: The Myth of Guandi, Chinese God of War." *Journal of Asian Studies* 47, no. 4 (1988): 778–795.

Ebrey, Patricia Buckley, and Maggie Bickford. *Emperor Huizong and Late Northern Song China: The Politics of Culture and the Culture of Politics*. Cambridge, MA: Harvard University Asia Center, 2006.

Esposito, Monica. "The Longmen School and Its Controversial History during the Qing Dynasty." In *Religion and Chinese Society*, Vol. 2, *Taoism and Local Religion in Modern China,* edited by John Lagerwey, 621–698. Hong Kong:

The Chinese University of Hong Kong Press; Paris: École française d'Extrême-Orient, 2004.

Faraone, Christopher A. *Talismans and Trojan Horses: Guardian Statues in Ancient Greek Myth and Ritual*. Oxford: Oxford University Press, 1992.

Fava, Patrice. *Aux portes du ciel: La statuaire taoïste du Hunan*. Paris: Les Belles Lettres and École française d'Extrême-Orient, 2013.

Fava, Patrice (Fan Hua 范華), and Wan Yilin 萬益林. "Hunan daojiao diaocha yanjiu—Chen Demei daozhang de fashi keyi 湖南道教調查研究 ——陳德美道長的法事科儀." In *Difang daojiao yishi shidi diaocha bijiao yanjiu: Guoji xueshu yantaohui lunwenji* 地方道教儀式實地調查比較研究：國際學術研討會論文集, edited by Lü Pengzhi 呂鵬志 and John Lagerwey (Lao Gewen 勞格文), 33–112. Taipei: Xinwenfeng chuban gufen youxian gongsi, 2013.

Goossaert, Vincent. "Bureaucratic Charisma: The Zhang Heavenly Master Institution and Court Taoists in late-Qing China." *Asia Major* 17, no. 2 (2004): 121–159.

——— (Gao Wansang 高萬桑). "Jindai Zhongguo de tianshi shoulu xitong: Dui *Tiantai yuge* de chubu yanjiu 近代中國的天師授籙系統：對《天台玉格》的初步研究." In *Shijiu shiji yilai Zhongguo difang daojiao bianqian* 十九世紀以來中國地方道教變遷, edited by Lai Chi Tim 黎志添, 437–456. Hong Kong: The Chinese University of Hong Kong Press, 2013.

———. "The Quanzhen 全真 Clergy, 1700–1950." In *Religion and Chinese Society*, Vol. 2, *Taoism and Local Religion in Modern China,* edited by John Lagerwey, 699–771. Hong Kong: The Chinese University of Hong Kong Press; Paris: École française d'Extrême-Orient, 2004.

Guo Zhaoxiang 郭兆祥. *Zhongguo Meishan wenhua* 中國梅山文化. Hong Kong: Tianma tushu youxian chuban gongsi, 2002.

Holquist, Michael. *Dialogism: Bakhtin and His World*. London: Routledge, 1990.

Hou, Ching-lang. *Monnaies d'offrande et la notion de Trésorerie dans la religion chinoise*. Paris: Collège de France, Institut des Hautes Études Chinoises, 1975.

Hsiao Teng-fu 蕭登福. "Shilun Ziwei dadi shen'ge: Jianlun Sichuan Dazu Shimenshan 10 hao ku sanhuangdong sanhuang shenfen de wenti 試論紫微大帝神格：兼論四川大足石門山10號窟三皇洞三皇身分的問題." In *Daojiao yu xingdou xinyang* 道教與星斗信仰, edited by Pan Chongxian 潘崇賢 and Liang Fa 梁發, 790–819. Jinan: Qilu shushe, 2014.

———. *Taisui yuanshen yu nanbeidou xingshen xinyang* 太歲元神與南北斗星神信仰. Hong Kong: Qiangseyuan chubanshe, 2010.

———. "Zailun Taisui yuanqi yu Taisui shen'ge de yanbian 再論太歲源起與太歲神格的演變." *Hongdao* 弘道 59 (2014): 4–23.

Hsieh Shu-wei 謝世維. "Writing from Heaven: Celestial Writing in Six Dynasties Daoism." PhD diss., Indiana University, 2005.

———. "Zaoqi Doumu Molizhitian wenben tantao: Yi *Xiantian leijing yinshu wei zhongxin* 早期斗姆摩利支天文本探討：以《先天雷晶隱書》為中心." *Chengda zhongwen xuebao* 成大中文學報 47 (2014): 209–240.

———. "Zhenxing, shentu yu lingfu: Daojiao sanhuangwen shijue wenhua chutan 真形、神圖與靈符：道教三皇文視覺文化初探." *Xingda renwen xuebao* 興大人文學報 56 (2016): 23–58.

Hu Fuchen 胡孚琛, ed. *Zhonghua daojiao dacidian* 中國道教大辭典. Beijing: Zhongguo shehui kexue chubanshe, 1995.

Huang Xiaoshi 黃小石. *Jingmingdao yanjiu* 淨明道研究. Chengdu: Bashu chubanshe, 1999.

Hucker, Charles O. *A Dictionary of Official Titles in Imperial China.* Taipei: Southern Materials Center, 1989.

Hudson, Wm. Clarke. "Spreading the Dao, Managing Mastership, and Performing Salvation: The Life and Alchemical Teachings of Chen Zhixu." PhD diss., Indiana University, 2007.

Hymes, Robert. *Way and Byway: Taoism, Local Religion, and Models of Divinity in Sung and Modern China.* Berkeley: University of California Press, 2002.

Idema, Wilt. "Some Remarks and Speculations Concerning *P'ing-hua*." *T'oung Pao* 60 (1974): 121–172.

Kaltenmark, Max. "*Ling-pao:* Note sur un terme du taoïsme religieux." In *Mélanges publiés par l'Institut des Hautes Études Chinoises* 2, 559–588. Paris: Collège de France, 1968.

Kao Chen-hung 高振宏. "Song–Yuan–Ming daojiao fengyuefa yanjiu 宋、元、明道教酆岳法研究." PhD diss., National Chengchi University, 2013.

———. "Xujing tianshi chuanshuo yanjiu: Biji, xiaoshuo yu daojing de zonghe kaocha 虛靖天師傳說研究：筆記、小說與道經的綜合考察". *Zhengda zhongwen xuebao* 政大中文學報 23 (2015): 131–170.

Katz, Paul R. *Demon Hordes and Burning Boats: The Cult of Marshal Wen in Late Imperial Chekiang.* Albany: State University of New York Press, 1995.

Kleeman, Terry F. *Celestial Masters: History and Ritual in Early Daoist Communities.* Cambridge: Harvard University Asia Center, 2016.

———. *A God's Own Tale: The* Book of Transformations *of Wenchang, the Divine Lord of Zitong.* Albany: State University of New York Press, 1994.

———. "*Sanguan* 三官, Three Offices." In Predagio, *Encyclopedia of Taoism,* vol. 2, 833–834.

Kong Linghong 孔令宏. *Song–Ming daojiao sixiang yanjiu* 宋明道教思想研究. Beijing: Zongjiao wenhua chubanshe, 2002.

Lagerwey, John. "*Lingbao yujian* 靈寶玉鑑." In Schipper and Verellen, *Taoist Canon,* vol. 2, 1018–1021.

———. "The Oral and the Written in Chinese and Western Religion." In *Religion und Philosophie in Ostasien: Festschrift für Hans Steininger zum 65.* Gerburtstag, edited by Gert Naundorf, Karl-Heinz Pohl, and Hans-Hermann Schmidt, 301–322. Würzburg: Königshausen & Neumann, 1985.

———. "Popular Ritual Specialists in West Central Fujian." In *Shehui, minzu yu wenhua zhanyan guoji yantaohui lunwenji* 社會、民族與文化展演國際研討會論文集, edited by Wang Ch'iu-kuei 王秋桂, Zhuang Yingzhang 莊英章, and Chen Zhongmin 陳中民, 435–507. Taipei: Hanxue yanjiu zhongxin, 2001.

———. *Taoist Ritual in Chinese Society and History.* New York: Macmillan, 1987.

Lai Chi Tim 黎志添. "Tian di shui sanguan xinyang yu zaoqi tianshidao zhibing jiezui yishi 天地水三官信仰與早期天師道治病解罪儀式." *Taiwan zongjiao yanjiu* 臺灣宗教研究 2, no. 1 (2002): 1–30.

LaMothe, Kimerer L. *Between Dancing and Writing: The Practice of Religious Studies.* New York: Fordham University Press, 2004.

Lee Fong-mao 李豐楙. "Cong xuannü dao jiutian xuannü: Yiwei shanggu nüxian de benxiang yu bianxiang 從玄女到九天玄女：一位上古女仙的本相與變相." *Xingda zhongwen xuebao* 興大中文學報 27 (2010): 17–54.

———. "Sanguan chuxun—Daojiao tuhua yu wenren yishu de cangpin yu zhanlan 三官出巡——道教圖畫與文人藝術的藏品與展覽." *Diancang gumeishu* 典藏古美術 315 (2018): 104–111.

Lee Fong-mao 李豐楙 and Zhang Zhixiong 張智雄. "Shufu yu fuhao: Zhengyi fufa de tuxiang jiqi xiangzheng 書符與符號：正一符法的圖像及其象徵." *Qinghua xuebao* 清華學報 40, no. 3 (2010): 327–364.

Lewis, Mark Edward. *Writing and Authority in Early China.* Albany: State University of New York Press, 1999.

Li Wuhan 李武漢. "Daxiongshan jingnei sishijiu zuo gu dian, si, antang de diaocha baogao 大熊山境內四十九座古殿、寺、庵堂的調查報告." In Chen and Arrault, *Xiangzhong zongjiao yu xiangtu shehui diaocha baogao ji,* vol. 1, 67–75.

Li Xinwu 李新吾. "Lengshuijiang Yangyuan Zhangtan shigong yu daoshi de yitong bijiao 冷水江楊源張壇師公與道士的異同比較." In Chen and Arrault, *Xiangzhong zongjiao yu xiangtu shehui diaocha baogao ji*, vol. 1, 271–303.

Li Yuanguo 李遠國. "Lun daojiao fulu de fenlei: Jianlun fulu yu Zhongguo wenzi de guanxi 論道教符籙的分類：兼論符籙與中國文字的關係." *Zongjiaoxue yanjiu* 宗教學研究 2 (1997): 39–47.

———. *Shenxiao leifa: Daojiao shenxiaopai yange yu sixiang* 神霄雷法：道教神霄派沿革與思想. Chengdu: Sichuan renmin chubanshe, 2003.

———. "Ziwei dadi xiaokao 紫微大帝小考." *Hongdao* 弘道 11 (2001): 62–65.

Li Yuanguo and Wang Jiayou 王家祐. "Tianpeng yuanshuai kaobian 天蓬元帥考辨." *Sichuan wenwu* 四川文物 3 (1997): 51–56.

Li Zhihong 李志鴻. *Daojiao tianxin zhengfa yanjiu* 道教天心正法研究. Beijing: Shehui kexue wenxian chubanshe, 2011.

Lin Qiaowei 林巧薇. "Shilun Yuandai Jixianyuan yu difang daojiao shiwu guanli de guanxi 試論元代集賢院與地方道教事務管理的關係." *Shijie zongjiao wenhua* 世界宗教文化 6 (2015): 38–44.

Lin Zhenyuan 林振源. "Fujian Zhao'an de xianghuaseng 福建詔安的香花僧." In *Minjian fojiao yanjiu*, edited by Tam Wai Lun, 129–165.

Liu Changdong 劉長東. "Benming xinyang kao 本命信仰考." *Sichuan daxue xuebao* 四川大學學報 1 (2004): 54–64.

Liu Guoqiang 劉國強, ed. *Hunan fojiao siyuan zhi* 湖南佛教寺院志. Hong Kong: Tianma tushu youxian gongsi, 2003.

Liu Tiefeng 劉鐵峰. "Meishan wenhua zhong daojiao jingji de ge'an kaocha 梅山文化中道教經籍的個案考察." In Chen and Arrault, *Xiangzhong zongjiao yu xiangtu shehui diaocha baogao ji*, vol. 1, 173–189.

Liu, Ts'un-yan 柳存仁. *Buddhist and Taoist Influences on Chinese Novels*. Wiesbaden: Harrassowitz, 1962.

———. *Chinese Popular Fiction in Two London Libraries*. Hong Kong: Lung Men Bookstore, 1967.

———. "*Siyou ji* de Ming keben 四遊記的明刻本." *Xinya xuebao* 新亞學報 5, no. 2 (1963): 323–375.

Liu Weishun 劉偉順. "Xinshaoxian Wenxiangguan diaocha baogao 新邵縣文仙觀調查報告." In Chen and Arrault, *Xiangzhong zongjiao yu xiangtu shehui diaocha baogao ji*, vol. 1, 76–94.

Liu Yonghai 劉永海. *Yuandai daojiao shiji yanjiu* 元代道教史籍研究. Beijing: Renmin chubanshe, 2010.

Liu Zhiwan 劉枝萬. "Raijin shinkō to raihō no tenkai 雷神信仰と雷法の展開." *Tōhō shūkyō* 方法宗教 67 (1990): 1–21.

———. "Tenhōshin to tenhōju ni tsuite 天蓬神と天蓬呪について." In *Dōkyō to shūkyō bunka* 道教と宗教文化, edited by Akizuki Kan'ei 秋月觀暎, 403–424. Tokyo: Hirakawa Shuppan, 1987.

Liu Zhongyu 劉仲宇. *Daojiao shoulu zhidu yanjiu* 道教授籙制度研究. Beijing: Zhongguo shehui kexue chubanshe, 2014.

———. *Fulu pinghua* 符籙平話. Beijing: Zongjiao wenhua chubanshe, 2013.

———. "Wulei zhengfa yuanyuan kaolun 五雷正法淵源考論." *Zongjiaoxue yanjiu* 宗教學研究 3 (2001): 14–22.

Lü Pengzhi 呂鵬志 and John Lagerwey (Lao Gewen 勞格文), eds. *Difang daojiao yishi shidi diaocha bijiao yanjiu: Guoji xueshu yantaohui lunwenji* 地方道教儀式實地調查比較研究：國際學術研討會論文集. Taipei: Xinwenfeng, 2013.

Lui Wing Sing 呂永興 and Li Xinwu 李新吾. *Shi Dao heyi: Xiangzhong Meishan Yangyuan Zhangtan de keyi yu chuancheng* 師道合一：湘中梅山楊源張壇的科儀與傳承. Daojiao yishi congshu 道教儀式叢書 2, edited by John Lagerwey (Lao Gewen 勞格文) and Lü Pengzhi 呂鵬志. Taipei: Xinwenfeng chuban gongsi, 2015.

Luo Jieyong 羅傑勇. "Xinhua maochang leitan de shoutu shoujiao jianshu 新化懋昌雷壇的收徒授教簡述." In Chen and Arrault, *Xiangzhong zongjiao yu xiangtu shehui diaocha baogao ji*, vol. 1, 455–460.

Matsumoto Kōichi 松本浩一. "Sōdai no raihō 宋代の雷法." *Shakai bunka shigaku* 社会文化史学 (1979): 45–65.

Meulenbeld, Mark R. E. "Civilized Demons: Ming Thunder Gods from Ritual to Literature." PhD diss., Princeton University, 2007.

———. "Classifying a Local Cult in Hunan: Daoist Ritual, Ideology, and Efficacy of the 'General Who Quashed Bandits'." In *Daoism and Local Cults: Rethinking the Paradigms*, edited by P. Clart, V. Goossaert, and S. W. Hsieh. Forthcoming.

———. "Dancing with the Gods: Daoist Ritual and Popular Religion in Central Hunan." In *Difang daojiao yishi shidi diaocha bijiao yanjiu: Guoji xueshu yantaohui lunwenji* 地方道教儀式實地調查比較研究：國際學術研討會論文集, edited by Lü Pengzhi 呂鵬志 and John Lagerwey (Lao Gewen 勞格文), 113–184. Taipei: Xinwenfeng, 2013.

———. "The Dark Emperor's Law: How Daoists of the Yuxu Gong Codified Liturgies in the Land of Meishan." *Studies in Chinese Religions* 4, no. 1 (2018): 66–111.

———. *Demonic Warfare: Daoism, Territorial Networks, and the History of a Ming Novel*. Honolulu: University of Hawai'i Press, 2015.

———. "From 'Withered Wood' to 'Dead Ashes': Burning Bodies, Metamorphosis, and the Ritual Production of Power." *Cahiers d'Extrême-Asie* 19 (2010): 216–267.

Meyer, Marvin, and Paul Mirecki, eds. *Ancient Magic and Ritual Power*. Leiden: Brill, 2001.

Mollier, Christine. "La méthode de l'Empereur du Nord du Mont Fengdu: Une tradition exorciste du taoïsme médiéval." *T'oung Pao* 83 (1997): 329–385.

———. "Talismans." In *Divination et société dans la Chine médiévale: Étude des manuscrits de Dunhuang de la Bibliothèque nationale de France et de la British Library*, edited by Marc Kalinowski, 405–429. Paris: Bibliothèque nationale de France, 2003.

Mozina, David J. "Daubing Lips with Blood and Drinking Elixirs with the Celestial Lord Yin Jiao: The Role of Thunder Deities in Daoist Ordination in Contemporary Hunan." *Cahiers d'Extrême-Asie* 19 (2010): 269–303.

———. "Living Redactions: The Salvationist Roots of Daoist Practice in Central Hunan." *Daoism: Religion, History and Society* 11 (2019): 1–61.

———. "Oaths and Curses in Divine Empyrean Practice." *Journal of Chinese Religions* 48, no. 1 (2020): 1–28.

———. "Summoning the Exorcist: The Role of Heart Seals (*xinyin* 心印) in Calling Down a Demon-Quelling Deity in Contemporary Daoist Thunder Ritual." In *Exorcism in Daoism: A Berlin Symposium*, edited by Florian C. Reiter, 231–256. Wiesbaden: Harrassowitz Verlag, 2011.

Murphy, Rachel. *How Migrant Labor Is Changing Rural China*. Cambridge: Cambridge University Press, 2002.

Ngai, Pun. *Made in China: Women Factory Workers in a Global Workplace*. Durham, NC: Duke University Press, 2005.

Nikaidō Yoshihiro 二階堂善弘. *Dōkyō, minkan shinkō ni okeru gensuishin no hen'yō* 道教、民間信仰における元帥神の変容. Suita-shi: Kansai daigaku shuppanbu, 2006.

———. "Taisai In gensui kō 太歳殷元帥考." *Ronsō ajia no bunka to shisō* 論叢アジアの文化と思想 3 (1994): 1–26.

———. "Tongsu xiaoshuoli yuanshuaishen zhi xingxiang 通俗小説裡元帥神之形象." In *Shengzhuan yu shichan: Zhongguo wenxue yu zongjiao lunji* 聖傳

與詩禪：中國文學與宗教論集, edited by Lee Fong-mao 李豐楙 and Liao Zhaoheng 廖肇亨, 513–547. Taipei: Zhongyang yanjiuyuan Zhongguo wenzhe yanjiusuo, 2007.

Ōfuchi Ninji 大淵忍爾. *Chūgokujin no shūkyō girei, dōkyō hen* 中国人の宗教儀礼, 道教篇. Tōkyō: Fūkyōsha, 2005.

Ownby, David. *Falun Gong and the Future of China.* Oxford: Oxford University Press, 2008.

Pai, Hsiao-hung, and Gregor Benton. *Scattered Sand: The Story of China's Rural Migrants.* London: Verso, 2013.

Palmer, David A. *Qigong Fever: Body, Science, and Utopia in China.* New York: Columbia University Press, 2007.

Patton, Kimberley C. *Religion of the Gods: Ritual, Paradox, and Reflexivity.* Oxford: Oxford University Press, 2009.

Perdue, Peter C. *Exhausting the Earth: State and Peasant in Hunan 1500–1850.* Cambridge, MA: Council on East Asian Studies at Harvard University, 1987.

Pregadio, Fabrizio, ed. *The Encyclopedia of Taoism.* 2 vols. London: Routledge, 2008.

Qin Guorong 秦國榮. "Guangchangong changyong benjing yu 'neichuan kougong' 廣闡宮常用本經與 '內傳口工.'" In Chen and Arrault, *Xiangzhong zongjiao yu xiangtu shehui diaocha baogao ji,* vol. 1, 160–173.

Qing Xitai 卿希泰, ed. *Zhongguo daojiao shi* 中国道教史. 4 vols. Chengdu: Sichuan renmin chubanshe, 1992.

Raz, Gil. *The Emergence of Daoism: Creation of Tradition.* New York: Routledge, 2012.

Reiter, Florian C. "The Discourse on the Thunders 雷説, by the Taoist Wang Wen-ch'ing 王文卿 (1093–1153)." *Journal of the Royal Asiatic Society* 14, no. 3 (2004): 207–229.

———. "A Preliminary Study of the Taoist Wang Wen-ch'ing (1093–1153) and His Thunder Magic." *Zeitschrift der Deutschen Morgenländischen Gesellschaft* 152, no. 1 (2002): 155–184.

Robinet, Isabelle. *La révélation du Shangqing dans l'histoire du taoïsme.* 2 vols. Paris: École Française d'Extrême-Orient, 1984.

———. *Taoist Meditation: The Mao-shan Tradition of Great Purity.* Albany: State University of New York Press, 1993.

———. *The World Upside Down: Essays on Taoist Internal Alchemy.* Edited and translated by Fabrizio Pregadio. Mountain View, CA: Golden Elixir Press, 2011.

Robinet, Isabelle, Miura Kunio, and Yamada Toshiaki. "*Sanyuan* 三元, Three Primes, Three Origins." In Predagio, *Encyclopedia of Taoism,* vol. 2, 856–858.

Robson, James. "Among Mountains and between Rivers: A Preliminary Appraisal of the Arrival, Spread, and Development of Daoism and Buddhism in the Central Hunan (Xiangzhong) Region." *Cahiers d'Extrême-Asie* 19 (2010): 9–45.

———. "Signs of Power: Talismanic Writing in Chinese Buddhism." *History of Religions* 48, no. 2 (2008): 130–169.

Schipper, Kristofer M. "Master Chao I-chen (?–1382) and the Ch'ing-wei school of Taoism." In *Dōkyō to shūkyō bunka* 道教と宗教文化, edited by Akizuki Kanei 秋月観暎, 715–734. Tokyo: Hirakawa, 1987.

———. "An Outline of Taoist Ritual." In *Essais sur le ritual III*, edited by Anne-Marie Blondeau and Kristofer Schipper, 97–126. Louvain-Paris: Peeters, 1995.

———. *The Taoist Body.* Berkeley: University of California Press, 1993.

———. "Taoist Ordination Ranks in the Tunhuang Manuscripts." In *Religion und Philosophie in Ostasien: Festschrift für Hans Steininger,* edited by Gert Naundorf, Karl-Heinz Pohl, and Hans-Hermann Schmidt, 127–148. Würzburg: Königshausen und Neumann, 1985.

———. "The True Form: Reflections on the Liturgical Basis of Taoist Art." *Sanjiao wenxian: Matériaux pour l'étude de la religion chinoise* 4 (2005): 91–113.

———. "Vernacular and Classical Ritual in Taoism." *Journal of Asian Studies* 45, no. 1 (1985): 21–57.

Schipper, Kristofer M., and Franciscus Verellen, eds. *The Taoist Canon: A Historical Companion to the Daozang.* 3 vols. Chicago: University of Chicago Press, 2004.

Schipper, Kristofer M., and Yuan Bingling. "*Daofa huiyuan* 道法會元." In Schipper and Verellen, *Taoist Canon,* vol. 2, 1105–1113.

Seaman, Gary. *Journey to the North: An Ethnohistorical Analysis and Annotated Translation of the Chinese Folk Novel* Pei-yu Chi. Berkeley: University of California Press, 1987.

Seidel, Anna. "Imperial Treasures and Taoist Sacraments: Taoist Roots in the Apocrypha." In *Tantric and Taoist Studies in Honour of R.A. Stein,* edited by Michel Strickmann, 291–371. Brussels: Institut Belge des Hautes Etudes Chinoises, 1983.

———. "Traces of Han Religion in Funeral Texts Found in Tombs." In *Dōkyō to shūkyō bunka* 道教と宗教文化, edited by Akizuki Kanei 秋月観暎, 21–57. Tokyo: Hirakawa shuppansha, 1987.

Shahar, Meir. *Oedipal God: The Chinese Nezha and his Indian Origins.* Honolulu: University of Hawai'i Press, 2015.

Skar, Lowell. "Administering Thunder: A Thirteenth-Century Memorial Deliberating the Thunder Rites." *Cahiers d'Extrême-Asie* 9 (1996–1997): 159–202.

———. "Golden Elixir Alchemy: The Formation of the Southern Lineage of Taoism and the Transformation of Medieval China." PhD diss., University of Pennsylvania, 2003.

———. "Ritual Movements, Deity Cults, and the Transformation of Daoism in Song and Yuan Times." In *Daoism Handbook,* edited by Livia Kohn, 413–463. Leiden: Brill, 2000.

Smith, Jonathan Z. "Trading Places." In *Relating Religion: Essays in the Study of Religion,* 215–229. Chicago: University of Chicago Press, 2004.

Staal, Frits. "The Meaninglessness of Ritual." *Numen* 26, no. 1 (1979): 2–22.

Stein, Rolf A. "Aspects de la foi jurée en Chine." *L'Annuaire du Collège de France,* 67 année (1968): 411–415.

Strickmann, Michel. "History, Anthropology, and Chinese Religion." *Harvard Journal of Asiatic Studies* 40, no. 1 (1980): 201–248.

———. "The Longest Taoist Scripture." *History of Religions* 17, no. 3–4 (1978): 331–354.

———. "Sōdai no raigi: Shinshōundō to dōka nanshū ni tsuite no ryaku setsu 宋代の雷儀：神霄運動と道家南宋についての略説." *Tōhō Shūkyō* 東方宗教 46 (1975): 15–28.

Sullivan, Lawrence E. "Sound and Senses: Toward a Hermeneutics of Performance." *History of Religions* 26, no. 1 (1986): 1–33.

Tam Wai Lun 譚偉倫. "Cong Yuebei Yingde de 'nanwu' jiaoyi kan minjian fojiao 從粵北英德的'喃嘸'醮儀看民間佛教." *Minsu quyi* 民俗曲藝163, no. 3 (2009): 71–115.

———, ed. *Minjian fojiao yanjiu* 民間佛教研究. Beijing: Zhonghua shuju, 2007.

———. "Yinsu Pu'an (1115–1169) zushi de yanjiu zhi chutan 印肅普庵 (1115–1169) 祖師的研究之初探." In *Minjian fojiao yanjiu,* 205–243.

———. "Zhongguo dongnanbu jiaoyi zhi sizhong xingtai 中國東南部醮儀之四種型態." *Lishi renleixue xuekan* 歷史人類學學刊 3, no. 2 (2005): 131–156.

Tambiah, Stanley Jeyaraja. "Form and Meaning of Magical Acts." In *Culture, Thought, and Social Action: An Anthropological Perspective,* 60–86. Cambridge, MA: Harvard University Press, 1985.

———. "The Magical Power of Words." In *Culture, Thought, and Social Action*, 17–59.

Tan Yihui 譚翼輝. "Yuedong de xianghua heshang yu xianghua fojiao keyi chuantong 粵東的香花和尚與香花佛教科儀傳統." In Tam, *Minjian fojiao yanjiu*, 115–128.

Tao Jin 陶金. "Qin'an yizhen: Qin'andian cang Song Huizong yujian yu shier leijiang shenxiang hua 欽安遺珍：欽安殿藏宋徽宗玉簡與十二雷將神像畫." *Zijincheng* 紫禁城 5 (2015): 66–81.

ter Haar, Barend J. *Guan Yu: The Religoius Afterlife of a Failed Hero.* Oxford: Oxford University Press, 2017.

Todorov, Tzvetan. *Mikhail Bakhtin: The Dialogical Principle.* Translated by Wlad Godzich. Minneapolis: University of Minnesota Press, 1984.

Tuan Chih-ch'eng 段致成. "Shilun Weng Baoguang *Wuzhenpian zhu* de neidan lilun: Yi 'lianji xiuxing' zhi fa wei taolun hexin 試論翁葆光《悟真篇・注》的內丹理論：以 '煉己修性' 之法為討論核心." *Chengda zongjiao yu wenhua xuebao* 成大宗教與文化學報 20 (2013): 85–110.

van der Loon, Piet. "A Taoist Collection of the Fourteenth Century." In *Studia Sino-Mongolica: Festschrift für Herbert Franke,* edited by Wolfgang Bauer, 401–405. Wiesbaden: Franz Steiner, 1979.

Verellen, Franciscus. "The Dynamic Design: Ritual and Contemplative Graphics in Daoist Scriptures." In *Daoism in History: Essays in Honour of Liu Ts'un-yan,* edited by Benjamin Penny, 159–186. London: Routledge, 2006.

———. "Tianshidao shangzhang keyi: *Chisongzi zhangli* he *Yuanchen zhangjiao licheng li* yanjiu 天師道上章科儀：《赤松子章曆》和《元辰章醮立成曆》研究." In *Daojiao jingdian yu Zhongguo zongjiao wenhua* 道教經典與中國宗教文化, edited by Lai Chi Tim 黎志添, 37–72. Hong Kong: Zhonghua shuju, 2003.

Vološinov, Valentin. *Marxism and the Philosophy of Language.* Translated by Ladislav Matejka and I. R. Titunik. Cambridge, MA: Harvard University Press, 1986.

von Glahn, Richard L. *The County of Streams and Grottoes: Expansion, Settlement, and the Civilizing of the Sichuan Frontier in Song Times.* Cambridge, MA: Harvard University Press, 1987.

———. *The Sinister Way: The Divine and the Demonic in Chinese Religious Culture.* Berkeley: University of California Press, 2004.

Wang Shuigen 王水根. "Cihuasi jiqi Pu'an zushi shulun 慈化寺及其普庵祖師述論." *Zongjiao zhexue* 宗教哲學 56 (2011): 99–111.

Wang Yucheng 王育成. "Donghan daofu shili 東漢道符實例." *Kaogu xuebao* 考古學報 1 (1991): 45–56.

———. "Tang–Song daojiao mizhuanwen shili 唐宋道教密篆文釋例." *Zhongguo lishi bowuguan guankan* 中國歷史博物館館刊 (1991): 82–94.

———. "Wenwu suojian Zhongguo gudai daofu shulun 文物所見中國古代道符述論." *Daojia wenhua yanjiu* 道家文化研究 9 (1996): 267–301.

———. "Zhongguo gudai daojiao qiyi fuming kaolun 中國古代道教奇異符銘考論." *Zhongguo lishi bowuguan guankan* 中國歷史博物館館刊 2 (1997): 25–50.

Wilkinson, Endymion. *Chinese History: A New Manual.* 5th ed. Cambridge, MA: Harvard University Press, 2018.

Wright, Dale S. *Philosophical Meditations on Zen Buddhism.* New York: Cambridge University Press, 1998.

Wu Xinfu 伍新福, ed. *Hunan tongshi: Gudai juan* 湖南通史：古代卷. Changsha: Hunan chubanshe, 1994.

Yang Yongjun 楊永俊. "Nanquan Puzu menxia de kejia xianghua heshang: Jiangxi Wanzai 南泉普祖門下的客家香花和尚：江西萬載." In Tam, *Minjian fojiao yanjiu,* 166–201.

Ye Mingsheng 葉明生. "Fujian Taining de Pu'anjiao zhuixiu keyi ji yu yujiajiao guanxi kao 福建泰寧的普庵教追修科儀及與瑜伽教關係考." In Tam, *Minjian fojiao yanji,* 244–278.

———. "Min xibei Pu'an qingwei dengpai diaocha 閩西北普庵清微等派調查." In *Min xibei de minsu zongjiao yu shehui* 閩西北的民俗宗教與社會, edited by Yang Yanjie 楊彥傑, 384–451. Hong Kong: Guoji kejia xuehui, 2000.

Zeng Di 曾迪. "Xinhuaxian daojiao yuanliu ji Julangong leijiao chanshi 新化縣道教源流暨聚嵐宮雷醮闡事." In Chen and Arrault, *Xiangzhong zongjiao yu xiangtu shehui diaocha baogao ji,* vol. 1, 204–242.

Zhang Shihong 張式弘. "Anhua daojiao de diaocha baogao 安化道教的调查报告." In Chen and Arrault, *Xiangzhong zongjiao yu xiangtu shehui diaocha baogao ji,* vol. 1, 31–66.

———. *Meishan wenhua* 梅山文化. Hong Kong: Tianma chubanshe, 2009.

Zou Shengyun 鄒昇雲. "Xinhua Miaotianguan songcao fashi de chuancheng 新化苗田觀送曹法事的傳承." In Chen and Arrault, *Xiangzhong zongjiao yu xiangtu shehui diaocha baogao ji,* vol. 1, 395–426.

Index

Page numbers in **boldface** type refer to figures and tables: **f** refers to figures; **wf** refers to web figures; **wv** refers to web videos. Thus, **51**f1.4 refers to figure 1.4 on page 51; **273**table A1 refers to items on page 273 listed on table A1; **27**wf1.3 refers to the mention of web figure 1.3 on page 27; **180**wv3.4 refers to the mention of web video 3.4 on page 180.

altar spaces: and Chen Diwen's performance of the Banner Rite, 162, **162**wf interlude 1, 263–266, **263**wf post.1, **266**f post.1; constructed by Chen's lineage in the Guanyin Temple, 78; and the eight trigrams in the Posterior Heaven, 287–288n28; placement of the Banner Rite manual an altar table, 180; and visual imagery of Yin Jiao, 77–78, **77**f2.1, **79**f2.2, 129

Andersen, Poul, 289n43, 289n47, 300n19, 301n21, 304n60, 306n27; analysis of a transformation of the body ritual sequence in Taiwan, 302n31; on distinctions made between the Dao and ancestral *qi*, 306n13; on the nine steps of the *bugang* movement, 304n62; on ritual as having meaning in a relational sense, 13

Anhua county: black tea grown in, 28, 277n3; and Chen Diwen's schooling in his youth, 27; geographical location of, 25, **51**f1.4, 278–279n16; and the Jiang-Li lineage Chen Diwen entered, 200; and the Meishan region of central Hunan, 36–37; and the Tradition of the Primordial Emperor (Yuanhuangjiao), 35, 48. *See also* Fuqing; Le'an township

Anhua Daoist Association (Anhua daojiao xiehui), 62, 63

Austin, John L., 309–310n65

Bai Yuchan (fl. 1194–1229): introduction to the *Preface to the Abstruse Directives of the Thunderclap from Wang the Fire Master*, 117; on summoning and employing thunder gods, 121, 135

Bakhtin, Mikhail, linguistic notion of "utterance," 15, 276n16

Banner Rite [to Summon] Sire Yin (*Yingong fanfa*): and Chen Diwen's lineage, 1–5, 5–9; Chen Diwen's performance of, 183, 263–269, **263**wf post.1, **266**f post.1; and exorcistic power, 3–7; Jiang Shenzhi's redaction of, 177, 198, 200, 256; and the religious vibrancy of the Song–Yuan period, 76–77; and ritual communication between an officiant and the martial deity, 9

Banner Rite [to Summon] Sire Yin—manual: "copulation between the dragon and the tiger" (longhu jiaohui), 194–195; instructions and incantations for transforming into the divine body of Zhang Daoling, 182–183, 182f3.1, 186, 187wv3.4, 190, 190f3.2, 198–199; Palm Tracing of Golden Radiance (Jinguang zhang), 180–181, 180wv3.4; Proclamation by the yuanchen, 216f3.5; and the ritual method of the Banner Rite, 141; in ritual use, 180

Banner Rite [to Summon] Sire Yin of the Anterior Heaven (Yingong fanfa yizong) of Luo Congyao, 200–201, 201–207, 202f3.3, 203f3.3, 207f3.4; and the term yuanchen, 200–208, 299–300n4

Bickford, Maggie, 308n46

Boltz, Judith M., 289n43, 295n125, 302n35

Book of Changes (Yijing) trigrams: kun, 193, 288n31; symbolic language of eight trigrams (bagua), 182; symbolic language of trigrams kan and li, 192, 288n31

Buddhist generational poem used by Chen Diwen's lineage: first (thirty-six-character) poem of Chan Master Guoming, 57; second (forty-eight-character) poem by Chan Master Jin Bifeng, 57; text of, 55–57

Campany, Robert Ford, 134, 135, 141

Celestial Lord Yin Jiao (Yin Jiao tianjun): association with the asterism Great Year (Taisui), 104–105, 152, 155, 157, 290n61; depiction in the Hall of Reverent Peace (Qin'an dian), 133; emergence in the Great Rite, 89; Esoteric Rite from the Emperor of the North [for Summoning] Marshal Yin of the Earth Ministry (Beidi disi Yin yuanshuai bifa), 129–130; title as Earth Minister Who Conquers with Mighty Power, Great Year of Utmost Virtue, Patrolling Emissary of the Nine Heavens, 139; title as the Top General of Luminous Militarism, the Worthy of Upmost Virtue, the [God] Great Year of the Earth Ministry Who Takes Charge of Killing, 147. See also heart seals

Celestial Lord Yin Jiao (Yin Jiao tianjun)—alternate names: Prime Marshal Yin Jiao (Yin Jiao yuanshuai), 2; Thunder General Yin Jiao (Yin Jiao leijiang), 2

Celestial Lord Yin Jiao (Yin Jiao tianjun)—diverse visual representations of, 19–20; and altar spaces for Chen Diwen's lineage, 77–78, 77f2.1, 79f2.2, 129; and the amalgamation of various esoteric Buddhist elements, 127, 132; and distinctions between original forms (benxiang) and morphed forms (benxiang) of deities, 132; and divine child and royal prince iconography combined in hagiographical tales, 134–137; and divine child and royal prince iconography combined in the Plain Tale, 142–145; and the liturgical history of Chen Diwen's lineage, 76; as youthful according to Peng Yuantai, 132–134, 156–157; as youthful prince-cum-warrior in In Search of the Gods, 145; as Zhenwu's demon-slaying accomplice (Yin Gao) in Journey to the North, 145–148

Celestial Worthy of Primordial

Commencement (Yuanshi tianzun): embodiment of same cosmic power as the primordial spirit at the core of the practitioner, 203–204; on the origins of the Emperor of the North, 96–97; teachings transmitted Wang Wenqing, 114–115

Chan: Chan Master Guoming, 57. *See also* Compassionate Transformation Monastery; Jin Bifeng

Chang Ch'ao-jan: on "inner transmissions" (*neichuan*) in the Shangqing tradition, 175–176; new Song liturgical movements compared with those of "classic" (*jingdian*) Daoist traditions, 196–197

Chen Chun-chih, 132. See also *yuanchen*

Chen clan, Daxiong Mountain region lineage members, **272–274**table A1

Chen Diwen: birth in Le'an village, 25, **25**wff1.1–1.2; and Buddhist names associated with, 56; employment before becoming a Daoist master, 29–32; interest in ritual music, 30, **30**wf1.8; ordination (*jiao*) as a Daoist-Buddhist master, 25, **25**f1.1, 161–163, **162**wf interlude 1, 168–175, **169**wf3.1, 244–250; *Secret Transmission* text taught to him when he received the *yuanchen*, 171–175, 223; and the spread of Buddhist practices to the lineage of, 48–58, **51**f1.4; Yin Jiao summoned with the Banner Rite, 1–5, 76, 210–216

Chen Diwen—lineage: and boundaries between Pu'an Buddhist, Daoist, and local *shi* traditions, 48, 281n43; Celestial Lord Yin Jiao recognized by, 2; local liturgical dominance of, 305n2. See also *Banner Rite*; 1806 genealogy; generational poem of Chen Diwen's lineage; Shen the Realized One

Chen Shouyuan, 98

Chen Yisong, 278n14

Chinese Communist Party: and the Falun gong, 70, 284n73, 284n75; villagers' committees (*cunmin weiyuanhui*) established by, 68. *See also* Cultural Revolution

Chongkan huitu sanjiao yuanliu soushen daquan, Ye Dehui's printing of, 295–296n131

Chuliang (Hailong), ritual tradition transmitted to Fuqing, 38, 40–41, 60

Collected Fundamentals of the Dao and Ritual (DZ 1220 *Daofa huiyuan*): first fifty-five chapters identified as Pure Tenuity texts, 294n112; *Great Rite [for Summoning] the Earth Minister of the Heart of Heaven* (*Tianxin disi dafa*), 89; *Hidden Texts of the Thunder Crystal of the Anterior Heaven* (*Xiantian leijing yinshu*), 118, 300n18

Compassionate Transformation Monastery, and the 1806 genealogy, 49–50, 57

Copp, Paul F., notion of "material efficacy," 222–223

Correct Rites of the Heart of Heaven liturgical tradition: *Correct Rites of the Heart of Heaven of the Shangqing Tradition* by Deng Yougong, 101, 184, 195, 232–233, 239; and *Demon Codes of the Spinal Numinous Writ of the Shangqing Tradition* (*Shangqing gusui lingwen guilü*), 98, 106; and inner cultivations (*neixiu*), 100; and the liturgical context surrounding the portrayal of Yin Jiao, 76, 94, 97–98; and Peng Yuantai's Great Rite ritual text, 97, 103; and Rao Dongtian, 97–99, 101–102; visualization of divine, exorcistic *qi*, 233; and Zhang Daoling, 98, 100–101, 188

Cultural Revolution (1966–1976): carved wooden image of Yang Faqing rescued by Chen Diwen's grandmother during, 27; ending with Mao Zedong's death in 1976, 66; Li Yezhen's courage during, 31, 64–65; ritual traditions suppressed during, 5; slogan heralding the destruction and replacement of the four old things, 65, 283n69; trauma suffered by Chen Diwen's transmission master's generation during, 5–6, 71

Daoist-Buddhist practice: and the amalgamation of esoteric Buddhist elements, 127, 132; Chen Diwen's ordination as a Daoist-Buddhist master, 25, **25**f1.1, 161; and *Esoteric Transmissions for Daoist and Buddhist [Rites] and their Templates (Fo Dao michuan ji kuanshi)* by Jiang Shenzhi, 46, 48, 281; and the half Buddhist, half Daoist character (*banfo bandao*) of Chen Diwen's lineage, 24–25, 35, 45–50, 52–54; introduced to Fuqing by Jiang Sanlu, 59–60, 71; and Li Yeshi's views of the Falun gong, 70; and Pu'an's master of exorcistic ritual techniques, 46–47

Daoist canon: and contemporary practitioners defending their practices, **155**wf2.1; and Divine Empryean teachings, 113, 292n81; incantations in early ritual texts in, 147

Daoist generational poem of the Daxiong Mountain region: and Chen Diwen's Daoist lineage, 37–38, 40–45, 54, 58; tabulation of lineage members, **270–273**table A1; thirteenth *gong* generation, 60, 61, **272**table A1; twenty-character lineage poem (*paixushi*), 37

Daoist masters: and the Academy of Scholarly Worthies (Jixianyuan), 89, 131. *See also* Bai Yuchan; Jiang Shenzhi; Jiang Yucheng; Li Yeshi; Li Yezhen; Min Bin the Iron-Hearted Man of the Dao; Peng Yuantai; Rao Dongtian; Tan Zixiao

Daxiong Mountain region: Chen Diwen's birth in Le'an village, 1, 25; and the Meishan region of central Hunan, 36. *See also* Daoist generational poem of the Daxiong Mountain region

demons: and the Emperor of the North's rule over Fengdu, 96–97, 108–109; and the term *taibao*, 297n147; Thirteen Great Guardians (Shisan taibao), 146; and Yin Jiao as Zhenwu's demon-slaying accomplice, 145–148

Deng Bowen: transformation into Marshal Deng, 117–118; and the Yellow Emperor, 117

Deng Cihuang, 1806 genealogy collected by, 281–282n47

Deng Xiaoping, reform and opening up, 66

Deng Ziyang (d. 739), 95

Divine Empyrean (Shenxiao): and depictions of Yin Jiao, 19; *Great Rite of the Five Thunders for Interrogation and Execution in the [Office of the] Jade Pivot in the Divine Empyrean on High*, 213; master Sa Shoujian (fl. 1141–1178?), 117, 163, 240, 308n50; True King Jade Clarity (Gaoshang shenxiao yuqing zhenwang), 114–115, 116. *See also* Bai Yuchan; Lin Lingsu; Wang Wenqing

divine power: and "divinely powerful *qi*," 6; and the term *shentong*, 200n16. *See also* exorcistic power

Duara, Prasenjit, 158

1806 genealogy: and Pu'an's Compassionate Transformation Monastery, 49–50; on the two Buddhist poems used in the Buddhist generational poem of Chen Diwen, 57

1888 colophon to a Daoist liturgical manual (*Dongyuan sanmei*): Fu clan production of, 61; history of Chen Diwen's Daoist lineage in, 38–40; line of transmission from Chuliang to Fuqing, 60

Emperor of the North (Beidi): Deng Ziyang's founding of a lineage devoted to, 95; and the liturgical context surrounding the portrayal of Yin Jiao, 76; underworld of Fengdu ruled by, 96–97, 108–109; Yin Jiao's ties of obligation to, 5, 8, 19, 21

Esoteric Rite from the Emperor of the North [for Summoning] Marshal Yin of the Earth Ministry (*Beidi disi Yin yuanshuai bifa*), 129–130

exorcistic power: of the Emperor of the North, 158; and proper performance of the Banner Rite, 3–7; and talismans, 225, 229, 231–232

Falun gong, 70, 284n73, 284n75

Fang and Fu clans: Daxiong Mountain region lineage members of, **272–274** table A1; and the spread of Chen Diwen's lineage to Fuqing, 41

Fava, Patrice, 278n14; on the divinatory significance of the shape of knots in banners, 312–313n3; on lineages in Xinhua, 43, 278n14, 307n31, 308n39

Fengdu underworld: Emperor of the North's rule over, 96–97; and the liturgical context surrounding the portrayal of Yin Jiao, 76

Fu clan: ritual manual colophon (1888) produced by, 61; and the spread of Chen Diwen's lineage to Fuqing, 41

Fuqing: Daoist-Buddhist practices introduced by Jiang Sanlu, 59–60,

71; Daxiong Mountain region lineage members, **272–274** table A1; and the spread of Buddhist practices to Chen Diwen's lineage, 51f1.4; spread of Chen Diwen's lineage to, 41–42, 60

Ge Hong (283–343), 257; *Traditions of Divine Transcendents* (*Shenxian zhuan*), 134

generational poem of Chen Diwen's lineage: adoption by lineages around Zhenshang township, 44–45; half Buddhist, half Daoist character (*banfo bandao*) of, 35, 45–50, 52; and lineages originating in the Jade Void Palace, 40. *See also* Buddhist generational poem used by Chen Diwen's lineage; Daoist generational poem of the Daxiong Mountain region

Gong clan: Daxiong Mountain region lineage members of, **272–274** table A1; Gong Qianshen, 60; intermarriage with the Jiang clan, 274; and the spread of Chen Diwen's lineage to Fuqing, 41

Great Rite [for Summoning] the Earth Minister of the Heart of Heaven (*Tianxin disi dafa*): and the Heart of Heaven movement, 97, 103–106; Peng Yuantai's colophon to (1290), 93–94; Peng Yuantai's preface to, 89–91, 178; and the story of Yin Jiao's revelation to Liao Shouzhen, 89–91, 137–138; Yin Jiao visualized as a boyish prince in, 156–157

Great Year (Taisui): as a baleful star, 298n158; Yin Jiao associated with, 104–105, 146–148, 152, 155, 157, 290n61, 298n153

Guanyin Temple (Guanyinsi): construction of altar spaces by Chen's lineage in, 78; geographical location of, **51**f1.4,

282n58; rebuilding of, **67**wf1.20–
1.21; and the spread of Buddhist
practices to Chen Diwen's lineage,
54–55

Hailong (Chuliang), and the spread of
Buddhist practices to Chen Diwen's
lineage, **51**f1.4
Hall of Reverent Peace (Qin'an dian) in the
imperial palace, 133
He clan of Songshan village, ritual manuals
mentioning their lineage, 40
Heart of Heaven practice. *See* Correct Rites
of the Heart of Heaven liturgical
tradition
heart seals (*xinyin*): and flower signatures
(*huaya zi*), 239–240, 307n38; and
Huizong's signature, 240, 308n46;
of Marshal Wang Lingguan, 237,
237f4.9, 240, 308n39; of Sa Shoujian,
308n50; of Shen the Realized One,
260; and signatures, 239; of Yin Jiao,
237, **237**f4.9, **244**f4.10; of Yin Jiao
inscribed by Chen Diwen, 244–250,
252–254, **252**wv4, **253**f4.12,
253wv4.12, **254**f4.13; of Zhang
Daoling, 240–241, 247
*Hidden Texts of the Thunder Crystal of the
Anterior Heaven* (*Xiantian leijing
yinshu*), 118–119, 176–177, 251,
*294*n107; on the Vermillion Crow
as a moniker for Marshal Zhang Jue,
310–311n70
Hongwu emperor (Zhu Yuanzhang, r. 1368–
1398), and Jin Bifeng, 57, 283n62
Hongzhu (base of Master Chen Yisong),
geographical location of, **51**f1.4
Huang Shunshen (1224–after 1286), 127,
286–287n24
Hudson, Clarke, 192
Huizong. *See* Song Huizong
Hymes, Robert, 289n43

Jade Void Palace (Yuxugong): founding by
Zeng Rushou, 39–40, 44; and the
spread of Daoist practices to Chen
Diwen's lineage, 39–40, **41**f1.3;
temples affiliated with, 280n23
Jiang clan: Daoist-Buddhist tradition of,
59–60, 71; Daxiong Mountain region
lineage members of, **272–274**table
A1; intermarriage with the Gong clan,
274; and the Li clan, 41, 274; local
liturgical dominance of, 305n2; ritual
texts collected by, 60–61
Jiang Feiqing (1888–1971), 61–64, 68,
70–71
Jiang Rui, and Yin Jiao's search for
accomplices, 82–83
Jiang Shenzhi: and the Banner Rite manual
used by Chen Diwen, **207**f3.4; *Banner
Rite [to Summon] Sire Yin* redacted by,
177, 198, 200, 256; commentary on
the *Secret Transmission*, 224, 281n35;
*Esoteric Transmissions for Daoist and
Buddhist [Rites] and Their Templates*
(*Fo Dao michuan ji kuanshi*) by, 46,
48, 281; *Genealogical Investigation of
the Practice over Ten Lifetimes of the
Celestial Lord Yin Jiao, Great Year the
Controller of Killer Spirits of the Earth
Ministry* (*Disi tongsha taisui Yin Jiao
tianjun shishi xiuxing maikao*) redacted
by, 79, **80**f2.3, 153–155, 284n3;
Marshals Yin Jiao and Wang Lingguan
painted by, **77**f2.1, 78; paintings of
deities by, 67, **77**f2.1
Jiang Yeqian, as Chen Diwen's guarantor
master (*baojushi*), 33–34, **34**wf1.10
Jiang Yucheng, 168, 254; as Chen Diwen's
presenting master (*yinjinshi*), 33–34,
34wf1.10; on the local liturgical
dominance of the Jiang and Li clans,
305n2

Jiang-Li lineage. *See* Chen Diwen—lineage

Jiangxi, Compassionate Transformation Monastery in, 57

Jin Bifeng: and the forty-eight-character Buddhist poem used by Chen Diwen's lineage, 57; Numinous Vulture Shrine founded by, 57; and Zhu Yuanzhang (later the Hongwu emperor), 57, 283n62

Journey to the North (*Beiyou ji*), recounting of Zhenwu's becoming the Dark Emperor, 145–146, 157

Kao Chen-hung, 132

Katz, Paul R., 158

Lagerwey, John, 301n22, 306n12; Pu'an-related texts collected by, 47, 281n38

Le'an township: adoption of the Longmen lineage poem by local Zhengyi Daoists in, 44, 278n14; ceramics industry in, 28–29; and Chen Diwen's grandfather's house in Mount Xiashan, 25, **25**wff1.1–1.2, 162, **162**wf interlude1; geographical location of, **51**f1.4; migrant laborers from, 29, **29**wf 1.5–1.6; tobacco industry in, 28

Lee Fong-mao, 307n31; original forms (*benxiang*) and morphed forms (*benxiang*) of deities distinguished by, 132; on Shen the Realized one, 286–287n24; on Zhengyi notions of *yuanchen*, 209–211

Li clan: Daoist-Buddhist tradition of, 61; Daxiong Mountain region lineage members of, **272–274**table A1; and the Jiang clan, 41, 274; lineage poem (*paixushi*), 37; local liturgical dominance of, 305n2. *See also* Li Feimao; Li Manjuan; Li Yeshi; Li Yezhen

Li Feimao, 62–63, 172

Li Manjuan (b. 1860), 61, 172

Li Xinwu, on adoption of the Longmen lineage poem by local Zhengyi Daoists, 278n14

Li Yeshi: as a village head Party member, 68–69; Falun gong viewed by, 69–70, 284n75; ordination of, 68

Li Yezhen (d. 2007): Buddhist name Li Mingzhen, 56; as Chen Diwen's transmission master (*dushi*), 31–34, 67, 162–164, 168–173; home near the Guanyin Temple in Guanxi, 55; Li Shenming as his transmission master, 67; reputation for courage during the Cultural Revolution, 31, 64–65; as a would-be member of the eighteenth *ye* generation, 37, 63

Li Yuanguo, on Deng Ziyang, 95

Lin Lingsu: Huizong convinced he was the Great Emperor of Everlasting Life by, 113; and Zhang Jixian, 116–117, 127

lineage poems. *See* Buddhist generational poem used by Chen Diwen's lineage; Daoist generational poem of the Daxiong Mountain region; generational poem of Chen Diwen's lineage; Quanzhen Longmen (Dragon Gate) lineage poem

Lingbao tradition: Great Rites of (Lingbao dafa), 127, 307n31; *Jade Mirror of the Numinous Treasure* (*Lingbao yujian*), 232; and the Pure and Bright Rites (Jingming fa), 127, 294n108; *Wondrous Scripture of the Upper Chapters on Limitless Salvation from the Numinous Gem* [*Corpus*] (*Lingbao wuliang duren shangpin miaojing*), 96, 292n81. *See also* Celestial Worthy of Primordial Commencement

Liu Tiefeng, 278n14

Liu, Ts'un-yan, 297n144, 297n146

Liu Zhongyu, 311n72

Longmen generational poem. *See* Quanzhen Longmen (Dragon Gate) lineage poem

Lü Dongbin, *Secret Transmission of Primordial Qi from the Anterior Heaven [as Revealed] by Patriarch Lü (Lüzu xiantian zuqi michuan)*, 173, 191

Lui Wing Sing: on adoption of the Longmen lineage poem by local Zhengyi Daoists, 42–44, 278n14; and the public notice for the funeral of Daoist Li Xuanming, 59

Luo Congyao (b. 1813), Banner rite of, 200–207, **202**f3.3, **207**f3.4

Luo and Zhang (clan), Daxiong Mountain region lineage members of, **272–274**table A1

Marshal Deng (Deng yuanshuai): blood offerings accepted by, 118, 122, 158; Deng Bowen's transformation into, 117–118; as the Great Deity of Sudden Flames (Huhuo [or Xuhuo] dashen), 119, 120; and other thunder deities associated with Yin Jiao, 118–119, 122–123, 135, 168, 294n106

Marshal Yin. *See* Celestial Lord Yin Jiao

Meicheng township: and Daxiong Mountain region lineage members, **272–274**table A1, 278n14; geographical location of, **51**f1.4

Meishan region of central Hunan: geographical overview of, 36; Yao and Miao native peoples of, 36

Meulenbeld, Mark, 142, 152–153, 278n14, 298n154; on the domestication of martial deities, 17

Min Bin the Iron-Hearted Man of the Dao (Tiexin daoren Min Bin), 177–178

Ming dynasty: and the Quanzhen order, 42; Yongle emperor (r. 1402–1425), 133. *See also* Hongwu emperor

Mount Nanquan Monastery of Compassionate Transformation, and the spread of Buddhist practices to Chen Diwen's lineage, **51**f1.4

Mount Qingcheng, 82

Mount Xiashan, Chen Diwen's grandfather's house, 25, **25**wff1.1–1.2, 162, **162**wf interlude1

Nikaidō Yoshihiro, 132

Peng Yuantai: image of Yin Jiao as youthful, 132–134; and the preface to the *Great Rite,* 89; and Yin Jiao's association with the asterism Great Year (Taisui), 104–105, 290n61; on Yin Jiao's revelation to Liao Shouzhen, 89–90

Precious Scripture of the Jade Pivot Spoken by the Celestial Worthy of the Nine Heavens Who Transforms All with the Sound of Thunder Responding to the Prime (DZ 16 *Jiutian yingyuan leisheng puhua tianzun shuo yushu baojing*), 130

Pure Tenuity tradition: and the first fifty-five chapters of the *Daofa huiyuan,* 294n112; and Huang Shunshen (1224–after 1286), 127; and the liturgical context surrounding the portrayal of Yin Jiao, 76

qi: ancestral *qi* of the primordial chaos (*hundan zuqi*), 223, 306n12; exorcistic *qi,* 223, 231–233; talismans imbued with ancestral *qi,* 218–223, **220**wv4.1, 226, 229, 233, **233**wf4.5, 257–259; without numinous *qi* (*meiyou lingqi*), 219. *See also Secret Transmission of Primordial Qi from the Anterior Heaven [as Revealed] by Patriarch Lü (Lüzu xiantian zuqi michuan)*

Qin Guorong: on banners that fail to knot at an ordination, 312n1; on heart seals used for Yin Jiao and Wang Lingguan, 308n39

Quanzhen Daoism: and the Ming court, 42. *See also* Quanzhen Longmen (Dragon Gate) lineage poem

Quanzhen Longmen (Dragon Gate) lineage poem: adoption by masters in Xinhua, 42–44; not adopted by certain lineages, **41**f1.3, 44–45; and the Zhengyi tradition, 43–44

Rao Dongtian, Correct Rites of the Heart of Heaven tradition (Tianxin zhengfa), 97–99, 101–102

Republican period, 62–63, 70

ritual communication: and Austin's investigation of speech acts, 309–310n65; and the exorcistic power of the Banner Rite, 4–5, 9, 13, 75; and the *Golden Banner Talismanic Rite for Manifesting the Dao of the Five Thunders* (*Wulei xiandao jinfan fufa*), 309n59; and performed action, 9–13, 256, 263–269, **263**wf post.1; and the talisman of the Banner Rite, 259–261. *See also* altar spaces; talismanic inscription; *yuanchen*

Robinet, Isabelle, 250, 301–302n26, 309–310n65

Robson, James, 311n71

Schipper, Kristofer M.: Daoist ritual viewed as "liturgical structure by," 9–11, 276n8; liturgical officiants likened to puppeteers, 11–13; on one-way communication between masters and martial deities, 14

Secret Transmission of Primordial Qi from the Anterior Heaven [as Revealed] by Patriarch Lü (*Lüzu xiantian zuqi michuan*): ancestral *qi* defined by,

191–192, 223–224; and Chen Diwen's lineage, 172–173, 191–192; on extracting from *kan* in order to replenish *li* (*choukan buli*), 192, 193–194

Shangqing tradition: and the *Correct Rites of the Heart of Heaven of the Shangqing Tradition* of Deng Yougong, 101, 184, 195, 232–233, 239; and Heart of Heaven texts, 102; "inner transmissions" (*neichuan*) in, 175–176

Shanxi, Numinous Vulture Shrine (Lingjiu an) on Mount Wutai, 57

Shen the Realized One (Shen zhenren): and Chen Diwen's "family letter" (*jiashu*), 162–163; esoteric names in the Banner Rite of, 246, 249–250; heart seal of, 260; Huang Shunshen identified as, 286–287; Yin Jiao's allegiance to, 4, 77, 83–88, 138–141, 152, 153, 156–159, 243–250, **244**f4.10, 264

shi traditions (*shijiao*): and boundaries between Pu'an Buddhist, Daoist, and local *shi* traditions, 48, 281n43; and Pu'an, 46; and the Tradition of the Primordial Emperor (Yuanhuangjiao), 35, 48

Smith, Jonathan Z., 256

Song Huizong (r. 1100–1125): collation of the new canon of Daoist texts under, 99; as Great Emperor of Everlasting Life (Changsheng dadi), 113, 115; signature created by, 240, 308n46; and thunder rituals presented by Zhang Jixian, 101

Song dynasty: and the asterism Great Year, 290n61; heart seals and individual expression in calligraphy during, 240; and the Meishan region, 36; religious vibrancy of, 76–77; Song Shenzong (r. 1067–1085), 36. *See also* Song Huizong

Song dynasty—Northern Song dynasty (960–1127), Meishan region of central Hunan, 36

Song dynasty—Southern Song dynasty (1127–1279): emergence of Yin Jiao during, 89; and *Hidden Texts of the Thunder Crystal of the Anterior Heaven,* 118–119, 176–177, 251

Songshan village: Chen Diwen's lineage poem adopted by Daoist master in, 278n14. *See also* He clan of Songshan village

Strickmann, Michel, 292n81

Sullivan, Lawrence E., 9

talismanic inscription, 217–261 passim; of the circular graph for the Golden Radiance, 233, **233**wf4.1, **233**wv4.2; communication with the celestial sphere, 217–222, **220**wv 4.1, 230–231, 258; graph denoting decrees of high gods, 234–235, **234**f4.7, **234**wv4.2; graph for Golden Radiance, 233, **233**f4.6; graph of "dog" in the *Banner Rite* manual, 248–249, **248**f4.11; and graphs for the "Emperor of the North decrees," 226–235, **226**wv4.2, **227**f4.4, **229**wv4.2; and graphs for the Three Terraces, Three Officers, and Celestial Guideline, **229**f4.5, 231–232; and material efficacy, 222–223; and without numinous *qi* (*meiyou lingqi*), 219; and the taboo names of the Three Officers, 232–233, 307n31; visualization by masters, 305n5. *See also* heart seals

talismanic language: and Austin's investigation of speech acts, 309–310n65; intelligibility of, 258–259; penetration (*tong*) of Yin Jiao, 8

talismans: and exorcistic power, 225, 229, 231–233, 235; imbuing with Golden Radiance, 233, **233**wf4.5, **233**wv4.2; scholarly literature on, 312–313n73; "spinal numinous writ" talismans (*gusui lingwen*), 101; of thunder gods, 294n106

Tam Wai Lun, 47, 281n42, 282–283n62; on "incense and flower monks," 51–52; on the *Pu'an zushi lingyan ji,* 281n38

Tan Zixiao, and Rao Dongtian's rites, 98, 101

Tang dynasty: Daoist cultivation practiced by Ye Fashan (616–c.720), 114; heart seals and calligraphy during, 240; and the Loyalty and Filiality (Zhongxiao) tradition, 127; Tang Xuanzong (r. 712–756), 95

Tang–Song transition: and the Correct Rites of the Heart of Heaven movement, 97–98; emergence of Fengdu ritual methods during, 105

ter Haar, Barend J., 158

Three Primes (Sanyuan): festivals of, 307n30; three modes of *qi* of (dark [*xuan*], primal [*yuan*] and commencing [*shi*]), 231

Three Primes (Sanyuan)—Three Officers of Heaven, Earth, and Water: and the cosmogonic breaths of the Three Primes, 231; purification of the talisman by, 232; taboo names of, 260

Three Sovereigns and the Five Emperors (Sanhuang wudi), 119, 293n98

thunder gods (*leishen*): Bai Yuchan on summoning and employing them, 121, 135; and the exorcistic power of the Emperor of the North, 100–101, 159; Five Thunders (Wulei), 112–119, 184, 212; talismans of, 294n106; thunder generals under Yin Jiao's command,

299n1. *See also* Celestial Lord Yin Jiao; Correct Rites of the Heart of Heaven liturgical tradition; Jiang Rui; Marshal Deng

Wang Lingguan: heart seal of, 237, **237**f4.9, 240, 308n39; Marshals Yin Jiao and Wang Lingguan painted by Jiang Shenzhi, **77**f2.1, 78; and Sa Shoujian's heart seal, 308n50

Wang Wenqing (1093–1153): Divine Empyrean teachings revealed to him by Wei Huacun, 113; *Great Rite of the Five Thunders for Interrogation and Execution in the [Office of the] Jade Pivot in the Divine Empyrean on High* (*Gaoshang shenxiao yushu zhankan wulei dafa*), 119, 204, 213; on his transmission from the Fire Master, 114; *Numinous Writ of the Jade Pivot on the Great Rite of the Five Thunders from the Jade Ministry of Upper Clarity* (*Shangqing yufu wulei dafa yushu lingwen*), 114, 117; *Preface to the Abstruse Directives of the Thunderclap from Wang the Fire Master* (*Wang huoshi leiting aozhi xu*), 117, 185–186, 212, 292n84

Wei Huacun: Divine Empyrean teachings revealed to Wang Wenqing by, 113; esoteric transmission dictated to her by realized ones (*zhenren*), 131

Western Spring Monastery (Xiquansi), **51**f1.4; founding of, 50; and Pu'an's brand of exorcistic Buddhist practice, 54, 57–59, 71; ritual spaces of, 282n52

Xiantian yuanyang zhengjiao jiefan xiandao zouzhi qiuming jiaoshi, 168

Xinhua: adoption of the Quanzhen Longmen lineage poem by monastic lineages in, 42–45; geographical location of, **51**f1.4. *See also* Zi River

Yang Faqing, wooden statue of, 27, **266**f post.1

Yangde (1585–1663), 52–53

Yangxi township, Daoist Masters in, 43, 308n38

Ye Dehui (1864–1927), *Chongkan huitu sanjiao yuanliu soushen daquan* printed by, 295–296n131

Ye Mingsheng, 47, 282n48

Yellow Emperor (Huangdi): and Deng Bowen, 117; and Marshals Xin and Zhang, 119

Yin Jiao. *See* Celestial Lord Yin Jiao

Yuan Miaozong, 99

Yuan dynasty (1279–1368): Academy of Scholarly Worthies (Jixianyuan), 89, 131; *Hidden Texts of the Thunder Crystal of the Anterior Heaven*, 118–119, 176–177, 251; religious vibrancy of, 76–77; Yuan Shundi (r. 133–1380), 57

yuanchen: and the Banner rite, 200–208, 299–300n4; Chen Diwen's "calling upon the *yuanchen*" (*kou yuanchen*), 171–175; Chen Diwen's "receiving the *yuanchen*" (*shou yuanchen*), 171–174, 223; and Chen Diwen's successful attainment of his primordial self, 212–216, **212**wv3.5(1:09–1:29); and divination blocks (*cigua*), 171, **171**wf3.2, 173–175, **174**wf3.3, 300n6; Proclamation by the *yuanchen*, **216**f3.5; as a term, 299–300n4; and the Zhengyi tradition according to Lee Fong-Mao and Zhang Zhixiong, 209–211

Zeng Rushou, 39–40, 44

Zhang Daoling: Chen Diwen's transformation into the divine body of, 179–190, 187–189, **187**wv3.4, 207–208; and Emperor Huizong, 101; as first Celestial Master, 101, 107, 168, 240; and Heart of Heaven practice, 98, 100–101, 188; instructions and incantations in the *Banner Rite* manual for transforming into the divine body of Zhang Daoling, 182–183, **182**f3.1, 186, **187**wv3.4, 190, **190**f3.2; and Marshal Zhao Gongming, 186, 240

Zhang Jinghua, 307n31; Abbey of Cultured Transcendents (Wenxianguan) established by, 39

Zhang Jixian (fl. 1092–1126, thirtieth Celestial Master): and Chen Diwen's "family letter" (*jiashu*), 162–163; and Divine Empyrean cosmology, 117; and Heart of Heaven methods, 101, 126; lineage of, 39, 291n65; and *Petition by Celestial Master Xujing to Excise [Ritual] Impropriety* (*Xujing tianshi powang zhang*), 241

Zhang Shihong, 66, 265

Zhang Zhixiong, on Zhengyi notions yuanchen," 209–211

Zhengyi (Orthodox Unity) tradition: and the Celestial Masters on Mount Longhu, 39; and the *Esoteric Rite [to Summon] Marshal Zhao of the Mysterious Altar of Orthodox Unity* (*Zhengyi xuantan Zhao yuanshuai bifa*), 186, 240–241; and Heart of Heaven methods, 101; and the Ming court, 42; and notions of *yuanchen,* 209–211; and the Orthodox Unity Celestial Masters lineage, 2; and the Quanzhen Longmen monastic lineage, 43–45; and talismanic graphs associated with the Three Officers, 307n31. *See also* Zhang Daoling

Zhenshang region, **51**f1.4; Chen Diwen's generational lineage poem adopted by lineages in, 37–38, **41**f1.3, 44–45, 278n14; Daxiong Mountain region lineage members, **272–274**table A1, 278n14; Longmen generational poem not adopted by lineages in, 44; ritual manuscripts from, 38; and Western Spring Monastery (Xiquansi) in the Daxiong Mountains, 50. *See also* Songshan village

Zhenwu: and Chen Diwen's "divine body" (*bianshen*), 180–181, **180**wv3.4, 189–191, **189**wv3.5, 194–195; and the Fengdu masters, 108; as guardian deity of the Ming dynasty, 133. See also *Journey to the North (Beiyou ji)*

Zhu Zhizhong, and Wang Wenqing, 185–186, 212–213, 292n84

Zi River: and the spread of Buddhist practices to Chen Diwen's lineage, 39, **51**f1.4; and the spread of Daoist practices to Chen Diwen's lineage, 39, **41**f1.3

About the Author

David J. Mozina studies contemporary Daoist and Buddhist ritual in central Hunan, and the roots of that ritual in Song, Yuan, and late imperial ritual traditions.

Titles in the New Daoist Studies Series

The Writ of the Three Sovereigns:
From Local Lore to Institutional Daoism

By Dominic Steavu

A Library of Clouds: The Scripture of the Immaculate Numen
and the Rewriting of Daoist Texts

By J. E. E. Pettit and Chao-jan Chang

Knotting the Banner: Ritual and Relationship in Daoist Practice

By David J. Mozina

Heavenly Masters: Two Thousands Years of the Daoist State
(Forthcoming)

By Vincent Goossaert